About the Author

Rev. Pamela Ann Frances Crane (formerly Pam Bennett) was born on January 19th 1943 in Selly Oak, Birmingham, UK, at 22h18 War Time.

Her first encounters with astrology and esoteric ideas came in the early 1960s when visiting France and living in London; these began to bear fruit in 1969 as a student with the Faculty of Astrological Studies under the late, great Jeff Mayo. In 1973 she gained her Diploma from the Faculty, together with the Margaret Hone Award for Interpretation. Since then she has worked in the UK as an astrological counsellor, served on the Council of the Astrological Association of Great Britain, and edited its newsletter *Transit* between 1974 and 1975 before going on to *The Astrological Journal* as its Assistant Editor for five years.

After qualifying, Pam spent many years as a tutor and examiner with the Mayo School of Astrology, while starting her own classes and astrological societies in Kent and Cornwall. For three decades she has written many articles for *The Astrological Journal*, *Astrology*, *CAO Times* and other magazines overseas, appeared internationally on radio and television (including her presentation of the nativity of Jesus on the much-praised 1997 'Everyman' on BBC) and has become a popular speaker at society meetings and conferences in the UK and abroad, with both fellow astrologers and the general public. With the advent of the Internet, she first published her work regularly in the email bulletin *Small World*, which went out for the first time on March 3rd 1998 at 5h30 pm from her home in Ospringe, Kent, later explored new ideas in an online blog, and now has a comprehensive website at www.theholytwelve.co.uk, where you can find not only *Small World* and almost every article she has published, but also her collected poetry and haiku.

In addition to the Faculty Diploma, she holds the Honorary Diploma of the Mayo School of Astrology. Back in 1982 she formed her own correspondence college – the Pamela Crane College of Horoscopy – in order to provide tuition in a spiritually oriented astrology, and specifically to teach Draconic astrology to a high level of ability, having made a special study of it since 1977. From the 1990s onward, and especially since ordination in 1992, Pam's research, consultancy and tuition have been greatly extended into a fully Interdimensional and Christ-centred Astrology. The correspondence courses have now closed, but Pam Crane continues to teach through her writing, lectures and workshops.

The present book is a result of years of study, and of requests from astrologers in Britain, Europe, the USA, Canada, South America, Africa and Australasia who have studied with her and have been enthused by her ideas.

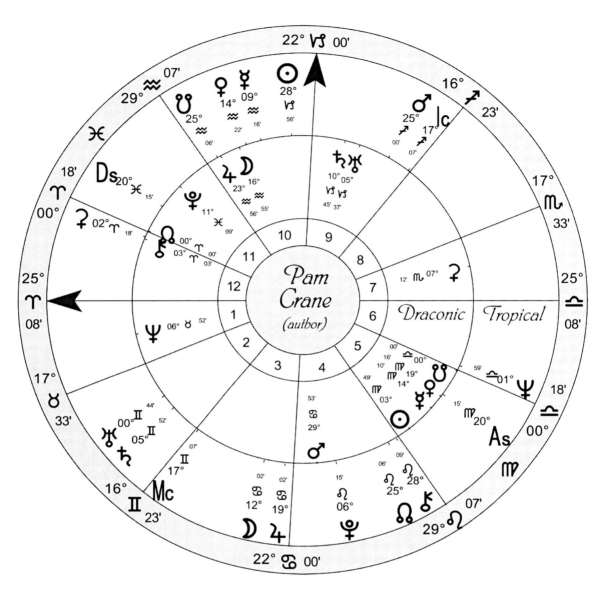

The Author's Horoscope
Draconic (Inner Wheel), Tropical (Outer Wheel)

The Draconic Chart

Reverend Pamela A.F. Crane

Flare Publications
The London School of Astrology

LSA
The London School of Astrology

This edition published in 2013 by Flare Publications
in conjunction with the London School of Astrology
BCM Planets, London WC1N 3XX, England, UK
Tel: 0700 2 33 44 55
www.flareuk.com and www.londonschoolofastrology.co.uk
email: admin@londonschoolofastrology.co.uk

A CIP catalogue record for this book is available from the British Library

ISBN: 978–1–903353–12–7

Cover design: Craig Knottenbelt
Cover image: Abbie Read
Additional images: Shutterstock

Text editing: Jane Struthers, Pamela Crane, Sy Scholfield

Charts: Solar Fire (Esoteric Technologies)

Layout: Frank Clifford

To my beloved Teachers,
and Father Frank –
who *knows* now.

My grateful thanks go to all the fathers and mothers of this book:

Those whose own pioneering work has inspired it, those who prepared its way by inviting me to speak on its subject, and the many students and practitioners of astrology all over the world who have responded by asking for it to be written.

Thank you, too, to all the people whose patient research has provided the astrological community, and so this book, with the birth-data central to its existence; to those who have pioneered and perfected the new generation of computer programs with which astrological knowledge and teaching has progressed by leaps and bounds; and to my friends who have given so much help along the way to make this work possible. You know who you are!

In particular:
Dennis Elwell, who sowed the first seed; Bruno and Louise Huber, and Haloli Richter, the first of many good friends to invite me to speak on Draconic; Colin Miles, who wrote the very first Draconic program for me; Martin Davis and Roy Gillett, who have been the souls of kindness as I struggled to master machines and software; Graham Bates, for his generous help with fine-tuning; Elizabeth Phillips, who gave me a peaceful place to write the first edition in 1985; Zerda Barlow, for offering valuable data; and my much-missed friend Jacob Schwartz for so many years of sharing and affectionate support, with added asteroids! – also especially, for making this new edition and its current revision possible, Jenni Harte and my publisher Frank Clifford, true visionaries both.

…And most of all, my dear patient husband, Gerard, without whose constant encouragement and support I could have accomplished little, and so who has loved this book into being … thrice!

Contents

Which Way, and For How Long?

Weird life.
All that time, that rolls
Before and around me like an irregular sea.
A pulse of the world's breath beats like a hill;
Miles of time
To move in the mind of the tortoise,
Spacious years
For living and dying
The day-dance of may-flies over the water.

I have borrowed the slow heart-beat
That shortens the day
And swallowed time in a step too vast
To heed the scurry of rabbit-paths in the thickets.
I have ticked an hour into more aeons of time
Than can be counted or conceived by men
Stripped of empathy and
Armed with stones.

The ant burns away a long life, And the tree, In the onward rush of seasons.

Trees grow no taller than I;
They watch my life as I would watch an ant.
My day is a second in time – Their day is eternity
To a may-fly.

So what of my strange metabolism
Flung between the particle and the cosmos?
To what end my journeys, lonely as love,
To the last forts of reason?
Which way,
Through lands of a million clocks that tell no more
Than a dandelion puffed away in the wind?

Pamela Ann Frances Crane, Autumn 1966

Draconic Astrology: An Inspiring Light

Foreword to the original volume
by the late Jacob Schwartz, PhD

My own astrological career was just beginning in the mid 1970s when an unintentional introduction to the Draconic system changed it. British astrologer Dennis Elwell was lecturing in my home city Philadelphia; a friend, Lonnie Moseley (who later authored definitive computer manuals for Microsoft programs) was among the group huddled around him at the end of the lecture listening for further new perspectives, when she heard his offhand remark about another astrological system orienting to the Lunar North Node rather than the vernal equinox. She rushed home, played with Draconic, and was amazed at the increased interpretive accuracy and insights. Thank goodness she shared the discovery. My astrological life has not been the same since!

Next came the sudden realisation that including the Moon's Lunar Node in the equation filled a vacuum – the Moon's absence in astrological orientations. No wonder Draconic explained events and experiences so much better: Draconic integrated the force of both luminaries. Our Sun had always dominated horoscope orientations because the Sun determined the vernal equinox, and collections of other Suns in the Constellations had dominated Indian Vedic systems for five thousand years at least.

Equipped with examples of Draconic charts clarifying the lives of famous personalities, and with the zeal of a missionary to solicit horoscopes from strangers in an audience and elicit from them specific statements based on Draconic, my own stage was set for events that were soon to follow in the States and Russia. Consequently, Pamela Crane's planned American lecture tour in late 1988 was a much anticipated event.

Pam and I had met three years earlier…

Some days are quite predictable with experiences quite ordinary. Other days flow with wonders and new events, destined to go well, as though in the command of a benevolent spirit. Such a day was May 29th in 1985 when my travels took me from London to that first meeting with Pam at her home in Faversham. Our conversations roamed from healing to astrology, from the awesome correlations of cosmic and mundane experience in Draconic charts to our favourite British composers. Riding together on double decker buses through the rolling hills of Kent to visit Canterbury's awe-inspiring Cathedral, was a most novel experience for me (I half expected the bus to tilt over at any moment!) but more so was being able to share a transcendent language with a kindred spirit, as we discussed the different levels of the human condition revealed through Draconic, Tropical and Vedic. Combining these distinct zodiacs transcends schools; their unity is an expression of a holistic universe we can just barely appreciate. Within it our thoughts and actions combine in a curious blend of destiny and freedom, with astrology providing some clues to the difference. Uncertainty is transformed and becomes order.

It was a glorious day!

… So when Pam said, hours after arriving in New York, that she had to cancel her tour and return to England because of sickness in the family, a mutual friend suggested I substitute for her at whichever venues were mutually agreeable. Pam was very happy with this arrangement, knowing by then how much I shared her passion for Draconic astrology.

One significant place on the itinerary was Cape Cod, where astrologer, writer and computer wizard Robert Hand put me up for the night. Like a good missionary, that opportunity was used to introduce the miracles of Draconic in his chart and especially in his relationships. Robert Hand and his associate Patricia White attended the lecture next day, and soon after this his computer products sold through Astrolabe were expanded to include Draconic options. Throughout my later tour of Russia, Ukraine and Uzbekistan in 1990-92, Draconic astrology was always a major component of the lecture and teaching repertoire. It was in this way that Muscovite Vladimir Bogdanov was introduced to the system. When he left Russia to join Matrix Software in the mid 1990s, he programmed the Draconic options requested by our growing band of pioneers into Matrix's flagship programs Win*Star (Windows) and Prima (Dos). In retrospect this whole series of events seems to have been programmed itself, as though directed for a purpose.

So at last, after five thousand years of a dominant Sun-Earth based astrology, the Moon, via her Nodes, receives overdue recognition as a point of orientation rather than one "planet" among many. The Sun is 400 times larger than the Moon, and the Sun is 400 times more distant than the Moon, a curious coincidence that results in the Sun and Moon appearing to Earthlings to be the same size. Denizens of other planets in our system would never experience this phenomenon. The inhabitants of Earth are the only ones to perceive the equality and hence equal necessity of Sun and Moon. Isn't it about time this balance was acknowledged in the reckoning of astrological orientation?

Draconic astrology is an essential complement to the more traditional Tropical or Vedic astrology. Each has a distinct place and purpose, but each is necessary for a perspective on the whole. After all this shared hard work over more than two decades, it does seem that modern astrologers are finally ready to acknowledge another system, one which – as I see it – balances masculine and feminine, yang and yin, projective and receptive principles. Pamela Crane's book serves as a clear and thorough introduction to a far-reaching astrological idea whose time has emphatically come.

Chapter One

Angels, Dragons and Wandering Stars

An Astrologer's Journey

Prologue: August 8th 1972, 12h10 pm, Belgravia

The two young women are sitting in semi-darkness. The older can barely see what she is writing on the tiny notepad she holds against the thin ray of window-light; her friend is drinking in words from the old lady comfy as a cushion in the plain chair before her, thirsty for meaning and ashamed of herself at the same time.

She hears extraordinary things from the stranger that she knows to be true – and then to her consternation the flattering phrase, '… and you will be famous for prophecy'. Everything is written down in her friend's small, neat hand to be kept and read and re-read as life is unrolled by the accelerating years. She is a very new, very obscure astrologer, and still thinks that 'prophecy' means foretelling future events. As this is something she refuses to do, the kindly old clairvoyante is going to be proved wrong. The prospect is understandably a little disappointing.

What has brought her to this point?

She doesn't realise it yet, but she has been following her dragon. Her first dragons were red and green, orange and blue, and their wings sometimes fell off. They would play together under Auntie Tet's table until her rainbow fingers smelled richly of Plasticine. Dragons always had nice faces. She was immensely cheered when later in her growing-up she discovered that China was full of smiling dragons with important jobs to do in landscaping and climate control. Unlike their embattled and consequently ill-tempered European cousins, they were allowed to go about their cosmic business without some dimwit in an iron dishcloth making a nuisance of himself during their most delicate assignations and making off with some protesting princess.

At the age of seven she found herself in a classroom on the outskirts of Manchester with a bookshelf along the back wall. For a year she read obsessively from one end of the shelf to the other, utterly absorbed by the drama and magic of the Roman gods, the Greek myths, the heroes of Asgard. At ten, she was still asking for more; at eleven the stories came into her hands as the prize for a good exam. By her mid-teens the pretty stones and enticing symbols of popular astrology had caught her eye as the breath of the spiritual world began to blow through the curtains of her imagination. She sang. She painted. She poemmed. She dreamed.

She was good at French. One sweltering May day in 1961 as a couple of small rocks waltzed together against the stars near the end of Aries, she was obliged to spend the afternoon with the rest of her class composing an essay, in French, about the pros and cons of building a Channel Tunnel. Every eighteen-year-old in Europe was chewing their pen over the same task. The Dragon had his eye on them; he had been once right around the heavenly circuit since they dropped into the world and he hid the little dragon inside them, and at eighteen destiny was calling. Great Dragon called to Little Dragon. As above, so below. None of them knew. The Great Dragon was taking an especially close look at his astrologer-to-be. She had no idea. But after finishing earlier than anyone else, and escaping with relief into the sunshine, and then catching German measles, and forgetting all about the essay-writing day … a letter came, and off she went with a couple of hundred other vivacious adolescents for a ten-day holiday in Paris. (The two little rocks were called 'French' and 'Chalonge' – Challenge.)

It was in Paris that she bought her first astrology book.

But it was in French, and it was one thing debating the finer points of underwater tunnels, and quite another making any sense out of words and phrases that couldn't be found in her dictionary! So her little Marabout–Flash copy of *L'Astrologie* was tucked away for seven whole years.

Only when she had married, moved to the seaside, had a first baby, and met her friend Jackie did the Dragon swirl out of the clouds again to breathe secretly down her neck. He whispered to a librarian (the first of many Franceses) to send her friend home with the astrology books and let her keep them as long as she wished. He brought another friend, Joan. The three worked together fluently – as threes do – until they were ready for his next surprise: westward across the fields, their first real astrologer, who would teach, befriend and open doors to the rest of her protegée's life. The astrologer would herself become renowned all over the astrological world as Olivia Barclay, the restorer of William Lilly's *Christian Astrology* and a pioneer in the revival of the great Horary tradition.

So our novice stargazer applied to learn with the Faculty of Astrological Studies, joined the Astrological Association, worked hard, earned her Diploma, won a prize, took on clients, started classes, encouraged students, played with ideas, went to conferences, made new friends, wrote innovative articles, talked to WIs, lectured at meetings. But no sooner had she stamped and mailed her envelope to the Faculty than the heavenly troops spotted the signal and went over the top…

It was May 28th 1971, she was twenty-eight, mother of two, babies napping, husband on 'lates', labouring in longhand over her first-ever client analysis (unpaid) – and her hand unaccountably taking on a life of its own. Shock! What was this? Let free, the hand with its pen wrote words that weren't in her head. Weary of upright, the letters plunged in circles, ran along upside-down, looped extravagantly, stretched like lions, and spoke of things she had never dreamed or encountered. Who was doing this? She thought she was saved by the bell – her doorbell – which, answered, revealed friend Joan, who was now recruited into the drama. Together they asked questions, teased answers: the writer, this unsought visitor, said he was Robin Gard, an American known as 'Bud', whose plane had been shot down over the Channel (a walk away) in the Second World War. But the drawing he asked the dumbfounded astrologer to do was a seated goddess holding a globe to her forehead, clothed in orange and green. And he started the drawing from the feet. She was spooked.

Then he went. And after wide-eyed discussion her friend went. Next morning she biked through the town, frantic to find some kind of help, some insight, some security in her chaotic new reality. 'Are you looking for something?' enquired stranger after stranger. She was led to a small house and an old couple who welcomed her like a daughter. They fed her tea and smiles and cakes and books and wisdom; they sent her forth again stronger, braver, resolved to stay open to this mystery, but to stay in charge. Their names were Herbert and Doris Lancaster, and she blesses their memory.

It wasn't easy – you try holding a coherent conversation with someone you can't see, can't hear, can't touch but who insists on drawing your attention to his existence in a world you never trusted your sanity to believe in! You try tracking him down through military records and directories – and fail. Then he graciously departs and leaves you, already exhausted with the sheer physical and nervous strain, to cope with an influx of ever more formless minds whose swirling script tells you that they are 'of Aer – [scribble] of Aer' – and begin teaching things that like these words you have never encountered before. 'That word you can't read is *Aeons*,' said her husband, blessedly supportive. 'It's Gnostic.' She had thought it meant long stretches of time, but eventually discovered that *Aeons* were also – in the Gnostic tradition, which so far she knew absolutely nothing about – emanations of the supreme Deity! She didn't know – and they indubitably did – that she was intended, many years and personal dramas later, for work in a little jewel of a Christian Church that would be condemned by the Establishment as 'Gnostic'. They said the world was full of angels – Angels of Aer – and those who were 'of the earth, earthy'.

The next development was the oddest feeling that – over the sink, on a bus, anywhere – something not her own was trying to ooze out of her mouth like toothpaste from a tube. Words, ideas... unable to cooperate or cope, she and her friend went to the Christian Spiritualists. On the 18th July 1972 at around 7 pm she and Mrs Halfpenny both saw a ladder. It was the very first time she had ever been aware of anyone else's image visiting the private inner screen of her mind, and she was ecstatic. After that, there was no stopping her. Visions crowded in, jostling for attention; minds pushed into her body through the back of her neck on Tuesday evenings so they could greet old friends and family. Sometimes she could smell them too. That year she knew the Dragon was busy; but she still didn't realise how much yet lay in store. She dreamed rich dreams of digging for buried treasure while the Dragon smiled his enigmatic smile and kept hidden the astonishing prize that he knew she was destined to find. He was also smiling because he knew – and she didn't – that his very name, Drakon, arose from a Greek root: *edrakon* was a past tense of *derkesthai* – to see clearly. Hence, clairvoyance. Of course.

> You must not meet a dragon's gaze, or you will be powerless; and the dragon will speak to you, in riddles, and will seem to know as much about you as you know yourself.
>
> Peter Dickinson, *The Flight of Dragons*

And now we are at the scene in Belgravia where she is being shown her path. After this disconcerting visit life arranged itself obligingly so that she could travel to astrological meetings once or twice a month, meet the correct people (probably very old friends!) who would ask her to start local groups, hold beginners' classes, write articles, join projects, teach by post, edit newsletters and serve on the Council. She had been to her first Conference and had her mind invigoratingly blown; now she came to her second. This was the one where she stood up in a crowd of two hundred or so total strangers and explained to the revered teacher on the speaker's platform that she thought the 5th harmonic was connected to the genetic code. The roof did not fall in; instead she collected the first of many transatlantic friends who whisked her back to the Cambridge College a month later to join him in a lecture on a subject far too huge and complex for either of them to handle sensibly – particularly in front of several rows of icy academics. This was the first really big double lesson: Know Your Audience, and Learn How To Speak! Her two years at drama school hadn't come anywhere near preparing her for this sort of thing. It took years, and her second funny, musical, dramatic husband, to turn her from a keen but anxious mouse into a confident, unhurried speaker who could hope to spin her ideas to the back of a hall.

She had lots of ideas. She played – what else do you do with a full 5th House? And the more she played, often happily adrift on a sea of grids and charts well into the small hours, the more the ideas came. Some of them had come already to other astrologers, which was reassuring; some were, if not brand new, certainly untried. Some excited interest, some went down like the proverbial lead balloon. It interested her to see that the people who picked up the new ideas and ran with them were themselves still novices or still in the process of establishing themselves. It seemed harder for many of her more settled, experienced colleagues to move beyond bounds they had set for themselves to explore fresh fields. The exceptions became her teachers and her friends, came to her talks as often as she attended theirs, printed her articles and sent her their own to read.

One day she visited American friends in London, and one spread cards on the rug. The Empress turned up. The vivacious girl fixed her with a serious gaze: 'You,' she said solemnly, 'are going to do karmic astrology.' As this meant nothing to her at all, she didn't think about it for long, and for the next few years worked happily on the *Journal*, her projects, and settling into a new home and new life on the chalk downs above the river Medway.

January 1977

But on her birthday in 1977 the Dragon cosied up to her again when she wasn't looking and left her a fortune that turned her life upside down. And a few angels got into the act, too. And the Archbishop of Canterbury. What happened was that a neurophysiologist from the Institute of Psychiatry in south London developed a powerful interest in the paranormal experiences of his patients. He wanted more people to study, couldn't think where to start asking, so went to the top. The Archbishop remembered the Religious Experience Research Unit (RERU) at Oxford, and put the neurophysiologist in touch with its Director. So Dr Peter Fenwick met Edward Robinson. Now it happened that our spiritual pilgrim had been in correspondence with the said Unit since Derby Day in 1972 when, instead of being glued to the racing she had been in her sunny kitchen listening to *Woman's Hour*, which had a riveting item about RERU's work at the top of the programme. By then, she had plenty to write about. Subsequently BBC's *Horizon* picked it up, and clogged the family's living-space with cameras, cables, mikes on booms and many people for a whole day to secure three minutes of film. (That was the day she first met a Liberal Catholic priest. But she didn't know!) Therefore Edward Robinson put his new young friend in touch with Peter Fenwick, and they met at Great Ormond Street on her birthday.

This began an interesting year, wrestling with charts of Peter's epileptic patients, trying to find some sort of pattern to their seizures. Sometimes she felt she was coming close – but then the patterns would slip away again. The data were poor; so few people could offer more than approximate times. She wanted precision, and it never came. In the end she admitted defeat. Oh, to be twenty years ahead, with the bright brain and swift images of her laptop to count for her! In 1980 she would buy a TRS80 with a tacky cassette deck – and scarcely use it. It all kept her nice and busy.

April 1977

The next trick up her Dragon's secret sleeve was to book her for a talk about Mars and Venus – full of erotic possibilities! – in a village just far enough away for her to spend the night with friends. (Aer, no doubt, had one of their really good dreams lined up for that night; they usually saved them up for visits to strange beds.) The arrangement was that during the talk, a very unhappy and extremely nice man would sit a few rows back with his wife and think to himself, '*I'd* like a lady like that!' Then they would meet, he would ask if there were classes, she would say 'not yet', each would expect the other to get in touch, and neither would in fact set eyes on the other until his Solar Return nine months later, at another talk, in another town. And so it went.

September 1977

In the meantime there was another Conference to go to. The scheming Dragon slipped into her plans, brilliantly disguised. He waited for his moment. A full theatre. A keynote speaker… he whipped off his disguise with a triumphant flourish as she gasped at the treasure pouring into her mind! The Dragon had a zodiac! It sang duets with the Tropical! It opened up the soul! It laid bare its deepest motivations! They were being shown dramas of Sun and Mars that had always been there and never been seen before. A quick bit of mental arithmetic, and she realised he was talking about her, too – the pioneering, the racing to win, the short fuse, the love of a challenge, the battle of wits… the courting and fear of pain… O Dragon, what gifts you spilled from your golden nest that day!

November 1977

On the 1st of November Urania herself, dancing before her Maker, removed another veil. The image of Chiron was revealed to astronomy as the Dragon stretched himself luxuriously from the top to the bottom of the heavens, breathing the fire of eternal, maverick Truth into the future of a reborn humanity. We were to learn about karma.

A few weeks later, an American envelope thumped on the astrologer's mat, and delivered to her the first ephemeris of the wonderful Centaur. To Dennis Elwell's gift of the Draconic zodiac was added Al H. Morrison's gift of Chiron. She had a client all that day, who had what she could only describe as 'boot-button' eyes. They were bright and black and keen; they looked as if they often twinkled out from behind a rock or a tree. When he had gone, and she was at last playing with Chiron, she found that her client had it exactly rising. Her client had Chiron eyes.

Needless to say, at the moment of the ephemeris' arrival, Chiron was on the Midheaven.

14th December 1977, Tenterden Town Hall

Roger Elliott has spoken, scores of curious people have been greatly entertained. Whether they will remember what the bluff and popular astrologer had to tell them, heaven only knows, but the small contingent from the Medway towns will for sure; he is a friend of our friend. She rises to stretch her legs, turns – and there beaming at her from the back row is the lively little bearded man she met in April. He is on his own. Why hadn't she phoned? Why hadn't *he* phoned? Never mind, here they were, and she is able now to ask him to classes. The group is up and running.

In January he joined the class – alone. He made himself Useful. He plugged and unplugged things, tidied trailing leads, checked recording levels, handed out worksheets, and so on. He was a nice person to have around.

The Dragon could relax for a bit now, as he had set everything necessary in motion for the next thirty-odd years and more, including the new relationship that would take both of them out of unproductive and often dismal marriages into a life charged with delight and spiritual purpose. He chuckled in his scales – these two had no idea what was about to hit them! He could now leave the field to Neptune, which had already put skids under her IC. All that had seemed secure, mundane, inevitable was being washed away from under her as plotting angels rearranged all her plans. First of all, they whisked her husband away with four hundred other aspiring PCs (the helmeted variety, the only kind we knew!) to sit an exam. It would win just one of them the honour of becoming the solitary British Transport Police Officer in the length of Cornwall. Cornwall, you will observe from your map of the British Isles, is as UK counties go not very wide, but noticeably long. It is also – again by island standards – a long, complex and weary drive from far-flung Kent. Then they fixed the result: he came back with a dazed look on his face and informed his astonished family that they had to up sticks and move all the way to Truro. This would mean his starting work down there almost immediately, with visits home only one weekend a fortnight, which suited the celestial scheme perfectly, as it gave the astrologer and her smitten student plenty of time in which to get to know each other.

Which they proceeded to do. What she didn't know, and he didn't know, was that he was a natural-born healer; so she didn't realise what was happening when he put his hand on her shoulder one day and she wanted to feel that touch again and again and again. Over the next five sunny, heady months, friendship turned to passion and to love; no common sense, no conscience, no duty could stop it – because it was a spiritual, not a material issue. Aëreen eyes observed with satisfaction an appointment kept, despite the spoke nearly thrown into their wheel by a lady reading cards over coffee without so much as a by-your-leave… 'You have a choice to make,' she said sternly. 'There are two men, two paths. If you take one, you will have joy beyond any expectation. If you take the other, you will regret it bitterly for the rest of your life. And I am not permitted to tell you which is which.' What a terrifying scenario! What a responsibility! What was she meant to do?

She did, in fact, the only thing she could do: pray hard, and trust her astrology. The fruits of both tugged her heart in a new, alarmingly different direction, and the rest is history. A fortnight after arriving in Cornwall she knew she had to go back, and a year later Neptune's seismic wave lifted her out of the old life into the new. They called their new home Arcady.

They were only there for two years, but during that time the Dragon was wide awake again, all fired up, and zealously going about his business; aided mightily by his celestial companions he stepped up his efforts to a quite implausible degree. Why, for instance, should a duty visit to an ordinary trade fair shock her Gerard into the realisation that he was intended to be a healer? Why should a peaceful evening session of prayer and absent healing four months later turn into an unscheduled meeting with a jolly, Irish – and disembodied – priest? How was the small group that gathered around the reluctant channel each week thereafter supposed to respond to the additional visits of a teacher who was only a voice that came from the sleeping man, and yet filled the sitting-room with a presence that was simply awe-inspiring?

'Have you a name we can call you?' they eventually asked after many weeks. 'No', replied the deep and beautiful voice, 'but you can think of me as The Tibetan.' Which meant nothing to any of them.

Another evening, their teacher addressed the astrologer. 'You must write your book,' he said. 'It's very important.' She had made such strides with her work in Draconic astrology that people had started asking her to do this. There was no literature about it to speak of, apart from a sprinkling of pages in two of Ron Davison's books, some early work in France that never really made it across the channel, and her own few articles over the past couple of years. But on the other hand it was still such a young subject; she didn't feel ready, let alone capable. An article of half a dozen pages was one thing, a full-length book quite another! The day she had stepped into Blackwell's bookshop, overwhelmed by the acreage of dense print that confronted her, she vowed never, ever to add to that massive weight of verbiage if she could possibly avoid it. Anyway, it was only astrology. What could be so important? The whole idea was too flattering, so she didn't trust it. She made a half-hearted attempt to get the project going and petered out after three pages.

Then they went to Belgrave Square.

And they met Cheryl. On the way home after unexpected reflexology from those long, sensitive brown fingers, the Dragon's protegée suddenly felt as if every vehicle on the road was driving straight through her; and all she craved – this lifelong carnivore and lettuce-hater – was lentils and salad.

June 15th 1980, 4 pm, Clapham

Another small room of muted light; the astrologer and her man have been pulled like twin meteors into the orbit of the glorious woman whose modest home now enfolds and startles them. For the best part of an hour the eyes of the seer have searched through her own and into her mind, her soul, as the tape-recorder whispered nearby. At six minutes past six o'clock the seer will marry them, but neither of them knows this yet, and now serenity changes to wonderment, for she has taken the astrologer's hands in her own and said, 'These hands must write the Word of God!'

She cannot imagine any circumstance in which this might happen. Despite her penetrating insights, about this Cheryl has surely to be wrong.

They went to Egypt with Cheryl and Dennis Stoll. The decision had been made way back at that first meeting: it was either Egypt or a new roof for Arcady; and in the event the day before they left in September 1981 for three weeks' pilgrimage into their deep past, the house was sold, nail-sick roof and all. And now it was also their honeymoon, as everything had continued as aërially intended and a wonderful wedding had taken place on a sunny day in August. All their healing friends had been there. Nina from Seeboard laid out a feast for them in a garden marquee; Howarth from the 'Light Op' played piano and sang like an angel through several bottles of Glenfiddich till two in the morning. Earlier still, in March, after fidgeting for lack of space, they found their home. So in a blue-gold sunset on Bonfire Night they at last settled into the Mayor's Arms, where next year she would start her own correspondence college.

They used the 'snug' for healing. It had its own door; no-one had to come through the rest of the house. People who responded to the touch from Gerard's hands, the flow of divine love through crown and heart and palm, became friends. Over the next few years the spiritual energy in the house increased. Visitors noticed, remarked on the lovely atmosphere, felt happy there. Meanwhile, good advice from a friend sent the recalcitrant author away to a small, old-fashioned hotel near her old home by the seaside. There, with a few books, drawing tools, music and a typewriter she was able at last to commit the essence of Draconic astrology to paper. It took three weeks; the typescript was submitted and accepted, and the finished book appeared in public in January 1987. But the book was not all that her friends Upstairs had planned for life in Ospringe.

'Ospringe' means either 'ox spring' or 'God's spring'. From the vantage point of 1999 eclipse year as this is written, either will do! At a service in the chapel at Tonbridge School, the two were introduced to a Liberal Catholic Priest. It was July 21st 1984, the date appointed for the Dragon and the Centaur – with a little help from their friends – to join forces and blow magic dust on their pupil's spiritual preconceptions. It was time to start in earnest the next stage of training for the unusual task she was chosen to perform. The process had started on Good Friday: one determining life-surge had connected her back to the Christian Church, through the priest at the local Roman Catholic Presbytery. For another year, while she spent surprisingly happy evenings preparing herself, with Father Frank, to enter the Church which had nourished her husband's youth, that same husband was discovering a treasure he had sought hopelessly for forty years, in the esoteric teaching and rich symbolic liturgy of the Liberal Catholic Church.

Angels and Dragons always have their way; by the summer of 1985 she had been coaxed to the altar at an unfamiliar service, to make her Communion for the very first time. Lights blazed on in her head, her entire being was astounded! She was a walking, breathing exclamation! It was her Damascus Road, the epiphany from which she could never turn back. In August she dragged all her astrological gear to their first week-long Church Congress – and scarcely touched it. The liturgy compelled her. Her soul soared. Poetry came flooding into her mind, singing the poignant joy of this re-involvement with Christ that lit her and set every flaw in sharp relief. The angels fed on the incense gilding the sunbeams and were glad; they knew she would be pleased with the present they would give her before the week was out, and would use it well. Nobody touched it until she came to the book table; and she was very pleased indeed with her history of the worldwide visions of Mary… especially with her words to the children at Medjugorje, telling them that August 5th, not September 8th, was her birthday. This was ever so close to the dreamed-of August 4th that you will read about in Chapters Five and Nineteen.

Al Morrison had been sending her asteroids. Amor and Atropos, Love and Death, had starred in many of her charts, and she knew by now that the tiniest heavenly bodies were of the greatest significance in the drama of life. She had begun to use Bach Flower Remedies (how quickly she learned them!) and was vividly aware of the inverse laws of power and scale. The greatest destruction on earth resulted from the splitting of its minutest atom; the deepest healing of the mind came from the memory of petals in water. The most precise description of events and people was found by fine-tuning the astrological chart and plotting its relevant asteroids. A list from California showed her that among them were Mary and Maria. She made Tropical/Draconic charts of the Marian visions, and of the visionaries. Mary and Maria were written against the horizon, the meridian, the Sun, the Moon. The Idea was demonstrably present in the moment; Mary was there. When the old bishop preached eloquently on Mary and the Moon at the tiny oratory in Folkestone, she was irrevocably decided – she would ask for Confirmation into this Church, and they would start services at the Mayor's Arms. These began on October 25th 1985 at 10h30 am, and they called their church the Oratory of the Holy Spirit. Unnoticed by them, as at their wedding, as at the moment when Gerard was told to heal, the Uranus-Chiron opposition was electrifying the horizon.

Unusual and enlightening events were therefore bound to occur. One Sunday a member of the small but growing congregation placed in her hand a picture of 'The Tibetan', DK, or Djwal Kuhl. It was a greying photocopy, and as an experienced print-colourist she thought it would be cheered by the addition of some colour. Out in the July sunshine with a rainbow in a box, the plan stalled. *What* colour? His Himalayan face smiled above the folds of a robe – should it be pale yellow like the chanting monks wore in her clear dream twenty years ago? Impossible to decide. '*You* do it!' she challenged, out of patience … and remembering that first encounter at Walmer, the drawing of the seated figure, the moving hand no longer her own. She let go. The hand no longer her own went to the box and drew out flesh tones and soft gold; the face with its aureole shone. Next a green-yellow like daffodil buds brightened the undergarment at his neck; lastly the monk's robe was given its deep dye of madder brown, a little closer to crimson than mahogany. This was a surprise! Whatever had happened to the 'saffron robe'? He looked wonderful, and soon small photographs of the image were being tucked into purses and wallets, while the original, framed, took pride of place on the wall. Strange, though, these colours.

Months later a television documentary took its viewers high into the Himalayas to learn about the life of the Buddhist monks still living and praying there. Over the green-yellow undergarment each one wore his robe of madder brown.

Aër breathed in her ear, urged her mouth to move, left sentences in her head that had to be written. She tried valiantly to go where she was put, do as she was asked, marshal the irruption of ideas, assemble them on paper, but it made her so tired. It couldn't be what she was really meant to do; others were channelling far more freely than she. Again she failed. But her people were closer to her, and she was at last beginning to flow with their desire.

1986, Oratory of the Holy Spirit, Ospringe

Perhaps *this* is what was meant by 'the Word of God' – her husband's birthday dream of a chapel where the two spare bedrooms had been, has become reality. Now he assists with the Christian sacraments at their own altar, and she sits quietly hour after hour (as she sat hundreds of years before?) copying scriptures carefully onto vellum to be read at their Sunday services.

She enters holy orders – unwillingly at first. She is quite well known among astrologers now; how can she take on two major commitments? How will her friends, her colleagues, receive her?

The Dragon whispered to her, 'Look up at the *stars*! And stand in the Sun!' It was time to remind her of her next task. How could she be content, after all, with only two of the many dimensions of astrological truth? His Master, *her* Master, would refer to it as 'your Royal Truth'. This work on the blending of energies between Tropical and Draconic must lead on further now to embrace the wider sweep of the ancient Sidereal framework, and then the deep close focus of the real geometries around the Sun. The Dragon goaded the Centaur in her sky, pulling her back toward her path. She loved this detective work, revelled in the truth laid bare before her day after enthralling day. Structures were emerging, ideas multiplying. Old, old, fractured astrologies were recombining into a magnificent, vibrant whole; nothing was superfluous, all was contained. Everything yet undiscovered, whether revolutionary or antique, could be subsumed without loss of integrity into an all-encompassing interdimensional astrology. All agreements, all paradoxes. It had the complexity and simplicity of music; and so she returned to music itself, and then to the subtler frequencies of colour, and then to the resonant crystalline structures of matter, building layer by layer a conceptual portrait of the vibratory universe from macrocosm to microcosm.

She took her work to Devon. It was June 1989, and the two of them had been invited to a week's retreat that would send their lives spinning once again. Roy, their friend, had left the Liberal Catholic Church. He had fallen out with the current Presiding Bishop, who was a weak and unimaginative man, to concentrate on building his own spiritual community. Roy had been consecrated during the winter, by an Oklahoma bishop in charge of another, healthier and perfectly legitimate branch of the Church, and asked his friends to attend. The spark that had lit the souls of Gerard and the quiet American now flared into a mutual joy: for hours they strolled the garden exchanging thoughts, swapping histories, while the newly-priested Lancashire tenor taught the bishop how to sing the Liturgy. They celebrated Mass together. They parted as firm friends. Moreover, during the most solemn part of the one service his wife did not attend (for the work was flowing), at the invocation of the head of the Great White Brotherhood, a familiar voice that had not been heard for nearly nine years resonated in the stillness of Gerard's mind… 'Now you know!' He wrote an account of this remarkable week in the Oratory's newsletter, *The Dove*, and sent a copy to his Presiding Bishop.

And the roof fell in.

It was impossible to continue under such an intolerant jurisdiction, the Ospringe congregation agreed. Unanimous, they left the parent church in a hail of abuse, and Gerard paid his first visit to Oklahoma. A synod was scheduled, he was to be vetted by the assembled bishops – and they moved the venue to Flagstaff, Arizona! He hadn't anticipated driving the length of the legendary Route 66 by night and day, being bitten in his sleep by a scorpion, having one of the most profound spiritual experiences of his life, and coming home as bishop-elect – but that is how it was. 'Why Flagstaff?' he asked John, his new Presiding Bishop and loved friend. His reply, 'You wanted to see the Grand Canyon, didn't you?'

This was a measure of the generosity of the man, the total opposite of his British counterpart. He had already demonstrated it in his active concern for his new bishop's wife, rescued by radical surgery from grave illness, and so weak that she could do nothing for nearly two months but speak, read, and learn to walk again. Every night he telephoned from Tulsa to send his love and keep them in good spirits. Every evening, relaxed after a meal, she would feel him vividly present, his healing energy restoring her. They blessed John Schwarz every day.

Work was impossible. The book on Interdimensional Astrology that she had been planning since the Dragon's surprise February visit, was on ice. He had uncoiled again, chuckling with anticipation, and allowed her to glimpse and then hold another jewel. Her dreams had changed: the treasures she found in secret places no longer eluded her. Instead she brought them away with her, keeping them safe from loss or destruction. But she could do nothing. To while away the time she went back to her box of rainbows and worked out a wonderful way to display the uniqueness of a birth chart purely through an interplay of colours. Once again the crafty angels had found a way to teach her the next thing she needed to know; soon her files were over-flowing with gloriously kaleidoscopic skies – and she found that not only she, but others too, could feel the presence of the person through the play of colour on the page. Soon she was writing again, and the skies full of colour poured into her book.

There was a conference, surely, of her unseen friends; she was due to ride the Dragon again, to leap another divide – and the only spur was to rob her of her astrology. Unthinkable! And quite impossible. Yet there was a way: they sent her off to Walsingham. Properly known on all its signposts as Little Walsingham, but now much greater than tiny Great Walsingham, this small Norfolk town is 'England's Nazareth'. It found its unique destiny back in 1061 when the Lady Richeldis de Faverches had a vision commanding her to build the Holy House of Mary and Joseph there on her land. Pilgrims came for nearly five hunded years – and then the appalling Henry VIII, amid the usual bloodshed, pillaged and burned its treasures, closed and ruined the Priory. Only in the 20th century was the shrine resurrected; pilgrimages began once again in 1934, and now Walsingham with its two major, and several smaller shrines, is a vibrant centre of Marian devotion.

Walsingham welcomed them both in a true, loving Christian embrace. They walked, prayed, sang, drank from its holy well, and would happily have stayed. Shortly after their return home she found herself standing by the telephone with her astrology crumpled around her feet like an old coat dropped on the floor. How else could she describe the vivid, invisible experience that now so shocked her? And how could this happen? The laughing Dragon waited for her to react. She did exactly as he expected: she said, 'Well, Mary, if you want me to give up the most precious thing in my life for you, then that is what I must do.'

The problem that nagged at her was that she had promised others beside herself that she would write her Interdimensional book, and it was barely started. A responsible soul, she felt that at the very least she ought to try to fulfil that commitment, even if all her other astrological work was finished for ever. Also, she had to find something else to do! The Dragon breathed on the window of her 5th House and rubbed it with his scaly elbow; the Sun shone through. She caught the creative thought – she would *knit*. But what should she make? Knitting had never been a strong point; the results were somewhat shapeless. Charity blanket squares had been her only notable success! So if knitting had to be in straight lines and fill her empty hours, then scarves were the answer. (The angels clustered round attentively; the Dragon inched closer …) Next question: who were they for? And how to choose the colours? It was not possible for her to start anything without the sense of a clear goal, and the goal was… what? Somebody up there whispered in her ear, a magic word. Of course! She would knit a *chart*!

Now at last the adrenalin was running, as she had found a challenge again. The watchers of her life breathed a sigh of relief and settled back after their series of delicate manoeuvres. She was happily engaged now with the problems of how to present the elements of a birth chart in a straight line, in their correct relationships, with an absence of symbols. There had to be a given number of rows for each degree. The colours were easy – she had worked them out by logic, tradition, trial and error for a year, a distinct shade assigned to every one of the thirty-six decans, and the work she had shared with the brilliant Michael Heleus from 1972 onwards provided the planetary spectrum. But using these colours to pinpoint the true positions of specific planets and angles along the length of the scarf presented real difficulties. To plot the Sun, for example, ideally needed one line of colour. But what *was* that line? She had to fine-tune. How about a harmonic? Ah, now, how about the 12th harmonic? And even better, since the colours were concomitant on the decanates, why not use their own natural subdivision into the dwad? This was a system she had never investigated, though dwads appeared from time to time in work from the USA; it was ripe for exploration, and off she sailed again on a familiar ocean of charts! Cheers went up in the Invisible as they watched her eyes widen and widen at the crisp new accuracy that the dwad positions – precise to degrees and minutes – delivered to every nativity. The gamble had paid off: the enforced stop and re-start had pointed her in exactly the right direction, and now she had nearly everything she needed to tackle the most daunting work of all. And she had great fun with her scarves.

October 25th 1992, Kent

Her mother has died.

It happened only four days after her birthday back in January, a Sunday chosen for her ordination as Sub-Deacon. The last conversation mother and daughter had was over the telephone on the 22nd – 'Happy Anniversary, Mum!' and the usual loving chat and intimate silliness. The next morning her world changed forever. A legacy meant she could buy her first computer and so start the long, hard haul up its legendary learning curve to the astonishingly expanded world of astrology that the company of heaven had finally flung open to her.

She is sitting at the desk her father gave her five years ago, staring at a blue screen, thoughts unstructured and melting into daydream … into whose opening pool drops an idea. She thinks it is her own – but as ever, who is to say? There is no power on earth like that of an idea whose time has come, and this one will drive her its own unguessable way for at least the next four years. This idea, born of the sudden realisation that Jesus' own perfection was the key to his Nativity, is in fact the fruit of her past fifteen years' work on the Draconic zodiac. She knows now beyond a shadow of a doubt that the description found in a person's Draconic chart unveils the deep principles by which they live; and those people born when the eclipses happen in spring, with the dragon's head and the Spring Equinox together in the sky so that their two zodiacs coincide, are the very souls who most practise what they preach.

If anyone ever practised what they preached, it was Jesus.

Therefore, if ever a person had to be born in a year of spring eclipses, it was he; and as the Jesus she is growing to know in her own heart is the divine human perfection toward which most struggling souls can only aspire, then the union of principle and practice, of Draconic and Tropical, of Dragon's Head and Equinox, must be absolutely exact.

This is something she was never going to do, this search for the Christ's Nativity. Too many good astrologers have made the attempt, and clearly failed, as the birth charts they produced could have belonged to any half-decent man. Thinking as astronomers, or historians, or simply as non-Christians, none have been able to see the inadequacy of their efforts. None have fully acknowledged the first and central requirement: that they search for the birth of *God*. And she is going to fail, too, of course – but at least it is a fresh approach.

There are eighteen years between one set of spring eclipses and the next. Knowing already the limited time-frame in which they had to fall – between the famous series of Jupiter-Saturn conjunctions of 7 BC and the death of Herod in 4 BC – there is only a small chance that the idea will work at all. The astrology software is good for ancient dates, and there is an ephemeris she can run; soon figures are sliding out of her printer. Astonishingly, the conjunction is going to happen… in which year? In 5 BC. In which month? It is going to be May. And the day? The day is coming up as May 7th, at 16h23 GMT. She still has no idea what she will see when this feeds into her program and prints an astrological chart.

It is 5h25 pm: the astrologer is looking at the birth of God. The Jesus of the Gospels has come alive in her hands, and she cannot believe what she sees. She knows what is required of a great Master; the tradition is that he is born at noon, sunrise or sunset – and this, at Bethlehem, was sunset. Jupiter is always powerful in priestly charts, symbolising both greatness and wisdom, humour and generosity, openness to the world and to God; combined with the other mighty planet Saturn, the pair represent both the spirit and the letter of the Law, all freedoms and all structures. Here Jupiter is setting in mid-Taurus with the Sun, exactly thirty degrees from Saturn, in the sunset position (the Descendant) meaning not 'I' but 'Thou' to whom this limitless gift of holy love and joy is being out-poured. She sees more, and knows the pattern is perfect.

But this Nativity is not the end of a journey; it is just a beginning.

Now indeed she must try to write the word of God.

Chapter Two

The Draconic Zodiac
A Sleeping Prophet Rouses Astrology

Dear Reader, let us begin our adventure into the new astrology by looking at the birth chart below. It is of a person – Subject 'A' – born on August 13th 1917, in Cincinnati, Ohio. You will observe the strength of Cancer and Leo, Mercury and Venus in Virgo, Jupiter rising in Gemini, and the culminating Uranus in its own sign. It is always useful to read other people's analyses of nativities, and so shall we do here. The following is most interesting:

'We find the soul and spirit entity took its flight, or its force being present and bringing the present entity's completeness, from … Venus' forces, with those of Jupiter, Mercury, Neptune being the ones in the assistance to the conditions bringing to forces to this present plane's development, with afflictions in those in Mars and in that of Septimus. Arcturus being in the greater force for this development upon this plane, [the soul] receiving then the greater force by the influence of Arcturus, with … the dwelling-forces of Neptune. The Moon's forces being those that have brought, and will bring, many of the influences from the forces of Venus.'

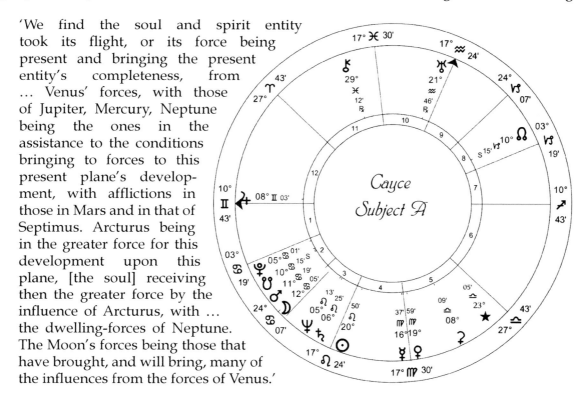

As these, we find those inclinations:

> 'With the strength of Jupiter forces, with that of Venus and Neptune … one given to letters, and of high exalted positions of self and all concerned therewith. Given to make show, or display, of that element that gives the greater expression of self Hence, will must be directed, else with the influence of Venus' forces [it] would give detrimental elements in the life. One whose forces from … Mercury will turn in the middle portion of life to those elements pertaining to the chemical forces, with that of Arcturus' forces giving strength to the elements that are directed in the entity.'

Whether or not this writer is familiar to you, in both style and content his approach is quite different to anything else you may find in published astrology. The language has an archaic ring, and is tortuous to follow. And what does it mean? References to Jupiter, and to the 'Moon's forces' – assuming the sign of Cancer – can be comprehended: but the remainder is baffling.

Here is another chart – Subject 'B' – a noon chart for a birth on 16th January 1919. The commentary states:

> 'Through Aries associations, there are the abilities of a high mental development; yet there are rather those warnings for this entity regarding accidents to the head. Injuries of some nature may come … either during the next four months or early portion of 1934. These warnings are from influences that come from Aries or head associations with Mars. Hence, as to the greater astrological activities from sojourns in environs, Uranus is the greater influence for the present experience.'

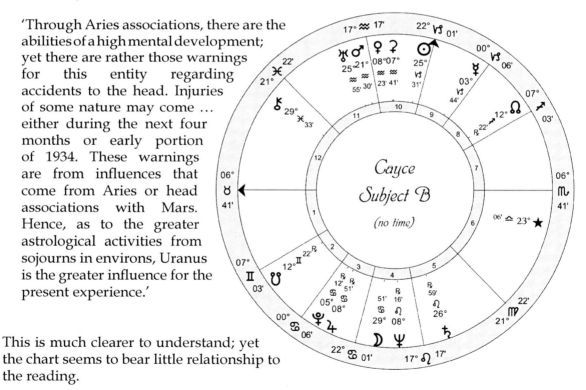

This is much clearer to understand; yet the chart seems to bear little relationship to the reading.

A further example is that of a man, Subject 'C', born on February 26th 1915, near Norfolk, Virginia at 5h56 p.m:

'There have been periods when the entity apparently has been blocked in the preparation for this or that activity, this or that association with individuals, and circumstances that would have changed or do change the whole course of events for the entity.

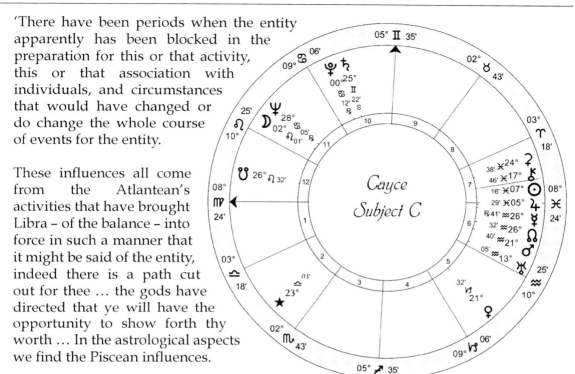

These influences all come from the Atlantean's activities that have brought Libra – of the balance – into force in such a manner that it might be said of the entity, indeed there is a path cut out for thee … the gods have directed that ye will have the opportunity to show forth thy worth … In the astrological aspects we find the Piscean influences.

In Venus as combined with Mercury, and the activities in Uranus, we find the interests in things mechanical as well as those that require the application of such by the material hands.'

But where is Libra's dominance of this chart? Who is the author of so many obscure and unfounded statements? What kind of astrology is this supposed to be?

Let me answer the second of these three questions first. These readings were never written by their author; all are extracts from transcriptions of Life Readings given in self-induced 'sleep' by the extraordinary Edgar Cayce. Margaret Gammon, in her indispensable book, *Astrology and the Edgar Cayce Readings,* reminds us that 'of the 2,500 life readings which Cayce gave from 1923 to 1945, almost all refer to past incarnations and specific astrological or planetary influences bearing upon the present [life]', and yet these were concepts totally foreign to the man. A devoted Christian, the Holy Bible was his constant source of inspiration and knowledge; his self-appointed task each year was to read the Word of God from the first verse of Genesis to the last syllables of Revelation. His singular gift was a deep trouble to him, as it appeared to run quite contrary to what he consciously understood of the law of God, and it took a great deal of persuasion on the part of those who knew him, respected his integrity, and yet could see the value of his gift, to allay his anxiety and prompt him to undertake his strange new work. Since childhood, Cayce had been capable of slipping at will into a kind of hypnotic sleep; in this state he was by some means able to learn, to obtain information and understanding that could not be reached or grasped by him in the waking state.

The work that came to dominate the last forty-two years of his life was the logical development of this. At the request of ever-increasing numbers of the sick, the anxious, the seekers of hidden truths, he would allow himself to pass into that apparent sleep which freed his consciousness to rise through the planes of spiritual awareness to the exalted hall where are preserved those records of every individual human life known to metaphysics as the Akasha. To begin with, and for the first twenty years, these heights were neither sought nor attained; he saw his role as a helper to the physically sick and, entering the knowledge of the body with his mind, was capable both of precise diagnosis and exact prescription, to the extent of locating the remedy to save a patient searching high and low for a scarce medicine or little-known herb.

It was one Arthur Lammers who, realising the dizzying potential of Cayce's gift, proposed that questions of a metaphysical, moral and religious nature be asked in the course of a consultation. This was in 1923, and proved to be the inception of the 'Life Readings' drawn by the mind of Cayce from the Akashic records.

In one of the readings, he describes the process of up-reaching to the hall of the Akasha:

'I see myself as a tiny dot out of my physical body, which lies inert before me. I find myself oppressed by darkness and there is a feeling of terrific loneliness. Suddenly, I am conscious of a white beam of light. As this tiny dot, I move upward following the light, knowing that I must follow it or be lost.'

He goes on to describe a series of changes of peopled environment, at first grotesque, then increasingly light and pleasant:

'There is more and more light, the colours become very beautiful, and there is the sound of wonderful music. The houses are left behind, ahead there is only a blending of sound and colour. Quite suddenly, I come upon a hall of records. It is a hall without walls, without a ceiling, but I am conscious of seeing an old man who hands me a large book, a record of the individual for whom I seek information.'

Similar descriptions of the spiritual 'levels' can be found in ancient texts such as *The Tibetan Book of the Dead*, and in very recent communications, as the account given by one determined seeker, Sir Arthur Conan Doyle, through his medium Grace Cooke, and published by White Eagle in *The Return of Arthur Conan Doyle*.

Astrology and the Edgar Cayce Readings is, then, the source of the astrological commentaries relating to the three nativities as shown, and – all too brief – an answer to our second question. This book has a further purpose, so let us proceed, and return to our first question.

I have three more charts to show you, Subjects 'D', 'E' and 'F'. Study them; they bear a relationship to the first three.

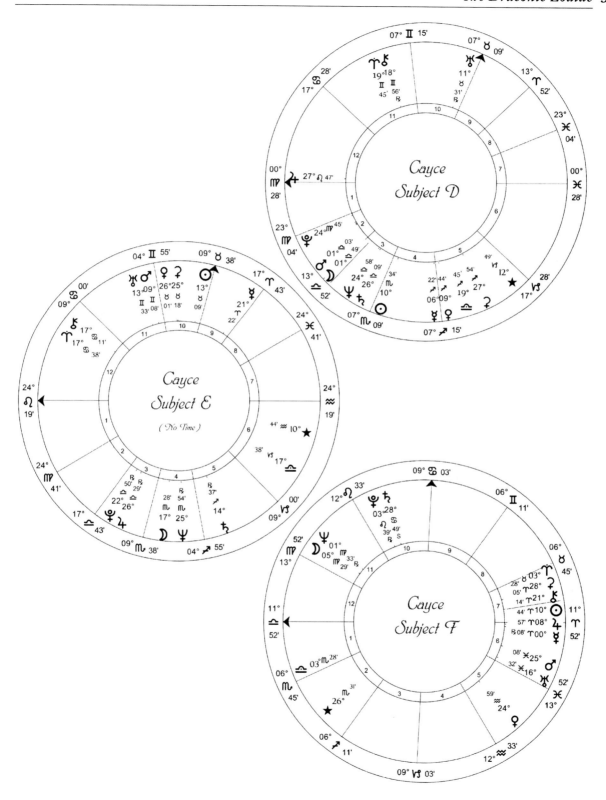

Has the relationship become apparent? Clearly, the planetary distribution in the houses is identical, between subjects 'A' and 'D', 'B' and 'E', and 'C' and 'F' respectively; the patterns of aspects and angularities are exactly the same. In short, only the signs, the degree-placements of the planets, Ascendant and Midheaven are different. Something is missing, however, in the second set of three charts: the Nodes of the Moon have disappeared, and a new symbol – or pair of symbols – has found its way into the structure.

What has happened?

Let us look at these new charts more closely.

In the chart of Subject 'D', four planets have been placed in Libra – Mars, Moon, Neptune and Saturn. Mercury is in 6°22' of Sagittarius, and Venus in 9°44' Sagittarius. Neptune's position in Libra is 24°58'; Arcturus (symbolised in these charts by the star ★) – that vast sun around which our own Sun and its planetary system is said by Cayce to revolve – has moved into 12°49' Capricorn.

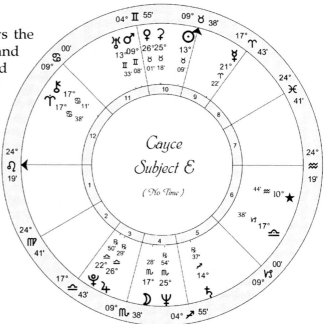

The horoscope of Subject 'E' shows the Sun and Venus in Taurus, Moon and Neptune in Scorpio. Mercury has moved into Aries at 21°22', Mars into Gemini 9°08', and Uranus to Gemini 13°33' opposite Saturn at 14°37' Sagittarius. Lastly, Diagram 7 for Subject 'F' has Venus at 24°59' Aquarius, Uranus in Pisces 16°32', Neptune at 1°33' Virgo with the Moon conjoined in 5°29', and Saturn at 28°49' Cancer. Libra rises.

We have just answered the first question. You see, the second three charts *are* the first three charts, but transposed into a fresh zodiac – not the Sidereal zodiac, or any variation thereupon (and there are many, as any thorough student of astrological history will testify!) – and now we see that for Subject 'C', Libra holds the Ascendant, an indisputably strong position in the overall pattern, when re-presented as Subject 'F'.

Look at Subject 'E'. The commentary on its original, Subject 'B', stated clearly that there were associations with Aries and mental development; here in the new version we have an Aries Mercury, and not only this, for 'head associations with Mars' are also emphasised by the mutual reception of Mars in Mercury's sign Gemini, at 9°08'. Uranus remains in its conjunction with Mars, moving to Gemini 13°33', very highly suggestive of the kind of wilful, impulsive energy that warns of accident.

When Subject 'A' becomes Subject 'D', 'Venus' forces' are greatly increased by the fourfold occupation of Libra, and the Sagittarian planets augment 'those of Jupiter' already strong through the presence of the great planet so close to the rising degree in either pattern.

We are beginning to see why Cayce was able to say in the course of one Life-Reading, 'Were this entity's experiences given from the purely astrological science, *as accepted in many quarters*, this would vary entirely from this [record] which may be given here, or that is viewed from here' (my italics). In other words, the astrology with which the modern world has become familiar paints a character picture which may bear scant resemblance to the patterns and meaning of Akashic astrology. In another reading he says: 'As to those [influences] of the constellations or of the zodiacal signs in the life of this entity, these are merely the wavering influences in the life, and not *those directing forces ever present in the inner soul of this entity*. These we find in opposition to much that is at present taught or given in [the] earth plane' (my italics). Elsewhere, he enlarges on the zodiacal theme:

'… the Egyptian and the Persian records are quite varied. If the entity would study astrology, do not put the signs in the Egyptian calendar but in the Persian, for the Persian interpretations are more proficient than the Egyptian. This is not belittling the efforts of the entity nor of the Egyptians in those periods, but *the variations in time* have been corrected by the Persians and not by the Egyptians. The Egyptian calculations are thirty degrees off … For as we have indicated, there are two, yea, three phases or schools through which such information, such charts, such characters have been carried – the Egyptian, the Persian, the Indian. The Persian is a combination and the older of all of these, and these are as logos, or as charts that have been set' [my italics].

Compare the above statements with Cyril Fagan's view, expressed somewhat forcibly in his book, *Astrological Origins*:

'The striking thing ... is the fact that with all the major nations of antiquity from the beginning of recorded history, the zodiac began with the lunar mansion of the Pleiades and ended with those of Aries the Ram. Why, then, in the classical period was the Hindu zodiac altered to commence with Aswini in Aries 0° having regard to the fact that Indian astrologers claim their zodiac always was sidereal? ... The sidereal is not just another zodiac – some new-fangled toy that has mushroomed into being in recent years. It is the great-granddaddy of all zodiacs. It was the only vogue in Egypt in the 3rd millennium BC. On the other hand, the western world's first introduction to Hipparchus' Tropical zodiac was when Proclus' *Paraphrase of the Tetrabiblos* appeared in the 5th century AD. Even then its reception was tardy.'

It would seem at first glance that Cayce is arguing for a return to the Sidereal zodiac, especially in view of his remarks about the Persians' proficiency. Cyril Fagan has no doubt in his mind that both Persia and Egypt used the stellar zodiac in some form. Yet again, Cayce states that the Egyptians were 30° out of phase – and if this applies to the Sidereal zodiac, then it must, in his view, be incorrect! There is no mention whatsoever at this point of the Greek contribution to Western astrology, the Tropical zodiac, commencing at the Vernal Equinox. And there is this strange remark: 'Hence the entity was born into the earth under what signs? Pisces, ye say.' And this was true; in the Tropical zodiac the Sun was at 28° of the sign ...'Yet astrologically from the records, these are some two signs off in thy reckoning.'

No Sidereal/Tropical argument can account for this!

How can one zodiacal system be at variance with another by both 30° *and* by 'two signs off'?

Without invoking two new zodiacs, there can be only one explanation: that the astrology referred to by Cayce is based on a moving zodiac (in comparison to the 'fixed' zodiac of the constellations), and one which moves more rapidly than any zodiac to which we have become accustomed, its Aries Point travelling through the whole circle of the Sidereal, and even the Tropical zodiac, over a relatively short period of years.

Such a zodiac exists: it is the Draconic zodiac. Its circle begins at the Dragon's Head, which is the name given by the ancients to the North or Ascending Node of the Moon, known also as 'Caput' (the Head, opposite 'Cauda', the Tail) and in India as 'Rahu', opposite 'Ketu'. We are at the beginning of the answer to our third question.

Each of the three example charts has been transposed into the Draconic zodiac, and it is with reference to this zodiac that Cayce's interpretive statements fall into place.

It is time to take a closer look at the first chart. This time the two zodiacs have been combined in a bi-wheel, below, with the Draconic positions in the outer ring. (This time I have not included the Draconic Aries and Libra Points.) To begin with, it is clear that Cayce is not merely employing astrological references as character description; he is not simply correlating trait with planet and sign, nor even does he seem to be taking a symbolic approach. He says 'the soul and spirit entity took its flight from Venus' forces', from which we plainly understand that the person *is* soul, *is* spirit, that these two aspects of the discarnate being combine, and that there is a place of departure (if 'place' is the right word) prior to manifestation on Earth. The departure takes place from 'forces' and this

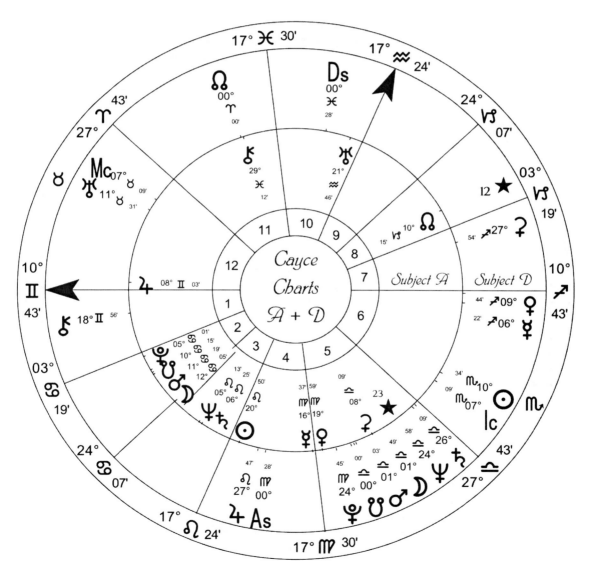

term recurs throughout the Life Readings. The implication is that we spend at least some part of our discarnate existence in vibrational states or 'planes' associated with certain planets; but whether these are found in the environs of the planets as we observe them, or whether the entire orbits are their home, or whether indeed they are unlocalised and abstract states of consciousness, may be debated.

The strength of 'Venus' forces' – far from evident in the Tropical map – stands out in the Draconic chart, with four planets (Moon, Mars, Neptune and Saturn) in the sign of Libra, Uranus and the Midheaven in Taurus, and, clearly seen for the first time, now that the two patterns have been drawn together, Venus herself in 9°44' of Sagittarius, less than 1° from the western horizon of the Tropical chart. While it is extremely difficult to make complete sense of Cayce's words, the grammar being very strange in places, we can understand that the forces of Jupiter, Mercury and Neptune are helping the individual's present life-progress, and observe not only Jupiter conjoined bodily with the Ascendant, but the Draconic Jupiter less than 7° from the Tropical Sun in Leo, and two Draconic planets in Sagittarius, Jupiter's sign. Mercury is one of these, and also close to the degree of the Tropical 7th House cusp. In the Tropical circle Mercury is very prominent, squaring a Gemini Ascendant from Virgo, and with Jupiter and Venus also falling in the Mercury signs.

Neptune is at first a puzzle; Pisces is untenanted by planets, and Neptune does not seem to be strongly positioned. But read on:

'Arcturus being in the greater force for this development upon this plane, [the soul] receiving then the greater force by the influence of Arcturus, with … the dwelling-forces of Neptune.'

Neptune and Arcturus are linked, and also with the 'greater force for this development …' For if you look again at this bi-wheel, you will see that the superimposition of the two zodiacs brings Draconic Arcturus into conjunction with the Tropical Moon's North Node, the Dragon's Head itself – indeed a force for development – and Draconic Neptune falls conjunct Tropical Arcturus. Thus the three forces are interlinked. *Forces*, mark you! Astrology is coming *alive*!

The inference is that the Nodal axis of the Moon – the Dragon – is the key to the individual's soul and spiritual reality. Caput and Cauda in the Tropical chart are indicative of the soul's path through the incarnation, and the zodiac originating at the Dragon's Head illumines our understanding of the nature of the incarnating being. Contacts between the two zodiacs, Tropical and Draconic, would then serve to 'materialise the Spiritual, and spiritualise the Material'.

In this light, the 'afflictions in those in (*sic*) Mars and in that of Septimus' can be understood, as Tropical Mars is found in the sign of its fall, Cancer, conjunct the South Node of the Moon; Tropical Pluto is close by, and may be the planet referred to as 'Septimus'. It is the South Node which is held to pull a person back to his evolutionary past, to that which is completed or sufficient, to his mistakes, and to wrongdoing – even Godlessness. It is strange that the Moon herself is not mentioned in this connection, being so intimately linked with Mars and Cauda; yet she may represent a part of this person's history that is simply past, and remains benign. However, the 'Moon's forces' are interpreted as 'those that have brought, and will bring, many of the influences from the forces of Venus', and indeed we find the Draconic Moon in Libra, expressive of the soul's link to the Venus forces, while Pluto in the Moon's own sign in the Tropical circle is linked to the Virgo Venus through its Draconic degree. Thus the Cancer planets and the Moon belong also to Libra and to Venus, bringing the Venus experience of the soul into potential manifestation.

Jupiter, Venus, Neptune and Mercury are all specifically mentioned as strong forces in the character here, and from this we can learn something of the criteria for planetary strength in Draconic astrology. Jupiter is close to an angle – the Ascendant – and this applies in both charts; Venus in the Draconic chart falls on the place of the Tropical Descendant, and so is angular again; Neptune is doubly connected with the developmental path of the North Node, since Tropically it conjoins Saturn, the Node's dispositor, and its Draconic degree conjoins Tropical Arcturus whose Draconic place, as we have seen, is close to the Tropical Dragon's Head itself. Mercury as well as Venus augments the 'Jupiter forces' from a Draconic position in Sagittarius, close to the Tropical 7th House cusp, and also on the Jupiter axis. Yet if angularity is so important, why are Sun and Uranus passed by in Cayce's commentary? Look again, and you will see that neither planet forms any additional contact to planets or angles in the Draconic chart, nor do they connect with the Nodes. **True planetary strength, therefore, may well depend on these sympathetic links between the Tropical and the Draconic, between the earthly and the spiritual, thereby illustrating the qualities of soul that are being brought most actively into the incarnation.**

In this case the Venus characteristics are not altogether helpful; Cayce refers to the possibility of 'detrimental elements in the life' unless the will is directed. The Tropical North Node in Capricorn and the 8th House clearly asks for this, in order to tackle a strong tendency to backslide into that Moon/Mars/Pluto conjunction in the soft Cancerian South Node. 'Arcturus' forces giving strength to the elements [that are] directed in the entity' can be understood in this context as the presence of that great star in Draconic Capricorn, calling to the soul to follow its right path to a more sober, disciplined, patient and purposive way of being.

The bi-wheel (of Subject C and F) on the next page is worth exploring further, for we have only observed so far that Libra has, in the Draconic chart, been brought onto the Ascendant. Cayce lays great stress on the sign though, '... that it might be said of the entity, indeed there is a path cut out for thee – the gods have directed that ye will have the opportunity to show forth thy worth.' Not only does Libra hold the Draconic Ascendant, but its ruler, Venus, falls in 24°59' Aquarius, closely conjunct the Tropical North Node and Mercury with Mars nearby. Here, in sharp contrast to the first chart, everything aligns to encourage a willing soul onward and upward, the path is pointed clearly and the way has been chosen. Much may be accomplished by this man. The pattern formed by the two zodiacs conjoined plainly shows 'Venus as combined with Mercury, and the activities in Uranus' – ruler of the sign in which this powerful conjunction falls. 'The Piscean influences' speak for themselves.

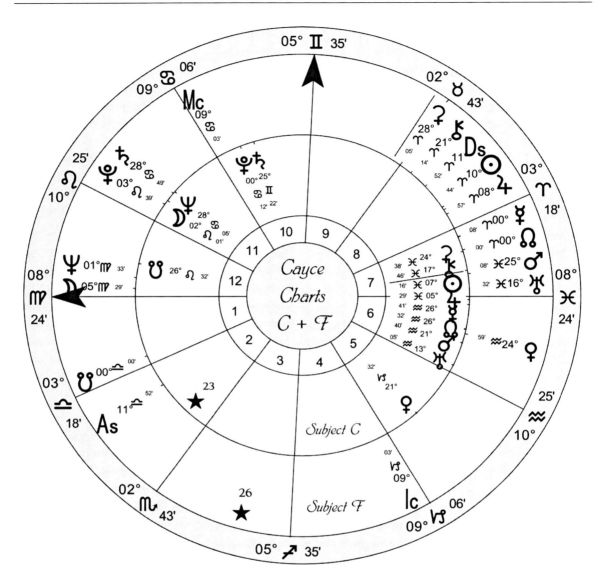

The reference to some kind of blocking is intriguing, since nothing in the pattern makes a square or opposition, save for a very wide confrontation between Venus and Neptune. It is true that Tropical Venus is in the Saturnian sign of Capricorn, and also forms a semi-square to the Pisces Sun, yet this does not appear strong enough to warrant special attention. When the Draconic positions are taken into consideration, the reason for this blocking becomes immediately apparent: the conjunction of Saturn and Pluto on the cusp of Gemini-Cancer moves to the Cancer-Leo cusp, falling on the 11th House Neptune and Moon, and widely opposing that same Tropical Capricorn Venus in the 5th House. *Here* is the blockage particularly, vis-à-vis the 11th House, in 'this or that association with individuals'. This pattern gains in personal significance since the conjunction of the Moon and Neptune moves in the Draco circle close to the degree of the Tropical Ascendant, creating a 'chain of significance' similar to those found to be operating in the first example chart.

One thing that consistently emerges from the Cayce readings is the *partial* response of most subjects to their horoscopes; and this is directly linked to the relative importance of a few key planets, as seen in the three example charts. They are important not because they have prominence in the familiar birth-map, but because they are environs in which the entity has dwelt and achieved a given measure of conscious awareness, the planetary principles having been absorbed into the individual being. The planet is alive in the person, as a 'directing force'. And it is such a planet, or group of planets, which comes visibly to prominence in the Draconic map, and the combining of the Draconic with the Tropical, as illustrated.

It is worth devoting the remainder of this chapter to extracts from the Life Readings which clarify Cayce's unique overview of astrology and the spiritual life of Man, since in the subsequent chapters we shall be leaving Cayce's work behind, in order to examine the Draconic horoscope in greater breadth and depth.

'Not as a physical body as known in the earth, but as a body adaptable to the environs of Jupiter; for there's life there (not as known in earth), as there is in Saturn, Sun, Moon, Venus, Mercury, Uranus, Neptune, Mars: all have their form – as about the earth, the inhabitants of the air, fire, water – in and out of the earth. The elements about same are inhabited, if you choose, by those of their own peculiar environment.'

Edgar Cayce (630-2)

So, firstly, there is the whole point of human life and growth:

'In the developing, then, that the man may be one with the Father, [it is] necessary that the soul pass, with its companion the will, through all the various stages of development, until the will is lost in Him and he becomes one with the Father.

The illustration of this we find in the man called Jesus. This man, as man, makes the will the will of the Father, then becoming one with the Father and the model for man …

When the soul reached that development in which it reached earth's plane, it became in the flesh the model, as it had reached through the developments in those spheres, or planets, known in the earth's plane, obtaining then One in All.

As in Mercury pertaining of Mind.
In Mars of Madness. [Anger seems meant here.]
In Earth as of Flesh.
In Venus as Love.
In Jupiter as Strength.
In Saturn as the beginning of earthly woes,
that to which all insufficient matter is cast for the beginning.
In that of Uranus as of the Psychic.
In that of Neptune as of Mystic.
In Septimus [Pluto?] as of Consciousness.
In Arcturus as of the developing.

For Life is a continuous experience. And the mind, the soul, the will, are those influences that act through material manifestation for the improvement, the development, or for retardment to the whole of the experience.

For each soul enters each experience for a development, that it may be prepared to dwell with that which it seeks as its goal. Hence the necessity of each entity ... [to set] its ideal in each experience. Hence we find in the developments through those activities of an entity in a material sojourn or through an astrological experience are but the evolution, or making practical. For it is not what an individual or an entity may proclaim that counts, but what each soul ... does about that it has set as its ideal in relationships to ... individuals about same.'

So Man is meant for God; he must follow his dream, his ideal; he must live by deeds, not words; and no man is an island unto himself. To be less serious for a moment, there is a delightful song that Bing Crosby used to sing, which I shall not quote in full, but part of which goes:

> '*A pig is an animal with dirt on its face,*
> *His shoes are a terrible disgrace!*
> *He has no manners when he eats his food;*
> *He's fat and lazy and extremely rude,*
> *And if you don't care a feather or a fig,*
> *You may grow up to be a pig!*
> *Or would you like to swing on a star?*
> *Carry moonbeams home in a jar?*
> *You'd be better off than you are –*
> *Or would you rather be a fish?*'

Man must choose which path he will follow, and he has the freedom of will with which to make the choice. Cayce dwells on this theme often: 'For, will is that factor in the experience of each entity in material manifestation which gives the ability to choose that as may be for the development or the retardment.'

Often, his remarks on the subject of human will followed a question about the role or validity of astrology:

Questioner: Is it proper for us to study the effects of the planets on our lives in order to better understand our tendencies and inclinations as influenced by the planets?

Cayce: When studied aright, very, very, very much so. How aright then? In that influence as is seen in the influence of the knowledge already obtained by mortal man. Give more of that into the lives, giving the understanding *that the will must be the ever guiding factor to lead man on, ever upward.*

Questioner: Should an astrological horoscope be based on the time of physical birth or the time of soul birth?'

Cayce: On time of physical birth; for these are merely *inclinations*, and because of inclinations are not the influence of will. *Will* is that factor of the spiritual forces or the gift, as it were, to man. as he came into material form, with which choice is made.

This remark is followed by the references to the Persian chart I quoted earlier, apropos of which he then says:

'… but the world does not govern *man*, Man governs the world! And the inclinations astrologically show whether man has or has not applied will! Then the inclinations are good, but they may be stumbling stones if one submerges will to listen at inclinations! Not that there are not definite helps to be attained from astrology, but those who live by the same the more oft are controlled rather than controlling.'

'… as to the astrological sojourns, these are where the soul entity is out of the material body and present with spiritual forces, that are only of a higher vibration yet are of the same materials of which matter is brought into experience as the soul enters or possesses a body in a material world; yet each experience, each phase, each realm, is that ye may become more and more consciously aware of being in Him, abiding in that divine creative force that only is that which is manifested in thine material surroundings as harmony, colour, sound, movement, those powerful forces that are the basis of all that is good, lovely, precious in the eyes and in the whole of Him that would have thee one with Him.'

Edgar Cayce (818-1)

'The strongest power in the destiny of man is the Sun, first; then the closer planets, or those that are coming in ascendancy at the time of the birth …'

(The strength of planets contacting the horizon from either Tropical or Draco configurations has been shown in the examples above.)

'… but let it be understood here, no action of any planet or any of the phases of the Sun, Moon, or any of the heavenly bodies surpass the rule of Man's individual will power – the power given by the Creator of man in the beginning, when he became a living soul, with the power of choosing for himself … With the given position of the Solar system at the time of the birth of an individual, it can be worked out – that is, the inclinations and actions [can be worked out] without will power taken into consideration.

The study from the human standpoint, of subconscious, subliminal, psychic, soul forces, is and should be the great study for the human family, for through self man will understand its Maker when it understands its relation to its Maker, and it will only understand that through itself, and that understanding is the knowledge as is given here in this state.

But from the astrological we find the influences innate, and some are to be cultivated, that may grow, that may expand, and become more a portion of the influence; just as others are to be curbed and a lesson gained and applied rather than allowing self to drift.

We find that there are those urges latent and manifested, in the personalities and individuality of this entity.

Personalities in the material plane arise from the application of the entity's urges in earthly sojourns. Individualities arise from what an entity would [do] or does about the entity's ideal in a material experience or sojourn in the earth.

Personality is that ye wish others to think and see. Individuality is that your soul prays, your soul hopes for, desires. They need not necessarily be one; but their purpose must be one, even as the Father, the Son and the Holy Spirit are one. So must body, mind and soul be one in purpose and in aim.'

(This is the core of Draconic Astrology, and led to its most important developments and discoveries.)

'But their thoughts and … the emotions of the body, are seldom in accord one with the other – or their individuality and their personality don't reflect the same shadow in the mirror of life.

… may the individuality that is the entity be brought [into] its activities so that its personality may contribute to the factors necessary to keep this entity in the direction needed.

The individuality is the sum total of what the entity has done about those things that are creative or ideal in its varied experiences in the earth.'

To summarise what I understand from Cayce's statements, the incarnating entity is the Individuality, which can be seen in the patterns of the Draconic chart. The Personality is represented by the patterns of the Tropical chart, which not only describes the earth experience but also the 'inclinations' which may tempt man or woman to surrender the God-given Will. The degree of harmony between the two is then shown by the interconnections from Draconic to Tropical, as are the planets whose planes of experience have helped form the growing soul and so stand prominent in the overall pattern. The will of the Individual is free – yet may choose either to follow God's will for his path in the direction of the Moon's North Node, or to assert his freedom completely by willing to remain locked to his past, symbolised in the South Node of the Moon. The degree to which he is likely to fall back or surge forward can be gauged by the sympathy of both Tropical and Draconic patterns to either the head or tail of the Dragon.

'As we find, the sojourns in the environs about the earth are the dwelling places or consciousnesses of the entity between the material or earthly sojourns, and are represented as places by the planetary forces given or named Venus, Jupiter, Mars, Mercury, Saturn, Uranus or the rest of those that are represented also by *the zodiacal signs that make for the relations of the earth to the Moon and the Sun* or to the activities about same.' (my italics)

Edgar Cayce (1494-1)

The Draconic positions of Sun and Moon – especially the sign of the Draconic Sun – are the keys to the Ideal embraced and followed by the reincarnating soul, supported by the spiritually influential planets.

There are astrological references in the Edgar Cayce readings which remain to be fully clarified; it may be that we have further dimensions to discover and explore in the fresh unfoldment of spiritual astrology. But there is no doubt at all in my mind that the resurrection of Draconic astrology has validated the once obscure astrological passages in the Cayce transcripts, and that these in their turn already teach us much of the significance and interrelationships of both the Draconic and the Tropical horoscopes, which we shall now proceed to study in increasing detail over the following pages.

'These conditions, mind of the soul, mind of the physical body, mind of the spiritual entity, are separated that one may gain the knowledge of their action. In the mind of the spiritual entity, we have that mind wherein the entity manifests in the spiritual plane. The mind in the physical body is the subconscious, the conscious, through which the entity manifests in the physical world.'

Lytle W. Robinson, in *his book Is It True What They Say About Edgar Cayce?* states, "In the same discourse he elaborated on the mystical superconscious:

'The superconscious is the divide, that oneness lying between the soul and the spirit force within the spiritual entity. Not of Earth forces at all, only awakened with the spiritual indwelling and acquired individually. It comes to the fore after death when the conscious mind is dropped and replaced by the subconscious or unconscious.'

Cayce's explanations make a certain amount of sense, nevertheless, there is no way of substantiating them," wrote Robinson.

Chapter Three

A Little History

'One of the earliest dragons to leave a permanent mark on the world (he is depicted in white glaze against a blue background on a gate in ancient Babylon) appears to have the head and horns of a ram, the forelegs of a lion, a scaly, reptilian body and tail, and the hind legs of an eagle.'

David Phillips, *Dragons* from *Man, Myth and Magic*

The Moon's Nodes and The Draconic Zodiac
Principal Dates and Authors

Babylonia: earliest traceable records of a probable Draconic (Dragon) zodiac. Lunar Nodes (Dragon's Head/Caput and Dragon's Tail/Cauda) little referred to or understood until:

1927	G.H. White, *The Moon's Nodes and their Importance in Natal Astrology*
1936	Dane Rudhyar, *The Astrology of Personality*
1949	Walter Friedjung, *The Significance of the Moon's Nodes* (*Astrology*, Spring 1949)
1949	George H. Bailey, Letter attacking above article (*Astrology*, Summer 1949)
1949	Walter Friedjung, Letter of reply to Bailey (*Astrology*, Autumn 1949)
1950	Arthur Gauntlett, *Significance of the Nodes* (*Astrology*, Winter 1950/51)

The **Draconic Zodiac** brought to astrology's attention:

1951	Cyril Fagan, *Zodiacs Old and New*
1959	Maurice Froger, *The Nodal Horoscope* (*Astrology*, Summer 1959)
1959	J. Coward, Letter of congratulation to above (*Astrology*, Autumn 1959)
1959	Ronald C. Davison, Lecture to Astrological Lodge, *Some Astrological Controversies* (London, 28 September)
1963	Ronald C. Davison, *Astrology* (Arco, p. 164)

| 1966 | Ronald C. Davison, *Every Planet Has Its Own Zodiac* (*Astrology*, Summer 1966) |

Lunar Nodes brought further into focus by:

1971	Dane Rudhyar, *Person-Centered Astrology* (an entire handbook/chapter)
1973	Zipporah Dobyns, *The Node Book* (Lunar and Planetary Nodes)
1975	Martin Schulman, *Karmic Astrology: The Moon's Nodes and Reincarnation*

The **Draconic/Nodal/Lunar Zodiac** beginning to be used seriously:

1977	Ronald C. Davison, *Synastry*
1977	Dennis Elwell, *Multidimensional Transits* (Lecture to Astrological Association Conference; article in Winter *Journal*, 1977)
1980?	Marc Penfield, *The Reincarnation Chart* (article)
1981	Pamela Crane, Address to the First Astrology World Congress, Zurich, April.
1987	Pamela Crane, *Draconic Astrology* first published by Aquarian Press.
1980s-2000s	Pam Crane, Jacob Schwartz, travelling and teaching Draconic astrology; Tom Jerome Roma founds the NCGR DracSig.; Draconic charts included in all major astrology software.
2000	Pamela Crane, *The Draconic Chart* first published by Flare Publications.
2013	*The Draconic Chart* revised and updated with new material.

Stars and Serpents

With very few exceptions, astrologers in the modern Western world start to learn and continue to practise their horoscopy in the Tropical zodiac. The twelve equal divisions of the Tropical zodiac begin their sequence at 0° Aries at the point in space where the Sun's apparent path, the ecliptic, crosses the equator – the position of the Spring Equinox. On the first day of our northern spring, this is where the Sun stands in the sky. This is the beginning of the first sign of the zodiac, Aries, and the end of Pisces, the last of the twelve.

Different cultures adopt different measurements, however, and many Occidentals are now becoming familiar with the Sidereal zodiac of the East, a most ancient astrology that has never suffered the disrespect and neglect in its native lands that have been the lot of the Western system. The Sidereal or star zodiac, as its name implies, is based on the constellations. Its First Point is a matter for animated conjecture to this day, and no doubt will be for years to come; but it is held by many to be determined by the position of the fixed star Spica as 0° of the autumn sign, Libra. (Should we now be looking also to Arcturus, its longitudinal neighbour, despite its great celestial latitude?)

The Tropical Aries Point moves backwards against the stellar background at a rate of approximately 1° every seventy-two years. These two zodiacs aligned around the beginning of the Christian era, but now have moved out of phase by about 24° of ecliptic longitude.

(The entry of Tropical 0° Aries into Sidereal Aquarius will mark the beginning of the much-heralded 'Aquarian Age'.) But among the zodiacs less familiar to the world of astrology is our rediscovery: the Draconic zodiac. The earliest reference to its existence that I have come across is the following paragraph from Cyril Fagan's book, *Zodiacs Old and New*:

> 'According to a Babylonian myth Marduk (Jupiter) created the Great Dragon, putting its head into the Moon's ascending Node, and its tail into the descending Node, making it carry six of the zodiacal constellations on its back and six under its belly. This is pictorially illustrated on a Babylonian Boundary Stone of King Nabushumishkun, and suggests that Caput's sidereal longitude on 1st Nisan was Aries 0°00'...'

This implies that the Babylonians considered that the positions of the planets in the Draconic zodiac (i.e. distances from the Node) were of consequence.

> 'Herne the Hunter is also a dragon of a kind. One of his old names was Cernunnos, the horned one. On the Gundestrup bowl he appears with a torque in one hand and a snake in the other; on Gaulish monuments he holds two snakes, each of which has a ram's head. The Dogon also know this criocephalus, or ram-headed serpent, for he is the image of their god Amma, who turns into a four-coloured rainbow when he is not haunting the bogs and watery places at night, as a will o' the wisp, a Puck, or a bog spirit.'

> Francis Huxley, *The Way of the Sacred*

Fagan's book appeared in 1951. In 1959 *Astrology*, the quarterly journal of the Astrological Lodge, printed an article by Maurice Froger entitled 'The Nodal Horoscope'. This was followed in the next issue by a congratulatory letter, from J. Coward, and the subject was raised at the Lodge meeting of 28th September that year in a lecture by Ronald C. Davison. In 1963 Mr Davison went into print, writing of the Draconic zodiac – in his term, the 'lunar zodiac'– on pp. 164, 192-193, 196 and 204 of his book *Astrology*, referring to it as 'the legacy of the past' in the context of three example delineations.

But 1977 was to be the Year of the Dragon – by a happy coincidence also marking the end of the year of the Fire Dragon in China, and the start of the year of the Fire Serpent – for it was in that year that Ronald Davison's *Synastry* was published, with yet more material on the Draconic zodiac; and in September of that year (the 3rd to be exact, at 5h30 pm BST) Dennis Elwell introduced the Draconic zodiac to the Astrological Association's Cambridge Conference, held that year in Churchill College.

Meanwhile across the Atlantic another astrologer, Marc Penfield, had been reading Ronald Davison's *Astrology* and experimenting with the 'nodal' zodiac; in 1980 I came across some of the fruits of his labours as published in an article entitled *The Reincarnation Chart*. By that time my own investigative and clinical work with the Draconic level of astrology had so fired me with confidence that I was certain that it provided the astrological world with answers to many unresolved questions, and I was therefore encouraged – but not surprised – to find that Penfield too considered that 'the horoscope now answers all the questions that an accomplished journalist asks during an interview ... the "why" is now arrived at through the lunar zodiac chart'. Penfield's approach differs from mine in one crucial respect: he does not – indeed, emphasises that one must not – translate the angles and cusps from Tropical to Draconic. Much of his reading rests on the placing of Draconic planets in Tropical houses. While this approach is indeed very important as part of the overall analysis, I do not feel that it goes far enough in exploring the full implications of the Draconic level of being.

Every journey begins with the first step; and now our first step on a remarkable astrological odyssey must be to determine the start of this zodiac in a chosen chart, and to learn its calculation.

Chapter Four

Be a Tree!
Introducing the Draconic Chart

The use of the Tree as a symbol and teaching aid is very ancient. Norse mythology conceived of a World Tree, Yggdrasil; Jack's Beanstalk is another symbolic tree. In the Classical world, trees carry rewards for those with the courage and virtues to earn them – rewards such as the Golden Fleece won by the hero Jason, and the coveted golden apples of the Hesperides. One of the mysterious rhymes we learned to sing as children goes, 'I had a little nut-tree/Nothing would it bear/But a silver nutmeg/And a golden pear …' The Holy Bible begins and ends with the most powerful tree imagery, first in Eden where only the fruit of the Tree of Knowledge was forbidden to the first man and woman, and finally in Revelation where the Genesis theme is recapitulated like the last movement of a mighty symphony as we are shown the City of God with the Tree of Life growing 'on either side of the river' bearing twelve kinds of fruit – clearly the twelve zodiacal signs; and of course Jesus used the analogy of the tree to powerful effect in his parables. There are many other biblical tree references, as for example in the famous dream interpreted by Daniel for King Nebuchadnezzar.

Tree imagery is found at its most stylised in the Kabbalah, where the Tree of Life becomes abstract, pure geometry and symbol, a potent ladder of light; and the natural tree is most beautifully combined with this spiritual Light-Tree in an image chosen by Manley Palmer Hall for his great volume, *Secret Teachings of All the Ages.* The reason I find his choice so significant is that it reminds us forcefully that this tree's roots are in the highest heavens where also is its true, spiritual Crown. What seems to be the crown of the tree is inverted on the earth, binding it to the phenomenal world. The crowns of such sacred trees bear silver and gold, Moon energy, Sun energy. Their roots go beyond the world we know, drawing us into the Mysteries. And so a tree is the image I now choose to show how the essential components of astrology both differ and fit together.

So, be a tree! You are planted in the world – in a forest, or a garden, or a wilderness – as a mere germ, a tiny seed, carrying all the information that will build a living thing that may be strong, balanced and beautiful or weakened, irregular, unexceptional, even ugly, as the environment and its changing conditions allow. The very first thing to emerge and extend from the germ is a root, without which the tree will thirst and starve and loosen and die. That root for a human life is the secret and vital link to its own spiritual reality, the truth of its heavenly origin, as it is now given a role to play in the incarnate world. As our root is in Heaven, our tree begins and ends its journey in the eternal Life.

With the root secure, a sapling stem may grow; life reaches out into the environment that both challenges and nourishes it. It makes some leaves; it may even flower a little, may even set a fruit or two. It is very young. It is like the newly incarnating soul that has known nothing of life on earth, and must spend its first incarnation getting used to gravity, climate, food, company, language, the demands of a totally alien life. As it grows – as the vulnerable but usefully flexible stem begins to firm into a trunk – each growing season, each incarnation, adds a fresh layer of experience, a growth-ring in the strengthening wood of the tree. This growing, broadening trunk provides the support needed by the tree in order to grow successfully from season to season. Our own 'trunk' is the wealth of accumulated experience from all our previous life-times, that has made us what we are today, stamped us with a clear identity, built into us principles born out of the crucial questions our previous lives have required us to answer … and the current 'season's' growth will add to all that has gone before, enriching our understanding, broadening our knowledge-base, reinforcing those parts of ourselves that are strong and good (only rarely adding distortion to distortion), changing parts of us that are weaker, less developed, no longer useful to us as individuals or to the world in which we play our part and, inevitably, since we are fallible, sometimes spoiling or killing off nascent qualities that had briefly shown promise and new possibilities.

We had a golden acacia tree outside our front window in Sittingbourne; it grew first as a pampered maiden in a Kent nursery. So it was unprepared for the shock of one September gale that pounded it on our exposed lawn, and it lost all its fragile young branches – nearly dying. We took pity on the sad twig, and took it with us when we moved to Ospringe, planting it by a high wall close to our house, expecting little. But our wind-sensitive sapling had learned from the experience. The whipping of the wind had changed its cells and made them grow stronger; and for six years the tree flourished, to overtop the wall. Then, in 1987, we had The Hurricane! Readers in the UK may remember that this terrifying wind was a southerly; our garden faced due south. The acacia took the full force of the storm, and by first light had lost half its upper branches. Nothing could take the force of that vicious wind and remain undamaged – yet the tree had learned; this time, with the memory of past trauma, the strengthened cells kept the trunk and half the crown intact, and several summers later it had regrown so dramatically that it needed a visit from the tree surgeon to prune it back to more manageable proportions … from which it once again romped away to dazzle the neighbourhood!

And so we grow. One life will knock us back, another find us insecure and vulnerable, another throw challenge after challenge at us until we are re-trained to be upright and strong. In one life we find ourselves protected; in another constantly exposed; in another, at the height of success, robbed of everything we own and forced to start over with different values and goals. One life is sweet and easy; we flower, we fruit, host to many happy visitors, sheltering the home-seeker, brightening the landscape with our beauty, our gifts and our offspring. Another life is hard, bitter, clouded, cold with little chance to do more than toughen up and survive until the life to follow. If spiritually we flourish, our Gardener rejoices, tends us, affords every opportunity for further growth, 'For whosoever hath, to him shall be given, and he shall have more abundance.' However, if soul and spirit become diseased those sick or weak parts will be pruned to prevent the healthy branches from dying: '… but whosoever hath not, from him shall be taken away even that he hath.' One life lays down in our heartwood a generous, wide ring, another a pinched, narrow one. So run the seasons of our spiritual growth.

The zodiac with which we in the Western world are most familiar, the Tropical (which you may find here occasionally abbreviated to GT, geo-tropical) is the ever-changing crown of our tree, the growing tip of its branches and twigs, the leaves that last only for a season, the flowers and the fruits resulting from the work our tree has been able *and willing* to do, and the conditions under which that work has had to be done. A tree's growth and performance will be affected if it is over-crowded and therefore competing with too many others for needed resources, also if there is too little – or too much – nourishment from sun, rain, air quality or soil conditions. If it is unattractive, and so unvisited by the birds and the bees, butterflies, furry friends climbing for fruit, the tree cannot breed – without skilled intervention by the Gardener! And so it is with us. All these immediate variables, the drama of changing individual circumstances and needs that shape our appearance and experience for an earthly season, and teach us new attitudes, new skills, these are the domain of the Tropical zodiac, the annual crown of our tree, by which we are recognisably ourselves.

And the trunk is the Draconic. Interestingly, sacred imagery often – particularly in Genesis – pictures the serpent, the Dragon, coiled around the trunk of the tree (just as it is coiled around the Caduceus) as guardian of sacred knowledge and hence symbol of our souls' expulsion from the Garden of innocence and 'fall' into mortal incarnation.

Everything we have already been, we substantially still are; and through these attributes we are also – more deeply, recognisably ourselves, just as the tree is unmistakable in its winter silhouette. The structure, strength and health of the trunk and main branches supports the on-going and entire future life of the tree; what it has become used to, and fit for, will determine its response to the unending challenges of the environment … just as we, faced with our own material and moral challenges, fall back for reassurance, strength and support on those principles, those central belief-systems which have developed in us and sustained us from life to life, to the point that we are not only committed to them but in fact identify with them. They are the oldest, deepest, most ingrained parts of our individual psyche. Returning to that level of self when life throws us its worst curves gives us a chance to re-focus, gather our strength, and start afresh like my golden acacia, stripped of her season's growth, after the storms and surgery.

You can pollard a tree to the point that it seems to die – yet if the trunk is whole and healthy, fresh life springs forth, often richer and stronger than ever. A human life can be cut short by accident, by disease, or foul play, and always ends in the natural winter of death – yet the life in the spirit-sustaining soul goes on when incarnate life seems extinct, and after sufficient rest comes back to animate another vehicle for its growing identity.

You can take a chain-saw to the base of a tree and cut it down right to the root – but if there is life in the root, with food and water to sustain it, even the trunk of that tree may grow again, as indeed stems grow up in a coppice; and if a human being so betrays his or her soul that everything they have ever been, and could ever become, effectively dies, as long as the eternal spirit at the root which is the Crown survives, that soul can hope for the grace to start again. 'We believe … that all His sons will reach His feet, however far they stray.' Extending the image of the coppice, where many new growths spring from a single rootstock, it is tantalising to wonder whether we too spread our energies and opportunities for growth through a number of brother-and-sister souls, to make up for lost time after we have made such serious mistakes and been so chastened.

The prime fruit of our tree is the silver nutmeg and the golden pear; whether Tropical or Draconic, the ideas expressed through the Sun (especially) and the Moon are of central importance. But *everything* in the heavens at birth has significance, so the whole of the familiar Tropical chart has to be transformed into the Draconic before attempting a Draconic analysis. In the course of this, you will find in many cases tremendous contrasts between the two sets of zodiac positions, and in all but a few, distinct differences. This mirrors the ambivalence common in human nature, the rift – sometimes a chasm – between what we practise and what we preach. What we practise is Tropical; what we preach is Draconic. We are not, generally speaking, WYSIWYG! What you see is Tropical; what you frequently get is Draconic. The only groups of people who approach WYSIWYG status and can reasonably be expected to practise what they preach are those whose Tropical and Draconic charts are virtually identical, i.e. who are born when the Dragon's Head is at or very close to Tropical 0° Aries, the Spring Equinox.

As you experiment with your favourite charts, following the guidelines in the next chapter, you will begin to see what I mean.

Chapter Five

Calculation
Setting Up the Draconic Chart

Before we embark in earnest on the calculations, one important point needs clearing up:

The Use of the True or the Mean Node

Discussing this matter with Dennis Elwell, I found that his preference was for the Moon's Mean Node in Draconic calculation, and in fact I also used it for some time. However, the appearance in recent years of accurate printed and software ephemerides for the True position of the Node has made it very much easier to compare the two. As a node of any kind is a point in space generally ungraced by the presence of any physical body, it is so abstract in its nature (the geometric and astrological realities of planes and gravity fields notwithstanding) that there seems little definite basis for symbolic argument as to the relative propriety of a mean, average position or one precisely calculated for midnight and noon each day. So, apart from the understandable feeling that a 'true' position speaks for itself, we are left with the testimony of trial and error.

I cannot say for sure which of these two positions is more reliable, though my own eventual preference, as you will see, is for the True Node. In preDraco days I was experimenting with Nodal Returns on the eighteen-year cycle. Trying out this idea during the chart-work for one of my clients, I found that strings of planetary midpoints based on the return of the Mean Node to its natal place, specifically at the time of that day when the subject's birth angles were repeated, produced a startlingly accurate picture of the degenerative course which this particular individual's life had taken over the ensuing years – and this was read straight out of Reinhold Ebertin's *Combination of Stellar Influences*. There is no faulty subjective assessment here and no room for wishful thinking. The same approach worked well in two further cases of people who led extremely different lives. So much for the Mean Node.

Next we find the late Al H. Morrison of New York (an under-appreciated, tireless and selfless pioneer) pointing out that tracking the progressed True Node through the ephemeris highlights the years that mark the real turning points in the life, when the Node literally turns in relation to us and goes Stationary to Direct or back to Retrograde again. And so far, the True Node's performance in this respect has proved consistent. The crunch for Draco came when it was time to tackle the Draconic Solar Return. Examples follow later. Suffice it to say at present that it was the True Nodal Sun's return to its natal place which yielded the most eloquent picture of the following year.

'In astronomy the dragon relates to the nodes, two diametrically-opposed points of intersection between the paths of the moon and the sun. To the mystic, the dragon symbolises the place of encounter between the moon and the sun within. The dragon can either devour the moon, seen symbolically as the mystic spiritual heart, or it can serve as the place or container of conception. By entering the dragon when the sun is in the nodes, the moon or heart conceives. Thus, in full consciousness of the perils, one must enter the dragon in order to await the eclipse in its cosmic womb.'

Laleh Bakhtiar, The Sufi

Calculation

The Tropical zodiac with which we are so familiar has its beginning at 0° Aries, the Spring Equinox, the point on the celestial equator where the Sun in its journey along the ecliptic passes from south to north declination.

The Draconic zodiac – with which we are about to become very familiar! – has its beginning at the Dragon's Head, the Moon's North Node, the point on the Moon's orbit where it passes from south to north latitude of the ecliptic. The Spring Equinox is just as much a 'node' as the Dragon's Head; both points mark the intersection of one important celestial plane with another, linking two critical dimensions of energy. We shall return to the deeper implications of this later on; for now let it suffice to show that from a node (one that satisfies certain requirements) one can infer a zodiac invariably to be generated as a natural consequence, and the node itself becomes the Aries Point. Planetary and cuspal elongations from that node therefore become elongations from a new Aries Point.

You may be used to working in signs and degrees; for myself I find it more straightforward to work in Absolute Longitude. All that is necessary is to subtract the position of the Tropical North Node from any Tropical planet or cusp to find the related Draconic planet or cusp position:

Planet/Cusp – Moon's North Node = Draconic Planet/Cusp

If the Node is further on in the zodiac than the planet or cusp, you will have to add 360° to the planet/cusp position before making this subtraction.

In time you may well get used to seeing these distances directly on the chart in front of you; but another useful aid to the visual astrologer is the superimposition of one copy of the chart upon another, either using a transparency or having a smaller wheel rotate within a larger. In this case, align the Equinox on the outer wheel with the Dragon's Head on the inner, and read off the new zodiacal positions.

Just as we place the Moon's Nodes in the Tropical chart, so in the Draconic chart we can place the Equinoxes; and for these I suggest the use of the symbols ♈ and ♎, for Aries and Libra (these in the text are from the Wingdings font). Unfortunately, not all of the current software (up to December 2011) is set up to insert such symbols, unless you have, for example, Solar Fire Gold; for some of you they will have to be entered manually in the Draconic chart.

'The male cries above and the female cries below and he changes.'

The Yuan Kien Lei Han

Setting up the Draconic Chart

As suggested above, it is possible to present the Tropical and Draconic charts together, superimposed by the rotation of one copy of the Tropical chart against another. If, however, you arrive at the Draconic positions by calculation or visual scanning, the following options are open to you:

1. Erect the Draconic chart on its own, in its completeness.

2. Draw the Tropical chart, and in an inner or outer ring mark the rotated sign positions for Draco; 0° Aries Draconic will be aligned with the Tropical Dragon's Head.

3. PREFERRED: On the Tropical chart, against its outer rim, mark in the Draconic positions as if they fell in the Tropical pattern: this shows up the resonances, the axial interrelationships between the two levels. This also enables you to try Penfield's approach, where the Tropical House placing of the Draconic planet is taken into account.

4. Against the outer rim of the complete Draconic chart, place the Tropical planets; this will show up the alignments as before, but opens up another tantalising avenue: the possible significance of Tropical planets in Draconic Houses!

N.B. Steps 1, 3 and 4 can all be easily displayed and printed by the majority of Astrology programs for the PC, such as Solar Fire, Win*Star, Astrocalc, Electric Ephemeris, Kepler. More are continually coming onto the market. A bi-wheel of Draconic with Tropical can also be displayed in AstroPocket (for the Palm) and Astracadabra (for Pocket PC.)

Bear in mind that when the complete Draco chart is erected, there will be a whole new set of House rulerships to consider, throwing quite different emphases on vital parts of the pattern. Aspects between planets and cusps, and midpoint structures, all remain the same as before. These exist in their own right, independent of any zodiac.

When analysing the Tropical/Draconic interactions on paper, it is helpful to ring the planets concerned, using one distinctive colour for Tropical and another for Draconic, and then marking the alignments in such a way that they cannot be confused with the internal aspect lines. A wavy line can be of use here.

'Ulysses Aldrovandus' *Historia Serpentium et Draconum* tells of an expedition to Florida where a winged serpent was killed and 'the natives took great trouble to remove the head of the dead beast; which they deduced was due because of some superstition.'

Peter Dickenson, *The Flight of Dragons*

The Aries Point

Few astrologers look on the Spring and Autumn Equinoxes as points to be reckoned with in the birth chart; but be assured that just as the lunar Nodes have their sign and degree placing in the Tropical zodiac, so indeed do the Equinoxes have their special place in the Draconic zodiac.

As with the rest of the chart, the Dragon's Head is subtracted from the place of the Spring Equinox to find the Draco position of the latter, the formula here of course being simply 360° – Dragon's Head = Aries Point. And the Libra Point falls opposite.

The Equinoxes, thus translated, maintain precisely the same relationship to the planets and Houses as they did originally – and the sudden appearance of aspects from planets to these points only serves to remind us that in fact any planet or cusp (I include angles of course) which falls close to the end or beginning of a sign is in fact in aspect to these important intersections in our home space. And we are thereby also reminded that the equinoxes do have House positions, which may be trying to tell us something.

What all this may be saying is this: that going by our earlier discussion it is no accident that Aries is known as the exaltation of the Sun, and Libra as the Sun's fall, and that if we are to answer the call of the spirit at the most personal level, we are likely to hear its voice from the House in which stands the Spring Equinox, while those planets and angles which find themselves on the cusps of the signs are those which will most readily spur us in that direction – or the opposite!

In the Draconic zodiac the Aries Point has a sign of its own, keying the soul into this new phase in its growth. In this context it is important to note that Tropical Node and Draconic Equinox placings come always in predictable pairs, i.e. Aries Node always means Pisces Equinox, Taurus always pairs with Aquarius, Gemini with Capricorn, Cancer with Sagittarius, Leo with Scorpio, Virgo with Libra, and so on and vice versa. People on a subjective path are distinguishable from those on an objective path. How significant this is in adding to our understanding of our personal mission in life I do not know yet; all I have found for certain is that cross-aspects involving the Equinox in the Draconic chart are rather too common in synastry to be dismissed as coincidental, so it is certainly worthy of deeper study than I have had time to devote to it so far. Therefore, if you can, it is interesting and helpful to include the Aries Point ♈ and Libra Point ♎ in the Draconic birth chart, even though I have not felt sufficiently confident in their interpretation to include them in the example charts in this book.

Before we leave this chapter, I think I should tell you about a dream I had, way back in the early 1970s, long before Draconic astrology came on the scene, long before I ever used the analogy of the Tree. In this dream, after a prelude relating back to my school years, I found myself with a whole group of astrologers dancing in a circle around an ancient oak tree. On its massive trunk was written the one word, *Prakriti*. The final part of the dream took me into a town and a phrase was spoken: 'Gunboat Maryland, Fourth of August.'

I had no idea what *Prakriti* was, or what language it came from. It was my friend Ken Fretwell, who had studied Sanskrit, who first told me what the mysterious word meant. Here is the *Encyclopdia Britannica*'s definition:

> 'Sanskrit PRAKRITI ('source'), also called PRADHANA ('principal'), in the Samkhya school of Indian philosophy, [is] material nature in its germinal state, eternal and beyond perception. *Prakriti, when it comes into contact with the 'soul' (Purusha), starts on a process of evolution* that leads through several stages to the creation of the existing material world. (Author's italics.) Prakriti is made up of three gunas ('strands', or constituent cosmic factors) that characterize all nature. In the Samkhya view, only Prakriti is active, while the self is incarcerated in it and only observes and experiences. Release (Moksha) consists in the self's extrication from Prakriti by the recognition of its total difference from it and noninvolvement in it. In early Indian philosophical texts the term *svabhava* (Sanskrit: 'own being') was used in a similar sense to mean material nature.'

Astonishing. All those years ago in that dream came the first clues to all the developments that eventually became InterDimensional Astrology – including the date of birth of Our Lady, Mary/Maria, the Mother of Jesus. (That story is told later in this book, in Chapter Nineteen.) Only the reference to the 'gunboat' so far remains obscure.

Chapter Six

The Guardian and The Treasure
The Meaning of Draco

In the Mesopotamian religion, there was a Sumerian deity called Ningishzida, the city god of Gishbanda, near Ur (in astrology-rich Chaldaea). Although he was a god of the underworld, he seems once to have been a tree god, his name meaning 'Lord Productive Tree.' He would have been identified with the winding tree roots; he was represented as a serpent. In his human form, two serpent heads grow out of his shoulders on each side of the human head, and his steed is a dragon. The son of Ninazu and Ningirda, he was the husband of Ninazimua, 'Lady Flawlessly Grown Branch'.

How remarkably this ancient imagery summarises all we have discussed so far! We are close to the source of modern astrology, we have a divine being who is three-in-one as god, human and tree, he is the embodiment of the root which is paradoxically the Source and the Destination, as the tree which fulfils its promise he is coupled in divine marriage with the perfect branch (echoes of Adam's rib), and he rides through the worlds on the Dragon.

Another renowned serpent is the Ourobouros, the emblem found in ancient Egypt and Greece. Coiled into a circle with its tail in its mouth, it continually devours itself and is reborn from itself. A Gnostic and alchemical symbol, the Ourobouros expresses the unity of all things, both material and spiritual, that never disappear but are perpetually changing their form in an eternal cycle of destruction and recreation. Here again is the serpent, the dragon, symbolic of cyclic and developmental experience through reincarnation.

'Ancient Chinese cosmogonists,' the *Encyclopaedia Britannica* informs us, 'defined four types of dragons: the Celestial Dragon (T'ien Lung), who guards the heavenly dwellings of the gods; the Dragon of Hidden Treasure (Fu Tsang Lung); the Earth Dragon (Ti Lung), who controls the waterways; and the Spiritual Dragon (Shen Lung), who controls the rain and winds. In popular belief, only the latter two were significant; they were transformed into the Dragon Kings (Lung Wang), gods who lived in the four oceans, delivered rain, and protected seafarers.' Here yet again we find Dragons that surely relate to dimensions of astrology as well as the phenomenal world. I shall resist the temptation to side-track, and simply draw your attention for now to Fu Tsang Lung, as it is the Dragon of Hidden Treasure which most beautifully symbolises our experience of the Draconic.

So let us now take a closer look at Drakon/Draco, the Dragon.

The reputation of dragons is in fact as varied as the human psyche, and always colourful. Variously, we believe or deny that they once roamed the earth, may still be found in haunted lakes and secret caverns, live on only in birds and lizards and children's tales, are to be fought, courted, or utterly shunned in the eternal battle between Good and Evil. In China, as we have seen already, dragons have been held in the highest esteem for thousands of years, honoured as the sovereigns of natural powers and universal laws. One story is that a dragon from the Yellow River presented the Emperor Fu Hsi with the eight Trigrams on which is built the entire philosophical structure of the I Ching. However, in the West we have been taught to fear the dragon as an emblem – even the essence – of the Prince of Darkness himself. To the Nordic myths, Christianity has added its own tales of dragon-slaying heroes; among these of course is St George, the patron saint of England, and, most exalted of all, St Michael the mighty Archangel of Light, vanquishing in the dragon all the fallen powers of darkness. Between the hemispheres of East and West, in the fontanelle of the world, Jesus the Christ was incarnate through a mother who, as Our Lady of Grace, is shown subduing the Serpent with her right foot. What clearer symbol of the heralded Piscean age?

But a wealth of dragon stories from the Western world, echoing the Chinese myth above, are of wresting a priceless treasure from its terrifying guardian. Psychologically this is interesting; do we see here the knight-errant of the more competitive hemisphere seizing by brute force that which a more cunning and cooperative Eastern hero would obtain through skill and persuasion? It may be our own spirit of antagonism which projects into our dragons the ferocity we so fear. In a lovely anthology on dragons compiled by Elizabeth Rudd, there is a poem by Brian Patten that puts this nicely:

'He went on a journey to where he imagined
the need for journeys would have ended.
Much he saw and would have liked to have owned
was guarded by monsters.
It didn't surprise him. Yet that he had conjured them himself,
out of fear, out of absurd jealousies,
was unknown to him.
No wiser from that journey all he learned
was how best to destroy monsters.
Many have vanished, but listen –
much of what they guarded and he wanted
has vanished with them.'

Brian Patten, *Monsters*

What are we rejecting when we reject the dragon? Very probably, only that projection of our own darkness, which like the symbol of the Tao holds within it the seed of our Light. Anathematised, both are consigned to the massive, collective human Shadow. I read a marvellous science fiction story some years ago (you may know this one) in which mankind had discovered the perfect means to rid itself of all its accumulated and undesirable garbage by dumping it through a portal in the space-time continuum. And of course, pay-back day came when through the cracking, shattering pavements a nightmare deluge of detritus erupted into the clean and tidy world, all but destroying an entire civilisation. If we make progress and expediency our gods, we get stuck in a groove of linear thinking which may eventually leave no room at all for its essential complement, the non-linear, cyclic and holistic understanding. ('Teach me to understand as well as know …') Discarded with this are all the truths, the province of 'commonsense', that are sovereign to mankind's right brain/left side. Here's an entertaining and instructive pastime – look at yourself in a mirror: which is the more mobile side of your face, the left or the right? Which side of your brain have you made your mind's habitual home? Happy are those whose faces are mobile and vital on both sides! – these are rich in life. We are designed for harmony and wholeness; not to be lopsided, blind in one eye, deaf in one ear, numb in half the head, half-paralysed in the soul!

As a species, we are plainly afraid of ourselves. We are constantly losing our heads and chasing our tails – our Dragons' Tails.

The rejected dragon is the natural order that links macrocosm with microcosm and is epitomised in the cyclic phenomenon of the zodiac. When Christ overcame the world, he did not destroy it, but overmastered it; when we seek our soul's treasure to build the Christ in us, when we strive to discover and perfect the Diamond Body, we do not destroy nature within us or around us but become masters of it, skilled in its understanding and proper use. Face to face with the Dragon in the sky, stretched between polarities in our birth charts, we must equally neither reject, nor ignore, nor destroy it, but instead seek the worthiest means to win its golden prize.

And what is this prize?

In a Japanese legend, the Buddha learned deep truths from the Dragon; the penultimate truth was that all living things must die. However, the Dragon refused to reveal the final truth until its hunger had been sated by human flesh. Accordingly, the Buddha offered himself as the sacrifice, and the Dragon then spoke: 'The greatest happiness is experienced after the soul has left the body', he said; at which words the Buddha bowed, and sprang into the Dragon's mouth.

The astrologer may understand this as the epitome of the courage and willingness we each must find, in order to meet the daunting requirements of the Dragon's Head, and by this means both know and save the life of the soul. 'For what shall it profit a man if he gain the whole world, and lose his own soul?' This is what we risk if, in our complacency, cowardice or ignorance, we keep on chasing our tails.

In a delightful little volume somewhat misleadingly entitled *Dragon Doodles*, written by Howard Kelly in 1946, I found the following paragraph. Pay particular attention to the last three sentences: 'Excursions into fantasy inspired by the dragon are many and varied. For he is chief among the four divine creatures, and his family is prodigious. There is the celestial dragon, the spiritual dragon, the earthly dragon, and the dragon of hidden treasure. The red dragon, the azure dragon, the yellow dragon … (the one that came to Fu Hsi) … and dragons with horns, and dragons without horns. Three-clawed and five-clawed dragons. But the beginning of all dragons was a four-footed, scaly monster which, like the alligator, hibernated in the swamps of the Yellow River, and as chief of scaly reptiles he acquired the power of transformation and the gift of rendering himself invisible and visible at pleasure.' Very Scorpionic! This is the bit: 'He ascended to the sky in the spring and buried himself in the watery depths in the autumn. He was an emblem of royalty and the representative *par excellence* of the watery element. He was a yellow dragon.' The reference to the spring and autumn skies is highly suggestive that, in spite of his watery connections, this dragon is a symbol of the Spring and Autumn Equinoxes, the zero points of Tropical Aries and Libra (in Fu Hsi's day somewhere against the stars of the Bull and the Scorpion), with the business end of the Dragon, his head with the truth-blazing, life-demanding mouth, in fiery Aries. There is plenty of support for this idea from Francis Huxley's account of ram-headed serpents in Africa, Europe and America, in his book '*The Dragon – Nature of Spirit, Spirit of Nature*':

> 'The Dogon hold the sun to be a radiant womb made of an eight-fold copper spiral, which sucks up the waters that the ram has let fall … For the *ram* is the hot-blooded incarnation of the water-spirits, and it can be seen plunging in the marshes during every storm, amongst the water-lilies, crying, 'Water is mine!' When the storm is over, it leaps into the clouds along the rainbow. In addition it has the moon on its forehead, just below the solar crown … its body is the earth, its eyes the stars; its fleece is water and green plants, its hind legs are the larger animals and its forelegs the smaller ones; its tail is the reptiles. It lives, *as dragons do*, by drawing up and then returning what it has drawn as the breath of the world: and its favourite number is eight.'

The italics are mine. He goes on to talk further about the number eight: '… the Chinese recognised that the Yin and the Yang made one dragon which had the eight trigrams for heads. And throughout the Old World, eight was the number of spokes in *the solar wheel which, in Europe as in Africa, was set in motion by the ram-headed serpent*.' (My italics again.) He goes on to speak of 'the snake belt ending in two rams' heads…', adding, 'On the north-west coast of America such a belt is the insignia of a warrior, and is thought to deal out thunder and lightning at one moment and a rainbow-like covenant at another. It must also have bridged the realms of life and death by virtue of its self-reflection …'

In the symbolism above there is the strong implication that the Ram and the Dragon's Head each functioned not only as the origin of important solar cycles, as a bridge between material and spiritual life, as a heroic challenge, as karmic reward and punishment, but also as an image of incarnation, as the carrying of the Cross, epitomised in their eight-fold cyclic symmetry. The Ram is the Dragon and the Dragon is the Ram. The Ram begins a zodiac, so therefore the Dragon also begins a zodiac. And remember there are four dragons! One to begin the Tropical zodiac, maybe, and another to begin the Sidereal; one of them may start the earthly cycle of the Houses; but assuredly one of them is the genesis of the Draconic zodiac at the point in the heavens that we ourselves know as the Dragon's Head, linking the Sun to the Earth through the orbit of the Moon.

Here we find this Dragon's wateriness, in his governance of the human soul. For without the Moon, he would have no life! Through her he is associated with her sign, her House – and our living past. Bound to her orbit about this lovely planet, he circles his treasure and guards the gate to our Gold, both a bridge and a barrier between the earthly and heavenly kingdoms. He is the symbol of the ensouling of spirit so that it may enter material experience, and of that soul's withdrawal when the body has served its purpose, the teaching and tempering of the growing spirit. **If modern man is still 'In Search of a Soul', then let him turn to the Draconic zodiac where he will discover the patterns of his older and ordinarily higher self; for the status of the soul is shown at the point of its entry into material life.** At birth, it is the embodiment of all it has come to believe and in principle uphold through its trials and its triumphs over many aeons of time. In that sense it portrays the true Identity, the being that must now work through a new becoming, the older Draconic manifesting through the newer Tropical self.

From its history, it can be seen that the Draconic zodiac has been fairly slow to come to the attention of the astrological world as a whole, and so far – astrologers being surprisingly conservative creatures in many ways – it is being taken up relatively slowly; but when people do come to realise its tremendous interest and importance they are galvanised into taking a stand on the issues involved, and align firmly with those who are concerned with the meaning and the purposes of the incarnate soul, willing to venture on its account into the rich territory of Draconic and allied 'vertical' astrologies. Those who are not so inclined will limit themselves to the purely 'horizontal' dimensions of psycho-analytic astrology or a somewhat superficial study of events. Even if in practice such analyses appear sufficient, the mind-set is woefully inadequate.

My own conviction is that it is more than ever essential now for astrologers to concentrate as recommended on lifting the spirit of man above its worldly preoccupations – not right away from them, because we live *in* the world, but we do not have to be *of* it, at least not all the time! It is a good thing to expand the human awareness wherever possible to an appreciation of the fact that every human being is a soul, is a spirit ensouled and then embodied; and as such each of us has a role to play in this world which stands very often aloof from our everyday psychological patterning. It is the task of the Draconic zodiac to show us what this role – or roles – may be. This can add a deeply significant new dimension to our life and to the experience of meaning in our lives, a true and illuminating sense of purpose. When examined in consultation, the very capacity of the Draconic zodiac to heal lies in its potent reminder of the reality of eternal life. Fearful souls are strengthened to know they do not die; the lost and the empty are restored to the drive, and joy, of a life recharged with meaning as their original vocation is rediscovered. So also are the fundamental principles which underpin their lives; in these, even an uncertain future can be more firmly and confidently rooted. The purpose of our relationships becomes extremely clear; and with the increase in understanding comes a flowering of love and patience.

It is the Draconic level which enables us to lift ourselves up to the energies that are available to us once this realisation has been attained. It can bring to an individual great inspiration to carry on when apparently life is at a standstill. In counselling you will find that it wonderfully inspires people to be presented with this aspect of their own life, and they go away with a greater light shining from them than when they entered the room. People tend to come to a counsellor when they are in crisis, but as a rule, even those professing casual interest are dealing with one or two major issues, and these will tend to emerge during the course of an hour and a half's discussion of the chart.

To sum up what has gone before, bear always in mind that when the Draconic chart is your focus it is the *higher principles* at work, the *purpose* behind a given development, the *meaning* inherent in an event, that are being examined to add unprecedented depth and insight to our interpretive skills. In so doing you will probably find, as I have over the course of three decades, that far more emerges of immediate and lasting value during a Draconic consultation than ever would if it were limited to the purely psychic and mythic levels of the newer Tropical self, however subtle and complex these may be. That these are of inestimable value we know from the wisdom and experience of those astrologers whose skills are highly developed in this area; but without the reminder that our true Self has an ancient, vivid, spiritual continuity and is therefore the root and guide and master of the tentative new incarnation, we risk building our own and our clients' houses upon sand instead of a deep, sturdy bedrock.

The more Draconic analysis came into my own work, the more I became convinced that it is one of the most valuable tools available to the astrologer today. As such, it is of inestimable value to a humanity both needing and wishing now ever more strongly to expand awareness, refusing to be limited by the material world, and desirous of beginning to live as a soul. Mankind is ready to be more aware of the soul nature, of the principles that are vital to each soul individually, of the lessons that must be learned, of the experiences that must be undergone, of the duties that must be performed. Each of us now is learning our individual capacity for self-sacrifice for the good of a larger whole – in other words the whole which is the soul-group of which each of us is a part. The concept of soul-groups is I think essential here; and indeed it reminds me that when I read Reinhold Ebertin's work *The Combination of Stellar Influences*, which is virtually the midpoint bible for astrologers, I was concerned that so often he neglected to mention any soul relationship in connection with the lunar nodal axis and instead emphasised associations with groups. Through the study of the Draconic zodiac and its implications this has been resolved, because it is clear that as an incarnate soul with a role to play which is larger than our immediate personality-needs and motivations, we are each part of a larger whole.

Indeed we are all part of one mighty Whole, one total, ultimate Unity, whether or not we directly experience this in any way; and that Unity is broken down – at least for the time being – into smaller unities in a series of hierarchies. Each of us has a place in some hierarchy, in some group (perhaps connected with a Ray group if you are familiar with esoteric astrology). You may instantly identify with a very obvious group such as the astrologers, or the musicians, or the magicians; or less obviously, the courageous, the sensitives, the loners; or the trailblazers, or the conservationists, or the peace-lovers, or the survivors, or the mothers of the world. There are many ways of identifying with a group of human beings, unlimited by geographical, national or racial boundaries; and when we look at our own progress as souls, it is clear that this is dependent very much on our interaction with other people. It would be rare, I think, for any individual to learn all the lessons of a lifetime in total isolation. No, we are brought together to learn our lessons. Even holy men and hermits are visited by those who seek something from them, and by the higher minds who teach them. We learn our lessons, both pleasant and painful, with those to whom we are connected through the soul links. Some of our karma is uncomfortable; some of it is extremely sweet and well deserved.

We have all had the experience of meeting people where there is a sense of recognition or of import about the encounter. If we fall in love, and the romance overwhelms our lives with its breathtaking, numinous quality, we may declare 'This thing is bigger than both of us!' to describe how dramatically we are carried away on the tide of this relationship. We seem to be out of control; it has a life of its own that takes us along with it. It is this kind of relationship which is often called 'karmic'; it has a deep significance far beyond any mere chemistry between the two parties, and it is this type of relationship which is of the greatest value and importance to the development of the soul. It tests us, it challenges us, it rewards us. It may be found in love, or in hatred, in family or at work, in lifelong friendship, in passing infatuations, in short-term or long-term commitments, in tedium or delight. We will always be involved with members of our group so long as we, as souls, are treading our path backwards or forwards, or standing still! The group will always be there; we will always be led together.

So the Moon's Nodes are linked with our purpose and with our people and with the life of our soul; and so is the zodiac of the Nodes, the Draconic zodiac. It speaks of roles that are well defined, and issues that are very clear. There are few of the tangled complexities that beset the psychology of the Tropical level, presenting constant challenges to the astrologer's skill. In view of this contrast between the two levels, why the clarity of the Draconic? Let us go back to Ronald Davison's phrase, 'the legacy of the past'. The South end of the Nodal axis is very clearly connected with the past of the soul, and the Moon herself by tradition is associated with history, roots, inheritance, memory and habit. How can a purpose be linked to the past? Look again at the clarity of conviction which accompanies the fulfilment of such purpose. It needs no tuition, and little encouragement. Dennis Elwell finds that in most people it is fully conscious (witness how much of our *Tropical* motivation lies uneasy and hidden!) and judging by the reactions in the consulting room I would agree. People need little reminding of the ideals and intentions that lie closest to their hearts. At the slightest prompting, the smallest excuse, these motives are primed for action. Have they been there all the time? Do we come into this life with them fully formed? Have we in fact brought with us the inner fruits of many different lives to share with the world during this incarnation, while at another level we work away at a new layer of selfhood? Are these principles and purposes indeed 'the legacy of our past'?

Of course, one could argue that the co-occurrence of the related Tropical and Draconic zodiacs in the one pattern is purely fortuitous. However, counselling experience and research by the leaders in this field confirm the vitality of the Draconic in every individual studied. We definitely have access to its energies, and that access seems to be easy for most people – often far easier than the retrieval of repressed aspects of the Tropical psyche. Yet one could still object that it need have no relationship, however persuasively argued, with the karmic past. Again, all I can say at this stage of our understanding is that in the very few cases where it has been possible for me to match the Draconic pattern against 'far memories' that have had sufficient power and impact to change both the mind and the heart and lead to real growth, the key elements in the memories and in the Draconic have gelled powerfully well.

'It is a conflation of two apparent movements, the fall into generation and the rise into the regenerated spirit, both of which can be figured as dragons. One dragon lives in water, like the Tarasque or his female counterpart the Melusine, who every Saturday beats the waters she swims in with her tail. The other breathes fire, like the fiery steed of the sun or the treasure-guarding dragons that haunt the tombs of famous men. This firebreathing dragon is associated with what the Greeks called the genius of a man – the ancestral principle embodied in his head, brain, spinal marrow, and penis.'

Francis Huxley, *The Way of the Sacred*

Philosophically, the very astronomy of Draco supports its connection with the soul. The Tropical circle is generated at the intersections of ecliptic and equator, linking the Earth's path around the central Sun with the plane of its own rotation, and therefore can be said to symbolise the joining of spirit with matter that is centred upon itself. By comparison, the Draconic circle is generated at the intersections of the ecliptic with the Moon's orbit around the Earth, linking thereby Sun and Moon and Earth. In this picture the Earth is Sun-centred only, not now self-centred; man incarnate, the material creature, centres himself on the spirit within. At the same time the Earth-centred Moon shows us the image of that gentle child, the reflection of the central spirit that is removed from the life of Earth, nevertheless constantly attendant upon it and affecting it, offering its own share of the light of the Sun. As the Stella Maris, Mary, mother of Jesus, is represented in Christian art as crowned by the twelve stars and standing upon the crescent Moon; in the Roman Catholic tradition, Mary – her name so closely resembling the Latin *Mare*, the sea – intercedes between humanity and God whose embodiment was in Jesus Christ, just as in another sense the soul is intermediate between matter and spirit, and in symbols we have the sequence of cross, crescent and circle. At the Nodes, all join. At the Moon's Nodes, consciousness can move from body-centredness to soul-centredness, from immediacy to far history, from human preoccupations to a soul's mission, from desire to principle, from individual identity to group identity. The Equinox kindles fire in the body; the Dragon's Head permits the solar quickening of the growing soul. The Moon is dependent upon the Earth for her status and upon the Sun for her light; the soul is dependent upon the body for its experience and upon the spirit, the divinity, for its grace and its life. In the Tropical zodiac we find the *human* conditions of the individual journey; in the Draconic is found what the *soul* brings to the experience – what it bestows, enjoys, or must endure.

'The dragon begins to speak. Yin and Yang are commingled.'

The Yuan Kien Lei Han

It is possible in this symbolic picture to read the whole story of Man's fall from grace and his redemption. As the Sun was progenitor of the Earth in the solar system, so God created the first man, Adam, in the Genesis story, and gave him rule over an idyllic Eden. Just as, in the distant past of the system, the Moon may have been pulled from the matter of the forming Earth to be its constant companion in orbit, so in the Bible legend God formed the woman Eve from Adam's rib, to be his constant companion and helpmeet. In the Garden of Eden were two Trees – the Tree of Life, and the Tree of Knowledge of Good and Evil – one symbolic of unity, the other of duality. At the nodal generative points of a zodiac there are two key experiences – one of unity, at the Aries Point, the other of duality at the Libra Point; i.e. at the North and South, Ascending and Descending nodes respectively. As already implied earlier through the symbolism of the Ram and the Dragon, the Descending node is a Libra Point, the Libra Point is a Descending node. In this we already have the idea of a fall into duality through the woman. The serpent, whether the Dragon of the eclipses or the worm Ourobouros that circles the Earth (between Equinox and Equinox?) links Aries and Libra, unity and duality, man and woman. Instead of following him to unity (into the Ascending node) Eve draws Adam at the beguiling of the serpent into the path of duality, falling into the Descending node. Instead of steering a straight, honest Arian course to union with the Divine, our first parents found themselves caught up in a jungle of pros and cons, thus obliged from then on to weigh every experience, every phenomenon, in the scales of Libra.

Thrown into a wilderness of choices, mankind's progress grinds almost to a halt. And halt it would, were it not that he sometimes hears that One Voice calling him urgently on, through the avatars, through the Christ, through the humble, through the conscience, through the significant 'accidents' of life. Redemption comes when the Divine is able at last to manifest through the woman, and Eve gives birth to Mary; and through Mary God enters mankind, bringing the Christ at last out of Adam. Here is the revelation of the eventual unity of God, woman, and man; of spirit, soul and matter; of Sun, Moon and Earth; of circle, crescent and cross. Woman, who first listened to the serpent and led mankind away from the One into duality, now listens to God and leads mankind back out of duality towards the One. In the Gospel of Thomas, Jesus says that unless a woman becomes like a man she cannot enter the Kingdom. Man was the first-created human in the Genesis story: he already embodies the Aries flame that would lift him back to his source. But it is the task of woman to seek and embrace that redeeming fire for herself – harder, for she has hitherto only known its reflection. The Aries Point, the Ascending Node, therefore, in the circle of the signs, is the crucial reminder of the path each of us must uniquely tread to make our way eventually back to the Source from which we came, while trying to make good the mistakes of our personal fall.

'As for the rainbow, it is a grand conception in the Bible to make it the token of God's first covenant with men, so that when the flood of his anger had abated, and the ark was grounded upon Ararat, he told Noah: 'And the bow shall be in the cloud: and I will look upon it, that I may remember the everlasting covenant between God and every living creature of all flesh that is upon the earth.' But it is not in the Bible that we shall learn why this jewelled bow of light is the token of such a covenant, or how it is that men try to hold God to his word by constructing a rainbow of their own in chimeric form and wheeling it about the streets of Metz or Tarascon. We can learn more from the Dogon, whose rainbow is a ram-headed snake that drinks the waters it has just poured down.'

Francis Huxley, *The Way of the Sacred*

The Draconic zodiac itself, generated as it is by the Moon's Ascending Node, implies a pattern, a status of the soul, that is perhaps as close an approach to perfection as the individual soul has so far been able to manage – which is a very conditional proposition! Necessarily so: our understanding of these things will always be constrained by the limits of incarnation. It is just that people appear always to do the best of which they are capable with their Draconic pattern. And the Tropical zodiac is clearly that which we are still in the process of perfecting, with the Dragon's Head, not its Tail, acting as our guide. If, for argument's sake, we were to generate a zodiac from a Libra Point – a Descending Node – all planets and cusps would fall in opposite signs to those from Aries. We would directly contradict our proper selves, made or in the making. No; we are meant to be what we see flowing from *Aries*, not its opposite. We are to join our wills to God's Will and to rise, not fall once again away from our selves and from our Source. Into and out of the mouth of the Dragon we mortals must come in our long search for that reunion; and there can hardly be a people in the world that has not made stories and images of the Dragon's ambivalent role in the human journey, including the alchemists of the Western tradition.

There are too many to relate here, but the accounts of Francis Huxley (in *The Way of the Sacred*) and others make enriching and provocative reading. It is also intriguing to speculate on the possible correspondences between the triune nature of humanity explored above, and threefoldness as expressed by other cultural philosophies such as that of the Essenes around the dawn of the Christian era, and the Huna of Hawaii. The latter knew of a low (*Unihipili*), middle (*Uhane*) and high (*Aumakua*) self, each inhabiting successively less dense subtle bodies, or *kinoaka* bodies, and each uses its own form of energy – *mana, manamana,* and *manaloa* respectively. Respectively, they express the natural, elemental self, the human self that is social and personally aware, and the self that has reached a degree of divine consciousness and wisdom. The first two inhabit the etheric and astral bodies. But whether *Uhane* and *Aumakua* are directly identifiable with the Tropical and the Draconic levels of selfhood I am not sure, even though the links are suggestive.

The Essenes conceived of an 'acting body' of love and wisdom, a 'thinking body' of wisdom, and a 'feeling body' of love. Within each body Man had three roles to fulfil: his individual evolution, his planetary function (his role on Earth) and his cosmic purpose. Again, it is debatable whether the bodies as here understood can be matched precisely to those known by the Huna, or to our own symbolism here, but the roles are suggestive of what we are beginning to understand. Perhaps for individual evolution we might look to the Draconic zodiac, for planetary (earthly) function maybe the Tropical – and our cosmic purpose could be taking us into yet another dimension. But a persuasive alternative could be this: that it is the Tropical that maps our individual evolution, the Sidereal describing our planetary function (see my recent work on the Sidereal and public/historic roles), and the Draconic itself that shows us the pattern of our cosmic purpose. We must of course be careful, when tempted to make comparisons between the ubiquitous groups of three, not to assume that all trinities are intertranslatable; for example, id, ego, and superego may appear very similar to the Huna low, middle and high self but in fact may not be exactly the same; they may simply be three aspects of *Uhane*, the middle self.

When all is said and done, the picture of the Draconic level that is emerging is both of a self and of a role, or set of roles, linked to the history of the growing soul, symbolised by the lunar astronomy; and of most poignant relevance in these years of crisis and change when it is remembered that man has at last become able to leave the Earth and set his physical foot upon the Moon. That small step indeed symbolised a great leap for mankind! In the evocative sequence of images that is the Tarot, one first confronts and meets the challenge of the Moon, and then is free to respond to the call of the Sun.

Chapter Seven

Principles and The Soul
Vocation, Conscience, Belief

In the Spring/Summer 1960 issue of *In Search*, there is a reprint of Maurice Froger's seminal piece on *the Nodal Horoscope* – i.e. the Draconic. The editors saw fit to comment on its inclusion: 'Maurice Froger is one of France's fine astrologers. We have reprinted this article on a zodiac commencing with the Moon's North Node since it could be important and has been neglected … for more information about such a Nodal zodiac see also Aldo Lavagnini's article in the Summer 1959 *In Search*.' That was over fifty years ago; and incredibly, despite every encouragement from Charles Jayne, Alfred Emerson and others, plus the hard work done by Froger, Davison and more recently by Dennis Elwell, Jacob Schwartz, and the author, the importance of and increasing need for an Interdimensional Astrology that addresses *all* the needs – temporal and spiritual – of many-selved humanity, have not yet been acknowledged as widely as one might have hoped or indeed expected.

After more than three decades' work with the Draconic zodiac both in and out of the consulting room, I am reasonably certain that activity at this level is generally for the good; therefore, most of the principles summarised below are those which can be held up as a human, if not a universal ideal – at least in the hearts of those that hold them. Here and there one finds an instance where the ideal has become distorted in its expression, especially where it is clearly tied up with past karma, and may even result in human disaster; but this may not be so much a reflection on the ideals themselves as on the weakness of the personality that contains them. Essentially, therefore, these are principles of perfectedness, and whether consciously honoured in the life's activity or not, may find expression in attitudes towards people in general. For example: 'A woman should sacrifice everything for her family'; 'Loyalty comes before everything'; 'People should be ready to fight for their beliefs'; 'In the end you have to be able to go it alone'. These are not assumptions about human psychology, such as are projected from the Tropical horoscope; they are assumptions about human – or absolute – ideals and purposes. They are based on the individual's own ideals and purposes, but are fully applicable to the soul-group to which the individual belongs, since members of a soul-group incarnate together to fulfil a common aim and to hear witness to the shared ideal. Here is found the reason for the Moon's Nodes' interpretive link with groups.

The Zodiacal Principles

Draconic principles show most clearly through the Sun, Moon and Ascendant. Naturally, they apply to all the planets and angles; but as the Lights are so overwhelmingly important (Sun, Moon and Earth are, after all, the very co-creators of the Dragon!) the summary below focusses on these, with some added comments on the Ascendant and personal planets.

Again I must stress that by far the majority of people express the positive and life-enhancing qualities of their Draconic Sun or Moon sign, and, for most of the time, only occasionally lapse into its mistakes. However, as a salutary reminder, the negative attributes of the twelve Draconic signs are also summarised!

A further point worth making is that we are all capable of psychological projection, and Draconic principles are not exempt from this human tendency; thus if you, gentle reader, are female, your Draconic Solar and Martian principles may reflect the deeper ideals you are looking for in a man, as well as those which you hold dear to your own heart, whether or not at this stage you are fully aware of them. Likewise, if you are a man, the values of your Draconic Moon and Venus may closely approach those you hope (consciously or otherwise) to discover in the woman you love: 'I believe that women (or indeed children, home life, or anything essentially lunar) should be like this / take an interest in these things …' Yet they are in reality your own beliefs about the nature, circumstances and conduct of intimacy, emotional matters in general, and the treatment of women and dependants.

I have done my best to stay gender-neutral in the following paragraphs; forgive me if here and there I resort to 'he' for the sake of simplicity.

Draconic Aries

People with Sun or Moon in Draconic Aries will believe deeply in the importance of some or all of the following, to the point of setting an example:

Moral and physical courage; the fighting spirit; honesty, straight dealing; self-reliance; activity; healthy competition; initiative; enterprise; speed; personal leadership; pioneering; inspiration; enthusiasm; strength of will, of body, of purpose; winning; self-development; personal freedom, being a man.

The Ascendant in Draconic Aries will approach the vocational life and karmic encounters with a driving compulsion, even a recklessness through which such principles are energetically manifested. Draconic Aries Mercury will apply them in thinking and all forms of communication; Venus and Mars in a fiery sexuality and a potentially hectic life-style.

Negatively there may be an equally strong belief in 'first come, first served', 'attack is the best form of defence', that 'what I say, goes'. Such arrogance is a potential pitfall for the Draconic Arian; it may be the legacy of a life or lives where the Aries has been used to leadership, action, warfare and getting his or her own way, and can undo much good progress if allowed to flourish unchecked. Likewise, a love of speed and quick decision-making can carry over as impatience that can grow into anger. The 'adrenalin high' is both seductive and addictive, it can be sexually thrilling; the soul wants more – spills more blood, rapes more victims, sets more fires, drives more furiously. All Draconic Arians need to watch out for signs of these flaws, and the dangerous long-term habits of hostility and bad temper that can develop from them. A faulty Aries is the last person to whom love of neighbour comes easily, and it is ultimately base selfishness, lack of love, that is the cause of all unhappiness, of all conflict, of all wars. But even a now belligerent Arian will eventually wish these all away.

Draconic Taurus

People with Sun or Moon in Draconic Taurus will believe deeply in the importance of some or all of the following, to the point of setting an example:

Provision of material, physical security; stability; the appreciation of beauty; stamina; husbandry; conservation of resources; care of the body; affection; pride of ownership; steadfastness of purpose, and in relationship; the labourer worthy of his hire; effort; building on firm foundations; comfort; respect for the Earth and its wealth; care for growing things; the singing voice.

The Ascendant in Draconic Taurus will approach the vocational life and karmic encounters with a steadiness, appreciation and common sense through which such principles are materially manifest. Draconic Taurus Mercury will apply them in thinking and all forms of communication, notably singing; Venus and Mars in a sensual sexuality and a hopefully comfortable and secure life-style.

Negatively the pleasure-principle or a commitment to material security could consolidate into an acquisitive selfishness, and comfort into hedonism, if the Draconic Taurean also believes that this life is all there is. 'Eat, drink, and be merry, for tomorrow we die!'; 'Get it while you can'; 'What's yours is mine, and what's mine is my own'; and the vulgar dictum, 'If you've got it, flaunt it!' Good stewardship can turn into possessiveness, and this can extend beyond property to people, bogging down the progress of relationships. A flair for fund-raising can deteriorate into unrelieved and soulless materialism. Fixed Earth by its nature is difficult to change, so if such a counter-productive attitude is brought into this life from the past it will need a lot of patient work with the help of wiser friends.

Draconic Gemini

People with Sun or Moon in Draconic Gemini will believe deeply in the importance of some or all of the following, to the point of setting an example:

Communications; ideas; versatility; kinship; agility; keeping in touch; youth and youthfulness; movement; mental stimulation; adaptability; variety; freedom of information; talking things through; learning and teaching; linguistics; speech; dance; speech and movement therapy; literacy; writing and authorship; thinking; journalism; Information Technology, the Internet and World Wide Web.

The Ascendant in Draconic Gemini will approach the vocational life and karmic encounters with a restlessness and appetite for knowledge through which such principles are keenly manifested. Draconic Gemini Mercury will apply them in thinking and all forms of communication; Venus and Mars in a sometimes fickle, sometimes cerebral, asexual or platonic sexuality and a constantly active life-style, thriving on stimulus and variety.

Negatively a Draconic Geminian may be so persuaded from the successful development of communications skills in previous lives that quantity and variety of contacts, journeys and information are to be prized above everything, that in this life depth and purpose can be lost, frittered away. Life becomes Trivial Pursuit. Without a proper focus, blown hither and yon on the flattering breezes of opinion, the Gemini may remain a scatter-brain, a social butterfly, interests and affections fickle and shallow. S/he may so be in love with talking that s/he may forget to listen. Youthfulness may become perverted to the futile pursuit of physical immortality, with all its attendant terrors of inevitable age and death. Clinging through artifice of every kind to an appearance and a vigour that in reality have long gone, slave to fashionable conceit, age loses all its dignity. Gemini needs reminding that Peter Pan is one metaphor among many of our *spiritual*, not our physical reality.

Draconic Cancer

People with Sun or Moon in Draconic Cancer will believe deeply in the importance of some or all of the following, to the point of setting an example:

The feelings; womanliness; motherhood; nourishing; intimacy; home and family; houses; roots; memories and recall; tenacity; caring sensitivity; patriotism; children and babies; protectiveness; the expression of feeling; responsiveness; the life of the psyche; knowledge of the Moon; water, oceans, mirrors, reflections, images, silver, souvenirs; collections; history and lineage; learning from the past; regression; emotional security.

The Ascendant in Draconic Cancer will approach the vocational life and karmic encounters with an emotional awareness through which such principles are sensitively manifested. Draconic Cancer Mercury will apply them in thinking and all forms of communication; Venus and Mars in a close, romantic, possibly dependent sexuality and an emotionally supportive, often nostalgic life-style.

Negatively a soul may incarnate believing that for its own safety it must cling to the past, or convinced from childhood that dependency has been protective and is therefore equally vital for the adult. This Cancerian can develop a clinging, demanding, ever-immature personality on such a basis. Self-indulgence deflects attention from the needs of others. The reverse can also be true: an equally deep-rooted mothering instinct can lead to great harm where it encourages dependency in the young when they should be spreading their wings; also through a common tendency to over-feed the husband, the child, the pet, damaging their health. Or there may be a potentially destructive lack of objectivity in respect of his or her cherished roots: 'my country (or, my family) right or wrong'. Most of this behaviour is well-meant, but ignorant. As with us all, if inner growth is not to be stunted, it is essential eventually to let go of our dependencies and of the past.

Draconic Leo

People with Sun or Moon in Draconic Leo will believe deeply in the importance of some or all of the following, to the point of setting an example:

Love; joy in life; spontaneity; the importance of play and education; human dignity; theatre; manliness; the intelligence of the heart; gold; the best of everything; light; pomp and ceremony; loyalty; fatherhood; magnanimity; all that is creative; innocence; setting a good example; hierarchy, natural authority, royalty; sport and entertainment; centring; self-expression and the achievement of selfhood; physical beauty; shininess, cleanliness; trust.

The Ascendant in Draconic Leo will approach the vocational life and karmic encounters with a dignity and integrity through which such principles are creatively, sometimes flamboyantly, manifest. Draconic Leo Mercury will apply them in thinking and all forms of communication; Venus and Mars in a powerful, loving, playful sexuality and as elegant and culturally rich a life-style as possible.

Negatively any Leo, Draconic included, runs the risk of believing that the world revolves around him or her. It is possible that many such incarnations are of people who are bringing with them their past experience of royal power or professional authority, and this can be very hard to let go, in a life which may be starkly contrasted to the one Draconically 'remembered'. Clearly, the best attributes of Leo need to be retained; but its potential self-centredness, bossiness, vanity and extravagance ('I deserve the best!', 'No expense should be spared') will hamper growth if indulged by a skilfully-recruited 'court' that thinks the sun shines out of you-know-where!

Draconic Virgo

People with Sun or Moon in Draconic Virgo will believe deeply in the importance of some or all of the following, to the point of setting an example:

Discrimination; usefulness; humility; modesty; being helpful, of service to others; fulfilling needs; orderliness; accuracy, precision and finesse; craftsmanship; having the right tools for the job; correct nutrition; fastidious purity of food, of environment, of body, of motives; the observation and removal of imperfections; hygiene and cleanliness; healing with substances or physical therapies; 'small is beautiful' and 'little things mean a lot'; caring for the underdog and noticing the fall of the sparrow; ordinary, humdrum everyday things and ordinary people; problem-solving; everything and everyone in their appropriate place; the power of the very small (e.g. homoeopathy, particle physics … and dwads, and asteroids!).

The Ascendant in Draconic Virgo will approach the vocational life and karmic encounters with a critical eye through which such principles are usefully manifested. Draconic Virgo Mercury will apply them in thinking and all forms of communication; Venus and Mars in an earthy sexuality and an unassuming but choosy life-style.

Negatively it is obvious that Draconic Virgo's discernment can easily degenerate into fussiness and neurosis, with the miseries of obsessive-compulsive disorder waiting at the bottom of the pit. The past-life perfectionist can be this life's nit-picker, and this of course extends to the Virgo's health, inspiring chronic hypochondria – great for pharmacies, hard on GPs! Preoccupation with material trivia can seriously distract from the demands of the true vocation; Virgos often can't see the wood for the trees. Also, the drive to be helpful can be such an irritant to those disinclined to be helped that it can further alienate an already downtrodden soul. Previously good habits and altruistic motives may have to be balanced with a new kind of discrimination in the context of the current life. If Virgo, on the basis of past experience, believes no-one takes any notice of him/her, then steps must be taken to start grabbing their attention and building confidence, otherwise s/he will forever remain a whingeing little no-account doormat only fit for others to wipe their boots on.

Draconic Libra

People with Sun or Moon in Draconic Libra will believe deeply in the importance of some or all of the following, to the point of setting an example:

Justice and fair play; kindness; balance; elegance; the giving and sharing of pleasure; femininity; making and keeping the peace; sociability; good behaviour; appreciation; beauty in all its forms; decoration; attractiveness; companionship and partnership; politics; dialogue and negotiation; tact, conciliation, diplomacy; cooperation; interest in and concern for others; seeing another's point of view; impartiality; harmony; happiness; sweetness; ease.

The Ascendant in Draconic Libra will approach the vocational life and karmic encounters with a graciousness through which such principles are harmoniously manifest. Draconic Libra Mercury will apply them in thinking and all forms of communication; Venus and Mars in a refined, considerate sexuality and a pleasing, undemanding life-style.

Negatively 'anything for a quiet life' sounds the death-knell for many a Draconic Libran whose purpose this time around is to enter the fray and, once in the thick of it, introduce the peace and harmony that were sorely lacking. The Libran skill is in pleasing people; but it can be simply out of vanity, or personal insecurity, in order to attract. If you have been beautiful in a past life, with many admirers, it is natural to want the same this time, but narcissism is another primrose path to spiritual decline. Maybe it's a Draconic Libran who is constantly dreaming up ways to make our domestic and working lives so much easier that our minds and bodies are atrophying for lack of exercise. 'Lazy Libra' is often a most unjust epithet, but nevertheless this is the sign's flip-side, and very destructive it can be, as this soul, incapable of self-sufficiency, then becomes parasitic, sucking energy from both family and society.

Draconic Scorpio

People with Sun or Moon in Draconic Scorpio will believe deeply in the importance of some or all of the following, to the point of setting an example:

Survival; power; self-transformation; profundity; passion; emotional discipline; privacy; secrecy; sexuality; research and revelation; persuasion; investigation; detection; healing power; hypnosis; confidentiality; knowledge as power; determination; depth psychology; the occult; warfare; big business; shared resources; plumbing the depths; self-mortification; confrontation with the darkness; watching and waiting.

The Ascendant in Draconic Scorpio will approach the vocational life and karmic encounters with a persistent thoroughness through which such principles are intensely manifested. Draconic Scorpio Mercury will apply them in thinking and all forms of communication; Venus and Mars in a driven, passionate sexuality and a secretive, sometimes self-mortifying, sometimes excessive, life-style.

Negatively the Draconic Scorpion may have come back from a life or lives of very dark experience. In most cases this will have strengthened, refined and deepened, rather than harmed, the soul, but a minority will be determined to keep on the same path. Therefore some will be dedicated to macabre or cruel practices; some will take pleasure in killing; some will be bent on self-destruction, some on revenge; some remain so possessive of their mate that more than one life is ruined by ingrained suspicion and jealousy. Some will take it for granted that all that counts in this world is the struggle for power and a monopoly of wealth, at however many people's or nations' expense. Only apparently less brutal is the Scorpio detective instinct gone bad: the nosey parker 'dishing the dirt with the rest of the girls' under a row of hair driers, or mud-slinging across the front pages of the tabloids. A new and particularly nasty manifestation of the Scorpio principle is the spread of hatred and violence via the Web. As I was starting this paragraph, the local television news reporting on a murder trial flashed up pictures of an Internet group who preach the elimination of 'nuisances' whose 'views do not coincide with ours'. Their symbol? The scorpion's tail. Be aware that once in a while you may have to deal with a soul so dangerously lost as this.

Draconic Sagittarius

People with Sun or Moon in Draconic Sagittarius will believe deeply in the importance of some or all of the following, to the point of setting an example:

Health in mind, body and spirit; optimism; faith; showmanship; exploration; travel broadening the mind; learning by experience; a holistic approach; lavishness; pursuit of truth; confidence; freedom of opportunity; conservation; intuitive wisdom; independence; the importance of relaxation; sportsmanship; enjoyment of life; nobility and riches; laughter, fun and bonhomie; natural living; animals; saying 'Yes!'; space; outdoor activity; religion, evangelism; generosity; understanding and guardianship of moral and natural law; higher education; freedom of speech, and of belief; the meeting of minds; good fellowship with all mankind.

The Ascendant in Draconic Sagittarius will approach the vocational life and karmic encounters with an openness and philosophical good humour through which such principles are buoyantly manifest. Draconic Sagittarius Mercury will apply them in thinking and all forms of communication; Venus and Mars in an adventurous sexuality and an expansive – or expensive! – life-style.

Negatively the lavishness of Sagittarian generosity, the insistence on the best of everything, can deteriorate into wastefulness, ostentation, gross sensual indulgence. A fund of good humour and jokes can coarsen until there are no limits to what will be said or done to raise a belly-laugh, and the popular story-teller can become a braggart, an insufferable show-off, a pompous bore. Belief in freedom can come to excuse licentiousness, and confident optimism justify sheer thoughtless folly. A soul reincarnating from a privileged background into more straitened circumstances may turn out as a con artist, an idle cheat who considers that the world owes him or her a living. One used to popularity may be corrupted into buying friendship and bribing colleagues. A travel addict may be nowhere to be found when his family needs him. And spiritual inflation is always a danger if Sag thinks s/he has a special relationship with God. The trouble is these Sagittarians always believe they are right; it is just that the rest of the world is out of step. How can they possibly be in the wrong? Their self-belief is so strong that they can charm their hundreds of friends into believing them too. That doesn't sound so bad – just lovable rogues? – but the true Sagittarian wisdom and religious instinct will never awaken if clumsy loud-mouthed souls are allowed for yet another life to get off scot-free with their greed and self-serving hypocrisy. The Draconic Sagittarian will never learn if the only person he listens to, in love with the sound of his voice, is himself.

Draconic Capricorn

People with Sun or Moon in Draconic Capricorn will believe deeply in the importance of some or all of the following, to the point of setting an example:

Purposeful activity; silence; patience; striving; excellence; self-discipline; being able to say 'No'; one thing at a time; self-sufficiency; mastery; the loner; respect for self and others;

high standards; initiative; common sense; wit; order; obedience; authority; moderation, thrift, simplicity; hard work; old age; timing; taking opportunity; planning for the future; empiricism; aspiration; responsibility; practicality; method; form, pattern and rhythm; listening; duty; statesmanship; perseverance; integrity; business sense, caution … and mountain climbing!

The Ascendant in Draconic Capricorn will approach the vocational life and karmic encounters with a matter-of-fact objectivity through which such principles are cautiously manifest. Draconic Capricorn Mercury will apply them in thinking and all forms of communication; Venus and Mars in an unromantic, physically necessary but controlled sexuality and a conventional, upwardly-mobile life-style.

Negatively we have yet another sign which prefers to be in the right, and to have everything and everyone under control. If you have spent at least one key life as a hard-headed executive or a statesman, this calculating efficiency and cold ambition is likely to come back with you. Unmodified, Draconic Capricorn is liable to be utterly ruthless in designing and attaining his or her ends; and once one goal is achieved, another will follow. This can all make for a cold marriage in which relationship can come a very poor second to the business or the position which supplies the family's needs. Friendships suffer too, if the self-sufficiency the soul has learned in the past gets in the way of forging important bonds in the present. People around such a soul end up feeling, rightly, used. Not nice. A polar problem with the Capricorns is that some have arrived from an earlier disadvantaged life which has left them feeling that nothing they do will ever be good enough – and so they won't even try. Also, if they have had to learn to economise, and fail to readjust, the mean-minded Draconic Capricorns court condemnation as cheapskates, skinflints, tightwads. They spend their lives moping like Eeyore in a prickly corner, pushing the world, its opportunities and all its real bounty away, determined to be miserable. Biblically, they started off with a God-given talent, but have buried it. Sad. Because this negative type will not hand over control to someone else, help and encouragement are difficult, and may never be accepted; they usually have to learn the hard way. But do try.

Draconic Aquarius

People with Sun or Moon in Draconic Aquarius will believe deeply in the importance of some or all of the following, to the point of setting an example:

Independence of mind; human rights; innovation and ingenuity; group activity; difference; friendship; people; reform; mass communications; democracy; rationality; unorthodoxy; technology; public opinion; liberty, equality, fraternity; rules made to be broken; science; the perception and speaking of truth; paradox; social justice; social work; New Age ideals, philosophy, therapies; 'Tomorrow's World'; change; science fiction; detachment; shock tactics; uniqueness; civil liberty; surprises; organised charity; analysis; asexuality; bisexuality; androgyny.

The Ascendant in Draconic Aquarius will approach the vocational life and karmic encounters with an emancipated friendliness through which such principles are inventively manifest. Draconic Aquarius Mercury will apply them in thinking and all forms of communication; Venus and Mars in an unconventional sexuality and an innovative, gregarious, even shocking life-style.

Negatively there may be some who have still not fully awakened to the ideal that fixed opinions, received wisdom and political correctness need to be replaced with an open, independent mind with the capacity to be inspired and to innovate. At its extreme, though, a truly independent-minded soul reincarnating could be so out of touch with the mores of the new environment that s/he is effectively alienated. This breeds resentment and rebellion; instead of changing himself the Draconic Aquarian may decide to spend his life disrupting the society that supports him. This may be through material outrage, or verbal shock, which will turn into an unhappy cycle of offence and rebuff until the misfit gives up, leaves or is ejected. This is a waste of citizenship. Aquarians don't compromise, but they do talk, and lines of communication need to be kept open to such souls until there is somewhere they can feel at home in society. After all, the Aquarian is among the most acutely socially aware, and usually a healthy antidote to the complacency in all of us. This social side does have its traps for the inadequate Aquarian, however, in his or her readiness over and over again to jump on the band-wagon of any new craze or cult for the sake of something different. Life as a New Age 'groupie' may be colourful and attractive, but is no lasting way for a fixed sign to find and follow its spiritual direction. In the process this soul may mislead many others along paths of dubious value.

Draconic Pisces

People with Sun or Moon in Draconic Pisces will believe deeply in the importance of some or all of the following, to the point of setting an example:

Ideals; compassion; gentleness; self-effacement; human vulnerability; redemption of the rejected; dreams; disguise; universality; unconditional love; music; magic; the fine arts; free giving; total union; divine obedience; sublimation and transcendence; cosmic consciousness; priesthood; communion; privacy; prayer, spirituality; eternal life; delicacy; being 'in the world, but not of it'; devotion, romance, 'the holiness of the heart's affections'; self-sacrifice; vision; divine healing; weeping; 'letting go', escape; poetry; the merging of identity – as in mediumship, in acting, in mystic union; the life of the psyche; the collective unconscious; chaos; fluids; fish; feet.

The Ascendant in Draconic Pisces will approach the vocational life and karmic encounters with a loving acceptance through which such principles are sensitively manifested. Draconic Pisces Mercury will apply them in thinking and all forms of communication; Venus and Mars in a lyrical, abandoned sexuality and an aesthetic or other-worldly life-style.

Negatively we find an escape clause built into the Draconic Pisces soul; it can spend life like a wimp running away from every imagined threat; until a series of emotional tidal waves carry it so far off course that it abandons ship. Heaven or hell: either is more attractive than life's maelstrom. Sensitivity, responsiveness, compassion, love … these are glories, not faults; but they bring sacrifice and pain, and a Piscean may simply be too weak or cowardly to cope, and opt for the easy way out – having it all to do over again in another trying incarnation. Frequently, all this can be laid at the door of the victim-saviour syndrome. A victimised past – even a salvific past – now seeks redemption or perpetuation through finding (or worse, creating) other victims to rescue. Surrendering to this compulsion can ruin lives; unrestrained romantic Pisces carries the seeds of chaos. In another soul, instead of a rich imagination we have a congenital liar. Less harmful but very annoying, there is also the I-shall-drop-litter-wherever-I-want-and-never-clean-up-after-myself brigade. In another, unguarded openness to the astral plane results in damaging psychic disorder. We also have the freaks, the degenerates, the rejects. Some have come to awaken compassion in us all; but there are those who wrongly insist on remaining the outcasts they were, and so through antisocial habits such as thieving, drunkenness and substance abuse, violate themselves, their families and anyone who tries to help them, conspicuously failing to make any inner progress. We may have to leave the wreckage of Pisces in God's hands.

Amongst the above summaries you will find some concepts which, like 'fluids; fish; feet' are not principles of aim, character or motivation, but nevertheless embody fields of work or experience that are of vital significance to the incarnate soul concerned, and of which he or she is not just actively but spiritually representative. In the pages that follow, example charts illustrate the working of the Draconic principles. These become active not only through the Draconic zodiac itself, but in a second fundamental way through the resonances set up between the Draconic and Tropical charts. All we have to do is to apply synastry to the two patterns and note the significant contacts. In a dream some years ago, before the work with Draco came to hand, I was given the term *'homologous duodynes'*. With only the vaguest idea of the meaning of 'homologous' and no notion of what a 'duodyne' might be, I went to my dictionary. Homologous, I found, meant 'agreeing; of the same essential nature, corresponding in relative position, general structure, and descent.' There was no sign of a duodyne; but a *dyne* turned out to be a specific unit of force, its root the Greek *dynamis*, power or force, and here we seemed to have two of them, or a double force.

I think we now have the answer to the conundrum. The phrase refers to the linking of one level of man's being with another, i.e. one pattern of that multilevel being linked with a second that is identical in general structure (the planetary and house geometries) but out of zodiacal phase with it; the overall significance of this linkage stemming from agreements of planets and/or angles in the same relative positions with respect to a nodal origin point – an 'Aries Point'. The idea of powers at work may refer to man's own powers as we understand them: the strengths, weaknesses and gifts of his mental, emotional, physical and spiritual bodies. But an interesting point arises, namely that Edgar Cayce in his Life Readings, given over a large part of his twenty-two years of public activity, constantly referred to 'planetary forces', where the astrological practitioner would normally employ some such term as 'influences' (old school) or 'effects', or 'significance', or 'correlation', or 'symbolism'. The more abstract and noncommittal nowadays, it seems, the better! Maybe we are determinedly ducking an issue which we of the incipient Aquarian Age are unwilling to face. Maybe Cayce the Piscean (Draconic Arian of soul) knew something the old astrologers knew and were not afraid to acknowledge. For my part, it has been well worth the struggle through the semantic jungle of the readings given in Margaret Gammon's book to harvest the material for the first chapter of the present work. If you read both, you may judge for yourself.

To return to the contacts between the two levels as shown in the Draconic and Tropical charts, these are active in two principal ways. Firstly, where a planet or angle aligns by conjunction or opposition to a planet or angle in the other chart (for example, Draconic Uranus conjunct Tropical Sun; Draconic Venus opposite Tropical Mars); secondly, where the Draconic planets and angles fall in the Houses of the Tropical chart (for example, Draconic Moon in Tropical 5th House) irrespective of any contact or none with Tropical planets or angles. The use of any 360° (ecliptic) chart-form with a double wheel intended for directions or synastry will organise the two levels of information very clearly; it is not necessary to cast an individual Draconic chart unless one wishes to 'get the feel of the person' entirely at this level. Simply enter the Draconic positions on the outer wheel of the Tropical map, and all the most vital alignments and the House focus will come clearly into the picture. Most current software will swiftly do this for you if you work with a computer.

Should one include Draconic house cusps? This depends on (a) your *use* of cusps, so enter whatever you consider to be significant, and (b) the accuracy of the chart: if the birth time is uncertain all cusps suffer grievously whereas planets (the Moon excepted) are virtually immune, and one can end up with some very dubious inferences. Are other aspects to be considered, as well as the principal alignments? I am unsure. A straight alignment provides direct access from level to level; think again of this as a resonant phenomenon, and that in a direct contact we have identity of resonance – two voices singing the same song. Indirect contact introduces a harmony, perhaps; squares bringing their reinforcing octaves. This is all very speculative; ultimately, experience is the best teacher. So far I have come across a few instances where squares or trines between levels (with tight orbs of a degree or so) were clearly key elements in that person's pattern, so watch for these.

'We do find cases where people are not really typical of their signs, and we find that some signs seem to produce a number of subtypes, which have nothing to do with decanates or other divisions of the sign ... I am inclined to think ... that in fact there are subinfluences, which can be attributed to the sign occupied in the Draconitic Zodiac ... which will give extra colouration. ... To summarise the system, things happen when several coordinates coincide ... if there is no overlapping, things tend not to happen, and you can make some very nasty mistakes ... each zodiac offers a different dimension of meaning, and I think that it is in the combination of them all that the solution to so many of our astrological problems may lie.'

Dennis Elwell, *Multidimensional Transits*

Chapter Eight

Practising What We Preach?
WYSIWYG Charts and Double Lives

To show you Draconic patterning at work, here is a selection of example charts of well-known people whose lives display vividly the principles found there. Put succinctly, the principled Draconic energies show what we preach, and those of the developing Tropical show what we practise. The ease or difficulty with which we combine the two depends very much on the position of the Dragon's Head and the subsequent 'synastry' between the two levels.

Where they are compatible, we are inclined to be WYSIWYG people! – on the whole we practise what we preach so that What You See Is What You Get. Where, however, there is clashing and contrast, principle and practice argue and fall out, and we can end up effectively leading double lives.

Bear these pointers in mind as you look at the lives of the following individuals – and, *most* illuminating, apply them to a frank and fearless scrutiny of your own life!

EDWARD BACH, Physician
Draconic Sun Aries, Draconic Moon Pisces

Edward Bach – for the greater part of his relatively short life a renowned and respected Harley Street doctor and medical researcher – gave his last six years to the discovery and development of the thirty-eight Flower Remedies that bear his name. He was born on 24th September 1886 in Moseley, Birmingham, England according to his biographer Nora Weeks (who carried on his work devotedly for many years) but no time of birth is given, so I have used a noon chart. The gentle, quiet kindliness of the man can be seen in the Libran Sun, the Moon in warm Leo, probably sextile Jupiter in Libra. His sensitivity and intelligence are marked by the Sun/Mercury conjunction in close trine with Neptune and Pluto, the Sun/Uranus conjunction adding originality to the point of eccentricity. Venus, the Sun-

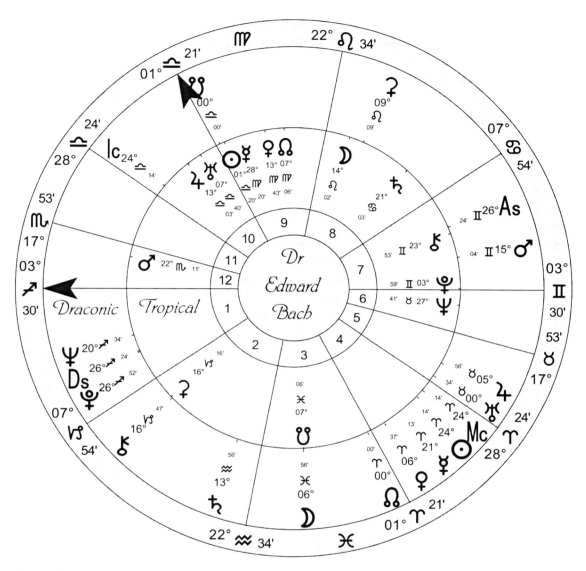

ruler, falls in Virgo: precise, practical, needing to serve. The Scorpio Mars contrasts the gentler side of his nature with a fund of deep and driving energy which nourished him in his unremitting search for the simple cure for all disease. In the Draconic chart, however, the Sun, Mercury and Venus all fall in Aries. Here is the pattern of a pioneer, a man 'no mere dreamer' with 'certainty … intensity of purpose … interest in all things'. 'Early in his search,' says Nora Weeks, 'he had gained the knowledge that *the personality of the individual was of even more importance than the body in the treatment of disease.*' Here is the Aries principle of 'the personality of the patient, the suffering human being … the patient's outlook on life, his emotions, his feelings.' With these last, the Pisces principles also come into their own: the Draconic Moon is in the sign of Pisces, and 'any human being, bird or creature in pain or distress aroused in him such compassion and desire to help their suffering that he determined, whilst still a boy at school, to be a doctor. This overwhelming compassion for others, which gave him so great an understanding of their distress, was one of his most striking qualities, and one which made him beloved by all who came in contact with him … He gave freely of his knowledge at all times.'

To Bach, the Draconic Arian, 'decision was instant action'; he was seen as 'a leader of scientific research' while engaged in the field of homoeopathy, and 'in his later work … the herbal remedies he discovered hold the power of so revitalising the mind and body that the wish to live and do one's work in life is regained, and with that desire good health returns.'

When he left London and his lucrative practice in 1930 to begin his search in earnest, 'he set out on his great adventure without one backward thought or regret … His enthusiastic nature and tremendous vitality made him appear far younger than his forty-three years. His courage – a courage that few possess – was unbounded, for he started out upon his quest with the knowledge that he must stand alone, with nothing but his own inner conviction of great new work to be done to help him through the years ahead. He wrote to a friend on one occasion, "What is called intuition is nothing more or less than being natural, and following your own desire absolutely."'

From the foregoing, it is easy to see how strongly the solar and lunar principles at the Draconic level of his being impressed themselves upon his life, how the gentle nature-lover found the strength, energy and purpose to achieve all he did despite periods of considerable poverty and recurrent ill health. One can see why his early dreams of healing coming directly from his hands became reality as he, the born sensitive, became even more delicately attuned to the spiritual life of people and plants. The last chapter of his biography sums up his character:

'Ever direct in speech, fearless of giving offence when he wished to emphasise the truth (Sun/Mercury in Aries) … he always refused to argue or reason with others (Tropical Libra) … He had the ability to perceive and instantly act upon the truth of any new knowledge he gained through his researches … His intense desire to help others to understand and learn as quickly as he did himself sometimes made him impatient at slowness (Aries) … but this mood would not last long, for he was possessed of infinite patience (Draco Saturn aligned with Tropical Moon in Leo) … and although he was quick to anger at injustice, unhesitatingly voicing it and siding with the weaker, he would encourage the weak one to fight his own battles and so regain his self-esteem. He experienced pain and disease, difficulties and hardships to the uttermost limit; but these he passed through with courage and gratitude, for he felt that through his own experiences he would eventually make the way easier for others. It was said of him that he slew seven dragons (!) so that others might be encouraged to slay one.'

In one of his notebooks he wrote:

'No man should be a leader amongst others for any length of time unless he were more expert in his special branch of knowledge than his followers … It therefore follows to be a leader against trouble, difficulties, disease, persecution and so forth, the leader must still have a greater knowledge, a more intimate experience, than, pray God, his followers need ever suffer.'

His biographer tells us that '… above all, he was one of those rare individuals who awaken in others a renewed sense of joy and interest in life, and a quickening of their observation and appreciation of the beauty in all around.' We see not only the love of harmony in the Libran nature, here, but the glorious fulfilment of the Draconic Aries Venus aligning with Uranus, Jupiter and the Sun. No wonder he was a man so loved in his lifetime, and still held so dear by those who are continuing the work his love and his genius began.

HAROLD EVANS, Journalist
Draconic Sun Aries, Draconic Moon Virgo

Harold Evans, born on June 28th 1928 in Manchester, England, opted for a life in journalism while still in his teens, first working on the *Ashton-under-Lyne Reporter*, then becoming Editor of the *Northern Echo* in Darlington, eventually appointed Editor of the prestigious *Sunday Times*.

Not only do the Sun, Mercury and Venus all fall in Draconic Aries, but in so doing, at the end of the sign, they conjoin Tropical Mars across the cusp in Taurus. With the Tropical Scorpio Moon, this adds up to an extremely vigorous and campaigning soul, never happier than when in the thick of battles he has come into life to fight. This is not nearly so obvious from the Tropical chart with its sextiles from emotional Cancer to steady Taurus, the Arian Uranus providing the only strong spur to a self-confessedly easygoing nature.

Let Evans the Draconic Arian speak for himself, in an interview published in *Quest 78*:

Question:	… you said that working up there in the North you felt 'like a barracuda in a boating pond'.
Harold Evans:	… I felt it was my job to be aggressive, to get very angry and to want to bite people. I wanted to bite politicians who refused an enquiry into the death of Timothy Evans. I wanted to bite Whitehall civil servants who wrote off the North East and cheerfully let parts of the region die. I wanted to bite local people who were smug and complacent as I saw it … I have a professional hostility … we started the campaign for a national programme for detection of cervical cancer in women … I reprinted pamphlets, and bombarded people with letters, and wrote articles … I always get an excitement out of publishing a news scoop, and I always get a sense of tremendous depression if we don't have a news scoop. I don't like being scooped. If … you are in a position of authority or knowledge and don't do anything about it and knowingly see that person's life wrecked, that is what angers me, and I think

it would drive me to murder and mayhem, and in journalism it drives me to anger and headlines and investigations.

The Draconic Moon in Virgo became very apparent as the interview progressed:

Questioner: … as an editor you also have to listen to other people's problems and try to help them develop their talents to the best.

Harold Evans: … I'm always conscious of imperfection … I'm always conscious of the infinite possibilities of making a newspaper better. Well, you begin to be modest at my age. You have to be, because things recede, you know. One can look back on certain successes, but

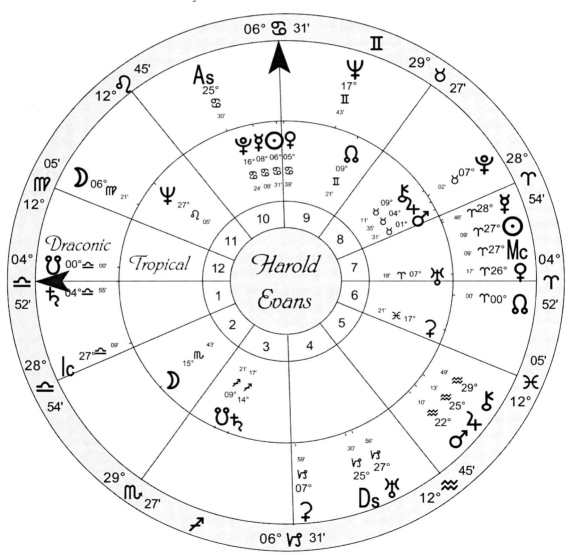

also on certain failures and limitations ... for the fine details of the argument and for the complexity ... print journalism is irreplaceable.

Question: Finally, let me ask you this: what would you hope to be remembered for more than anything else?

Harold Evans: I'd like to be remembered for making a contribution to journalism, and for journalism making a contribution, with all the teams and people associated with it, to improving peoples lives.

STEPHEN HAWKING, Physicist
Draconic Sun in Leo, Draconic Moon in Aries

By the age of twenty-seven, Stephen Hawking had already been elected a Fellow of his Cambridge College for distinction in science. Ever since his arrival there he had been totally absorbed in studies of General Relativity, and, ever since, his work has gone from strength to strength in his efforts to achieve in his lifetime what Einstein failed to accomplish in his own. But the outstanding factor in Stephen Hawking's work is that he undertakes it in the face of total and progressive disability: he contracted Amyotrophic Lateral Sclerosis (ALS) shortly after his arrival in Cambridge. He was born on January 8th 1942 (the same month that saw the arrival of that other highly publicised Draconic Leo, Muhammad Ali, 'The Greatest!').

With both Sun and Mercury in Tropical Capricorn trine Saturn, Uranus, Moon and Neptune (all in Earth) but the Mercury in close square to Mars, we would expect brilliance of intellect focussed on the physical universe and yet some problem with mental or nervous energy. In fact, ALS is a motor neuron disease that affects the body's musculature, eventually wasting it completely. So all the activity of that Mercury/Mars square is now locked into this man's quite extraordinary mind.

The Leo principle asserts itself strongly enough in his necessary focus inward onto the central truths of his existence. 'Who he knows he is, is what it is all about. He knows he's a husband and father with a family to support. He knows he's a professor at Cambridge with the Department of Applied Mathematics and Theoretical Physics.' He already knew he was seriously ill when he asked the young woman he loved if she would marry him. She accepted, and although the marriage was eventually dissolved she proved a tower of strength for many years, to equal his own. The *love* between them won through: he told James Bryce, 'My view of everything changed. My will to live and to continue striving was all because of Jane.' Bryce makes the following comment, which epitomises Stephen Hawking the Draconic Leo: 'It is the *inner man, the mind/consciousness* and brain, that Stephen is definitely putting to its best use. I believe that in his example of *pushing one's inner mind potential* there is a very strong message for all those who are seeking ways to cope with disabilities of any kind [my italics] ... The mind, if left to grow strong, is never really trapped at all. It can be trained to do wondrous things far beyond what any of

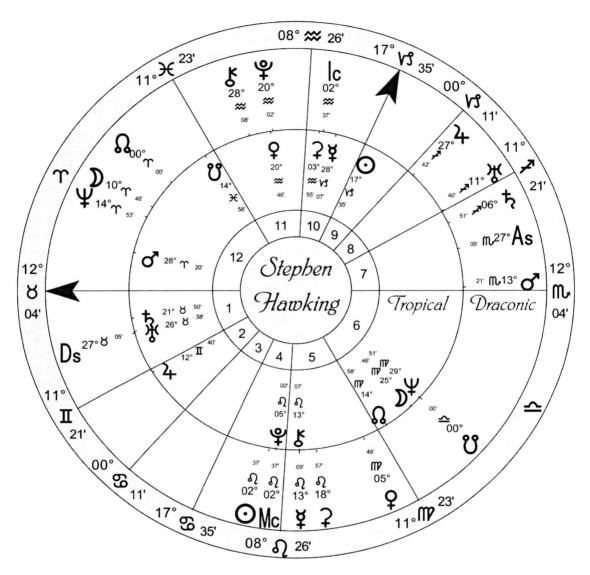

us can conceive.' And this extra power of the mind emerges from the Draconic pattern in the conjunction of Draco Sun with Tropical Pluto, the Survivor, the Transcender. Not only is it manifest in his work – his theoretical research into the ever-receding boundaries of space and time, touching the dawn of creation, and the as yet unknown universes of black holes, where all familiar laws of physics break down at the inconceivable trauma of the singularity – but also in his survival of his own physical breakdown, in the opening of his own inner universe, and in changing mankind's entire perspective on the space-time continuum. The whole of his life is transformative; his authority comes from his very centre. 'In fact at times,' says Bryce, 'it seems to be a major force in his ability to almost ignore that he has a disability at all.'

As Stephen was admittedly 'somewhat lazy and prone to being quite bored before his illness,' it may well be that Jane initially represented his Draco Moon in Aries; but she inspired and encouraged him to such an extent that all the latent drive and battling spirit and determination surfaced in its own right, and he has since been a vigorous and outspoken campaigner for better understanding of and facilities for the disabled.

In this context, one of the most interesting facets of the Draconic pattern here is the exact conjunction of Draconic Leo Mercury with Tropical Chiron. Both astrologers and astronomers are still learning about this small but deeply significant planet, in its orbit between Saturn and Uranus. Terms such as 'maverick' have been applied to it; connections with learning and teaching, with suffering and healing, have been firmly established. It is concerned with the transmission of knowledge, skills, wisdom and values; it is the province also of paradox – that which is neither one thing nor the other, the singularity, the utterly unusual, and the combining of things apparently irreconcilable. It makes bridges; between the rational and the irrational, between Nature and Man, between the forces of darkness and the forces of light, between order and chaos, between life and death, between material and spiritual, as necessitated in religious initiation and in psychological individuation, both of which require *the voluntary passage through a death in order to redeem the past and recreate the future*. And for Hawking, the teamwork of Mercury/Chiron has provided the means to speak the thoughts, convey the ideas, that seemed in such danger of remaining trapped inside his head – the brilliant voice synthesiser whose bizarre transatlantic tones now so characterise his pronouncements that his words are instantly recognisable; his voice has become a global icon in sound.

His ex-wife Jane has said, 'I have often thought that on some level somewhere Stephen has chosen the position he's in. We've both wondered about it. It seems he took the path he did so he could do nothing else but use his mind to achieve things that will forever enhance man's knowledge.' And again, to quote Bryce, '… It is the Unified Field Theory,' which Stephen Hawking has long sought for, and still seeks, 'that would join the two theoretical factions of Relativity and Quantum Theory into one unified whole, and form the basis for a single cosmic law by which everyone could understand the universe.'

JOHN McENROE, Tennis champion
Draconic Sun Leo, Draconic Moon Scorpio, Draconic Ascendant Aries

John McEnroe, over the years of his greatest fame, earned himself the unflattering title of 'Superbrat' among the sporting media – not just for the extraordinary power of his tennis, which has won him a large number of titles, but for his lamentable displays of short temper on court, ranging from a querulous petulance to vituperative rage. The chart is quite extraordinary in its symmetry, dominated by the acute tensions of that Fixed/Mutable Grand Cross and laced with the flashing brilliance of Mars, Uranus, Jupiter, Venus in the 5th/10th harmonics. Control is there, in a surprisingly good Saturn, which struggles, however, with that restless, wayward Gemini Mars.

It is a chart which I think brings home very clearly indeed the idea of 'the legacy of the past', for an inspection of the Nodal axis shows a need to move away from Aries principles and develop some Libra, especially as the Aries South Node is in his 1st House, not far from the Ascendant. His lessons will all revolve around the need to put others' interests before his own. So we can infer a certain amount of Mars karma to be worked out with that planet so much in tension and its negative qualities so often exhibited. This is not all; the self-assertiveness symbolised by that Aries South Node takes over completely when the pattern is transposed into the Draconic. The already maverick trio of Chiron/Mercury/Sun is now found in Leo, and the Moon/Mars pairing is in Draconic Scorpio, suggesting that we have here a soul with a history of power-seeking, and a deeply rooted belief in getting one's own way at whatever cost. He may have triumphed often, and have to learn now that victory is hollow unless won with grace and fair play. Interaction

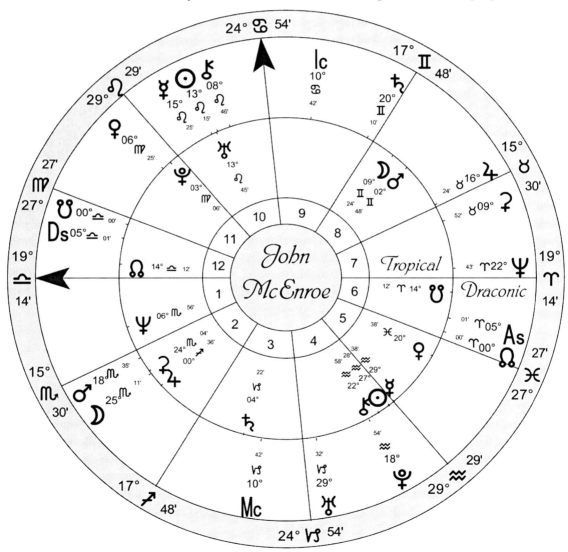

with the crowd through all the Air of his Tropical pattern would eventually see to it that he got his own power into perspective, developed consideration and goodwill, and bade farewell to the spoiled child. He has clearly been trying, and in his mature years he has noticeably mellowed – even though he could for a while still throw the odd tantrum. 'Getting angry on court is just a waste of energy,' he was saying later. For many years he was also much in love with Tatum O'Neal, who for the duration of their relationship was probably a wonderful Ellie to his Tom (see Charles Kingsley's *The Water-Babies*) with all the Saturn restraints she laid on him while bringing all that was royal and brave alive in his passionate soul. In 1985 I wrote, 'Eventually he'll make it, his higher self will win.' In 2011 I am sure that has happened. He spends much of his time as an expert commentator at televised matches, including Wimbledon. 'Trying to be your best is really what it's all about.'

ALBERT EINSTEIN, Scientist
Draconic Sun Conjunct Tropical Pluto in Taurus, Draconic Moon in Aquarius

I have written earlier about Stephen Hawking, the theoretical physicist who is attempting to complete and extend the work of his great predecessor, Einstein, by formulating and proving a Unified Field Theory. We found that he had Draconic Sun conjunct Tropical Pluto in Leo. Clearly, not every physicist delving into the mysteries of nuclear structures (if one can call the attendant phenomena 'structures') is going to have this pattern, but it is significant that both men have been/are transforming scientific thinking by tearing down the frameworks of obsolescent theories and building challenging, even daunting new constructions on those sound foundations that remain. This in itself is Plutonic activity; but one must also remember the material they are examining in such depth – the related concepts of matter and energy.

It was Einstein who first gave humanity the formula by which the interrelationship of matter and energy could not only clearly, but usefully, be understood: $E = mc^2$, where E is energy, m is mass, and c^2 is the velocity of light, squared. He proved that all matter is concentrated energy – or, as one might put it in the present context, Taurus is Pluto'd Sun! His pioneering role in his field is presented typically by the alignment of Draconic Mars to Tropical Sun, and emphasised by Draconic Pluto opposite Tropical Mars. Through his Special and General Relativity theories, Einstein had, in the words of Louis Untermeyer, 'wrought more of a revolution in science than the works of any other man … The explosion of the atom bomb – an explosion which converted a tiny bit of matter into the blasting power of 20,000 tons of TNT – proved that matter was merely unreleased energy, and that matter and energy were two different manifestations of a single cosmic entity.'

At this point a most fascinating fact arises; and I will continue to let Mr Untermeyer explain:

'A philosopher as well as a physicist, he believed that the mystic transcended the materialist (the chart is dominated by the 10th House Sun and MC in Tropical Pisces) and that it was impossible to draw the line between the physical and the metaphysical. "The most beautiful thing we can experience is the mysterious," he declared. "It is the source of all true art and science."'

And when we look at the two zodiac levels in combination we find that Midheaven in Draconic Taurus, close to the degree of Tropical Neptune. (Draconic Neptune is not far from the Tropical Cancer Ascendant.) Pluto also seems implied in the mystery:

'To know that *what is impenetrable to us* really exists, manifesting itself as the highest wisdom and the most radiant beauty … is at the centre of true religiousness.' He contended that 'the cosmic religious experience is the strongest and the noblest mainspring of scientific research.'

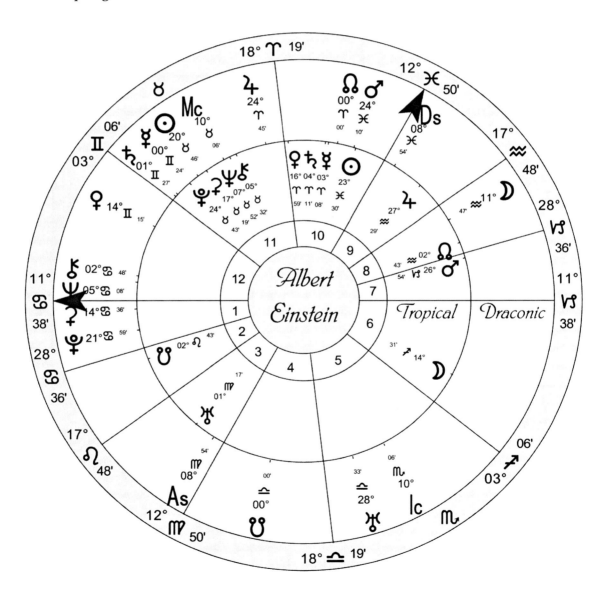

Now we come to the most interesting part:

> 'It was in the Dutch philosopher Spinoza that he found something which led him to discover the equivalence of matter and energy. "In Spinoza," said Einstein, "one finds the majestic concept that thinking (the soul) and extension (the naturalistically conceived world) are only different forms of appearance of the same 'substance'."'

This is reminiscent of the concept of *'Homologous Duodynes'* introduced earlier. Such is man? Such is all matter? The Ancient Wise, in all their guises, have taught us this from time immemorial. Ultimately all matter is energy, all manifestation is spirit. 'No scientist was so revered in his time since Newton,' says Isaac Asimov in his short biography of Einstein. This was due not only to his being 'the most influential scientist in the world,', but to his nature as a human being. The Tropical Pisces Sun and Sagittarian Moon combined their gentleness and generosity with the scientific, revolutionary but humanitarian Draconic Moon in Aquarius, and the always sweet-natured pattern of Draconic Venus aligned with the Tropical Moon: he was 'a lover of peace and a champion of the poor.' His devotion to the freedom-loving spirit of man had been declared in a series of pamphlets and papers. He valued, as a true representative of Aquarius, 'the quest for truth for its own sake.' And, true to Draconic principle, speaking for his Sun/Mars and his Aquarian Moon, he wrote, 'Let us not shun the fight when it is unavoidable to preserve right and the dignity of man.' It was this reaction which turned the congenital pacifist into the dedicated warrior for humanity. 'We must realise we cannot simultaneously plan for war and peace,' he said, reflecting in a new way the contrast between the pacific and the assertive principles in his own pattern. It is sad indeed that 'his ability to revolutionise physics was greater … than his ability to change man's heart' despite his stubborn endeavours, and we are still left with his unwanted child, the nuclear bomb, even though he was true to his own words when he said, 'We scientists will not change the hearts of other men by mechanisms, but by changing our own hearts and speaking bravely.'

Tropical Chiron in Taurus, conjoined by the Draconic MC, may represent the Unified Field Theory he so vainly sought. It is worth noting in this context that Draconic Chiron, falling in Cancer, is closely square the conjunction of Mercury and Saturn in the Tropical, and may be the indication of both the exhaustive effort and the eventual denial. This conjunction had also made him a decidedly late developer; he was asked to leave his school, says Asimov, 'by invitation of the teacher who said, "You will never amount to anything, Einstein."' The young man thus became the most unusual 'dropout' in the history of science. And we do have a double contact of Chiron to the angles in the combination pattern. I would also like you to consider Ceres, recently promoted to Dwarf Planet, now the equal of her demoted son-in-law Pluto. Ceres is immensely strong in both physicists' charts – here touching both Draconic Sun and Tropical Ascendant – and in view of her sovereignty over the natural world, she may also encourage the search for its fullest understanding in the Unified Field Theory dear to the heart of both men.

Taurus and Aquarius are, of course, signs in square; towards the end of his life, Einstein found it impossible to accept 'all the changes that were sweeping the world of physics,' despite his role as intellectual revolutionary. He would not accept Heisenberg's principle of indeterminacy, for instance, for he could not believe that the universe would be so entirely in the grip of chance. 'God may be subtle,' he once said, 'but He is not malicious.' The Sun may be conjunct Pluto – but it is in Taurus, not Scorpio!

RICHARD DIMBLEBY, Broadcaster
Dragon's Head Conjunct 0° Aries: Draconic Level Aligned with Tropical Level

This famous British broadcaster was born 'on the last Sunday of May 1913' – the 25th of the month – according to the biography by his son, Jonathan, and made his entry into the world at midday, in Richmond-upon-Thames. In so doing, he joined a very considerable group of people, born every eighteen years or so, who have in their pattern a conjunction of the Aries Point Tropical with the Aries Point Draconic, and therefore an identical pattern

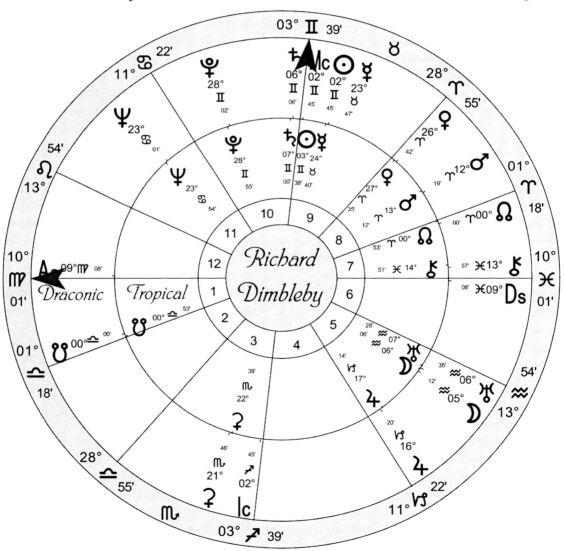

at each level of their being. The biography illustrates quite poignantly the tremendous activity there was at both levels in Richard's case, and the difference between them: on the one hand all the strengths, the compulsive destiny of the soul's role, and on the other the human nature and frailties of the personality that carried it.

The principal elements of the pattern are the Sun crowning the Midheaven in Gemini, conjoined with Saturn and square the Virgo Ascendant, but in a lovely flowing trine with Moon/Uranus in Aquarius in the 5th House; the vital Mercury is in the 9th in Taurus, sextile Neptune in Cancer and in a wide trine to 5th House Jupiter in Capricorn. Chiron sets in Pisces; the Aries Mars squares Jupiter. With this demanding flow of energy he threw himself into the thick of the action, as a young reporter on the family newspaper (*The Richmond and Twickenham Times*), as the BBC's first reporter and war correspondent, and later as the principal commentator on BBC television where he then became the chairman of the influential current affairs programme *Panorama.* All this activity in the news media is clearly an ideal outlet for a serious-minded and responsible Gemini with ambition and an innovative, creative bent; but it was more than that, for he undertook all he did because he *believed intensely* in the importance of bringing world affairs to public attention, and in bringing them *alive.* He broke quite a lot of rules in the process (Aquarian Moon/Uranus trine the Gemini Saturn) but thereby established new standards and new institutions in media news coverage. This was something he had come into this life to do, and which, through the course of his fifty-two years, strengthened this often wayward, often very touchy man. It made of him an institution, a familiar figure much mourned by colleagues and country at his early passing. I shall leave most of the commentary to Jonathan and to Richard himself, but first, quoting Michael Balkwill of the BBC:

> 'He found words that blew a wind of change through BBC bulletin style. Perhaps there was still the odd newspaper cliché, but he was beginning to find how to convey grandeur without being emptily pompous (that Sun/Saturn/MC was easily, and quite often, accused of pomposity), how to be vivid and colloquial without cheapness and gimmicks … he told his story to his audience, he did not broadcast *at* them.'

The principle of a detailed, painstaking Virgoan approach is plain here from Jonathan's comment: 'He did not deal in vague descriptions of "hundreds of acres inundated in the grim fight against the encroaching waters"; instead, Dimbleby found out and conveyed in his reports what the complete situation really was – and explained it in terms of exact locations, comparative water levels, pumping stations and sluice gates, with proper use of technical terms.' Michael Balkwill too, as editor of his early copy, became very aware of Richard's 'obsession with accurate detail'.

In just as much poignant detail Dimbleby described what he found in a deserted village near the Maginot Line during the war; and his son Jonathan makes another point about his nature in this context: 'Dimbleby was always offended by such scenes: to a man brought up in ordered security such desolation was a violation of human dignity. And he valued the right to dignity – to live in self respect without fear – above almost all else.' (Sun, Saturn, Midheaven.)

His colleague and confidant David Howarth said of him: 'Richard set about reforming the presentation of news by starting a kind of underground movement, infecting people here and there among the staff with his own excitement at his own ideas of radio reporting.' Kenneth Adam remarked, '*it seemed as if he had a sense of mission*, he never gave up – his energy was remarkable.' (My italics.)

At twenty-nine, Richard Dimbleby was becoming aware of his rôle and his image. He wrote to Sir Richard Maconochie, 'You are, willy nilly, just what in your letter you say one is not – "a diplomatic correspondent." It is something even more than that, because you are received not only as a working observer, not only as a personality, but as the official envoy of a very great and powerful national organisation.' Perhaps a little of the ego has crept into the role here, too?

'When he wrote scripts,' says Jonathan, 'he did not ponder them for long hours, they flowed from his pen at great speed, and hardly ever required alteration. His responses were those of Everyman (Moon/Uranus/Aquarius), speaking *from* as well as *to* the people. And, like Everyman, he conveyed the truths that mattered to him with much greater effect than those who, searching after greater truths, lost themselves on the way.'

He had as a gift the common touch. 'I'm intensely interested in people and their ways of life,' he said, and his son adds, 'He was curious about details with a child's pertinacity, never satisfied until he had a complete answer.' Dimbleby endeared himself to people through this very faculty of eliciting information about them – and then retaining it. People felt that they mattered. It is a way of loving. 'He clung fiercely to his political principles … loathed the extremes,' writes Jonathan. 'He abhorred the "detestable, arrogant, dangerous nationalism" which racialist South Africa then nurtured … He was outraged by General Peron in Argentina who was "fighting against freedom of speech, personal liberty, indeed democracy itself."' How strong is that Aquarian Moon!

Almost paradoxically – but befitting the Sun/Saturn/MC principles this time – he believed in monarchy, but to him the existence of the Crown was a guarantor of the British 'way of life' – the democracy that he cherished. His son tells us, 'He believed that Peers should live up to the image that ordinary people had of them; on a state occasion they should behave with fitting solemnity.' Richard Dimbleby *always* did. Nevertheless, his protests on a matter of principle could come across as primness and pomposity. Perhaps there was some snobbery in that Sun/Saturn/MC; one of the human frailties of the man. But the same pattern laid down his role as BBC commentator at the Coronation of Her Majesty Queen Elizabeth II … 'a sublime experience.'

Richard Dimbleby embraced the idea of the Outside Broadcast with fervour. 'The power of being in two places at once (Gemini!) is the newest that man has wrested from reluctant nature … The BBC has magnificently vindicated the noble idea of a public service,' wrote Maurice Wiggin of that historic broadcast. These were ideals that Dimbleby stood for. But he did not always please his superiors, and the man would show through the great commentator: 'His sensitivity to criticism … was nevertheless acute: when taken even mildly to task, he reacted with the fiercely defensive arrogance of insecurity.' This is the other side of the Sun/Saturn/MC square Virgo rising. Authority and position mattered to the man. 'Dimbleby had no doubt, as he once said, that "great commentators are born not made." The ability to translate instantly thoughts, colours and unexpected incidents into words, and to give form and shape to the sentences … Dimbleby derived great satisfaction from the particular skills required by television, which he knew (though he never mentioned it) that he possessed to a greater degree than anyone else.' (i.e. in body, mind and soul!) '… His art, his conscious purpose, was to make the essentially meaningless appear significant; his words were to make sense of a succession of otherwise incomprehensible pictures. In the process he created that sense of moment, of history, and mystique which made his words matter.' High praise from Wiggin the critic!

When he moved to *Panorama*:

'It fell to Richard Dimbleby to take the television audience by the hand and guide it gently into more tolerant, liberal ways. Intuitively sensitive to public attitudes, frequently sharing them himself, he had an acute sense of what was felt to be proper. Sharing many of the doubts and anxieties of his audience, having discarded yesterday the prejudices they held today, he was the perfect television mentor … his instinct was to inform and entertain, while gently pushing back the barriers of ignorance and intolerance … so accurately did he touch the public pulse that he soon attained the status of a televisual father of the people.'

Although there were occasions when 'his sense of propriety clashed with a powerful libertarian instinct,' clearly they were both essential to his purpose, and they combined as easily as did the man's public and private life. 'Some of his critics,' says Jonathan Dimbleby, 'were irritated as much by his virtues as his vices. Why was he always so calm? Never at a loss for the right word? Always so faultless? His mastery of the medium, so complete and so unrivalled, was a goad compelling them to envious protest. How could – why should – one man stand so apart and above the rest; so dominate the most powerful instrument of mass communications; seem so omnipotent, so omniscient, and – worst of all – so nice?'

The pattern is clear!

SIR FREDDIE LAKER, Entrepreneur
Dragon's Head *opposed* to 0° Aries; Draconic Level opposite in quality to Tropical

August 6th 1922 saw the birth of an entrepreneur destined 'to become through his innovations both a popular hero and a financier's nightmare.' The Draconic-Tropical pattern is interesting in that it provides an example of the characteristics of a man's personality being diametrically opposed to those of his soul and purpose, and yet so complementing them that they align closely and – hopefully – cooperate with them. In a two-page profile of Freddie Laker published in the *Observer Magazine* of October 2nd 1977, John Heilpern describes him as 'a tycoon very much in touch with the public. He is an apostle of free enterprise.' Surely a Leo with as much going for him as the late Sir Freddie Laker fitted the rôle of tycoon admirably; but the Sun is in *Aquarius* in the Draconic chart, and here we

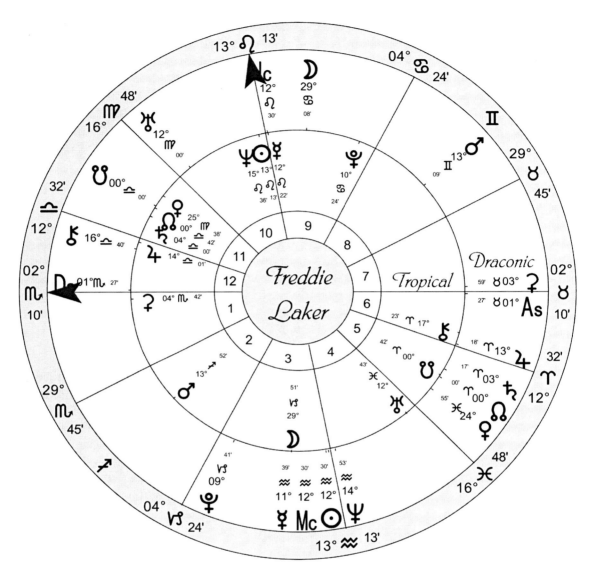

find the ability to identify with people, as well as the profound and guiding belief in free enterprise.

That insistence went as far as that other well known Aquarian activity: breaking or at least challenging the rules of the establishment. Frederick Alfred Laker did this with vigour, condemning the while the shock/horror of the major airlines with gentle observation: 'They certainly don't have to be imaginative. So if someone wants to change the rules, they object. It's understandable …' Freddie Laker was highly imaginative. It is not just the Sun that lies basking in Leo/Aquarius; it is joined with conjunctions of Mercury and Neptune. 'What is it about planes?' he said, from Aquarius! 'If you want a glamour industry, it's aviation! It isn't really the money. I love aeroplanes! Every minute of my day I think about them. I don't really think about anything else.' And he did so ever since he was a schoolboy and made his first epochal decision to go 'into aeroplanes.' He went to see *Those Magnificent Men in Their Flying Machines'* and that was his ration of cinema-going for four years or so!

The Leo personality imposed itself as strongly as one would imagine on his enterprises, with his name on every plane he flew … and with the impact of his personal warmth and energy on the travelling public. 'People shake him by the hand, ask for his autograph, shout, "Good old Fred!"' It was that energy and dominance that built his Skytrain idea of inexpensive walk-on, walk-off flights into the world's leading independent airline – until his traumatic collapse early in 1982 (which many people, including Heilpern, foresaw as a possible outcome of provoking competition).

One of the causes of this failure to fulfil the Aquarian ideal of providing people with greater freedom of travel, along with independence from the strictures of established airline procedures, may have been this: that he was operating on the assumption that 'what the public wants is cheap air travel.' He saw the booking conditions imposed by the major airlines as overprotective: 'Everyone wants to protect the people! But the people don't want to be protected. They want cheaper travel.' Was there ever a clearer voice of stifled Moon-in-Cancer conscience challenging typical Moon-in-Capricorn assumption! … (rightly or wrongly.) In this statement we find the two sides of Freddie at war with each other … and the human being, 'capable of stinginess as well as generosity' (Sun Leo, the morning Moon in Capricorn) seems to be winning. It is revealing that 'in fact he spends comparatively little money – rarely socialising or going out to any great extent.' This is highly suggestive that the policy of cheap fares is a projection of his own disinclination to empty his pockets or give anything away ('You don't give me a free drink in your club, and I don't give you a free seat in my planes') which is so common in men with a Capricorn Moon – one of the most uncomfortable characteristics one can encounter as it is so unyielding in so many ways. This ties in with his upbringing by a mother early deserted by his father and who 'for years of her life had to fight for survival. … 'The poor old sausage,' Laker said of her affectionately, 'She was a bit of a wheeler dealer. Bright! She knows how many beans make five…'

Perhaps the collapse of Skytrain was the soul's warning to take account of the opposite Cancer principle of true care and protection – which he found in himself as far as his beloved planes are concerned! 'He worries about them, in the manner of a proud father worrying what his children are up to. He has to know where his planes are, ringing his headquarters last thing at night and first thing in the morning to find out.' But the Capricorn purse strings and ambition kept winning over the higher call to listen to what the other airlines were trying to say to him, that other principles should be involved if the mission were permanently to succeed. That food, comfort, protection against disappointment or economic disaster were worth paying for in the long run. Our weaknesses can hinder the intention of the soul. At the time of first writing *Draconic Astrology* (March 1983) and once again in the 1990s, Sir Freddie Laker was trying to fight back yet again, calling on his usual flair for breaking impasses (Sun, Mercury and Neptune tri-octile Uranus, trine Mars, trine Chiron, sextile Jupiter), but for thousands of investors and passengers their last holiday booking with Laker may have been the most expensive undertaking of their lives.

EDGAR MITCHELL, Astronaut
Draconic Sun conjunct Tropical Neptune, Draconic Uranus opposite Tropical Sun

Edgar Dean Mitchell, astronaut, was born on September 17th 1930 in Hereford, Texas at 04h30 am CST, and was the sixth space voyager to set foot upon the surface of the Moon. The Tropical Moon is very prominent in his chart; it is in its own sign of Cancer, conjunct Mars, Jupiter and Pluto in the 11th House, a pattern in itself indicative of a strong yearning for adventure, and promising rich inner experience through the conquest of the Moon. The most striking facet of his Draconic/Tropical pattern is the double involvement of the Sun; the Draconic Sun lights up the Tropical Ascendant and conjoins Tropical Neptune, and the Tropical Sun is opposed by Draconic Uranus. An article by Caroline Myss in the first issue of *Expansion* magazine gives plenty of space to Edgar Mitchell's own words,

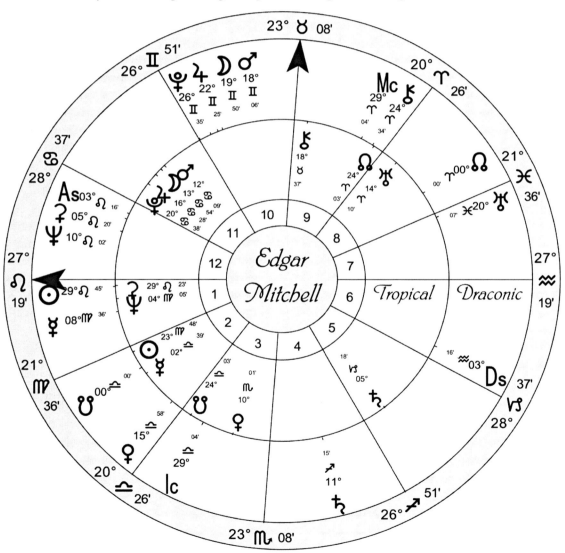

which express the vitality of the Uranian and Neptunian principles most beautifully, 'since he is one of the few individuals whose personal consciousness (Draconic Sun to Tropical Ascendant) is now as fluent in science (Uranus) as it is in mysticism and spirituality (Neptune)'. Mitchell's founding of the *Institute of Noetic Sciences* in Florida follows the transformative experience he had when gazing at the Earth from the Moon. 'It was an explosion of awareness (Sun/Uranus), an integration of a oneness with all that is, a fusion of consciousness for a period of time (Sun/Neptune) which resulted in insights that led me to think differently (Sun/Uranus). The Institute's rôle is to research *inner* space, the barely explored and scarcely understood realm of human consciousness. Seeing the Earth from so different a perspective, he said, '… makes you feel pretty small'.' Here is Draconic Uranus activating the Tropical Virgo Sun! 'My objective is to attempt to help create a new model, a new way of looking at the universe that takes advantage of the mystical basis upon which all religion is built as well as taking full advantage of scientific training …'; and then comes the Draconic Gemini Moon: 'We have to create models, we have to create maps of our reality in order to be able to communicate that reality to others.' The Draconic MC is also speaking here, conjunct Chiron right on the Tropical 9th cusp and Dragon's Head.

He is perfectly convinced of the validity of 'the whole range of psychic abilities. One has to first go within and *purify the thought process* and get in touch with oneself in order to develop these faculties.' Here speaks not only the Draconic Sun/Tropical Ascendant but Draconic Mercury in Virgo. Virgo and its rising ruler Ceres are strongly accented as representing the material, the physical:

> 'I guess I feel strongly that our task is to bring the divine idea (Uranus) into the material world. Ideas have to manifest in the physical before they do anything … Part of the process as I see it is the manifestation and perfection of the divine idea into material reality. *And that is only done through human consciousness.*' (Sun channelling Uranus, Ascendant manifesting higher Sun.)

The Draconic Gemini Moon in the 11th is busy through the Institute sponsoring seminars, research work and education, and joins the Draconic Libra Venus opposite Tropical Uranus in his concluding remark: 'Our work is very much oriented toward societal models – what we can do to help create better models *that will make society and human beings function in a more harmonious, satisfying way and to stimulate others to do their own questioning and thinking.*'

Since the first publication of *Draconic Astrology*, a lot has happened. In particular (happy the Virgoan astrologer!), thousands of asteroids have been tracked, numbered and named, so that we have, in addition to the great planetary archetypes, a vast and growing encyclopaedic dictionary of ideas swirling around the heavens. Knowing that I was going to meet Ed Mitchell at last, at a conference in Cambridge some years ago, I plotted the positions of relevant asteroids onto his chart, with spectacular results.

So when he gave me five minutes of his precious, pressured time, I took him over to my lobby exhibit and showed him his birth chart. He saw his Sun conjunct *Spacewatch* and

Houston, square *America*, opposite *Astronomia* and Draconic *Soyuz-Apollo*; he saw *Mitchella* (and *Noether*) on his IC aligned with Draconic *Skytel* on the Tropical MC; he saw *Unitas* and *Academia* rising (aligned with the Draconic Sun). It was like pinning on a conference ID badge.

'I don't know what I am looking at,' he said, and went to talk to the people with Degrees.

SATYA SAI BABA, Religious Leader
Draconic Leo Sun conjunct Tropical Neptune

The chart of the late Satya Sai Baba – born, according to his biographer Howard Murphet, at sunrise on November 23rd 1926, in Puttaparthi (or Padapati), India – is a particularly dramatic example of the differences and interaction between the Draconic and Tropical charts. Also it makes an interesting comparison with the case of Ed Mitchell, who has, like Sai Baba, the Draconic Sun in the last decan of Leo; this connects with his Tropical Neptune in early Virgo. In Sai Baba's case, the entire cluster of rising planets – Sun, Saturn, Venus and Mercury plus the Ascendant – move from Scorpio/Sagittarius into late Leo to resonate with the Tropical culminating Neptune. In repose, his face had all the sombre intensity of the angular Sun/Saturn in Scorpio; his practical life had all the simplicity, even asceticism, that one associates with such a pattern. Animated, Sagittarius glowed in his rounded face, the watchful look of Scorpio replaced by generous warmth and a kindly humour. His daily habits alternated between his addressing and mingling with massive crowds at *darshan* and retreating firmly into an inviolable privacy in which he occasionally conducted privileged personal interviews. The square from Tropical Neptune at the MC in the 9th House to the rising stellium still makes him an enigma to many who remain unconvinced of either his status as an avatar of the Divinity, his self-proclaimed rôle, or the miracles witnessed by so many of his devotees. With such strong contacts to the three outer planets and to Chiron, his *potential* for spiritual power and awareness is clear to the astrologer; but the hard aspects to that 1st House inevitably lead one to wonder whether after all he was deluding himself as to his real nature.

But look at the Draconic pattern! All those dramatic planets at the horizon now burn in solar Leo, channelling directly through the Tropical Neptune and bringing it vividly alive, the focal star in his sky. His daily dress was an orange robe – the colour of the Sun; he wore his hair like its corona. He was living through, professing, the principle and capacity for universal love, for divine understanding, for complete altruism, for total inclusiveness, and for miracle-making. And what was it that came through to his devotees? The very essence of love itself, the highest expression of Leo, became central to Baba's identity, the driving force and the guiding light of his worldly progress.

Now, were it purely *self*-love that he came to represent, and the cultivating of mass worship by fraud and trickery (the deceptive skills of Neptune), it is fairly unlikely that he would have found his vocation at so young an age (he was approaching thirteen when he first announced his mission to those closest to him), also improbable that he would have

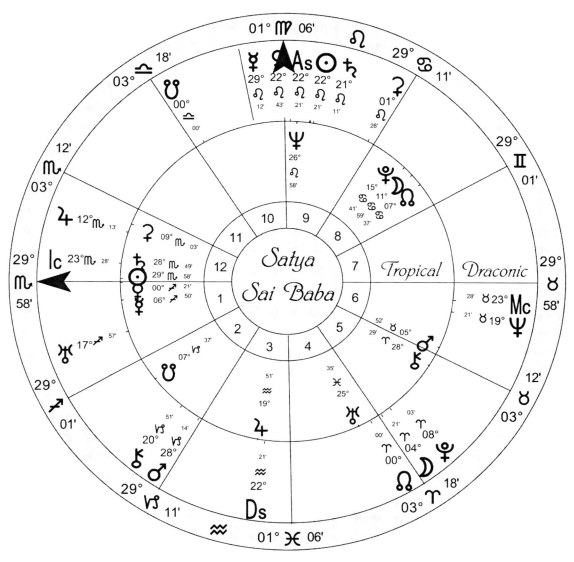

sustained this lifestyle in basically one place for so long. It would also be far less likely that he would – as he did – extol to all who would listen the very virtues proclaimed in the Christian Gospels and holy books the world over, while apparently putting them into daily practice … although, as we have seen frequently among evangelicals and gurus, the glamour of spiritual power can inflate the ego and carry it high and far on the storm of popular adulation. So often it has all ended in tears.

'By their fruits shall you know them.'

Some examples of his teaching will serve as useful illustrations:

'To a worldly man, a God-intoxicated person will appear mad and he will laugh at him for it. But to the God-intoxicated man, the worldly appear insane, foolish, misled, blind. Of all the insanities that harass man, God madness is the least harmful, the most beneficial.' (Neptune square the rising Draconic stellium.)

'My main tasks are fostering of the Vedas [Hindu Scriptures] and fostering of the devotees.' (Draconic stellium channelling into the 9th House Tropical Neptune.)

'Your innate laziness prevents you from the spiritual exercises necessary to discover the nature of God. This laziness should go. It has to be driven out of man's nature in whatever shape it appears. That is my mission.' (Draconic Moon in Aries.)

'I do not take anything from anyone except love and devotion … I call you to me and ever grant worldly boons so that you may turn Godward.' (Tropical Moon in Cancer conjunct North Node in 8th House; South Node in 2nd House in Capricorn, ruler Saturn exactly conjunct Sun.)

'No avatar has done like this before, going among the masses, counselling them, guiding them, consoling them, uplifting them and directing them along the path of *satya, dharma, shanti* and *prema* [truth, righteousness, peace and love].' (Draconic Mercury, Saturn, Venus and Sun in Leo; Mercury/Moon /Chiron/Jupiter/Uranus in quintile series.)

'The divine should be expressed in mind, heart and action; in thought, word and deed [Draconic Leo stellium] … You as body, mind and soul are a dream [Neptune square rising stellium, Tropical] … but what you really are is existence, knowledge, bliss. You are the God of this universe. You are creating the whole universe and drawing it in.' (Draconic Leo stellium conjunct Tropical Ascendant through Leo Neptune in 9th House.)

'It is the heart that reaches the goal; follow the heart. The pure heart seeks beyond intellect. It gets inspired. Remember, every song sung in praise of the Lord is a sword that cuts the knots of laziness. It is a fine piece of social service to remind all of their duty to the Almighty who watches over them.' (Mars in Taurus – voice in song – quincunx Mercury and triseptile Venus in Sagittarius – religious devotion – ruling Draconic Aries Moon and in 6th House of service.)

'One of the first principles of straight living is the practice of silence. For the voice of God can be heard in the region of your heart only when the tongue is stilled and the storm is stilled and the waves are calm. Silence is the speech of the spiritual seeker. Soft sweet speech is the expression of genuine love.' (Saturn conjunct Sun/ Mercury/Venus in Draconic Leo.)

'Inner cleanliness has its own soap and water – the soap of strong faith and the water of constant practice.' (Tropical Venus and Mercury in Sagittarius, Tropical Sun/Saturn in Scorpio.)

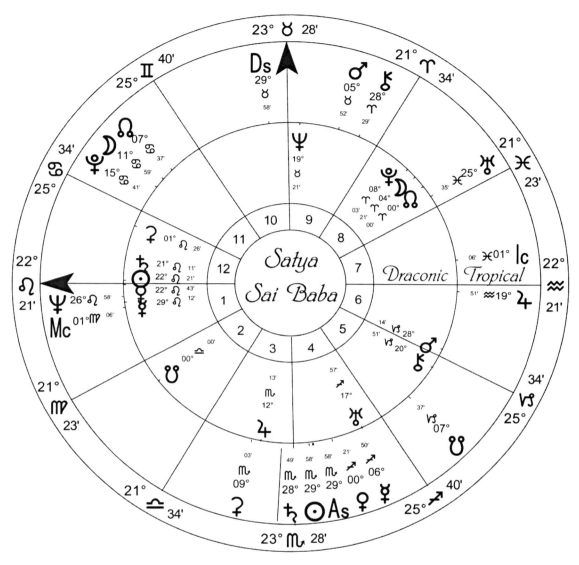

'… service is for you as sacred as a vow, a *sadhana*, a spiritual path. It is the very breath; it can end only when breath takes leave of you.' (Mars, ruler of Draconic Aries Moon, in 6th House.)

'Do you think that I would confront you with pain were there not a reason for it? Open your heart to pain, as you do now for pleasure, for it is my will, wrought by me for your good. Welcome it, as a challenge.' (Draconic Moon in Aries in the 8th House.)

'Bring me the depths of your minds, no matter how grotesque, how cruelly ravaged by doubts and disappointments. I know how to treat them. I will not reject you. I am your mother.' (Tropical Moon in Cancer with North Node in the 8th House.)

'Start the day with love, fill the day with love, end the day with love: this is the way to God.' (Draconic rising stellium in Leo, squaring Neptune and through Tropical Neptune in Leo in the 9th House.)

'Since I move about with you, eat like you, and talk with you, you are deluded into the belief that this is but an instance of common humanity. Be warned against this mistake. I am also deluding you by my singing with you, talking with you, and engaging myself in activities with you. But, at any moment, my divinity may be revealed to you … Since divinity is enveloped by humanness you must endeavour to overcome the *maya* (delusion) that hides it from your eyes.'

'I am neither guru nor God; I am you; you are I; that is the truth. There is no distinction. That which appears so is the delusion. You are waves; I am the ocean. Know this and be free, be divine.'

'The buildup thus obtained between the old and new positions shows how the legacy of the past affects the life pattern of the present.'

Ronald C. Davison, *Astrology*

CHRISTOPHER REEVE and FRIEDRICH NIETZSCHE
The Pluto Principle (1): Superman!

Although the figure of Superman as portrayed by the late Christopher Reeve bears little resemblance, in his supragalactic origins and paranormal powers, to the image conjured by Friedrich Nietzsche in *Also Sprach Zarathustra*, it is fascinating to compare the charts of these two apparently very different individuals and find so many points of similarity.

For there is no doubt that despite his overall acting talent, and his serious interest in classical music and sailing, Reeve made his name in the three films depicting the adventures of 'Superman' and therefore will always be associated closely with the comic-book hero. He was always an attractive man, to begin with, with the right kind of charisma and charm – as befits one so strongly Libran with a Fiery Tropical Moon, Mars and Ascendant; but the overriding factor here is Tropical Pluto rising in Leo, very close to the South end of the nodal axis, tensely square to the 10th House Jupiter, but sextile the conjunction of Venus and Neptune and trine the Moon/Mars. Fitted to the rôle, then; but look deeper, bring in the Draconic level of his being, and see how the Pluto power factor is magnified!

Whichever other parts this man played during his life, in or out of acting, he came into this incarnation to be known as the personification of the power of Good that confronts and conquers Evil. The Draconic Sun is now in Pluto's own sign, Scorpio, with Mercury and also the nearby Libra Point; the battle with the forces of Darkness – so often undertaken

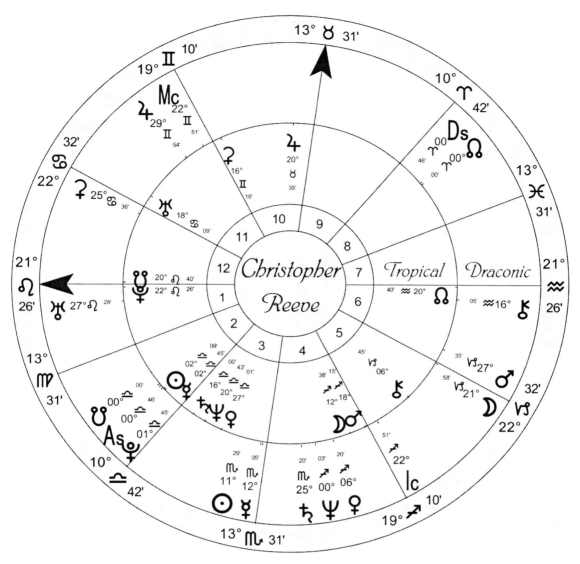

by Draco Scorpio natives, and willingly, to prove the value of courage in the relentless testing of the human spirit – is his battle. And it is to take place centre stage, as the Scorpio configuration falls close to the Tropical IC. I wonder if the Libra Point (not shown), at 9°20′ Scorpio, is the indication that he was so constantly fighting other people's battles? Surely this should be enough to set him on his path; but a second major picture emerges where the Draconic Ascendant/Pluto in the Dragon's Tail therefore moves into the second degree of Libra to channel its energies through the Tropical Sun/Mercury. And he was promised a double dose of limelight since in fulfilling his incarnate need to find and create that which is good and beautiful, he would identify the more closely with this higher personality of his and draw on its power to put its creative magic into effect. And so his star came into the Ascendant!

His ability to fascinate, and therefore to influence strongly for good or ill, is also tied into the 5th harmonic pattern of Moon/Uranus = Sun, but a third Draconic pattern comes in here, too, with Draco Uranus at the end of Leo, near to the Tropical Pluto and Ascendant, allying illumination with power, and Draco Moon in Capricorn aligns with the Tropical Uranus in the 11th House bringing something new to his audience out of his deep concern for common sense and a well ordered society. Yes, his Superman is a teacher too; setting an example of kindness, care, self-discipline and bravery, particularly to the children who admire him. Some of this may well be found in the tight square of Draco Chiron to the Tropical MC.

Now, the first version of the above commentary on Reeve's chart was written back in 1983-4. On May 27th 1995 at 15h05 EDT in Culpeper, Virginia, Christopher Reeve was thrown catastrophically from his horse and broke his neck. After that, as the world knows, this extraordinary man spent his life as a quadriplegic in a specially-equipped wheel-chair, fighting his way back to a productive and creative life with a courage and determination that would put even Superman in the shade! Every quality we have seen in the Draconic/ Tropical patterns above was tried in the fire and proved a flawless metal. Not only did he demonstrate his own ability to *survive* an extreme trauma, but he returned to acting again, finding the perfect rôle in *Rear Window*, was in demand as a speaker and campaigner, and set a high-profile example of courage and optimism to the physically disabled everywhere. As with all South Node rising people, his was a sacrificial life dominated by its overall spiritual purpose. Against the 'evil' that had befallen him, he remained, profoundly, the triumphant champion of the good.

Despite his conviction that he would walk again, after nine years of struggle Reeve died at last on October 10th 2004 at Westchester, NY. I do not have a time.

In Chapter 17 I shall return to his chart with its two slightly differing given times, and that of the accident, as these offer us a useful exercise in rectification.

Nietzsche, who first coined the term 'Superman', wrote of him thus:

> 'Man is something to be surpassed. What have you done to surpass man? … What is the ape to man? A laughing stock, a thing of shame. And just the same shall man be to the Superman: a laughing stock, a thing of shame … The Superman is the meaning of the earth. Let your will say: The Superman shall be the meaning of the earth!'

I think our views on the ape have become somewhat more enlightened since he wrote that in the nineteenth century; but accepting those values, one can see with his eyes the mighty leap he envisaged mankind taking to fulfil what he conceived of as human destiny.

Sun and Pluto oppose each other exactly across his sky, the idea of humanity taking on a godlike power from Tropical Aries, challenging sybaritic humanity itself in Libra in the 11th House. Sun Libra again.

'The people … are herdsmen, but they call themselves the good and the just! Whom do they hate most? The one who breaketh up their old table of values, the idolbreaker, the lawbreaker. He, however, is the creator …'

Where do we find this iconoclast, but in the movement of the Sun to Draconic Aquarius, to conjoin Tropical Neptune. *'I tell you: one must have chaos within one to give birth to a dancing star!'* Interestingly, this conjunction falls in the area of Reeve's Descendant/North Node/ Chiron; and both men have Draconic Moon channelling through Uranus, for Nietzsche's

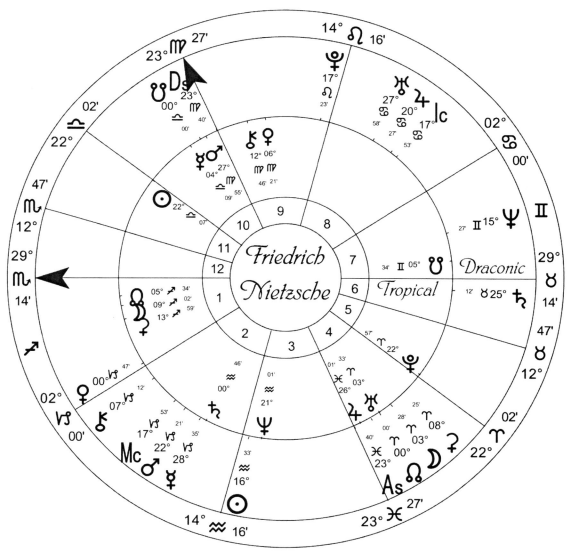

is in 3° Aries conjunct that planet, and right opposite Reeve's Libran cluster. Nietzsche has Scorpio rising, rather than Pluto, the Dragon's Head instead of the Tail; his Tropical Mars culminates, whereas Reeve's is joined by the Draconic IC. Both have Tropical Moon in Sagittarius, Tropical Mercury in the early degrees of Libra. Nietzsche's Tropical Sun lies close to Reeve's Neptune and Saturn in Libra. Both have Jupiter angular to the meridian. Their Draconic Saturns are directly opposed: Nietzsche has his conjunct the Descendant (testimony to his miserable and misanthropic loneliness), and Reeve's therefore falls on the philosopher's Ascendant.

In Reeve, was there ever such a picture of a man come into life with the determination not just to show something of what man can be by symbolising the flight of his spirit in this flying hero! … but to give the lie to all the false, dark, destructive images of the superman built up since Nietzsche, both by those who tried to fulfil his prophecies, and by those who were their grievous victims. God was absent from Nietzsche's universe; whether He is present in that of Christopher Reeve's Superman I am not certain, but one thing is indisputable – the Forces of Light and the Spirit of Love always come to our rescue, and have come spectacularly to his. And the Sun of Christ's Nativity shines on his MC.

SIR ALEXANDER FLEMING, Biologist
The Pluto Principle (2): A Power to Heal

A 'canny Scot who cannot bear to throw anything away nor even a contaminated Petri dish' was born in Ayrshire in 1881, under a 2nd House Leo Sun square Saturn and Neptune! This man, who might just as well have become an Ayrshire farmer, was pushed towards a career in medicine by his brother, and chose to study at St Mary's Hospital in London simply because he had once played waterpolo against their team, being an accomplished swimmer himself. This turned out to be a crucial decision (as one might anticipate, with the Moon in Sagittarius in the 6th House conjunct the Dragon's Head!) for the subsequent chain of events led to his becoming famous as Sir Alexander Fleming, the discoverer of penicillin.

He had already made good use of his Moon/Mercury/Neptune, Sun/Mars, and Venus/Uranus/Jupiter 5th-10th harmonic network in winning nearly every available prize in the school's sports, medical training, and ensuing research work, by the time the Great War broke over Europe and he was sent abroad as an officer in the Royal Army Medical Corps. His experiences on the battlefields left a profound impression on him; as a dedicated healer, the sight of wounded men dying, because medical aid was proving ineffective, was more than he was prepared to tolerate. So he poured himself into renewed efforts to find the key to natural immunity, and eventually discovered *lysozyme*, 'a bacteriolytic ferment which acts on certain bacteria and causes their rapid dissolution.' But the discovery which was to prove epochal for the world of medicine came in 1928, when one day he found a dish of staphylococcus germs growing a mould; not an unusual occurrence, except that in this case the area around the mould was, remarkably, quite free of germs. When Fleming inspected the culture more closely, he could see the staphylococci gradually disappearing under the influence of the mould. This 'triumph of accident' (Jupiter/Venus/Uranus/

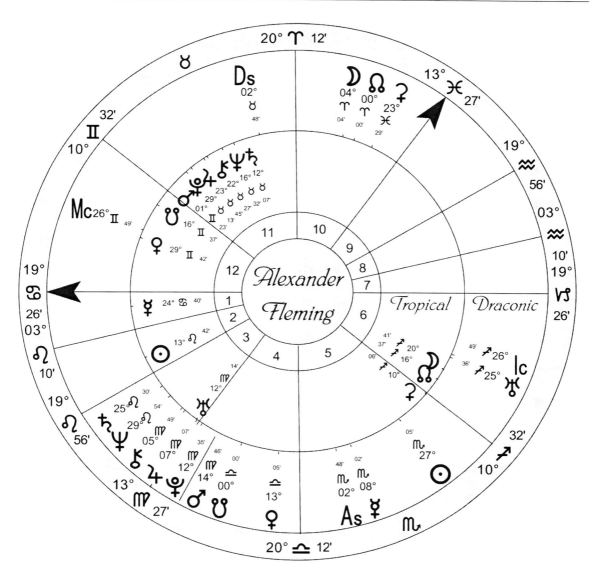

MC!) as he referred to the discovery, was to be the beginning of antibiotic treatment, and meant that when the Second World War broke out, the miseries of the First no longer had to be endured, with mass production of penicillin arranged in the United States.

Since then, many new antibiotic treatments have been developed, and diseases that would once have proved fatal or severely crippling no longer pose a threat to human life. Here is the principle of Pluto as a healing power at work: the Tropical pattern shows Fleming to be a most caring, gifted and practical man, with his future in the Health Service (North Node in Sagittarius in the 6th House). Unlike the actor Christopher Reeve, Pluto is not an especially dominant element in the planetary pattern *in coelo*, but again the Draconic Sun goes into Scorpio, opposing Tropical Pluto, and Draconic Pluto works through that happily accidental Tropical Uranus at the IC from Virgo, showing the career of committed, painstaking, selfless research. Here is Scorpio looking for a way for the human body to survive and renew itself, and testing Fleming's own dedication in the repeated testing of his material. Incidentally, even the original, accidental culture survives! It was never thrown away.

ORSON WELLES, Actor and Director
A Maverick Talent

Oddly, this physically bulky and personally charismatic man leaves one with the impression of terrible vulnerability. He was a magician – a conjuror – for most of his life; he liked to weave magic into his work, wherever he himself was presenter of his subject. The air of mystery goes further, pervading everything he did, lending an extraordinary atmosphere to his films whether he was actor or director.

When one considers the extreme sensitivity of the strongly Neptunian, that vulnerability and the love of illusion and magic can be seen to belong together – and in Welles' case it stems from the close proximity of Tropical Neptune to the Draconic Ascendant across the Cancer/Leo cusp. So, when he is living and working at the vocational level, he becomes so identified with the Neptunian idea as it manifests in the world, that he is its ambassador and its embodiment. He fell in love with film early in his life, and it was a love affair that would last. With Draconic Ascendant in Leo, Tropical Saturn just about to rise, and Draconic Sun on the Tropical Ascendant with Draconic Mercury, he wove spells on the vision with light and shadow, his gift enhanced by the quintile of Sun and Neptune, linked also to Venus.

A major problem for this extraordinarily creative and dedicated man was money. He openly expressed his distaste for fundraising. Tropical Neptune is in the 2nd House, – and therefore his art suffered many delays and setbacks from lack of finance. The rising Saturn, ruling the Tropical 8th House and joined to Pluto over the cusp of Gemini/Cancer, semi-sextile Neptune and semi-square his Sun, drove him to exert total control over his creation, so that rather than allowing those who would pay for his piping to call the tune, he would abandon set, actors, schedules for weeks at a time to earn the next pay cheque by his own efforts. He would accept parts in other people's films that did inadequate justice to his stature, and with the remuneration subsidised his own work and paid his crew.

Such an unclassifiable blend of creative dignity and what almost amounts to self-abasement, can only be described by one of two major squares in his chart – the tight conjunction of Tropical Jupiter/Chiron in Pisces in the 10th House to the Ascendant and Saturn/Pluto. This also channels the higher, Draconic energies of the other square between Sun/Mercury and Moon/Uranus, transforming the intractability and doggedness of Taurus/Aquarius into the maverick brilliance and versatility of Gemini/Pisces. He laid himself open to his own wounds; he made the inevitable enemies, I daresay, that a man does who refuses to follow accepted patterns of behaviour and who can embarrass by his very presence. He was like an uninvited king – or like the figure of Falstaff created by him in his favourite film, *Chimes At Midnight*, once the intimate of the wayward Prince Hal, and crying to his loved Liege from the social limbo into which he has been so rudely cast. There is such pathos in this abandoned figure, like the mute appeal of an animal helpless to escape the consequences of being simply what it is.

Curious, this sense of childlike innocence in such a charismatic giant of a man, who could deal with subjects of such psychological power, explore the darkness of the human soul in its complex searching, interpret the great human themes in Shakespeare with such a penetrating insight, take on himself the mantle of our own Shadow as in Citizen Kane and Macbeth. Marilyn Monroe also had it, and she too was born with Sun quintile Neptune. I have observed this as a recurrent theme in a number of charts. The other factor which has an important bearing on this quality is found in the Draconic interaction with the Tropical: Draconic Venus pours her love and kindliness through the Tropical Sun in Taurus, and I

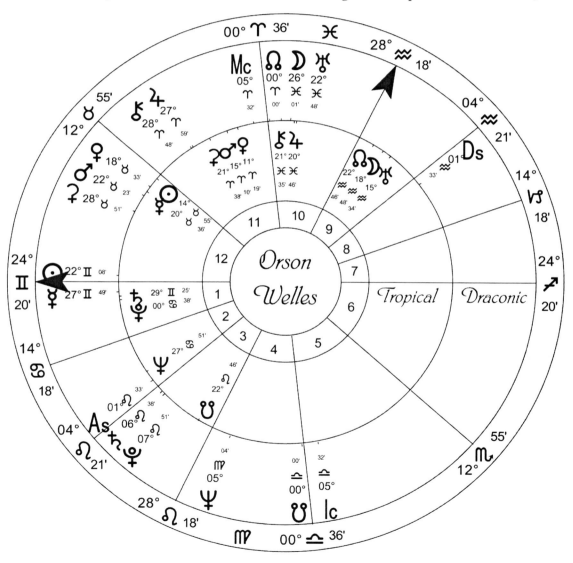

have yet to meet a man or a woman with this pattern who is not gentle and good at heart. Nor have I yet met one with the drive of Draconic Mars joined with Tropical Mercury, as Welles has, who does not show enormous mental and verbal vigour and an attendant delight in frankness! Add to this a rising Tropical Gemini, and you have a man who will disconcert by baring not only his own but the global human soul. It is analogous to going naked in public; it is a very Chiron quality too, the centaur bringing out the natural man in uncomfortable contrast to sophisticated society.

One can sense this tension running throughout Welles' work; as the storyteller he plays on it. Courage of the convictions, and great single-mindedness are shown in the Mercury patterns; and these are vital to a man building a life in directions that in order to bear fruit must break with established values and means, and take both creator and audience on his own unique visionary adventure.

Chapter Nine

Draconic Midpoints
A Higher Motivation

Although, clearly, midpoints in the Draconic pattern are identical to those in the Tropical, since the arrangement of horoscopic factors remains undisturbed despite the change of zodiacal longitude, it is necessary to realise that if the two levels of one's being interact dynamically in the way that we have already seen, then the dynamics of midpoint interaction must be examined. It should be possible for a Draconic planet to trigger action in two Tropical bodies through their midpoint; and it may also be possible for two Draconic planets to converge their energies on one Tropical. Later on, we shall see some fine examples of this activity in the chapter on astrologers and Urania; for the present, let us look at the chart of Dr Ludwig Lazarus Zamenhof.

As the inventor of a global language, Esperanto, he is an excellent choice, as the factor we are looking for is unquestionable: it must be Mercury, and probably working from the higher level to the lower. First of all, the presence of the Tropical Sun and Mercury in the last decanate of Sagittarius betrays a man of universal aspiration (the energies from the centre of our galaxy have their effect on such people) and his idealism is accentuated still further by their square to Neptune in Pisces. The ability and inclination to influence others through his ideas comes through the trioctile (also known as the sesquiquadrate) to Mercury and Sun from Pluto in the 7th House, and an unusual educative ability is shown by Tropical Chiron with the North Node in Aquarius, sextile the Sagittarius conjunction.

Communication between the world's disparate nations becomes a vocational issue when we find not only that the Draconic Sun and Mercury move into Aquarius themselves but conjoin the Tropical Dragon's Head there. This provides him with a doubly powerful motivation to be the creator of a new language that should unite the diverse tongues of the human family and bring down in lightning the tower of Babel, with all its confusion and misunderstanding. His devotion to his task stems in part from the following midpoints: Jupiter/Chiron and Saturn/MC = Mercury/Pluto; Sun/Chiron and Mercury/Chiron = Uranus; and Sun/North Node = MC. He is committed, eager to instruct, full of his visions for the new language that will break down all the old barriers, dedicated heart and soul to his aims.

And is the higher mind the source of his inspiration? Is he motivated from the Draconic level? Yes, indeed: Draconic Mercury subtends no less than seven midpoints: Tropical Sun/Neptune, Mercury/ Neptune, Moon/Jupiter, Mars/Chiron, Jupiter/Saturn, Uranus/Ascendant and Pluto/ North Node. This means that whenever any one of these pairs is active – and by implication they will activate together – the way is open for the higher mind to come through to stimulate active idealism, generosity, bridge-building, constructive vision, enterprise and ingenuity. In return, their activity is reinforced, but the Tropical Mercury/Pluto carries only two midpoints, Jupiter/Chiron and Saturn /MC, so the higher motivation is manifestly the stronger. As Chiron/MC is one of three *Draconic* midpoints which impinge on Tropical Mercury, it may well be indicative of the second mode of midpoint interaction, in this instance Zamenhof's powers of communication. It implies that these are dedicated to the service of the soul's mission to pursue a teaching career during his incarnation, that is, to disseminate the universal language. To complete the vocational picture, this remarkable and influential innovator has Draconic Uranus on the Tropical Jupiter/MC, Draconic Ascendant in Sagittarius opposite Tropical Uranus, Draconic Pluto opposed by the Sun and Mercury in Sagittarius. The 11th House Moon/ Saturn also comes strongly into focus, opposed by Draconic Venus in Aquarius, and from the Draconic level conjunct the Tropical Libran Ascendant, facilitating communication between equals who might otherwise remain mute.

As Esperanto has its own asteroid, it is well worth a look, before we close this brief but necessary chapter, for possible midpoint structures activating and activated by it. This proves rewarding! Tropical *Esperanto* is found close to the Ascendant of Zamenhof's natal chart, in 10°45' Libra; the corresponding Draconic position is at 28°59' Scorpio. By this angularity alone, you can see how the man identified with his etymological child. True to asteroid form, the over-riding preoccupation of his life, indelibly marking his identity for posterity as plainly as a conference badge, lies angular to the birth horizon. And when we search out its midpoints, allowing a 2° orb, we find these: Tropical *Esperanto* = Draconic Sun/Jupiter, Moon/Chiron, Uranus/North Node, the subject and object of his invention, his purpose, his study, his heart's delight. And Draconic *Esperanto* = Tropical Sun/Mars,

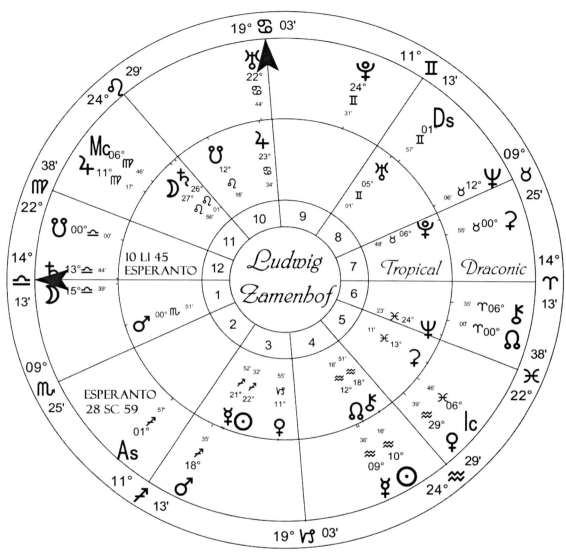

Mercury/Mars, Moon/Saturn, Chiron/Uranus. The whole principle of the global language sets his adrenalin running, structures his life, awakens the propagandist, the maverick teacher.

History has since shown that languages are more likely to spread through organic development, through expediency and human choice, rather than contrivance; so, while Zamenhof's invention has continued to gain adherents, it has never achieved the global popularity and power he would have wished. Instead, to many people's surprise, English has proved one of the world's most successful languages and now, along with much transatlantic culture, is wide-spread via the global media and the Internet. It may not be working out in quite the way Zamenhof hoped or intended, but the spirit of his vision is in some ways even more alive as we begin to taste the freedoms of the Communications Age.

Chapter Ten

Draconic Synastry

This Thing is Bigger than Both of Us!

The comparison of charts – 'synastry' – is one of the most interesting and rewarding fields of astrological endeavour. And this is all the more true when the Draconic dimension is added to each of the charts concerned. Just as the individual natal chart reveals its system of principles and its working purpose in the world through the addition of the Draconic patterns, so does the structure and purpose of any given relationship become very clear.

As usual, the two Tropical charts are examined in depth to ascertain each partner's special orientation and needs, and these are subjected to the techniques of synastry to pinpoint the degree and nature of interaction, the composite chart adding insight to the meaning of the relationship to each party. Inclusion of the two Draconic maps will take you onto a different level; first there must be the individual analyses as before, but when you come to the interactions there are three new possibilities:

1. A interacts with B purely at the Draconic level, indicating a bond between souls who have agreed for this life to pool their resources in a joint work, to share deeply held principles and base their relationship on these; perhaps to relive an old, old relationship and through its delights and trials bring it to a greater perfection or at least achieve a degree more understanding.

2. A at the Draconic level stimulates B at the Tropical and vice versa. In this case B may be aware only of a pleasurable or eventful partnership at a psychological or material level, while A will respond with a deeper sense of import and urgency to the contact, will have a feeling that the relationship is 'meant', is 'bigger than both of us', has a quality of inevitability about it at every turn, which B does not share and finds bemusing or inconvenient. But of course the presence of B in A's life does have added meaning; this is pointing him or her in a spiritually important direction, and in the process is likely to bring out the best in A. But B is reacting all the time at a level far closer to the 'little self' and, in failing to rise to A's active ideals, may

become a source of disappointment and even aggravation. In fact, where the bonds are forged across oppositions, through planets in polar signs, the contrast between one expectation and the other may become so acute that the partnership ruptures. A will continue to try hard; B will constantly thwart that effort in the pursuit of needs and desires heightened by the presence of A. The bond of conjunction, in turn, may inadvertently spark off a spirit of competition in B if he or she cannot rise to the more altruistic level of expression to which B unwittingly moves A!

3. The reverse applies with any two charts; B's Draconic planets and angles may be the stimulus to the Tropical in A. A composite may also be drawn between the two Draconic charts. Its structure, as regards the pattern of aspects between planets and angles, will be basically the same as that in the Tropical composite;

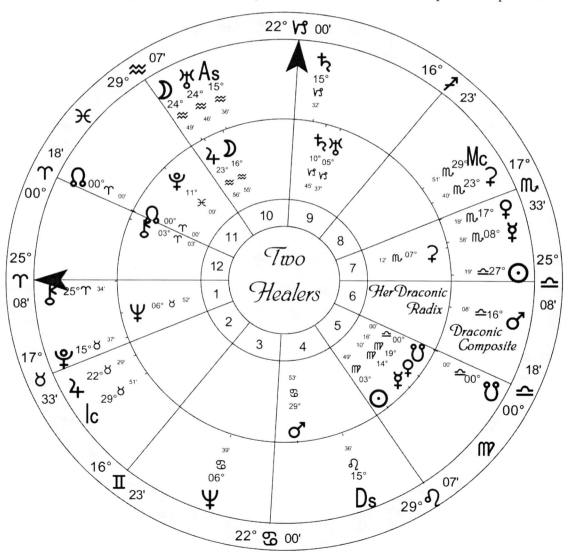

and you will better appreciate this if you realise that the composite Draconic map is essentially the same as the Draconic version of the Tropical composite. As you might expect, the function of this new chart is to illumine the purposive meaning of the relationship to each of the partners, as the focal degrees are mapped back by conjunctions and oppositions to the two versions of each natal chart.

There is a very nice example in the chart of two healers (pictured on the previous page). This couple, each of whom had been married previously, met through a common interest in New Age thinking and activities, developed a most harmonious friendship, and found this deepening into profound and committed love for each other. These facts are clearly illustrated in the Air trine between Sun and Moon, the exact conjunction of Moon/Uranus (meaning that in each of the nativities there is the identical but mirrored Moon/Uranus arc), and the powerful opposition to Pluto from Venus in Scorpio. Both sensed strongly a higher purpose in the relationship, she feeling more certainly married to this man than ever she had to her previous partner. Subsequently they have become jointly involved in spiritual healing, honouring the lovely trine of Mercury in Scorpio to the conjunction of Chiron and Neptune in Cancer. The patterns mapping back to her Draconic natus are outstanding. The Sun falls on its 7th cusp, the Ascendant conjoins the Moon, and the Moon itself conjoins Jupiter. A marriage indeed made in heaven!

JAYNE TORVILL AND CHRISTOPHER DEAN
The Creative Partnership

On 24th March 1984, the amateur career of Britain's Ice Dance champions came to a spectacular climax in Ottawa, Canada, when after a nearly six-hour delay in the programme due to a power failure at the Civic Centre Arena, they skated to their fourth World Championship. The music they had chosen was *Bolero* by Ravel; the continuity of rhythm and subtle acceleration in tempo almost flouting the rules laid down for Ice Dance, the programme itself a poetic and intense interpretation of the music as a story of lovers driven to suicide in the fires of a volcano – something never attempted before in the history of Ice Dance competition. It was nine years since the partnership began under the tutelage of Janet Sawbridge, and six years since Betty Callaway became their trainer in 1978. In that first year she brought them to their first of six British Championship Gold Medals – and the first of the perfect 6s that were to become their trademark, so immaculately did they polish every set pattern or free dance. In 1980 they were placed fifth at the Olympic Games in Lake Placid and awarded the MBE; among their later triumphs were three European Championship Golds, with the highest accolade of all – the Gold Medal at the Olympic Games in Sarajevo in 1984 – only a month before their last World Championship and final appearance in the amateur arena.

During this time there was much speculation – understandably, given human nature – as to whether Chris and Jayne would eventually marry. At the time of first writing *Draconic Astrology* the closest they ever came to acknowledging a possibility was a 'Wait and see'. But in every interview where the question was raised the answer was that they are 'very close … closer than friends, closer than brother and sister, closer even than twins. But

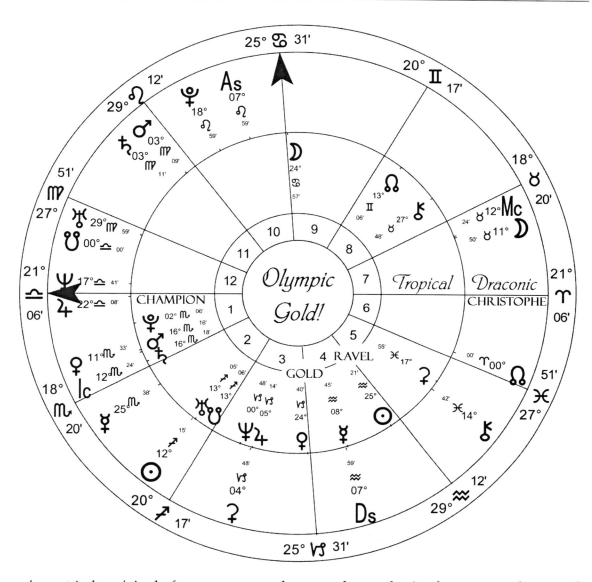

we're not in love.' And of course we now know each was destined to marry other people – Chris twice, as his first marriage failed; and he is currently (2011) separated from his second wife.

Jane Firbank, writing in the *Daily Mail* the day after that golden performance at Sarajevo, showed a deeper understanding than most people of the nature of the pair's relationship.

'Like other great artistic partnerships, theirs is fuelled not by sexual fulfilment but by the all-consuming drive for perfection. The energy that could have taken them into bed has gone instead into a relationship which transcends the merely sexual. They are dedicated, first, to being the greatest ice dancers in the world and only secondly to each other … It is the "peak experiences", when one is fully involved body, mind and heart, which give life purpose. Sex is only one of these. No one can doubt that for Torvill and Dean the ice rink is another, and a better.'

They 'reached the point when two bodies really did move as one,' said Linda Hawkins in the *TV Times*. 'It takes unfaltering determination and extraordinary self-sacrifice.' Further, 'With Chris, it seems, it was the straightforward urge to win.' 'The outstanding characteristic about Chris is his competitiveness,' says Jayne. 'He is fiercely determined not to be second best to anyone, anywhere.'

This side to Chris Dean is immediately visible in his Fixed T-square of proud Leo Sun, unbudgeable Taurus Mars, and Neptune in the fighting sign of Scorpio. Much of the creative imagination is also locked into this pattern, enhanced by the albeit wide conjunction of Uranus to Sun, and the potent Mercury/Pluto in sextile to Neptune from Virgo. I have always held the arc of Leo-Virgo-Libra-Scorpio to be the epitome of the perfectionist, and this is fully borne out by Chris and Jayne's joint dedication to precision. Now, I was unable to get a birth time from Chris, and only a vague time from Jayne ('quite early in the morning') and so I am working entirely from Sun-MC charts, useful in their own right where life achievements are under study, but he is highly likely to have either a Moon/Saturn conjunction or the Moon in Capricorn. If – as I suspect – the latter is the case, then not only is he the kind of enigmatically quiet man who is not content unless he is planning, organising or achieving something, but one whose very life's purpose is geared to a structuring of beauty within the bond of a working partnership. The Sun-MC chart and its associated Ascendant has a lot to say about the individual's contribution and response to their success; Chris Dean's true noon pattern has North Node and Jupiter rising in Libra, and he is indeed a man whose career has thrived on his own adventurous ideas, resilience, humour and self-confidence. The result? Still, in the new millennium, his creative spirit is bringing joy to global audiences as he continues to perform with Jayne and to bring the delight of Ice Dance to a whole new generation of skaters.

The Draconic version of this pattern reveals the Sun in early Capricorn working through the Tropical Cancer Venus, and conjunct the Tropical Moon. Now, this is also a very apt pattern for the keeping of the Queen's Peace – for the maintenance of law and order! But with the Moon's *South* Node in Aries his early experience as a police constable would tend to draw his Sun/Mars into potentially damaging areas. How much happier, then, that he turned towards the thing he enjoyed to develop his sense of the beautiful, and channelled the cutting edge of his desire, self-assertion and ambition into the creation of so much magic! Jupiter and Neptune embracing the North Node of the Moon have pulled him forward. When Christopher Dean is doing what he came into this life to do, he is silent, concentrated, disciplined, spiritually open – and all this focusses on his aesthetic sense. With Draconic Mercury/Pluto in Aquarius aligned with the Tropical Sun, he is constantly innovating, in a powerful mental overdrive that seeks to transform the medium in which he is working – and himself – into something far beyond the ordinary, and in so doing to lift the audience into an exalted state of inner participation. It may be highly significant that the Aries Point at 3°45' Virgo falls so close to the Tropical Mercury/Pluto; it can only add to the extraordinary charisma, the bright aura, of Pluto's power pouring

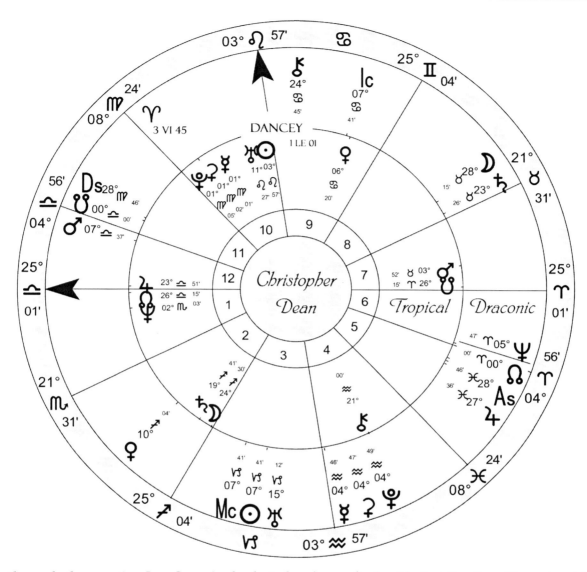

through the creative Leo Sun. And what else do we find with that Sun? … The asteroid *Dancey*! Which in Draconic Capricorn aligns exactly with his Tropical *Christophe!* Discipline is the *sine qua non*.

Of Torvill and Dean as a partnership, 'The real charisma,' writes Jane Firbank, 'springs from their unbelievable rapport – every movement, glance, expression in one finds its echo and counterpart in the other.' "It's uncanny," says Chris. "When I want Jayne to go in a particular way she moves with no apparent effort on her part and little persuasion on mine. We seem to have a telepathic understanding." Most certainly; here Jayne plays her part. She shares with Chris the charismatic union of Sun with Pluto – but here it is the Draconic Sun aligned with Tropical Pluto, linking directly with Chris's Mercury/ Pluto/Aries Point. And as the Draconic Sun falls in Pisces, it is Jayne who, in the dance, receives and flows with every unspoken nuance of Chris's intention. Born 'quite early in the morning', her Draconic Moon probably lies not too far from his Leo Sun and catches fire with it in the drama, joy and flamboyance of *Barnum* and *Mack and Mabel* that shone over the ice in a glory of golden costumes. 'Ordinary' she may have seemed in her days with the Norwich Union, but in her vocation the Leo self is regal. The *Daily Mail*'s Ian Wooldridge mentioned an incident in which Jayne was asked to arrange herself in a group photograph, at the centre and sitting on the floor. 'The ice queen' he says, 'was outraged. "I *never* sit on the floor," she snapped'– thus revealing a fraction of the character that made her unbeatable. We would not have expected a gentle, adaptive Pisces Moon to stand so firmly on its dignity!

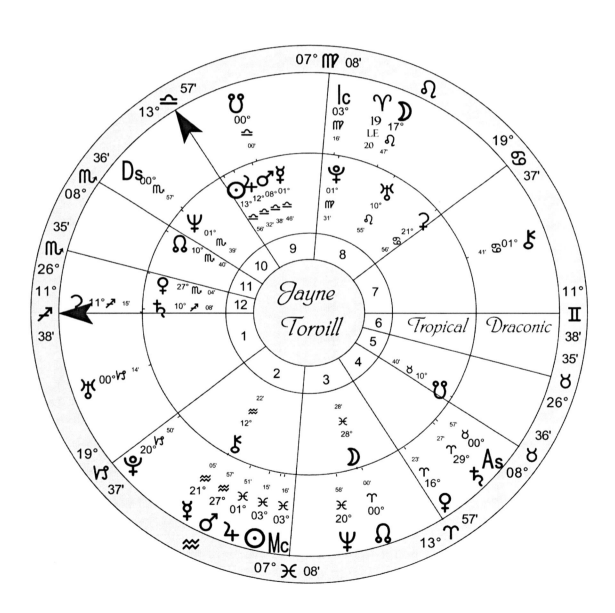

Also in common with Chris, we find Jayne with Sun and Venus combined – but again the other way round; her Draconic Sun works through her Pluto, while a Draconic Aries Venus (more snap and fire!) channels through the opposition to her usually placid and good-humoured Tropical Libra Sun/Jupiter. Here are two people who do what they do for love; twin ambassadors of the heart, and of the power of the human creative spirit in which we are 'a little lower than the angels'. We may note again that both have Mercury (Tropical with Chris, and conjunct the Draconic Moon with Jayne) aligned with the Aries Point. Could it be, then, that the Aries Point directs us to an activity, or a function, with which we are compelled to identify through our choice of life? The very thing which dominates these two people's lives and for which they have become so famous is their perfect skill and eloquence in movement.

And it is this very axis which first strikes the eye when examining the interactions between their patterns, for, as mentioned above, the Aries Point/Mercury/Pluto conjunction of Chris is bound up with Jayne's complementary Draconic Pisces Sun – a blending of the perfectionist with the idealist. Her Draconic Aquarian Mars is close to the axis, adding encouragement to his ideas and a daring vigour to her response. Confidence and a sense of adventure in the partnership come from the close union of Jupiter with her Sun. There is a further Mars link, and a strong one: Chris's Draconic Mars in Libra finds its echo in Jayne's Tropical Mars, their energies blending in a lovely harmony, her natural drive in its gracefulness answering to his higher competitive spirit. And his Tropical Mars, with its South Node tendency to get a bee in his bonnet and take inordinate risks (such as his insistence on hurtling down the bobsleigh run at the Winter Olympics, which could have killed or seriously injured him as it had others during the fortnight) is channelled and held in check by her higher Saturn in the last degree of Aries; part of Jayne's purpose is to offer discipline to Chris, furthering their joint vocation, and helping to calm him at times of impatience or tension, a rôle familiar to those who know them or follow them closely. Ian Wooldridge shows us this edgy side to Chris's nature in the following instance: 'Her partner, seemingly a perpetual study in blandness, proves at close range to be less cool then he looks. When he arrived here by train from Munich … he was in a miserable tizzy about his baggage and the instant availability of ice to practise on.'

There are other aspects to this partnership: her imagination feeds his confidence in what he has to do, and vice versa, as her Piscean Moon touches on his Draconic Jupiter. And in a double contact, Jayne's Venus aligns with Chris's Saturn from Tropical to Draconic, and her Tropical Saturn likewise conjoins with his Draconic Venus in Sagittarius. This may account for the blend of intensity and restraint in their affection for each other, each enjoying the other's seriousness. After all, it is a deeply serious relationship, founded as it is on hard, patient work, and long hours of exacting routine and repetition. In the moments of glory, it is Chris who is the first to be demonstrative to his partner (the noon rising Jupiter again!) while she, enraptured by success, is slower to share her feelings with him (*her* noon Ascendant conjoins Saturn!).

The last significant axial link between planet and planet is the conjunction of Jayne's Draconic Mercury with Chris's Tropical Chiron. Now, with our current understanding of Chiron, what I conjecture is this: that as the two of them expressed a desire to bring their unique talents to bear on the training and inspiration of up-and-coming skaters, it may be Jayne's way with people and her original approach through Aquarius that brings out in Chris gifts as a teacher that previously had lain dormant. For Chiron in his natal chart combines with the Mars/Neptune through quintile and tredecile (108°), and while one appreciates the 'maverick genius' contained in this pattern – together with the similar combination of Venus/ Jupiter/Uranus – either the healing or the teaching role is usually marked. (Their trainer, Betty Callaway, born on 22nd March 1928, has a Taurus Chiron in close sextile to her conjunction in Pisces of Mercury and Venus: wonderful for a teacher of dance!).

Finally, what does the composite chart show us? Its pattern gathers Mercury and Venus into a conjunction in Tropical Virgo – precision again – and sextile to Mars. A Jupiter/ Saturn sextile squares this and configures kindly with Chiron/Uranus. Neptune conjoins the composite North Node. The signs involved tell us something about the manner of execution of their dance. But it is the Draconic version of the composite (the correct chart made by combining the two Draconic patterns) that highlights the decisive originality of these two skaters in combination, with Sun, Mercury and Venus now all in Aquarius, linking back to the Tropical composite Moon, with its opposition to Uranus. Of even greater importance is the relationship of the composite mapped back to the two birth charts, illuminating as this does the meaning of the partnership to each of its two members. And in fact the Tropical map says very little to us, and were we to leave it at that, we might be forgiven for assuming that this approach to composite work was unenlightening and invalid. But look at the Draconic! Here are the telling contacts, the composite Sun falling on that brilliant axis of Tropical Sun/Draconic Mercury/Pluto in Chris's chart, bringing all his creative genius into flower, and the responsive, feminine Cancer Moon aligning with his Draconic Sun (and possibly Tropical Moon) announcing the spiritual inevitability and importance of this bond between man and woman.

In Jayne's case, it is the Mercury/Venus conjunction that sparks her Draconic Moon from the opposition (and perhaps her Tropical Ascendant), offering her the perfect avenue of aesthetic self-expression, grace and drama under the public gaze, in the spotlight. And the Draconic Mars falls directly on Chris's Tropical Saturn: sure testimony once more that it is this partnership that brings the crucial discipline to his fractious energy and sets it free. But you see, it is not till we get to the purposive, spiritual level of the Draconic chart that the reasons and dynamics of this relationship truly emerge – and then they emerge with great power. At the everyday Tropical level, the astrological signs of normal sexual chemistry are lacking; at the higher Draconic level the emphasis is on a profound and creative Aquarian friendship, with just the possibility of their joint vocation drawing them into conventional marriage. John Hennessy, their biographer, asked them, the day after their triumph, if they felt closer together as a result of *Bolero*. '"Yes," they both softly answered, but Jayne ruined the romantic mood I had hoped to establish by adding with a giggle, "because he's my friend, a bigger friend than he was yesterday, because he didn't fall down or anything."' Chris told John Hennessy, 'There's a chemistry between us that even we can't understand. I'm sure that neither of us could do what we do with any other partner, could we, Jayne? What's the chance of somebody else coming along with the same temperament, the right age, in the right place and at the right time?' And so far, nobody

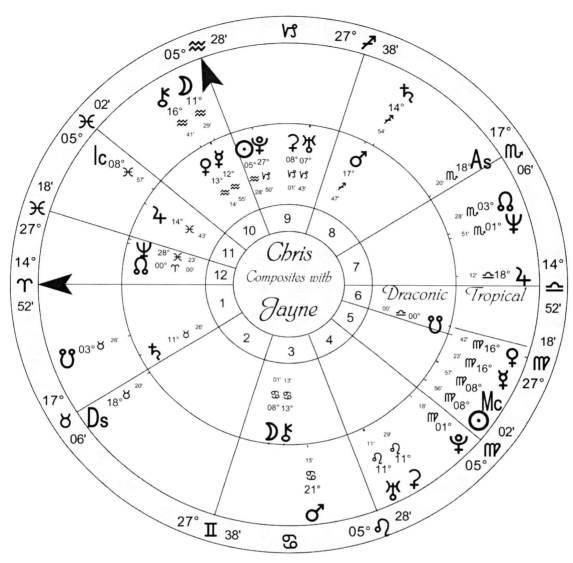

else has. As I revisit this chapter in 2011, despite occasional declarations that this tour or that show would be their last, they have been unable to stop the creative flow or quench the desire to keep on dancing together.

The piece of music that brought all these creative elements together in their climactic amateur triumphs at Sarajevo and Ottawa in 1984 was written by a man born with his Draconic Sun/Moon conjunct Tropical Mercury in early Pisces with Jayne's Draconic Sun/Jupiter; Tropical Venus and his own Draconic Saturn at the beginning of Aquarius opposite Chris's Leo Sun; Chris's Draconic Mars setting and Jayne's Tropical Sun/Jupiter on his own Draconic Jupiter/Ascendant. Even his culminating Leo Uranus is 0°25' from its position in Chris's chart! **Maurice Ravel**'s *Bolero* was composed when his progressed Tropical Venus conjoined natal Draconic Chiron in 2° Aries (on Betty Callaway's Sun)

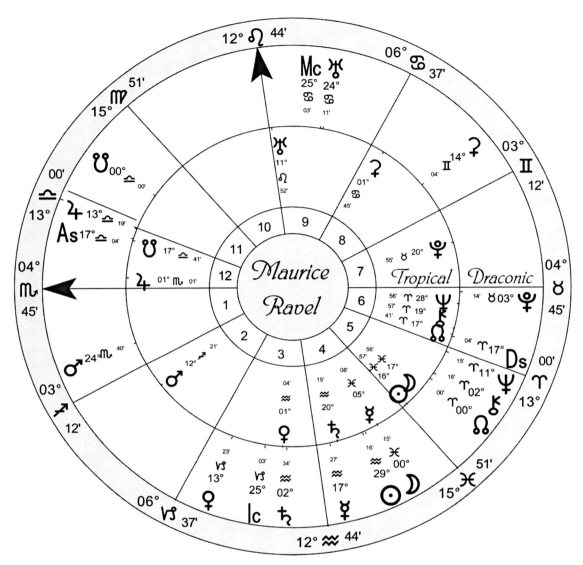

and squared progressed Mars in 2° Capricorn. It was probably his best known piece for orchestra and the least listened to. At the time when transiting Pluto moved into the first degrees of Scorpio and closed onto the composer's Ascendant, *Bolero* was brought back into the dance for which it was first written. It was given expression in a new medium, was recharged with dramatic and spiritual meaning, and all over the world Ravel was rediscovered. As the applause rang out in Ottawa, asteroid *Ravel*, now at Pisces 15° within orbs of the composer's Sun, was right on the IC, Draconically aligned with both *Christophe* and *Jane* from early Capricorn, on Chris's Draconic Sun/*Dancey* axis. What chords may bind us!

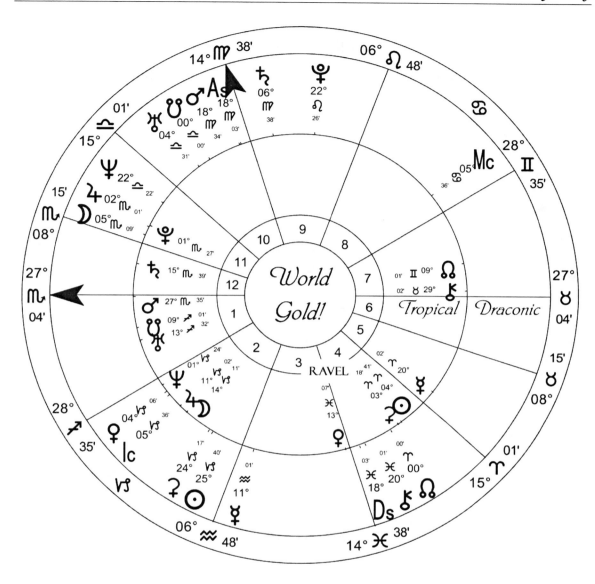

Sexual Fulfilment

This is a rather ironic title, since the marriage in question foundered when the husband was about fifty and the wife in her mid-forties. They had brought up a family, and proceeded for one reason or another to find each other a trial. The astrologer was called in at the stage when the husband was casting around for a new partner and he wanted to take a closer look at his married relationship for clues to its breakdown in case he ran the same risks again. The man was a sceptic, but a Scorpio; he refused to take anything on trust, but neither would he close his mind so long as the material presented an intriguing challenge. The synastry with his wife offered the usual mixture of delights and aggravations that one tends to find in any partnership of character. In this case it was she, Cardinal Aries, who left home, he the Fixed Scorpio who stayed. The midlife crisis claimed its victims. But there was one thing quite extraordinary about the synastry between these two once the Draconic level was drawn: they had every possible permutation of Venus/Mars between Draco and Tropical that you could imagine! They started off with mutual Mars/Venus sextiles, which is pretty healthy in itself, especially for two such vigorous individuals; but then we also find his Tropical Mars conjunct her Draconic Venus, his Tropical Venus conjunct her Draconic Mars, his Draconic Mars conjunct her Tropical Venus and his Draconic Venus conjunct her Tropical Mars! And for good measure the Draco Mars/Venuses make mutual sextiles too. If you also observe that their Nodes are trine, you will understand how this has come about.

Presented with the suggestion that their physical relationship must have been somewhat out of the ordinary and extremely compulsive, the Scorpio guard at last came down. 'If I ever doubted the accuracy of astrology, all my doubts are now dispelled,' he said. 'This was the only thing that was really any good – and it was, as you say, fantastic.' But it didn't save the marriage. The amusing postscript to this is that after a couple of abortive attempts to build relationships with ladies who, in at least one case, seemed perfect for him, he settled for one who, to the astrologer, seemed lacking in most respects but for *one thing* … And so our patterns repeat themselves!

MORECAMBE AND WISE, Bringers of Sunshine!

Eleven days before the first draft of this chapter, 'Little Ern', the straight man of the now immortal comedy duo, died in his sleep after a heart attack. Eric Morecambe's own big heart had stopped beating fifteen long years before, on May 20th 1984. He never seems to have left us, yet for Ernie these were interminable years of bereavement and struggle. A Sagittarian, he will always have put the cheeriest face on things, hiding the dreadful pain of a life full of laughter effectively at an end.

'Good comedy thrives on conflict', and in their composite chart you will find about as much of that commodity as anyone could hope for! 'We argued and disagreed at times,' said Ernie to one interviewer, '… The difference, you see, is that when opinions differed we did it as brothers.' This Morecambe-and-Wise composite is graced by a Fixed Grand Cross of Sun/Mercury/Venus, Moon, Saturn and Neptune that embraces Eric's own Ascendant Grand Cross, giving him in the partnership a perfect vehicle for his idiosyncratic humour. With Leo rising, Jupiter setting, Sun/Saturn squaring these and Neptune confusing everything from the Ascendant, the laughs come from his continual battle against insult and loss of innate dignity. He is like an over-grown, trusting child, bewildered when people and objects fail to behave as one might justifiably expect, triumphant when inspiration strikes and he can get his own back with a chortle of glee! Jupiter setting is a great giver, and he gave literally till his heart gave out.

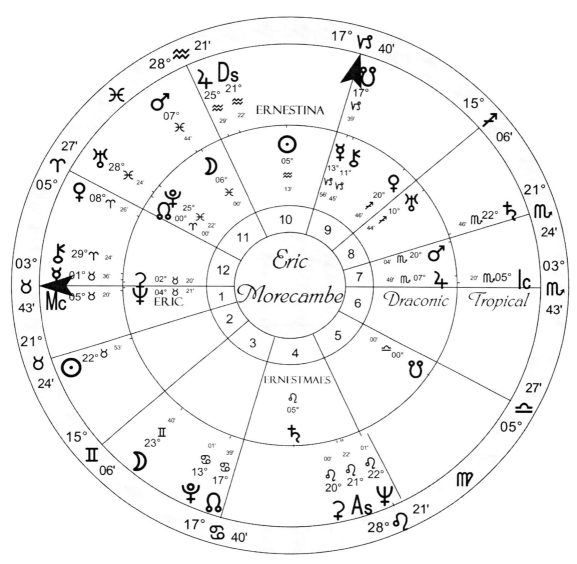

The Tropical Fixed Grand Cross finds the Sun in Taurus, and from this one might be led to expect a fairly staid, conventional man. However, the Draconic Sun has moved to Aquarius. Here, under the unassuming, ordinary, kindly exterior (Taurus now rising) beats the heart of rebellion, anarchy and iconoclasm! The fluent Gemini Moon goes into Pisces to meet his 7th House Mars and paint that familiar, loved picture of injured innocence that so tugged at our heart-strings as we waited for inevitable, delicious, funny retaliation. With setting Draconic Jupiter also aligned with Tropical Mercury and MC, he couldn't help but be funny, in private as well as public. With Draconic MC on his Capricorn South Node, he also worked incredibly hard at it to the point of self-sacrifice. Like that other wonderfully funny man, the magician Tommy Cooper, he died on stage.

That South Node/MC is one of the meeting points with Ernie Wise; his own Tropical Venus/Jupiter/IC conjunction is there. Here you can see how his 'straight' Capricorn humour fed and was in turn nourished by Eric's high standard in performance. And of course so many of the jokes were at Ernie's expense, all about his incorrigible stinginess with money, pomposity, and absurdly lavish projects. Born only six months before his friend, his and Eric's Tropical Saturns both straddle Eric's Draconic Scorpio Mars, vying for control; but Ernie's Mars undoes all this by constantly provoking Eric's comic onslaughts from its position close to the Draconic Jupiter/Tropical IC in Scorpio.

As we have come to expect, it is the Draconic composite that really shines. This is a union of souls, a shared incarnation, a joint vocation. The bond between these two generous, shiny souls is vividly displayed in the shifting of that Grand Cross so that

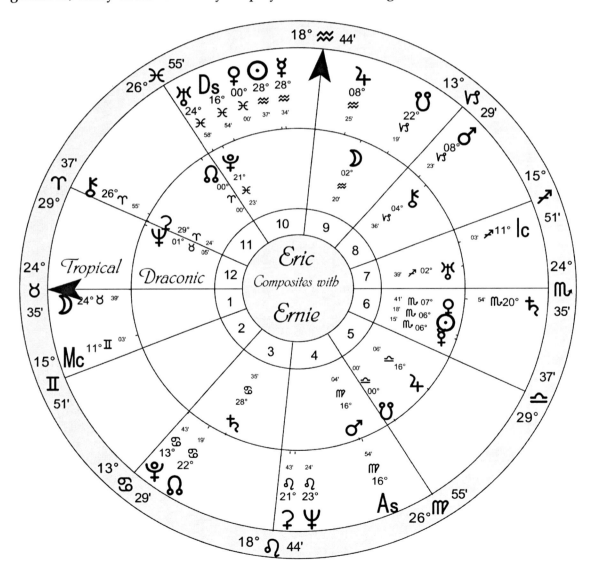

not only does its Moon approach Eric's Aquarian Sun, but also the opposition to Ernie's Draconic Sun in Leo. If these were man and woman it would be a marriage – and one made in Heaven. This configuration, with the Solar stellium on Eric's Descendant, is the heart of this chart, the soul of this partnership. Here is the Aquarian anarchist in inspired conflict with Leo's vanity, Eric's Taurus-rising pragmatist puncturing the conceit of Ernie's pretentious Gemini-rising wordsmith, while at the same time trying desperately to admire all those 'plays like what he wrote' (and in which public figures from newsreaders to Prime Ministers delightedly took part!).

Accordingly, I have chosen to display their bi-wheels with the Draconic positions at the centre – and for another reason too: it is here that the brilliant asteroid phrases in these two nativities shine most brightly. Eric first: he has his own asteroid, *Eric*, rising,

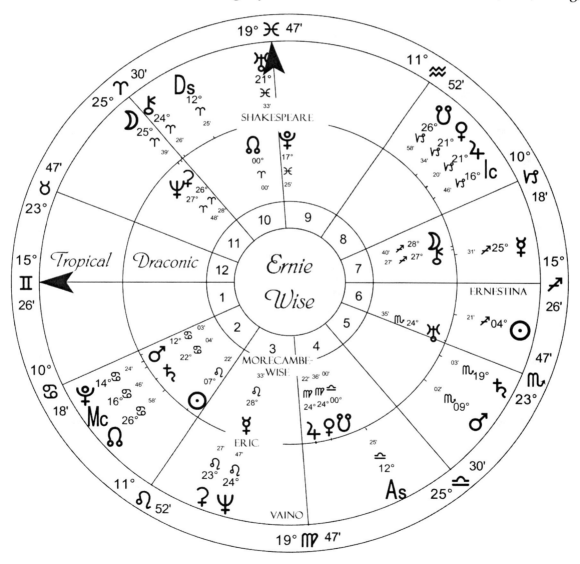

but Draconic *Eric* also exactly conjoins his Tropical MC where the clown's asteroid *Coco* rules the sky! On his Draconic MC, in the Capricorn South Node, is Tropical *Rabelais* – a gentle warning to avoid going too far so as to cause offence, in his enjoyment of racy physical humour. To the best of my knowledge he never overstepped the mark, and continually delighted with an innocent sauciness. Opposite, of course, at the Draconic IC (thus again doubly angular) is *Fantasia*. He always dreamed of getting the girl! So much of his humour was true fantasy, completely off the wall – this is why it is timeless, and audiences at the turn of the millennium love his stuff just as much as those of us who grew up with Morecambe and Wise. So where's Ernie? Only conjunct his Sun! That is, *Erna* is conjunct Sun by 4°, but *Ernestina* makes an exact contact from Tropical to Draconic in 5° Aquarius, opposite Ernie Wise's own Draconic Sun. Incidentally, you often find this. I met so many people who have asteroid *Pamela* on my own Sun or Ascendant degree that I began looking for this, and found it in other pairs of charts too, where the contact is of temporary or lasting significance. It doesn't happen every time, but often enough to be well worth observing. To complete our look at Eric's asteroids, there is lastly a descriptive little trio conjunct his Taurus Sun, of Draconic *Vaino*, *Witt* and *Fanatica*.

Ernie's asteroids are amazing (my apologies: I have only space for a small selection in the accompanying table) – and very interesting, because not only is his own name firmly on both angles again (Tropical *Ernestina*, with the slapstick, bull-in-a-china-shop

Name	Long.	Trav.	Lat.	R.A.	Decl.
* Eric 4954	05°♉56	+00°20'	+02°17'	146°42'	+15°49'
☍ ♃ 1°53' A	☌ ♆ 1°34' S		☌ ⚳ 3°35' S		☌ As 2°12' A
☍ Ds 2°12' A					
* Ernestina 698	18°♎05	+00°04'	-12°19'	311°37'	-30°45'
* Ernestmaes 7349	05°♌51 R	-00°13'	+04°08'	232°11'	-14°38'
☍ ☉ 0°37' A	☌ ♄ 0°44' A		# ♆ 0°05' A		
* Fantasia 1224	17°♋15 R	-00°13'	-07°16'	210°02'	-20°00'
☍ ☿ 3°18' A	☍ Mc 0°25' S		☌ Ic 0°25' S		
* Hilaritas 996	28°♐27	+00°19'	+00°09'	014°47'	+06°29'
* Morecambewise 1...	00°♐21	+00°22'	+00°00'	348°59'	-04°43'
* Shakespeare 2985	29°♑38	+00°24'	+00°22'	044°43'	+17°21'
* Smiley 1613	08°♍41 R	-00°08'	-09°33'	265°42'	-32°56'
☍ ☽ 2°41' A					
* Sunshine 3742	09°♑42	+00°23'	-01°10'	025°49'	+09°26'
☌ ⚷ 2°02' A					
* Vaino 2096	21°♉20	+00°04'	-00°56'	160°14'	+07°19'
☍ ♂ 1°15' A					

Eric Morecambe - Draconic ↑ & ↓ Tropical Asteroids

Name	Long.	Trav.	Lat.	R.A.	Decl.
* Eric 4954	23°♌35	+00°20'	+02°17'	250°02'	-19°52'
☍ ♃ 1°53' A	☌ ♆ 1°34' S		☌ ⚳ 3°35' S		☌ As 2°12' A
☍ Ds 2°12' A					
* Ernestina 698	05°♒45	+00°04'	-12°19'	054°06'	+06°40'
* Ernestmaes 7349	23°♏31 R	-00°13'	+04°08'	341°03'	-03°32'
☍ ☉ 0°37' A	☌ ♄ 0°44' A				
* Fantasia 1224	04°♏54 R	-00°13'	-07°16'	327°27'	-20°51'
☍ ☿ 3°18' A	☍ Mc 0°25' S		☌ Ic 0°25' S		
* Hilaritas 996	16°♈07	+00°19'	+00°09'	126°08'	+19°28'
* Morecambewise 1...	18°♓01	+00°22'	+00°00'	096°11'	+23°20'
* Shakespeare 2985	17°♉18	+00°24'	+00°22'	156°56'	+10°02'
* Smiley 1613	26°♐21 R	-00°08'	-09°33'	016°35'	-03°16'
☍ ☽ 2°41' A					
* Sunshine 3742	27°♈21	+00°23'	-01°10'	137°08'	+15°12'
☌ ⚷ 2°02' A					
* Vaino 2096	08°♍59	+00°04'	-00°56'	266°19'	-24°20'
☍ ♂ 1°15' A					

Name	Long.	Trav.	Lat.	R.A.	Decl.
* Eric 4954	28°♈34	+00°29'	+33°35'	162°50'	+44°01'
☌ ♆ 0°45' S	☌ ⚳ 2°05' S				
* Ernestina 698	17°♌40	+00°23'	-05°15'	252°40'	-27°46'
* Ernestmaes 7349	03°♋28	+00°23'	+02°13'	209°07'	-09°32'
* Fantasia 1224	25°♊49	+00°22'	-05°54'	198°49'	-14°20'
☍ ☽ 2°50' S	☍ ⚷ 1°37' A				
* Hilaritas 996	27°♎03	+00°11'	-00°06'	326°23'	-13°36'
☍ ♆ 0°45' A	☍ ⚳ 0°35' S				
* Morecambewise 1...	28°♌55	+00°31'	-02°03'	265°28'	-25°26'
☌ ☿ 0°22' A					
* Shakespeare 2985	23°♏39	+00°07'	-01°18'	351°54'	-04°54'
☌ ♅ 0°55' A	// As 0°00' A		# Ds 0°00' A		
* Smiley 1613	29°♋01	+00°20'	-06°04'	232°05'	-25°09'
* Sunshine 3742	29°♎33	+00°13'	-00°07'	328°48'	-12°47'
☍ ♆ 1°44' S	☍ ⚳ 3°04' S				
* Vaino 2096	21°♉41	+00°13'	-00°24'	169°25'	+04°06'
☍ ♅ 2°53' A					

Ernie Wise - Draconic ↑ & ↓ Tropical Asteroids

Name	Long.	Trav.	Lat.	R.A.	Decl.
* Eric 4954	25°♌33	+00°29'	+33°35'	263°40'	+10°18'
☌ ♆ 0°45' S	☌ ⚳ 2°05' S				
* Ernestina 698	14°♐39	+00°23'	-05°15'	012°44'	-00°14'
* Ernestmaes 7349	00°♏26	+00°23'	+02°13'	328°50'	-10°16'
* Fantasia 1224	22°♎48	+00°22'	-05°54'	324°10'	-20°29'
☍ ☽ 2°50' S	☍ ⚷ 1°37' A				
* Hilaritas 996	24°♒02	+00°11'	-00°06'	080°13'	+23°02'
☍ ♆ 0°45' A	☍ ⚳ 0°35' S				
* Morecambewise 1...	25°♐54	+00°31'	-02°03'	021°56'	+06°59'
☌ ☿ 0°22' A					
* Shakespeare 2985	20°♓37	+00°07'	-01°18'	108°54'	+20°59'
# ☉ 0°01' S	☌ ♅ 0°55' A		// ♇ 0°07' A		
* Smiley 1613	26°♏00	+00°20'	-06°04'	355°58'	-08°22'
* Sunshine 3742	26°♒31	+00°13'	-00°07'	082°56'	+23°09'
☍ ♆ 1°44' S	☍ ⚳ 3°04' S				
* Vaino 2096	18°♍39	+00°13'	-00°24'	287°01'	-22°55'
☍ ♅ 2°53' A					

asteroid *Toro*, on the Draconic Descendant, and 'Ernie Wise' translated as *Erna Wisdom* tropically on his Draconic MC) but his heroes are here too. With a rising conjunction of *Chaplin* and *Laurel*, plus Sun only 5° from conjunction with *Hardy*, Ernie would either have gone through life consciously patterning his comedy on theirs (which is not apparent, as Morecambe and Wise are unique) or purely and simply have been born to take his place in a glorious comedic tradition. Certainly the standard of comedic business and timing set by the immortal Laurel and Hardy was one which the Leo perfectionist in Ernie would have striven to attain. *Wisdom*'s second rôle is Norman Wisdom, not only another of this century's great sympathetic cinema clowns, but also a close friend. Sagittarians adore and thrive on humour; Ernie Wise surely spent every hour he could manage in cinemas enjoying the verbal and physical antics of those other great clowns … and yes, *Coco* (Draconic) with *Chant* (song) conjoins his Tropical Ascendant in Libra. And where's *Eric*? Conjunct Neptune, ruler of the Draconic MC, opposite the twin delights of *Hilaritas* and *Sunshine*, and aligned with his Tropical Aries Moon/Chiron. The Tropical quartet aligns in Leo-Aquarius with the trio of *Dancey*, Mercury and *Marconia*. (It is the easily-missed but equally important Dwad – see Appendix – of Tropical *Eric* that closely opposes Ernie's Sagittarian Sun, from 6° Gemini.) The Tropical Mercury/*Marconia* also turns up close to Draconic Moon/Chiron/*Fantasia*. Interesting that it is a Moon contact this time, with the partner's name! In Eric's case, Ernie is associated with the Sun. Once again, it looks so like a marriage; certainly the Aries Moon epitomises the ungovernable child in his partner. In the asteroids here we have the perfect picture of the two of them doing their funny dance at the end of the TV show (*Marconia*) and singing the song, 'Bring Me Sunshine', which will always be theirs. After all, Ernie had been a self-proclaimed and much-applauded song-and-dance man since early stardom in his teens.

The *pièce de résistance*, however, remembering all those Plays Like What He Wrote, and especially Ernie's incomparable versions of the Bard, is this wonderful line-up, straddling his Draconic Meridian with its angular Pluto/Jupiter/Tropical Uranus, of *Witt*, *Wisdom*, *Erna*, *Vaino*, *Fanatica*, *Babelsberg* and *Shakespeare! Most of these are entirely self-explanatory in view of what has gone before. Babelsberg* has a double connotation: first, as the tower of Babel, it is perfect for the linguistic acrobatics and constant misunderstandings that are the pivot of so much of the humour; secondly, it is the name of a major film studio, a German 'Hollywood'. *All* the Stars queued to be part of *Morecambe and Wise!* Additionally (and I quote Ernie's obituary in the *Daily Mail*), 'Ernie always saw Hollywood as the pinnacle they must conquer. Mentioned in the same breath as Astaire or Mickey Rooney, as a kid, he yearned to make movies there. Significantly, he chose *Still On The Way To Hollywood* as the title of his 1990 autobiography. But Eric would have none of it.' So Ernie contented himself and his wife Doreen with a Hollywood lifestyle. Back to the asteroids: bawdy *Rabelais* is worth noting here; like Eric, Ernie has this asteroid linked to the Nodes – but this time it is in the opposite sign, Draconic Cancer, conjunct *Smiley* and the Tropical *North* Node. He could be too po-faced, too respectable, too prim; he actually needed encouraging to indulge in something a little more risqué, so who better to egg him on than naughty Eric?

Do take another look at that Draconic composite; it has even more to reveal. I have shown it to you in a biwheel with the Tropical composite chart – remembering that all dimensions interact. The Draconic composite is at the centre. No wonder Eric and Ernie's life together established them in the public's affections, with the Tropical Moon in this chart firmly on the Draconic Ascendant! The Tropical Ascendant in turn picks up Draconic Virgo Mars ... so much of the comedy fires off from the trivia of the domestic situation, jibes, nit-picking, little things that raise big laughs. And just look what else the Draconic composite does with its angles: these intimately configure Eric's Tropical Ascendant and Fixed Grand Cross, suggesting that the soul of the double-act drew upon and was ultimately dependent on the tensions and incongruities in Eric's own personality. That this was largely so is evidenced by the tendency to look on Eric as the real star, and Ernie just as the perfect 'straight man' or 'feed'. But to this pattern, through the horizon axis and IC, comes Ernie's contribution, his *Draconic* asteroids, *Ernestina* and *Dancey* (he was in fact, as intimated above, a very good dancer), *Erna, Wisdom, Shakespeare* (of course!), *Witt, Fanatica, Vaino,* and *Babelsberg*. In other words, it was Eric and their double-act that gave Ernie's gifts the outlet they needed and deserved – and which would have been poorer without them. Of course they had script-writers (Sid Greene, Dick Hills, Eddie Braben) but no script-writer can create laughter without the inspiration and input of the performer's genius. You might say in a broader context, that the Draconic is the 'genius', the 'tutelary spirit', of the astrological chart.

Since originally writing this, a different birth time for Eric Morecambe has been published in a new biography by Graham McCann (*Morecambe and Wise*, published by 4th Estate, 1998.) He gives a time of 12h30 pm BST, half an hour later than the noon time initially believed to be correct. However, on re-examining the chart in this light, I see no reason to change what we have here. The later time moves the angles away from Eric's name asteroid; this is inconsistent with what I have observed for years now – that if the personal name is in the area of the Ascendant at all, it is either on it, extremely close or right opposite on the Descendant. The double angularity of 'Eric' that appears in the bi-wheel above is confirmation enough for me that it is the new time that is in error for whatever reason. And if you want further proof, take a look at this chart for their first ever TV series, that started at London's Shepherds Bush on April 21st 1954 at 21h40 BST. It is well-known that it was far from a success – this came later, as witness Draconic Jupiter on the Tropical MC – but even so this engagingly anarchic show with its powerful Chiron and doubly angular Venus was the beginning of a very long and exceptional television career that made both Eric and Ernie great stars. And here as you would expect are the angular contacts to Eric's *Noon* chart: life-changing Pluto right on his Ascendant opposed by the Draconic Aquarius Moon (the public applause); Pluto again (Draconic this time) square Venus, and Tropical Saturn opposite Sun, all configuring his natal, angular, Draconic Grand Cross. This disintegrates at a 12h30 pm birth time. As it is, it describes perfectly the impact on his life, his career, his personality, and also the initial struggle for recognition, the saturnine disappointments. Also the composite we have been looking at, based on Eric's noon pattern, is strongly configured at the time of their first show: not only the Draconic composite T-square in early Fixed signs, but significantly its MC and Ascendant (that Tropical Moon-Pluto again, and the horizon, and the Draconic meridian), while the Tropical Moon (the public image) falls directly on the composite Tropical IC.

I think we're safe with noon!

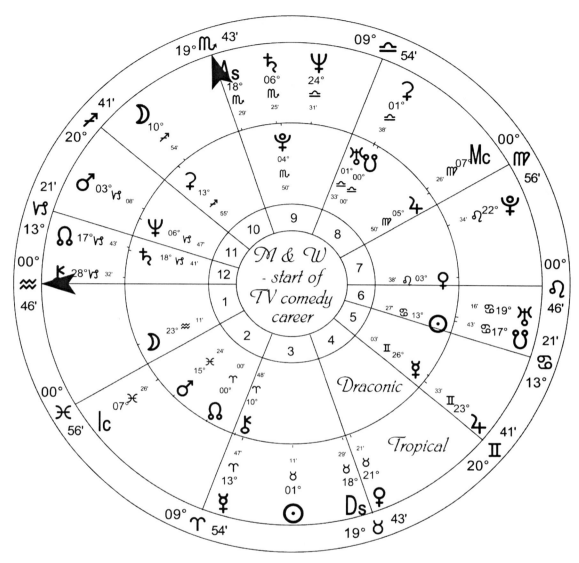

Ernie's Solar Return on November 26th 1998 while cruising in the Caribbean (the Return chart angles are therefore only approximate) still carried the current although separating conjunction of Pluto with his Sun, here in an 8th House stellium, squared by a Pisces Moon. This troublesome pattern was bound to the Draconic by its Saturn/Neptune square – the rising Saturn in Sagittarius closing on Ernie's Sun. He had suffered a number of strokes and heart attacks since officially retiring from his enforced solo career at the age of seventy; December brought two heart attacks, followed in January 1999 by a triple heart bypass operation in Florida. Over the next few months this Draconic Saturn joined the transiting Pluto axis at 10° Sagittarius, and further weakened his general resistance. When the end came, only two weeks after a depressed and homesick Ernie returned to England, it must have been a joyous release from suffering for him, and a loving reunion with his long-missed friend. He died under a 'happy Sun' that had only sweet aspects. Tropical Chiron

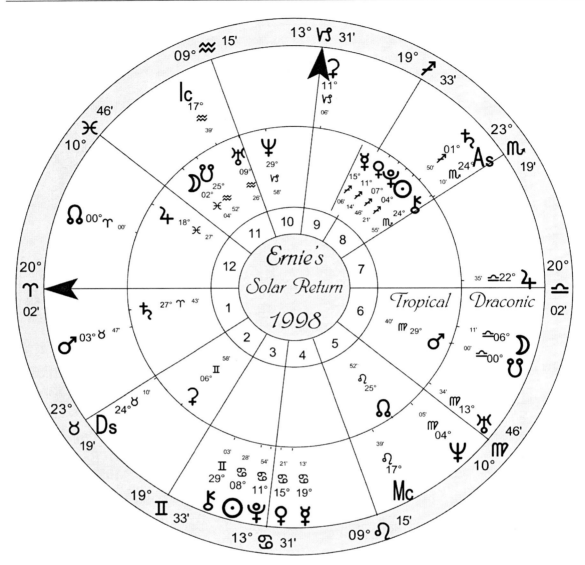

had reached his natal Sun, which had just risen Draconically at the stated time of death, 7h00 am. Draconic Chiron and Pluto embraced his Midheaven in Cancer, a late-Sagittarius Draconic Moon lay on his Draconic Chiron/ Tropical Mercury conjunction, and, square this, Draconic Uranus and Tropical Mercury transited his natal Draconic Jupiter. Jupiter itself was very close to his 7th House cusp; the Draconic Sun/Mercury opposite Tropical Venus/Saturn/Ascendant square Neptune touched all the elements of their Draconic Fixed Cross. Poignantly, the Dragon's Head in 21° Leo on the Draconic MC was all of 0°06' from Eric's Tropical Ascendant; as he pulled up his material roots at the Dragon's Tail, the soul of Ernie Wise flew up to meet his Maker, and his mate.

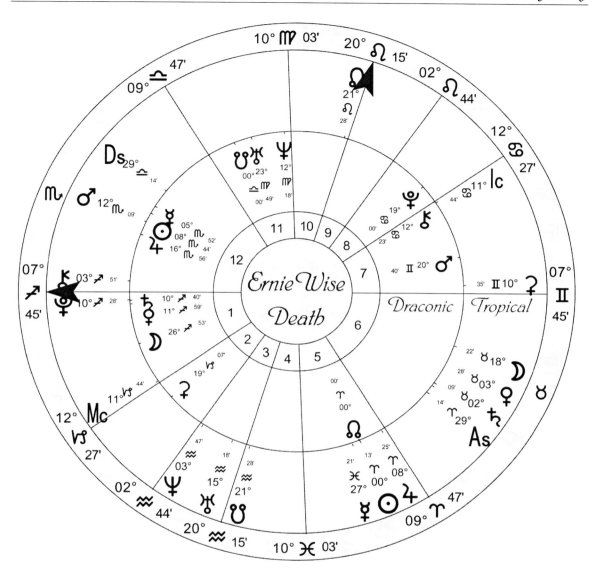

A Case of Reincarnation? Two Martin Luthers!

Having suggested that the Draconic chart holds the key to those capacities and convictions which each of us brings into the current life from previous experiences on earth, we have not yet been so bold as to compare two charts and infer that they may belong to one soul. I am not in any way going to come down firmly in this case on the side of reincarnation as an explanation for the strong similarities between the two patterns before us; all I intend to do here is to look at this as a possibility. Al H. Morrison, in *CAO Times*, has already

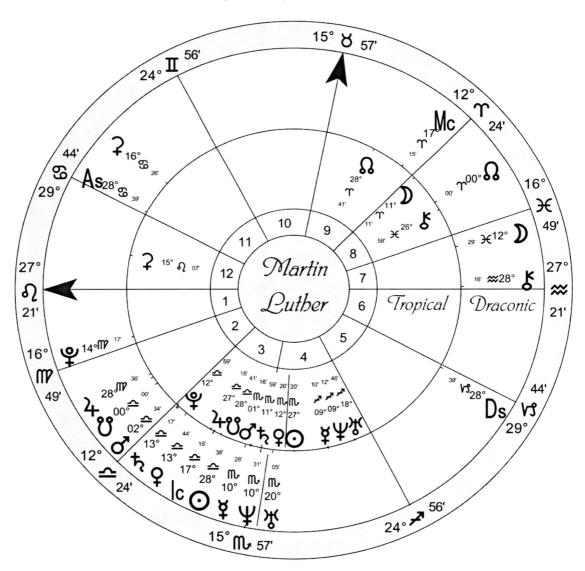

pointed out the 'spiritual continuity between the two men' that shows even in the Tropical patterns.

Martin Luther, prime instigator of the Reformation of the Church in Europe in the early sixteenth century, is a powerful blend of Scorpio, Sagittarius, some Libra, Aries Moon and North Node, with late Leo on the Ascendant. With that amazing concentration of planets in the 3rd and 4th Houses, the focus of his activity was upon the foundations of religious thinking and expression. Saturn and Venus dominate the IC, symbols of his profound dissatisfaction and the drive to root out old structures and replace them with better ones. This is better seen in the energy passing from Draconic Uranus through the Tropical Sun – so often seen in the charts of the determinedly unorthodox, the inventors and originators. The higher Mercury and Neptune, his own spiritual inspiration, feed that lifetime's drive for reform from the Scorpio IC, which in turn with Venus/Saturn lends real influence to the purgative Pluto in the 3rd from Draconic Libra. Now, there is some dispute as to whether calculations for dates so far back in history should be made from contemporary tables or from modern computer programmes; and in Luther's case this makes a difference sufficient to shift the Draconic Sun from Libra (modern) to Scorpio (ancient). Whichever is the true position on that cusp, the Draco Sun, his deepest conviction, fires his Mars energy to put up a relentless Scorpio fight, for him a South Node matter and tied in with the Tropical Libra Jupiter. Mars rules his North Node, so his whole purpose is focussed on what he already is and has come to give to the world, whether as a selfless mission, or for whatever other hidden reason. On the Draconic MC in Aries lies his Tropical Moon; the power of his feelings as a human being dictate this lonely path, find their outlet in his sense of spiritual vocation to establish a fairer but still firm Church, grounded in a critical reappraisal of the scriptures in their original form, and a liturgy that was no longer incomprehensible to an undereducated public. Draconic Sun linked to the Tropical South Node of the Moon is indicative of a driven life, deeply vocational, often sacrificial, even to the point of martyrdom for the cause.

And now we come to Martin Luther King, Jr. For the Reverend King also had this Draconic Sun/Tropical South Node pattern: moreover, *the Draconic Sun falls at the end of Scorpio almost exactly on his predecessor's Tropical Sun, his Tropical Ascendant is conjunct Luther's Tropical MC (on the Nativity axis – see Chapter 19), and his late Cancer IC is rooted on Luther's Draconic Ascendant.*

The distribution of planets is very different, King's being so spread out as to make a great splash in the sky – a tremendous contrast to Luther's tight pattern. But there are echoes in the configurations: both have a Sun/Moon/Pluto pattern strongly marked, also Moon/Venus/Pluto. Each has Sun/Venus in aspect by 15°, with Saturn involved in the same structure. Luther's Draconic IC conjunct Tropical Pluto is answered by King's wide Pluto/IC conjunction; Luther's Draconic MC conjunct Tropical Moon by King's Draconic Moon conjunct Tropical MC! Luther's Draconic Moon in Pisces is only 7° from King's Tropical Moon. Their Jupiters are not far from opposition across the Aries/Libra – Taurus/Scorpio cusp. Luther's Tropical Mercury is just 4° from King's Draconic Mercury in Sagittarius; King has Draconic Saturn at the end of Libra (opposed to Draconic Mars) conjunct Luther's important Draconic Sun, Tropical South Node and Tropical Jupiter; and

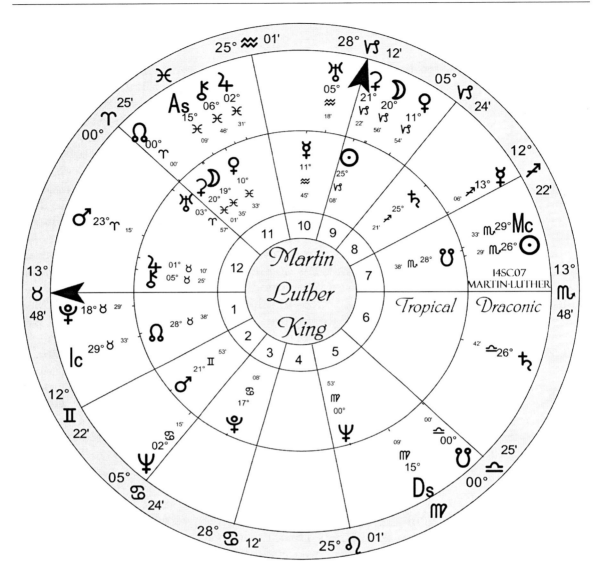

the latter's Draconic Descendant conjoins the Black clergyman's Tropical Capricorn Sun/MC.

The relationship between them is clearly very strong, even if they are not manifestations of one entity. The striving of the one for a purged and renewed Church must have inspired the other's sacrificial struggle for a respected and fully enfranchised Black community (Draco Capricorn Moon conjunct Tropical Sun/MC, opposition Tropical Pluto). King, unsurprisingly, has Chiron rising with Jupiter. When this chapter was first written I added, 'If only we had a Chiron position for Luther!' Now we do. There is Draconic Chiron at the end of revolutionary Aquarius right on Martin Luther's Tropical Descendant, preaching to the crowds.

Homing In

When one considers the singular importance of the Ascendant and Midheaven in distinguishing the pattern of one individual from that of any other, out of hundreds of babies being born at the same moment on a smallish patch of the Earth's crust such as the United Kingdom, the birthplace will always hold a special connection with its child; and when a child becomes famous, the citizens of that place will often honour the house in which he or she was born with a plaque and inscription, even though they may never have known the personage, and the time spent in the house may have been extremely short. In the majority of cases, the town or village of birth will have witnessed the entry of the soul, meaning that conception will have occurred there as well. Therefore it would seem reasonable to expect a pattern of links to appear between angles, Nodes and Aries Points in the nativities of the person born and the place itself. It is not a question of locating a given town in a matrix drawn to an Earth zodiac – this may be possible, it may also be desirable, but opinion is far too divided on this subject; it is a matter of matching the native to the map which most fairly represents a significant beginning in the history of the birthplace.

My own recourse was to *The Astrology of Towns and Cities* by Harold Wigglesworth. His research was carefully done, and most times are taken as 0h00 am Civil Time, a logical choice for two good reasons which are that in Britain we use 00h00 am as an inceptional moment for most statutory matters, and astrologically to focus on a place is largely to think of it as someone's roots, which is more IC than Ascendant (and far preferable in my view to the use of 12h00 noon which seems customary in the US). The Ascendant at 0h00 will figure strongly in what follows, as environment, relationships and identity are involved as well as heredity, history, home and security. Briefly, I used in my survey 154 charts out of my files which were timed to within half an hour of accuracy; most are probably accurate to a quarter of an hour. Over three-quarters of these showed strong – and frequently multiple – alignments between Tropical or Draconic Ascendants or MCs with Nodal axes and/or Aries Points in the patterns of native and birthplace.

To show you what I mean, have a look at a few of the more striking examples:

Male, born 19 October 1941, Bromley, 1h30 am BST.

Native: Tropical Ascendant Leo 21°, MC Taurus 7°, North Node Virgo 20°45', Draconic Ascendant Pisces 0°, Draconic MC Scorpio 16°, Aries Point Libra 9°15'

Birthplace: Tropical Ascendant Scorpio 17°, MC Virgo 5°, North Node Libra 8°13', Draconic Ascendant Taurus 9°, Draconic MC Aquarius 27°, Aries Point Virgo 21°47'

The above example shows six cross-correspondences, four of them extremely strong. A father and his two sons follow: the father, born in Maidenhead, has MC Capricorn 16° conjunct the town's North Node; his Draconic IC conjunct Maidenhead's Draconic Ascendant in Aquarius 15°; and his Draconic Ascendant on the town's Draconic MC and Libra Point (opposite the Aries Point) from Sagittarius 8° to Sagittarius 10° and 14° respectively. Both his sons were born in Chatham: Number One son follows Father's pattern in having his Draconic IC in Gemini 24° conjunct the birthplace Draconic Ascendant exactly, and with a slight variation so does Number Two son, with Draconic IC conjunct his town's Tropical Ascendant by 2° from Virgo 7°. Here is an elegant instance of spiritual roots being put down in two cases in the spiritual levels of the environment and, in one, in the material circumstances.

A mother and daughter repeat the pattern of Dragon's Head 6° conjunct the birthplace's Tropical MC; the mother was born in Reigate, the daughter in Barnsley. The girl also had MC conjunct the town's Draconic MC, and Draconic MC close to its Aries Point; the mother and Reigate have Draconic MC 4° apart.

One more example: two of the most famous children of the town of Nottingham since Robin Hood are of course Jayne Torvill and Christopher Dean. Nottingham's South Node in the first degree of Virgo lies on Dean's Aries Point, Mercury and Pluto; its North Node opposite in Pisces is conjunct Jayne Torvill's Draconic Sun; and her own Nodal axis aligns with Nottingham's 11° Taurus-Scorpio Ascendant/Descendant. These two souls came into the place which would help them to find and pursue their true vocation; and, indeed, at our moment of birth and throughout our lives by moving home, so do we all.

If you are interested in testing this out for yourself, there is now a greatly expanded database of British charts available to you on request. A few years ago I was able to make contact with Harold Wigglesworth's widow, and she kindly gave me permission to re-publish digitally all the chart data of towns and cities that her husband had so painstakingly prepared and published by hand. This project became an absorbing adventure into British civic history when I also found online a number of excellent sources of town charters, city foundations and grants of Arms. Solar Fire files of more than 1700 of these in England, Scotland and Wales are now on my PC and can be supplied by email; all you have to do is put in your request on my website, www.TheHolyTwelve.co.uk, and if there is data for your location, it is yours.

Chapter Eleven

The Horary and The Event
What is it Really About?

Horary astrology has a long history of very precise rules; and there is no doubt in my mind whatever that followed with care these rules will prove most reliable in answering correctly framed questions. But there is no reason why we should not explore the possibilities opened up by the application of Draconic astrology to the horary question; nothing ventured, nothing gained! Of course you may say this is nonsense, as a question cannot have a perfecting soul in the way that a person can – how can it apply? However, if we look on Draco as a dimension of being, it may also be argued that historic dimension of the soul life may have something to say about the meaning of the question, or the experience that gives rise to the question.

For our first example, let me show you the very first horary I ever did, in a real personal emergency, on April 27th 1974 at 9h15 am BST in Walmer, Kent, when I discovered that my husband's motorcycle was missing.

'Where is the motorbike?' was the clear question for the moment.

As you can see, the Moon was rising in Cancer – conjunct my own Moon – and so plainly indicative of the querent! The bike, a machine whose duty was to potter about locally and take my husband to and from his work in Dover a few miles away, is found as Mercury in Aries in the 11th House – conjunct my husband's Ascendant ruler – and as the Sun, also in the 11th, ruler of the 3rd House. In fact the venerable BSA was found, the next day as far as I recall, after following a number of leads and hunches, south-east of the house and not very far away. The young man who took it answered to the description of the Descendant ruler Saturn conjunct Mars in Cancer in the 12th, having red hair and still living with his parents. That Mars is only 6° or so from Moon/Ascendant, and we had met only a few days previously when he had called at our house to ask if we would sell the bike, as his own needed a new engine! We had obviously declined – and there in Capricorn/Saturn is his frustration. There are the facts of what actually happened.

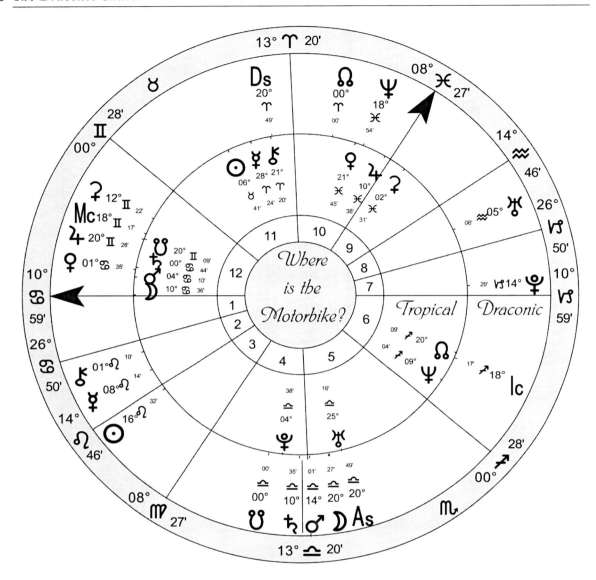

Now, if we have a look at the chart in the Draconic mode, what changes do we find?

First of all, 'I' have become Libran (and whether the Via Combusta has any effect at this level I do not yet feel qualified to say!) with Venus in 1° Cancer in the 10th; 'he' is now the setting Aries, but still signified by the Mars/Saturn conjunction in the 12th. The picture is becoming quite fascinating: the new Ascendant aligns sufficiently closely to the Tropical Uranus to identify the querent as someone who will approach the matter in an unusual way, namely through horary astrology! And see how closely linked the Venus is with that Tropical Saturn, when you consider that it was partly through the use of the horary that this young man was obliged to surrender the coveted machine he had stolen; and the latter is now also signified by Mars, ruling the Draconic 3rd. It must have meant a great deal to the poor lad. But look also at the other ruler of that 3rd House: Pluto in Capricorn in the 4th.

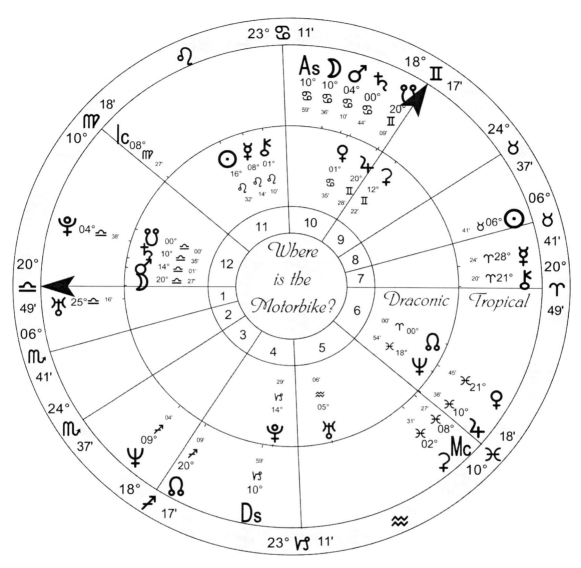

He was on the point of breaking it up for spares for his own machine that you will recall badly needed repair, in the back garden of his home a couple of roads away.

I think that nowadays we can legitimately include Chiron in the horary pattern; here Tropical Chiron falls on the Draconic Descendant by a couple of degrees, indicative of both the desperation of the young thief's act and the lesson he had to learn.

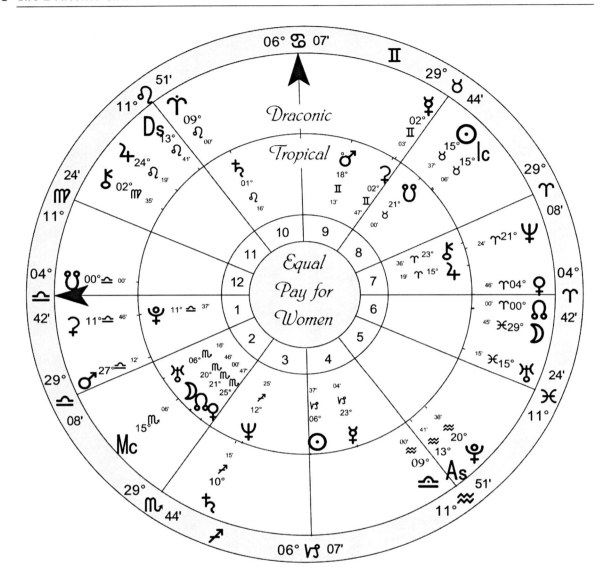

A Pattern of Legislation – Equal Pay for Women

How could one doubt the efficacy of Draco in adding meaning to the facts of horary after looking at this pattern? Legislation passed in the United Kingdom to oblige employers to pay their women employees on a par with the menfolk became effective as from 00h00 am Civil Time (which was also GMT) on December 29th 1975. The chart before you is cast for London.

The chart is potently radical, with a Moon/Venus conjunction in the Dragon's Head in the 2nd House, and fair-minded Libra rising with transformative Pluto opposite bountiful Jupiter in the 7th. Mercury, co-ruler of the legal 9th sextiles the 2nd House cluster from the

4th. There are rumblings of unease: the Sun, representative of both man and government, with an eye to a secure working structure in the years to come as signified by Capricorn, is squaring up to the Ascendant/Pluto, and uneasy also in its semi-square with the woman (Moon). The intelligentsia of Mars, ruler of the 7th in the 9th in Gemini, also feel insecure from Neptune's 3rd House opposition in Sagittarius: ideals are all very well, but …! However, Aries Jupiter in the 7th is there to cheer them and reassure them of a job well done.

But the man has to make this sacrifice; Draco puts him as the Sun into the Tropical South Node in Taurus. One woman's gain is another man's loss, so to speak. After all, at the Draconic level the Moon and Venus both arrive on the Tropical Descendant in Aries – now they are on a par with the man! The Moon is at a Node, the Equinox is in the 6th House, and she is doing a man's job. This is echoed by the Draconic MC's presence in Scorpio conjunct the Dragon's Head and Moon in the Tropical 2nd: any woman who works hard deserves to be rewarded accordingly, and she can now hold her head up and assert her own dignity and authority at work, she can stake her claim and take her place in the world of business, she has a future in equal partnership with the man. The aim of partnership is repeated by the Aries Point at 9° Leo close to the Draconic Descendant. What seems to some to be a rather unsettling ideal in fact reflects a higher order working to bring in the necessary new structure. But – as the Draconic Moon falls short of Tropical Aries by 16′ – will this measure in fact fall short of its intention? The Draco Sun falls opposite the Tropical Moon; in this position you either join forces or fight. It will no doubt take some time before those whose roots have been severely shaken will stop blaming the women for the inevitable economic crises of this turbulent and transitional age.

The Discovery of Chiron

It isn't every day that a new planet – even a very small one – is discovered orbiting the solar system, but it did happen on November 1st 1977 at 10h00 am in Pasadena, California, giving the astrologers something fresh and pleasantly controversial to argue about.

The chart of the discovery is rather spectacular, with every element except Chiron above the horizon united in a great shout to the world to throw out our accumulated mental and emotional rubbish, and transform, and look after each other; to let the past go, and work for a future of peace and justice. Surely the Draconic pattern would tell us something more?

Where there is doubt about the meaning of a new astrological factor, and we have a zodiac that concerns itself with meaning, does it not make sense to use it? Having studied the workings of Chiron assiduously ever since its first ephemeris dropped through my door, I find that the Draconic patterns make a group of very clear statements about this herald of humanity's next surge of growth.

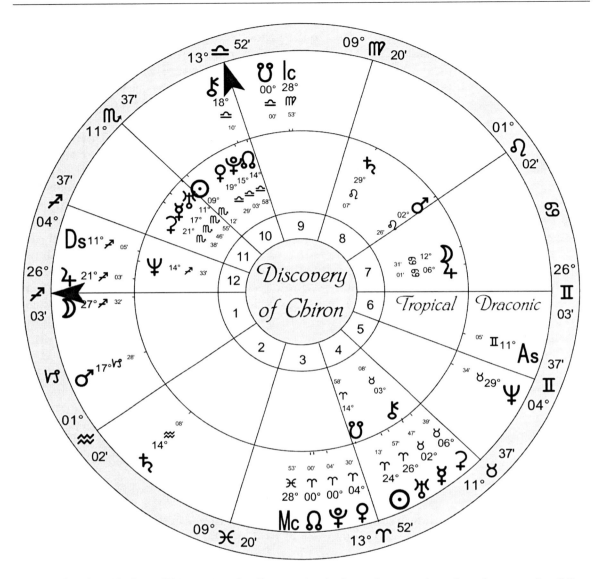

Firstly, the Higher Chiron, in the Draconic, is found crowning the chart at the Libra Midheaven, together with the Tropical Venus, Pluto and Dragon's Head. A resonant angularity of this kind is typical for a discovery or revelation pattern, identifying the object or idea manifest in the moment. This culminating Draconic Chiron says, 'I am the Bridge to peaceful Transformation. I am the gentle Guide furthering Mankind's growth and purpose, through union and love. Hand in hand, I call you onward and upward.'

Secondly, for all those who have gone out on a limb to experience Chiron's truth, we have the Higher Sun and Uranus in Aries saying, 'I am also the maverick; willingly I make the new thing happen; I stand alone, confident in my independence; with courage I break through. I am the stuff of which the old heroes were made.'

Thirdly, for all who honour the significance of myth, the Higher Moon and Jupiter stand in the last decan of Sagittarius, conjunct the Tropical Ascendant and the Galactic Centre. 'I am the centaur Chiron; the world's myth gave me this body in which I bring humanity its teaching and its healing, its wisdom, its adventure. I am all that is generous and free; and I am man's bond with the natural world in all its forms. My body of stars still points humanity towards its ultimate destiny.'

Fourthly, the Greek root of Chiron's name, *chiro* or *cheiro*, means 'hand'. The Higher Ascendant is found in Gemini, the sign of the hands. It is also the sign of the Twin Pillars of Light and Dark, between which falls the Veil, and behind which lies the journey towards truth. Opposite, on the Higher Descendant, is the Tropical Neptune in Sagittarius. 'I am the Doorway; you may approach me in faith and silence, in consciousness of your spiritual selfhood, and willing union with the divine. I who know will teach you, in the quiet place; and I am the hands which soothe and heal the suffering soul.'

Chiron orbits between Saturn's boundary and the strange territory of Uranus; the Tropical Saturn/Uranus midpoint falls at 5°31' Libra, bisecting the quintile between them on this day. Draconic Venus subtends their arc from the opposite position in 4°30' Aries. We are given the gift of passage from the known to the unknown, our delight and our victory if undertaken willingly, with courage and confidence. And the Higher Mercury, in Taurus, closely conjoins Tropical Chiron itself, the old Chiron in the past of the 4th House, the embodied Chiron, to emphasise the importance of the teaching still being given to the world by the Centaur.

There are many echoes of Huna. The old Hawaiians taught that the way for man to attain to his higher self, and thence to the Divine, was through his lower self, the Unihipili – much maligned and neglected by modern humanity so proud in its self-consciousness. Now we are at last realising the wisdom of listening to the body and losing our shame of the fleshly part of ourselves; throwing off the fig-leaf. Helped by the burgeoning Green movement, the enlightened among scientists and a media revolution – all Chiron's children – we are slowly growing toward a proper respect for the physical Creation; increasingly we behold and wonder at its intricacies, its subtleties, the delicate and potent interweavings of Gaea's ecosystems, the miracle of intelligent nature.

There may still be many physical scientists who cannot come to terms with astrology; but at least, as one of their number said on a recent radio broadcast, there are very few who do not believe in God!

An Inner Event

The accompanying chart is cast for 6h10 am BST, Truro, Cornwall, on October 7th 1978, at which moment a phrase rose prominently into my consciousness: '*No man cometh unto the Father but by me.*'

The straightforward pattern of this moment rests on the final degrees of the Mutable Grand Cross, with Virgo rising and Pisces setting. As it is not a question but a spontaneous statement originating from the New Testament and the teaching of the Christ, the idea of 28° of a sign on the Ascendant being 'too late' for the chart to be valid, according to the traditional rules of horary astrology, can hardly apply. The Ascendant ruler Mercury conjoins Sun and Pluto in Libra in the 1st House; the Descendant's co-ruler Jupiter is in Leo

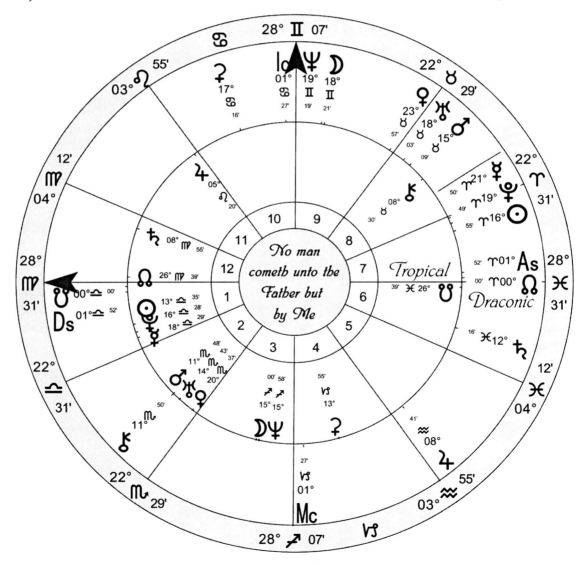

and the 11th, while the higher ruler Neptune falls in Sagittarius in the 3rd in the same degree as the Moon. As the phrase did not originate deliberately in the recipient's mind, and as the recipient was a woman, I think that here the Ascendant and 1st House clearly represent a much higher identity. The sensitive 3rd House Moon and Neptune-ruled Descendant must stand for the recipient. Therefore we can read this directly: the Dragon's Head just in the 12th but close to the Virgo Ascendant says, 'Be humble, develop self-knowledge at the deepest and highest levels, and come to me who calls you.' The conjunction of Sun (ruler of the 11th), Pluto (ruler of the 3rd) and Mercury (ruler of Ascendant and the 10th), asks everybody out there to commit their hearts, minds, identities and goals to that profound, unflagging search for transformation and spiritual serenity. 'Let your possessions be the treasures of deep experience, faith, thought and universal love,' say the rulers of the 9th, 3rd and 8th, and the ruler of the 5th in the 2nd House in Scorpio, 'and throw out everything else that is not worthy, which cannot transform you. Value courage and daring and hold to them; they will take you through every trial back to the Source.'

As the Moon's North Node is so close to the opposition of the Tropical Aries Point, the Draconic pattern opposes the Tropical, only serving to emphasise the importance of the Sun/Mercury/Pluto relationship. But that stellium, and the Ascendant, now stand firmly in Aries, reiterating our theme during the discussion of the meaning of Draco: that Aries – and particularly the nodal origin of a zodiac itself – represents the gateway to and from our divine spiritual origin, whatever name we may give that source and however it may identify itself in a given epoch or culture.

In the Tropical chart, 'I' and 'Thou' are in different houses, different places; 'I' is in itself, a Trinity of Love and Power, while 'Thou' is busy about her personal affairs and involved in creating his society. But at the Draconic level, 'I' and 'Thou' are found in the same house, as Mars and Venus in the 2nd – not closely conjoined, for we *are* not our Source, but linked by Uranus, ruler here of the 11th and perhaps symbol now of the soul group through which we may each ultimately come closer to the Divinity. I do not know why this meeting should be in the 2nd – perhaps it is because here we embrace spiritual *values*, that then make us spiritually *valuable*? But look, Draconic Chiron intimately conjoins Tropical Mars and Uranus; and the symbolism of Chiron runs in so many ways parallel to the story of Christ. Jesus said, 'I and the Father are One', and Chiron, aligning with Mars, still conjoins Draconic Mars from its Tropical position. If the 1st House is the Father, perhaps the 2nd House is the Father as expressed through the Son. At their respective levels in this chart, the axes of the Moon's Nodes, the angles and the equinoxes align closely with the arms of the archetypal Mutable/Cardinal Cross. We can only find our selves and our way by taking up the cross with humility and courage and each following our Example.

An Election Chart – To Open a Healing Clinic

The options were not completely open when this clinic was in the planning stage; for a number of reasons the only viable day for regular healing sessions was a Tuesday, so it would be necessary to find out if a venue existed that was both suitable for the purpose and had no regular bookings so far for that day of the week. Then it could not be hurried,

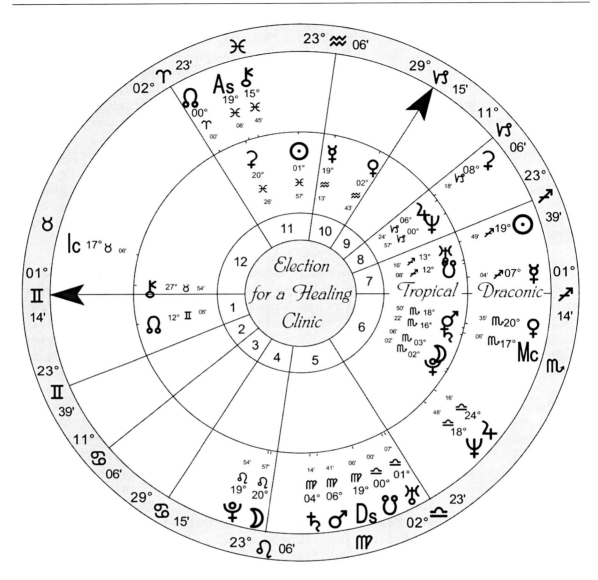

as other commitments had to be honoured before embarking on the project. With all these factors taken into account, it was decided to choose as a starting date a Tuesday when Sun, Moon and outer planets were harmoniously configured – and the nearest date that was clear of commitments offered precisely those conditions. So in a way the day, February 21st 1984, chose itself. And the time? As the clinic was to remain open for as many hours as possible to give as many people as possible the chance to visit in between their other activities, it had to be morning. And, the place being found and booked, it had to be after 9h00 am and at a sensible hour for the sake of those having to keep the books! So the healers settled for 10h00 am.

In many ways, the chart as it stands could hardly be better; we have the sensitive couple shown in the Tropical Sun/Moon water trine, given the power to heal through

Pluto, and Neptune near their midpoint in mutual sextile. There is a full 6th House Scorpio for healing service, for answering deep needs. The idea of self-sacrifice for the well being and enlightenment of others is contained in the 7th House South Node and Uranus in Sagittarius. And felicitously, Venus smiles kindly in the Midheaven, while Chiron the Wounded Healer, and the Teacher, rises.

But did they miss the point? Perhaps here, as an election, the too-soon rule applies? Only 1° of Gemini rises, and after trying to build up local interest and custom for nine months the couple had to close the clinic and return to healing at home. Those who did come benefited greatly, and a few were regular visitors; but people who got better ceased to come, and after a most promising and busy start fewer and fewer dropped in during the day to avail themselves of the 7th House free gift. Donations dwindled, and two well meaning souls found themselves with more time to themselves to catch up on their reading than they had bargained for. The point at issue is Dragon's Head in Gemini in the 1st! It is futile to chase your tail. And the Tail, here, was the clientele.

The chart as a whole is not entirely easy, of course; there are squares between Sun and Chiron/Ascendant, Moon/Pluto and Venus/MC, and Mars/Saturn and Mercury. Plain sailing could not be expected even though most of the hard aspects are separating. It is the Ascendant which closes into its square with the Sun within 1°, suggesting that this, plus the Solar Arc factors, may be indicative of the nine months they managed to stay open. I think the two healers are shown by the Twins on the Ascendant, and so their ruler is Aquarian Mercury, full of aspiring ideals in the 10th but squared by the 6th House Mars/Saturn: the work tended to go from one extreme to the other, either very demanding and tiring mentally and physically, or frustrating and tedious through lack of custom. Patients (the Descendant and its ruler Jupiter in the 8th with Neptune) were on the whole extraordinarily kind, generous souls who deeply appreciated the spiritual healing given – but they were few! Maybe, with Moon ruling the 4th (the venue) in Scorpio with Pluto, the place itself was too tucked away, not obvious enough despite posters and billboards and the flush of initial publicity. Now, even the ruler of the Draconic 4th is in Scorpio! This time the ruler is Venus on the MC, suggesting that, the nature of the place and its work being what it was, even self-publicity should be fairly discreet.

But things that are meant to prosper, do. And here there was a gentle decline. The indications of this inevitable failure are found in the Draconic/Tropical contacts: Draconic Saturn, with Mars, falls opposite the Tropical Pisces Sun, in the 11th, and the Draconic MC, with Venus, is almost exactly conjunct Tropical Scorpio Saturn. Here is the pattern of short-lived success, the lonely struggle to pioneer a new service in the community. Perhaps if the wife (Moon/Pluto in Draconic Leo opposite Tropical Aquarius Mercury) had fulfilled her brief to do more creative advertising? But (and here we can take a hint from astrologer Marc Penfield) she is focussing the Tropical 4th House, and in the end it was she who said they would make better use of their time and achieve more if they abandoned the public clinic and kept strictly to appointments at home. He (Draco Sun Sagittarius here and also in his own chart), naturally wanting to retain the opportunity for people to come and go freely, nevertheless had to agree to give up this ideal for the time being. There is not much option in the end when the ruler of the 11th is in the Dragon's Tail and your own work needs to take priority! Modern commerce assures us that it is possible and desirable to create demand (often a questionable activity) – but it is impossible to create a *need*, unless you yourself are the instrument of deprivation; if it isn't there, it isn't there and you may as well channel your time and resources elsewhere.

Events Heroic

Coincidentally ('merely' or not, according to your persuasion!) both the BBC and British commercial television chose the seventeen days preceding the inner event just described to relaunch two series that had already been run several times and always proved immensely popular – to the extent of each becoming a cult. BBC television began a rerun of *Star Trek* on September 19th 1978, and ITV in the SouthWest started showing *The Prisoner* again on the 1st of October. Most readers will be familiar with *Star Trek* and its famous split infinitive, 'to boldly go where no man has gone before!', and will need little or no introduction to its stars William Shatner and Leonard Nimoy, or its stories of adventure, danger, mystery and soul-searching among the stars on the Starship Enterprise.

The Prisoner

For the benefit of readers in the UK or overseas who may be unacquainted with *The Prisoner* it starred the late Patrick McGoohan, a multi-talented actor well known in the United States and the UK, and concerned the abduction of a man working as a secret agent, his confinement to an extraordinary 'Village' full of intrigue and illusion (plus a very large chess-board and a man-size, lethally self-propelled balloon called Rover) and his repeated attempts to escape or to expose the 'Number One' who controlled and manipulated the entire Village and its population. This identity remained hidden until the very last of many tantalising episodes; his executor, 'Number Two' changed his identity in almost every story. The Prisoner himself is known only as 'Number Six'; his repeated shout of defiance to his captors echoes that of every one of us who has in someone's files become nothing more than a consumer (no longer a customer), a statistic: '*I am not a number! I am a free man!*'

That shout is loud in the chart for the re-run of that first episode! Sagittarius rises, and the Sun/Mercury conjunction stands proud in the Midheaven. The Dragon's Head beckons the Prisoner to freedom in the 9th, alongside the Moon (his attempts at escape were often by sea or aided – naturally! – by a woman); but it is the deceiving Neptune, ruler of the Pisces South Node, that rises and continually ensnares and deludes him, squaring the 9th House Saturn, frustrating his efforts to be free.

With the Descendant-ruler Mercury, he of the dual nature, so closely conjunct the culminating Sun (which in turn disposits the Ascendant-ruler and sextiles it, despite its harassment from the Mars of the 4th/11th House Village) I think I can leave you to work out for yourself the outcome of the Prisoner's trials. Suffice it to say that the entire grouping

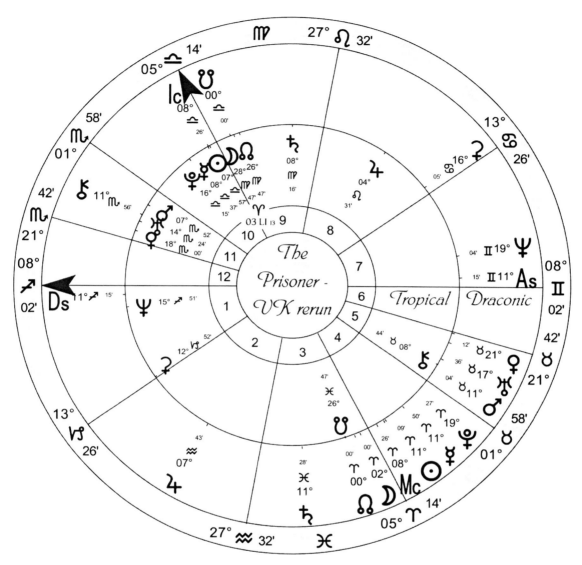

around the MC changes at the Draconic level into Aries, as you might expect, setting the heroic example, and implying what you have probably already guessed by now. The Aries Point at 3°13′ Libra lines up with the Midheaven, Mercury and Sun. The Draco Ascendant is in Gemini. So who is Number One … ?

Star Trek

At the rescreening of *Star Trek* again the Sun was angular, this time in the 7th, and right in the Moon's North Node. The story is once more of man heading in the right direction, now in search not of the dominant 'Number One', but of the Other; for the mission of the *Starship Enterprise* is to seek out new worlds, new beings, new cultures and establish peaceful relations with them.

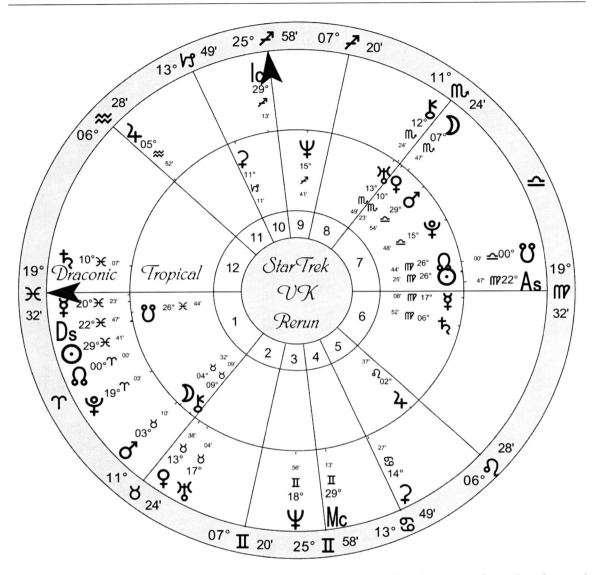

Needless to say. the ship and its crew are constantly threatened with physical disintegration by alien forces and beings, as one would expect with the Dragon's Tail ascending in Pisces! Time after time our heroes are nearly undone in the snares of fantasy and illusion spun for them with insidious skill and intent by the wicked, the envious or the cowardly encountered on their voyages, through Neptune in the 9th, squaring and threatening the Ascendant.

Daydreaming, woolly philosophising, and misplaced idealism will not do on board the *Enterprise,* or off it. Practical discipline, precision and discrimination are essential to the success of the mission and to the crew's survival. These are the Tropical, Virgoan criteria set for character and behaviour. But the higher motivations and purposes shown by the Draconic take us back into Pisces! Even the Sun with the Dragon's Head is just in the sign. And Mars, already in Tropical Libra in the 7th, goes into 3° of the other Venus sign, Taurus, to align with the Tropical Moon. If ever there was a mission of universal goodwill …! Draconic Pisces is the mystic, the sensitive, the idealist, the healer. The Draconic Scorpio Moon conjunct Tropical Venus/Uranus intensifies and emphasises this, as well as indicating the courage and determination to be tested and not found wanting in any encounter, no matter how harrowing.

The women on the ship, the efficient, supportive 'Yeomen', are shown in the Earth trine of Moon in the 2nd, Saturn in the 6th; but beware of the seductresses of the Moon's square to 5th House Jupiter and opposite the Scorpio Venus! They are part of the test; Draconic Moon in Scorpio with Venus is pure temptation, sent to strengthen the modern space-age Argonauts by their repeated and laudable refusal to succumb. The presence of Draconic

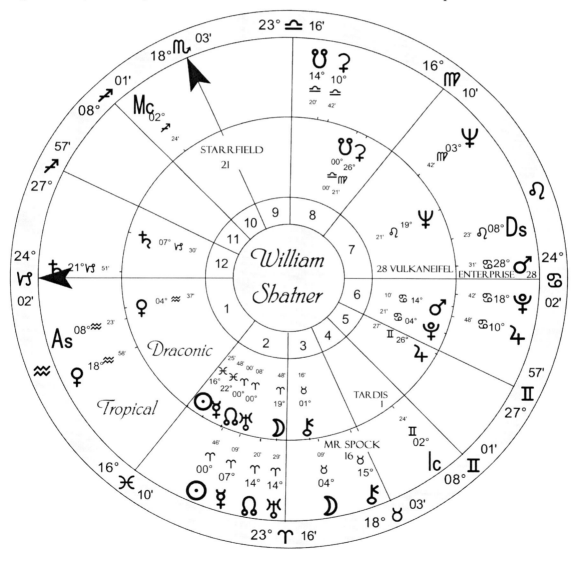

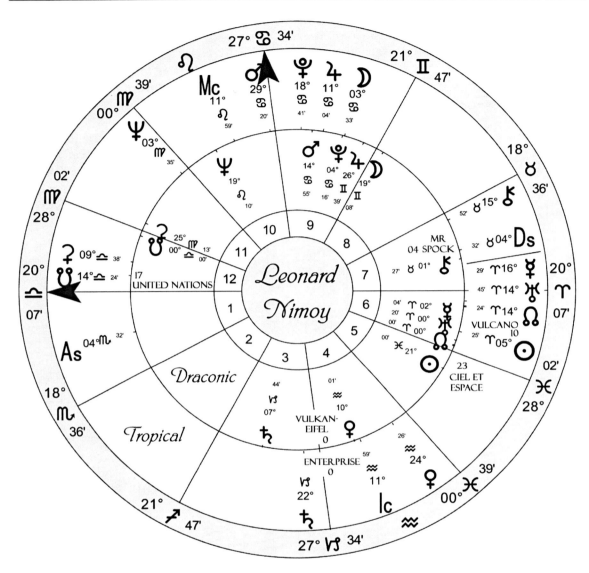

Sun and Mercury on the Tropical Ascendant and South Node testify to their collective resolve: to identify with universal ideals and mankind's great dreams, and work them out in practice whenever and wherever this is required in order to honour principle and spiritual debt.

And look where those principles lie! In the two hearts of the principal actors, William Shatner and Leonard Nimoy, playing Captain Kirk and his Vulcan side-kick Mr Spock. They were born only four days apart in March 1931, with all that joint Tropical Sun-Aries drive and vocation to play the hero, all their beliefs centred on the universal and the dream, on the same axis of Draconic Sun-Pisces. With Draconic Uranus conjunct the Sun, Tropical Mars on a Draconic angle and both the maverick Chirons interdimensionally angular, their task is to awaken the hero in us all. Their destiny aboard the *Enterprise* is written in the heavens: the Tropical asteroid *Enterprise* is on a Draconic angle in both charts – on William Shatner's Descendant, and on Leonard Nimoy's IC. Both have the Sun bodily conjunct *Interkosmos* and *Kapteynia*, and of course both were principal officers on the bridge of the starship. But William Shatner also has *James* on his Sun! ... as he heads into the *Starrfield* in his Midheaven, accompanied by Tropical *Mr. Spock* at his Draconic IC (with Tropical *TARDIS* ... the deceptively spacious craft of Doctor Who, launched three years before *Star Trek*, in 1963) and *Vulkaneifel* on his 7th cusp. As you might expect, this same asteroid is on Nimoy's IC; and Draconic *Mr. Spock* lines up neatly with his Tropical Descendant – opposite *United Nations*, which is his rising asteroid. *Vulcano* itself is conjunct his Sun, albeit a little wide, and opposite is *Stargazer*. The universe figures dramatically in Leonard Nimoy's chart (he has spent his life unfolding its wonders to the public through drama and documentary): we also find Tropical *Astronomia* close to his Draconic Descendant,

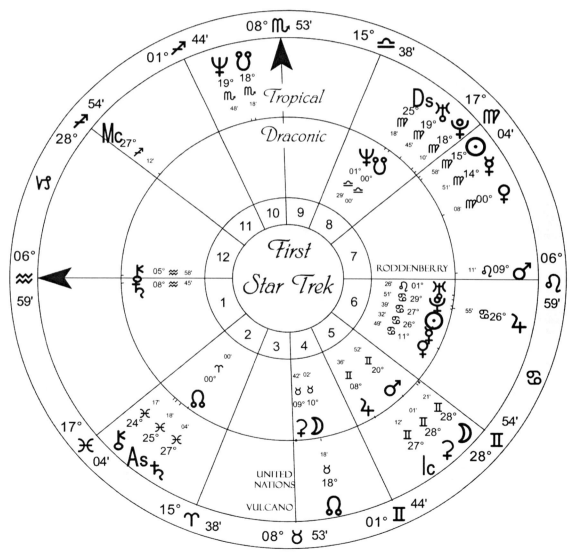

with *Spacewatch* opposite, and Tropical *Cieletespace* on his Draconic Pisces Sun. Gene Roddenberry who created *Star Trek* is also definitely present at both births – his asteroid is opposite Nimoy's Moon, and from its Sidereal position of 6° Sagittarius *Roddenberry* conjoins William Shatner's Tropical MC.

When this was first written I had no idea when Star Trek was first broadcast in the US; however, this data eventually came to light. That momentous event on NBC television happened on September 8th 1966 at 19h30 PDT in Los Angeles, and here for your delectation is the inceptional chart, focussed on Draco. Here as we would have hoped is the imagery of that great communal leap into the unknown with all its attendant dangers – Draconic Chiron and Saturn rising in Aquarius, opposed by Draconic Uranus and the Tropical Leo Mars. The Tropical Virgo stellium of Mercury/Sun/Pluto/Uranus translates to Draconic Cancer: the crew are a close and mutually dependent family, the starship is their only home. The Draconic Moon and Ceres *in coelo* at the IC, the women on board, bring stability, nurture and comfort into a constantly changing, often volatile environment; the Tropical pattern is almost completely mutable.

The Asteroids of the very first *Star Trek* are, again, spectacular! Setting at that moment is its creator's own asteroid *Roddenberry* at Draconic 8° Leo; *Chekhov* is nearby at Leo 4° together with *Jean-Luc* (anticipating Picard in *The Next Generation*) and *Stargazer*, with *Starr* at Leo 6°. These all line up on the Draconic Descendant

First Star Trek - Draconic asteroids

Name	Long.	Trav.	Lat.	R.A.	Decl.
* Chekhov 2369	04°♌40	+00°24'	+01°33'	174°10'	+04°12'
☌ ♅ 3°13' S	☍ ⚷ 1°17' A		☍ As 2°19' S		☌ Ds 2°19' S
* Enterprise 9777	21°♊09	+00°20'	+00°06'	131°56'	+17°59'
☌ ♂ 0°16' A					
* Interkosmos 2365	14°♏39	+00°06'	+01°04'	273°13'	-22°20'
* James 2335	12°♍43	+00°23'	-15°13'	203°03'	-26°02'
* Jean-Luc 9531	04°♌43	+00°24'	+00°17'	173°43'	+03°01'
☌ ♅ 3°16' S	☍ ⚷ 1°14' A		☍ As 2°16' S		☌ Ds 2°16' S
* Kapteynia 818	12°♊36	+00°19'	+07°54'	125°04'	+27°40'
☌ ♃ 3°59' S					
* Kelly 22312	29°♊33	+00°35'	-16°41'	135°16'	-00°27'
* Kirkpatrick 9902	00°♌27	+00°31'	-03°30'	168°18'	+01°12'
☌ ☉ 2°48' A	☌ ☿ 3°55' A		☌ ♅ 0°58' A		☌ ♇ 0°36' S
* Leonardo 3000	29°♋13	+00°24'	-01°05'	168°07'	+03°55'
☌ ☉ 1°34' A	☌ ☿ 2°41' A		☌ ♅ 2°13' A		☌ ♇ 0°37' A
* McCoy 4259	21°♌27	+00°22'	+01°31'	189°34'	-02°28'
* Mr. Spock 2309	12°♑03 R	-00°11'	+00°37'	332°13'	-10°45'
☍ ♀ 0°14' A					
* Pickard 5716	24°♍49	+00°19'	-00°34'	220°30'	-16°20'
* Roddenberry 4659	08°♌13	+00°23'	+00°36'	177°04'	+01°56'
☍ ♄ 0°31' A	☍ ⚷ 2°15' S		☍ As 1°14' A		☌ Ds 1°14' A
* Scotti 3594	20°♊37	+00°25'	+08°12'	133°45'	+25°56'
☌ ♂ 0°15' S					
* Skytel 3243	06°♒06 R	-00°12'	+00°23'	354°43'	-01°51'
☌ ♄ 2°39' S	☌ ⚷ 0°07' A		☌ As 0°53' S		☍ Ds 0°53' S
* Stargazer 8958	04°♌23	+00°23'	-00°22'	173°09'	+02°32'
☌ ♅ 2°56' S	☍ ⚷ 1°34' A		☍ As 2°35' S		☌ Ds 2°35' S
* Starr 4150	06°♌31	+00°26'	+01°53'	176°00'	+03°47'
☍ ♄ 2°14' A	☍ ⚷ 0°32' S		☍ As 0°28' S		☌ Ds 0°28' S
* United Nations ...	18°♓49	+00°01'	-13°31'	039°09'	+01°05'
* Vulcano 4464	19°♓17	+00°00'	+00°31'	035°04'	+14°32'
* Vulkaneifel 4611	24°♊22	+00°25'	+00°38'	135°20'	+17°37'
☌ ♂ 3°29' A	// ♇ 0°09' S				
* Xenophanes 6026	23°♐52 R	-00°07'	+03°59'	313°30'	-13°18'
☍ ♂ 2°59' A					
* Xenophon 5986	12°♉18	+00°19'	-01°35'	090°40'	+21°51'
☌ ☽ 2°16' A	☌ ⚳ 2°36' S		☍ Mc 3°25' A		☌ Ic 3°25' A

First Star Trek - Tropical asteroids

Name	Long.	Trav.	Lat.	R.A.	Decl.
* Chekhov 2369	22°♍59	+00°24'	+01°33'	219°22'	-13°44'
☌ ♅ 3°13' S	☍ ⚷ 1°17' A		☍ As 2°19' S		☌ Ds 2°19' S
* Enterprise 9777	09°♌28	+00°20'	+00°06'	178°00'	+00°58'
☌ ♂ 0°16' A					
* Interkosmos 2365	02°♑58	+00°06'	+01°04'	323°19'	-13°23'
* James 2335	01°♏02	+00°23'	-15°13'	256°53'	-38°11'
* Jean-Luc 9531	23°♍02	+00°24'	+00°17'	219°00'	-14°58'
☌ ♅ 3°16' S	☍ ⚷ 1°14' A		☍ As 2°16' S		☌ Ds 2°16' S
* Kapteynia 818	00°♌55	+00°19'	+07°54'	173°15'	+11°31'
☌ ♃ 3°59' S					
* Kelly 22312	17°♌52	+00°35'	-16°41'	178°49'	-17°44'
# ♇ 0°02' A					
* Kirkpatrick 9902	18°♍46	+00°31'	-03°30'	213°32'	-17°11'
☌ ☉ 2°48' A	☌ ☿ 3°55' A		☌ ♅ 0°58' A		☌ ♇ 0°36' S
# ☊ 0°05' A	// ☋ 0°05' A				
* Leonardo 3000	17°♍32	+00°24'	-01°05'	213°10'	-14°30'
☌ ☉ 1°34' A	☌ ☿ 2°41' A		☌ ♅ 2°13' A		☌ ♇ 0°37' A
* McCoy 4259	09°♎46	+00°22'	+01°31'	236°10'	-18°15'
* Mr. Spock 2309	00°♓22 R	-00°11'	+00°37'	017°00'	+07°54'
☍ ♀ 0°14' A					
* Pickard 5716	13°♏08	+00°19'	-00°34'	271°35'	-24°00'
* Roddenberry 4659	26°♍32	+00°23'	+00°36'	222°34'	-15°42'
☍ ♄ 0°31' A	☍ ⚷ 2°15' S		☍ As 1°14' A		☌ Ds 1°14' A
* Scotti 3594	08°♌56	+00°25'	+08°12'	180°46'	+08°37'
☌ ♂ 0°15' S					
* Skytel 3243	24°♓25 R	-00°12'	+00°23'	040°09'	+16°02'
☌ ♄ 2°39' S	# ♆ 0°00' A		☌ ⚷ 0°07' A		☌ As 0°53' S
☍ Ds 0°53' S					
* Stargazer 8958	22°♍42	+00°23'	-00°22'	218°28'	-15°30'
☌ ♅ 2°56' S	☍ ⚷ 1°34' A		☍ As 2°35' S		☌ Ds 2°35' S
* Starr 4150	24°♍49	+00°26'	+01°53'	221°16'	-13°59'
☍ ♄ 2°14' A	☍ ⚷ 0°32' S		☍ As 0°28' S		☌ Ds 0°28' S
* United Nations ...	07°♉07	+00°01'	-13°31'	085°30'	+09°51'
* Vulcano 4464	07°♉36	+00°00'	+00°31'	085°31'	+23°54'
* Vulkaneifel 4611	12°♌41	+00°25'	+00°38'	181°10'	+00°11'
☌ ♂ 3°29' A					
* Xenophanes 6026	12°♒11 R	-00°07'	+03°59'	358°52'	+03°51'
☍ ♂ 2°59' A					
* Xenophon 5986	00°♋37	+00°19'	-01°35'	140°51'	+13°38'
☌ ☽ 2°16' A	☌ ⚳ 2°36' S		☍ Mc 3°25' A		☌ Ic 3°25' A

with Tropical *Scotti* at 8° Leo and Tropical *Enterprise* at Leo 9° Boldly Going with Mars! Tropical *United Nations* and *Vulcano*, both at Tropical 7° Taurus, grace the Draconic IC (close to an exact Sidereal conjunction of *Spacewatch* and *Starrfield* at Taurus 12°) to bring an eclectic mix of intergalactic passengers and crew on board, including of course the Vulcan, Mr. Spock. His own asteroid, *Mr. Spock*, is found right on the Draconic Ascendant, connected from Sidereal 6° Aquarius. *Leonardo*, for actor Leonard Nimoy, is conjunct the Sun *in coelo*; in his Draconic position he meets with a happy conjunction of Tropical *Kapteynia* and Draconic *Kirkpatrick* – Captain Kirk! Wonderful.

Back to Number Six …

We have taken a look at two Draconic Pisces heroes; what about McGoohan? Here is our third March birthday (March 19th 1928, three years and three days before William Shatner was born), for a man described once as 'a rebel with a romantic streak.' Now, the relationship of this actor to his vehicle is fascinating, quite different to the foregoing. His psychology as shown by the Tropical pattern is indeed that of a restless, idiosyncratic romantic, very subjective in his overall approach to life and needing a lot of personal space. We find Draconic stellia in Capricorn and Sagittarius, and Tropical Saturn in the area of the South Node – all suggestive of someone who has learned a high degree of control and self-sufficiency, and who is just as happy, if not more so, communing with nature in a silent wilderness as sharing that peace with others. There seems to be an overall theme of privacy and independence in which to be free to fantasise, to invent.

The chart for the repeat screening of *The Prisoner* shows not only that tempting South Node nearly touching his Pisces Sun, but his own South Node is focussed by the Sagittarian Ascendant and dissembling Neptune! So his own Dragon's Head aligns with *The Prisoner*'s Descendant in Gemini, and the *The Prisoner*'s Aries Point falls directly opposite McGoohan's Uranus. If there is message and meaning in all this for the principal actor, it is 'Become other than you are! The only way out of the prison you have made for yourself in your determination to be free is to reunite with the Other and thereby discover your true identity.'

McGoohan's Draconic Sun is in Capricorn: first he has to experience the Prison … even so close to the Aries Point (at Capricorn 17°19'). And crowning his Tropical Midheaven, as a promise of the fruits to come, is the Draconic conjunction of his Ascendant and Mars – the planet found in the 12th House of his chart, the Free Man in the fantastic Prison. This Ascendant and MC are 1° conjunct the Ascendant of *The Prisoner*'s chart, in Sagittarius 7° –'*I am a free man!*' The cry is echoed by his own Tropical Ascendant in Aquarius, and its attendant Draconic Chiron.

In making an escape from (professional) restrictions, McGoohan was during his earthly life at least as active as his alter ego; nor did he fail to recognise the particular importance of the 4th House – his private life at home – in balancing and refreshing his public life as a cult hero. Saturn in the Dragon's Tail in the 10th did not trap him (it rules the Tropical 12th); after a series of frustrations he struck out on his own as a freelance and remained so to the end of his earthly life, his own man, a free man, completely in charge – Number One.

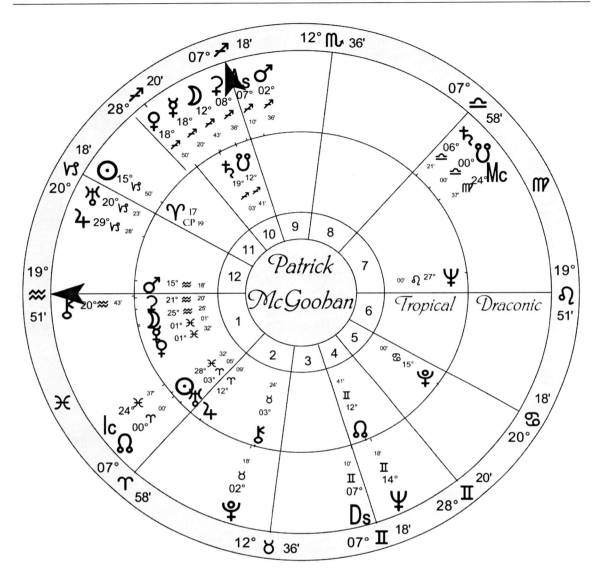

Before leaving this chapter and its exotic theme, I couldn't resist showing you the chart for the first ever episode of Doctor Who, briefly mentioned earlier. Doctor Who was – and is still! – a Time Lord, who can never die but only regenerate into a new body with its new personality while retaining total awareness of who he is and what he (as hero) must do. The broadcast (the day after the assassination of President John F. Kennedy) is said to have been delayed by nine minutes, but not so; the delay was a mere 80 seconds, and the transmission time 5h16pm GMT. The accuracy of this time is confirmed by the necessary presence of asteroid TARDIS on an angle – in this case radix Tropical TARDIS on the Dwad Pisces Ascendant; it appears nowhere special at all in the later chart. The other word we really need to stand out in this chart is 'Doctor'. Apart from one recently-named pebble, Dr.G., whose position I have no means of computing, the only asteroid among all the flying shingle that qualifies is DoctorWatson. And it is conjunct the Sun by only 2°09'. 'I am The

Doctor.' Not only is he the Doctor, the maverick alien traveller of Tropical Sagittarian Sun/ Draconic Chiron-Uranus/Pluto, but with his Draconic Leo Sun opposite Tropical Saturn, indeed a Lord of Time! … And a powerful one: he has not one but *four* major alignments with the charismatic, regenerative and godlike Uranus/Pluto, three of them including Chiron; that with the Tropical Sun, above; Sidereal Uranus/Pluto-Chiron with the Tropical IC-MC; Tropical Uranus/Pluto-Chiron stretched across the Draconic horizon; and Tropical Dwad Pluto exactly on the Tropical radix MC. Also in the Tropical wheel Dwad Uranus joins the Descendant (see page 347 for information on Dwads). High in the sky, embracing the Midheaven with Saturn is the Moon, approaching her first quarter. The Doctor will never 'get the Girl'; she is Tropical Aquarius – bright, enterprising, a people person; she is often a whole city full of people, sometimes a world. But as Draconic Scorpio she must always battle and suffer in order for her salvation to be won by the Doctor, the Solar hero who in turn must always leave her. What a moment to give life to a legend!

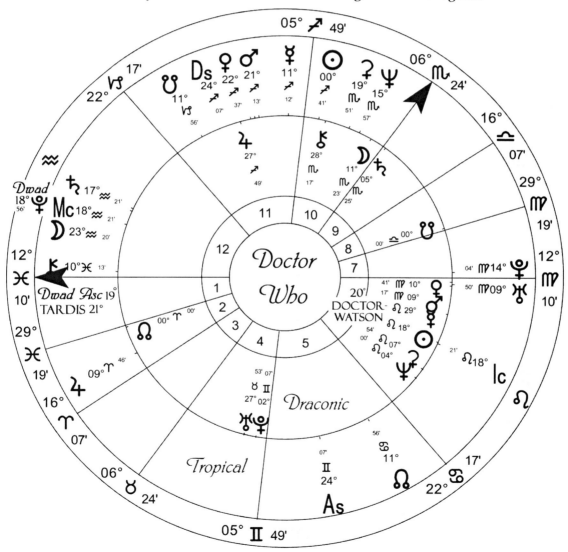

Chapter Twelve

The Draconic Pattern in Transits

It must be remembered that the Draconic level of astrology constantly coexists with the Tropical; it would be nonsensical to limit its application to the natal chart. Fully aware, now, of the higher activity of the human being, we must look to its stimuli. Normally, we go to our ephemeris to examine the transit patterns for the current date at a chosen moment; now we must either translate these patterns into Draconic, or make use of a specially prepared Draconic ephemeris. It has never been easier to do this, since in the past few decades so much good software has been written to facilitate charting in almost any chosen zodiac including Draconic – and indeed in any chosen harmonic. (We can now include the Dwad here, as Solar Fire Deluxe and Gold have a Vedic module enabling precise Divisional Charts to be made in not only the Sidereal but any zodiac you choose, specifically the Dwadashamsha.) Printed Draconic ephemerides are readily available as output from most of the major programs.

What we have to do now is to look at Tropical transits to both levels of the chart, and also at the Draconic transits to both levels. We started to do this on a small scale in earlier chapters. It seems reasonable to infer that while the familiar Tropical transits indicate conditions impinging on us which have their source in the knowable world, and which will naturally have their prime impact on the personality, the Draconic transiting pattern is of a higher order and may bring into our lives collective issues for us to deal with, spiritual promptings, or otherwise human and comprehensible events which nevertheless are charged with a special and vital significance (probably karmic) in the individual life. Sometimes we encounter situations that serve as reminders of our higher calling, our deeper drives, which we may have neglected. Those standing by, who notice, say 'Do you think Life is trying to tell him something?' The Draconic transits can act on the Draconic level, spurring it to action. They can also stimulate the effort to achieve self-knowing and self-realisation within the compass of the personality at the Tropical level. There is a suggestion of inevitability in the Draconic transits, where we might judge the Tropical transits as more fortuitous; as if the higher self takes over for a while and elects to unlock possibilities previously barred, or to put its foot down firmly on a familiar activity or attitude – and the lower self has little option but to comply. Learn about Draconic transits by watching your own as closely as you can; also those affecting other people whose lives are sufficiently open to you. Here are several examples to give you the flavour of what is happening.

It would be nonsense to write a volume on Draconic astrology without including the chart for the very lecture which introduced it for the very first time to me and to many other astrologers in the audience at Churchill College, Cambridge, on 3rd September 1977, at 5h30 pm. It has the distinction of being one of the nicest charts in the collection, a splendid advertisement for its own thesis! And it substantiates two other controversial factors into the bargain. Not only is asteroid *Urania*, Muse of the Astrologer, riding high on the MC, but it draws the opposing Moon, reactionary in Taurus, into a powerful alignment with 9th House Scorpio Uranus and Chiron in the 3rd, once these are transposed into the Draconic.

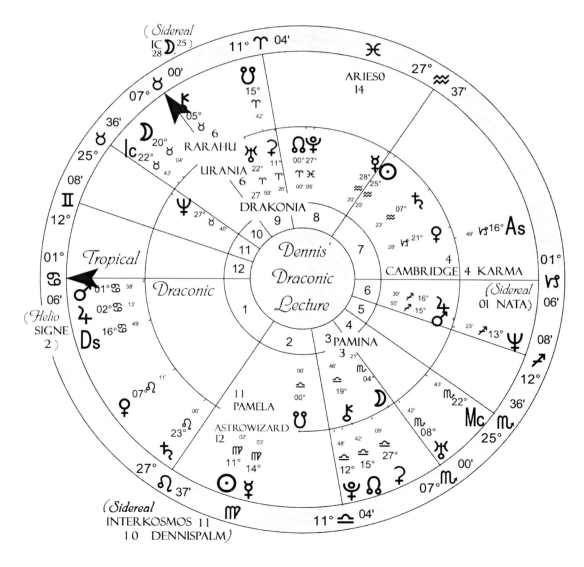

(This is why I have again chosen to place the Draconic chart at the centre of the bi-wheel.) Not only this, but *Tropical Rarahu* (exact) and *Tropical Drakonia* (wide, at 12°55' Scorpio) line up brilliantly with this important, purposive meridian that includes one very interested listener – *Pamina* conjunct the Moon! *Arieso* (Aries 0) configures equally impressively with Sun, Mercury and Draconic *Pamela*. *Cambridge* is setting, its Draconic degree joined by Tropical Karma and Sidereal Nata. With the Draconic Ascendant is Helio Signe. Draconic Drakonia takes its place in history at the Sidereal IC. Was there ever such a dramatic and descriptive pattern for bringing to the world's attention a profound, practical new Node-based astrology, a transformative teaching? I don't know how many Pams there were in the audience that afternoon with Draconic Dennispalm transiting their 7th cusp, but this one definitely got the message! Please note Tropical Mars on the Draconic Ascendant: the entire theme of Dennis Elwell's lecture was draconically active Mars. These double charts show you what the moment is *about*.

Because Scorpio rising people are rather private individuals, I will refrain from going into too many details at this point and simply observe that this lecture was clearly one of the more important things that Dennis came into this life to do, if one reads the pattern correctly, as this entire constellation aligns with his own horizon, Draconic *Urania,* and Nodal axis … and rising *Aries0/Pamina*, and 'setting' Draconic *Drakonia/Cambridge/Pamela*; and moreover, the Draconic Sun and Mercury of the lecture embrace his own Tropical Sun. Dennis also has natal Draconic *Rarahu* between his Tropical Aquarian Mercury and Mars. He was bound to come to that point in his life where his own fascination with Draconic astrology culminated in a Cambridge lecture that would catch the ear of at least one keen pupil going by the name of Pamela.

The lecture's Tropical Sun, on the other hand, was widely conjunct my own Draconic natal Sun, and the thought-provoking Sun/Mercury/Tropical Saturn alignment was shaking up the Nodes and Chiron. The Aries Point and Tropical Mercury fell on Draconic Mercury, and the major alignment coincided with my Aries Point. Taking these and other factors into consideration, the time seems to have been right for a positive response. If this event chart were of a person, I would say that they not only stood for the vision of the New Age, for the awakened intelligence, the self-aware individual with global concern, and for the deeper, cathartic understanding of the soul's history (Draconic Scorpio Moon on the IC), but were capable of putting astrology to work in the healing and enlightening of suffering people, and showing them how to build on the foundation of their past experience a more secure and happy future. They would be detached and circumspect in their deep probing, but possessed of a wonderful vigour and enthusiasm (Mars/Jupiter on Draconic Ascendant). They would be capable of simplicity, single-mindedness, staying power, and unique insight (1st/7th patterns). And these are the qualities of Draco. And with all its crucial asteroids so commandingly placed, inevitably they would use it!

'Significant relationships in the life are usually those which have previously been established in a past incarnation … positions … translated … into … the Draconic zodiac … may show through their cross-aspects to other nativities those contacts which have been carried over from a previous incarnation.'

Ronald C. Davison, *Synastry*

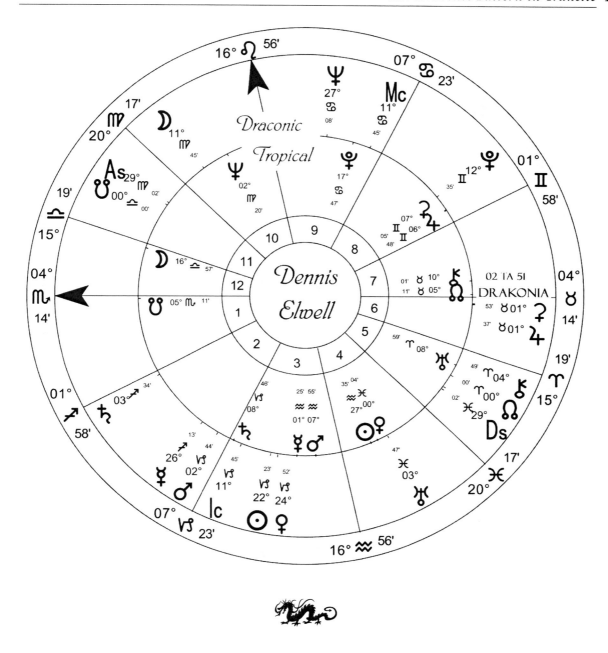

Young Man at a Crossroads

As far as Zerda knew, she was born in the morning of July 12th 1930. The exact time became an issue of some importance, however, when she entered the world of astrology, and eventually she settled on a rectified time of 6h51 am GMT, with an MC of 4° Taurus and 19° Leo Ascending. The Dragon's Head thus lies close to the MC, in Aries in the 9th, the tail in Libra in the 3rd near the IC. This, together with Chiron squaring the ascendant from

18° Taurus, has ensured that her life has had more than its fair share of challenge and trial, and the keys to this lie in the interaction between the Draconic and Tropical elements of her pattern.

What do we find? An exact Sun/Pluto conjunction close to the exact Mercury/Uranus square from Cancer to Aries, tied in to the Chiron/Ascendant square at the Draconic level, all emphasising the involvement in caring for someone plunged suddenly into the trauma of suffering and finding her own emotional and spiritual strength and courage through the crisis. Additionally, Draconic Mars falls in 29° Aries in exact alignment with the Moon's North Node in its 6° square with the Moon, and this in turn is found in Draco Capricorn and closely conjunct 5th House Saturn – typical of the woman who must find her way alone for much of her life and bear a burden for her children. The placing of Sun/Pluto/

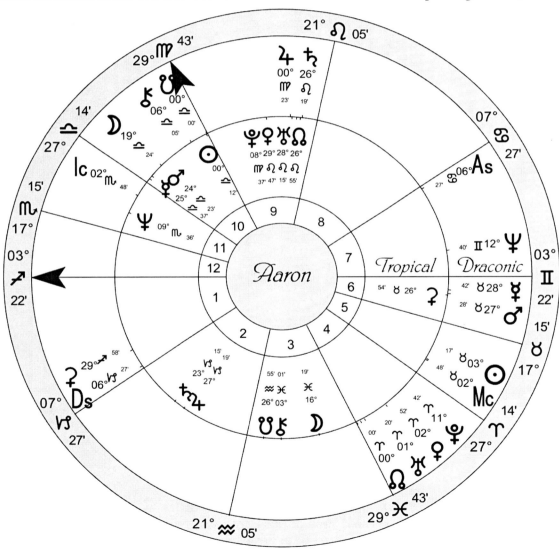

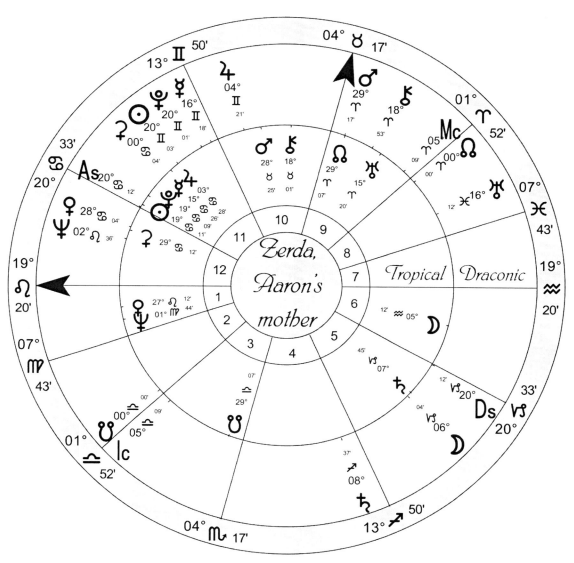

Mercury in Draconic Gemini indicates a rôle that is communicative and/or locomotive. Her son Aaron was born on September 23rd 1961 at 12h45 pm BST in Ramsgate, Kent. A tight square of Mercury/Mars in Libra to Saturn/Jupiter in Capricorn hovered rather close to Zerda's Nodal and Sun/Pluto axes and picked up their midpoints. A Venus/Uranus/ Chiron opposition aligned with her own Venus/Neptune conjunction and squared her Mars, and tied into this was the Nodal axis itself, in Leo/Aquarius, across the 9th and 3rd Houses. From this alone, one might well suspect that this son would bring problems into his mother's life through some difficulty in controlling or manifesting mental or physical activity in some way. The suspicion is confirmed when we look at the transits (for this is what they are, as well as being the synastry between mother and son!) involving Draco.

Aaron's birth Ascendant, when transposed to Draconic, lines up precisely with Zerda's Draconic Moon/Tropical Saturn, indicating that here is the child who is destined to test her patience, her practical organising ability, and also her wisdom and generosity, for Tropical Jupiter opposes her Saturn at her birth, and is close to Aaron's Draco Ascendant. Equally striking and pointed is the tight conjunction of the Draco Mercury/Mars of this birth with Zerda's own Tropical Mars at the end of Taurus, the Tropical Pisces Moon on her Draconic Uranus, and Draconic Chiron conjunct her Draconic IC. The Tropical Sun/Tropical MC/Draconic Venus/Draconic Uranus axis in Aaron's chart falls quite close to his mother's Draconic MC/IC. Thus are the elements of the unusual, the unexpected, the vigorous or violent, the courageous, picked out between the two maps. The one remaining part of the pattern which we have not looked at so far is the crowning of Zerda's Tropical MC in Taurus by her son's Draconic Sun/MC – and it is this which turns out to determine the timing of the events that were to put mother and son to the test.

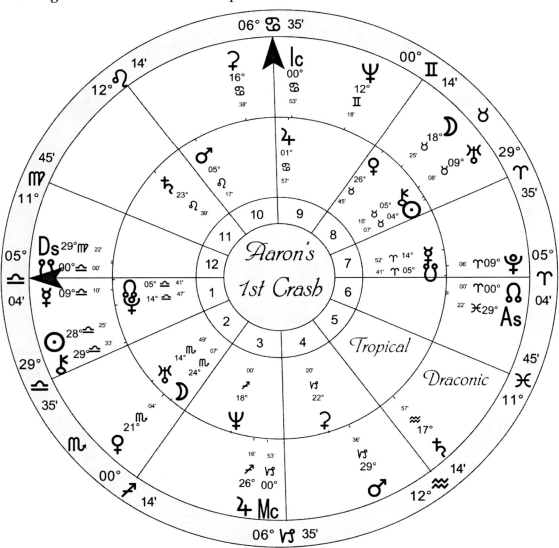

For it was on April 24th 1978 at about 5h15 pm BST, with the Sun in 4° Taurus right on that double MC and Aaron's Draconic Sun, that he was involved in a crash with a car at a crossroads not far from his home. The consequences for Aaron were not serious on this occasion; but, exactly one year later, on April 25th 1979, at roughly 12h30 pm BST, with the Sun standing in 4° Taurus again, it happened a second time. The difference was that Aaron's motorbike collided with a car coming from his right at the junction instead of his left – and the accident broke his back. One day Zerda was the mother of a strapping young adult working up to leaving home and leading a fully independent life; and the next she found herself with a stricken 17-year-old, full of ambition and drive utterly frustrated, dependent on her emotional and practical support, battling to come to terms with his perpetual wound in the paralysis of his lower body and a life on wheels that he did not anticipate.

Look again at his chart: like his mother, he has the square of Chiron to the Ascendant – and his is in the 3rd House, nor far from the South Node, and the Draconic Chiron also makes a wide link with the Tropical Libra Sun. The meaning of two lives is tied in to this double event, so what was going on by transit? The chart of the first crash gave solemn enough warning, in the Sun/Chiron conjunction square Mars affecting Zerda's MC/Moon square, her Draconic Moon/Tropical Saturn and Jupiter and Aaron's Draconic Ascendant/Descendant. This was picked out by the Tropical MC/IC of the collision. Their Tropical Mars/Draconic Mars/Mercury conjunction was focussed by the Tropical Moon and Venus in Taurus, and the sensitive axis of her Tropical Nodes and Draconic Mars to his Tropical Mercury/Mars triggered by the Draconic Sun/Chiron at the end of Libra. That powerful early Libra/Aries axis of theirs right on the horizon with the Moon's Nodes had already been marked by an eclipse one month before. The conjunction of Tropical Moon and Draconic Venus set off Zerda's Chiron/Ascendant square from its Draconic position in Scorpio.

So why was the outcome not immediately disastrous? I think the answer lies in the crash pattern itself; for the meaning of this event, in its own right, will be found in its own Tropical/Draco interactions – and here we find an angular Jupiter brought into further prominence by contact with the Draconic IC. Because of this, the purpose of the crash is to witness a relatively lucky escape on this occasion for the lad whose Draconic Ascendant conjoins that contact; and with the Draconic Venus/Tropical Moon conjunct Uranus, and Tropical Descendant conjunct Aaron's own Draconic Venus/Uranus, we can almost hear the quick sigh of relief that no tragedy had occurred. Nothing more threatening than Jupiter lay square to the Ascendant that day. But on April 25th, one year later, it was a very different story. Yes, he was lucky not to die – and we again find Jupiter at work on an angle, this time Draconic Jupiter on the Tropical Descendant and Draco Descendant with Aaron's Tropical Venus/Uranus; but he had come to a cross in the sky as well as his crossroads, for lying in wait for him that lunchtime were the afflicting planets of his birth.

The Ascendant was moving in a separating orb from its square with Chiron to close another with Uranus; and the destiny locked into this moment is made poignantly clear by the alignment of Draconic Sun/Chiron to the Tropical Uranus and of Draconic IC to Tropical Chiron. Aaron's angular Draconic Mars is echoed by the Draconic Mars/Tropical

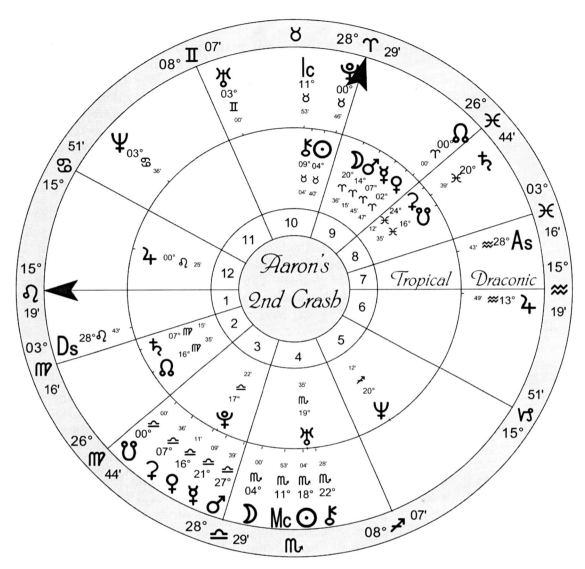

IC of the accident, opposed by the powerful Draconic Pluto on the Tropical MC, this entire axis striking yet again at the vital late Aries/Libra contacts between mother and son. The angles are in fact very close to Zerda's own; and nearby in 4° Scorpio we find the Draconic Moon, on her Tropical IC and close to that of the accident, opposite the Tropical Sun and her boy's Draconic Sun/MC, drawing the man and the woman in the drama into close and purposeful relationship whose difficult, lonely and karmic nature is shown by the Draconic Saturn in the Moon's South Node. Aaron's own South Node and Chiron are focussed by the Draconic Ascendant of the crash: the suffering to be endured and conquered is clear in the strong Draconic Scorpio – no Draconic Sun in Libra this time.

Look into these patterns and you will find more and more. The main elements were duly honoured in the joint struggle of mother and son which made of a wheelchair a useful and familiar extension of Aaron's body, created a home in which he could move with considerable freedom and independence, and ultimately enabled this young man with his strong need to achieve to involve himself again with vehicles and start running his own business from converted buildings on his mother's land. For her, it has been a test of love, ingenuity and patience; for him, a test of determination, practicality and staying power. For both, it has been tremendously hard work and a mutual fulfilling of spiritual obligation. For the astrology, one could not find a finer example of the way in which patterns of destiny gather to a head at the denser and subtler levels of human experience, to fulfil the purposes of earthly life and relationship.

'Say not, "I have found the truth," but rather, "I have found a truth." Say not, "I have found the path of the soul." Say rather, "I have met the soul walking upon my path." For the soul walks upon all paths. The soul walks not upon a line, neither does it grow like a reed. The soul unfolds itself, like a lotus of countless petals.'

Kahlil Gibran, *The Prophet*

Chapter Thirteen

The Draconic Solar Return
A Birthday Surprise!

By now you will have realised that there is nothing that you can do with Tropical astrology that you cannot do with Draconic astrology (except the Ebertin approach to midpoint analysis which takes relatively little account of zodiacal placing in its emphasis on interplanetary dynamics, and thus stands aloof from their dimensional context) and it will come as no surprise that we can draw up the Draconic Solar Return.

By this I do not mean the translation of the familiar Solar Return (or any other Return chart for that matter) into its Draconic form; I mean precisely the Draconic Solar Return – the return of the Draconic Sun to the exact degree and minute of its natal Draconic placing. As the Moon's North Node retrogrades through the Tropical zodiac at a rate of more or less 0°03′ of arc per day, it follows that this return is not going to occur neatly once a year; it will come up once every 11½ months or so (depending on the use of the Mean or the True Node to determine the Draconic Sun). Now that Draconic ephemerides are readily available the task of finding this return date and time has become much easier – especially important, as the motion of planets, Sun and Moon each day in the True Draconic zodiac, with the continual changes of direction and speed of its starting point in relation to the Earth, is so variable over the course of a few days. Some programs, notably Solar Fire, automatically calculate and display Draconic Solar Returns, True or Mean according to choice, making the astrologer's task effortless.

Work on this form of Return has established reasonably firmly that it is actually the True Node that we must use in our calculations. The Mean return and the True return fall close together in time, often only a few hours apart; but so far the True Return is eloquent of the events that stamp their import on the coming year, the Mean Return far less so. This is readily observed from planetary alignments to the angles of the Return chart. One thing that I do not include, but which would be worth looking at, is a strictly critical comparison of the Draconic Solar with the Tropical Solar. While Tropical Returns have always been of interest, they do not always seem to carry the drama of the Draconic charts; these may indeed be the patterns of the central events of our lives as active souls, those encounters and experiences we have chosen and therefore fated for ourselves at various stages of our earthly development. The examples that follow will serve to illustrate this point.

The Draconic Solar Return: Calculation

1. Not an easy task initially; if you don't have access to a Draconic ephemeris the date in the relevant year on which the Draconic position of the Sun falls conjunct its natal place must be found by painstaking inspection. It is made simpler if you first look at your natal Sun/Node relationship as an arc which may even be expressed as an aspect, and this may make the repeated relationship easier to see.

2. Once you have found the date, make sure you have worked out your Draconic Sun to the second of accuracy – which means similar starting accuracy of the True Node. As Neil Michelsen's positions for the True Node are given to the 10th of a minute (i.e. 6' of arc) these should provide a reasonable basis for the fine-tuning necessary.

3. Next, find the True Draconic positions for the Sun at 0h00 and 24h00 on that day by subtracting the Node from the Sun in each instance.

4. Take the earlier figure away from the later to find the arc travelled by the Draconic Sun during the day – faster than the Tropical as a rule, unless the Node is Direct.

5. Subtract the position at 0h00 from your own Draco Sun position.

6. Divide the result by the Draconic Sun's motion found earlier: now you have the proportion of the day that elapsed up to the Return, as a decimal figure.

7. Multiply this decimal by 24: this will give you the time of the return, UT, as a decimal figure.

8. Convert back to hours, minutes and seconds.

9. Check this by recalculating Sun and True Node for this time and ensuring that their difference equals your True Draco Sun precisely. If not, adjust.

10. You are now equipped to draw up the Tropical chart and convert this into the True Draconic Solar Return. As always, look at both levels, and at the interactions; not forgetting that you also have here a set of Draconic and Tropical transits to the natus. Some sexagesimal electronic calculators have a habit of tidying up their figures by dropping seconds or rounding off to the nearest minute. It may be safer, in the cause of accuracy, to work these figures on paper; the time it takes is minimal. Once you have worked out the time of the Return, the chart can be calculated by any means that suits you.

'In your longing for your giant self lies your goodness: and that longing is in all of you. But in some of you that longing is a torrent rushing with might to the sea, carrying the secrets of the hillsides and the songs of the forest. And in others it is a flat stream that loses itself in angles and bends and lingers before it reaches the shore. But let not him who longs much say to him who longs little, "Wherefore are you slow and halting?" For the truly good ask not the naked, "Where is your garment?" nor the houseless, "What has befallen your house?"'

Kahlil Gibran, *The Prophet*

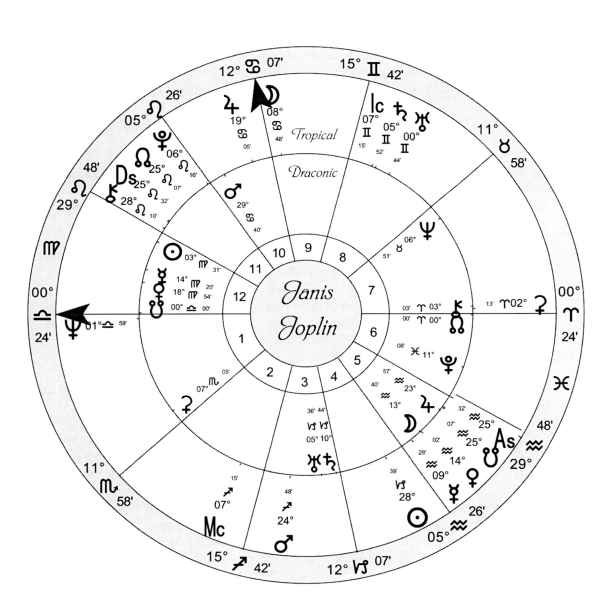

The Draconic Solar Return: Death of a Blues Singer – Janis Joplin

Janis Joplin was a rebel. She was born and brought up in a comfortable middle-class family in a comfortable middle-class society in an unlovely Texan town; hated its complacency, her school, the values it instilled; was lonely, unpopular, intelligent but bored; majored only in art and then shook the dust of Port Arthur from under her feet to sing, drink and hitch her way into the hub of the sixties culture – California. 'They laughed me out of class, out of town, and out of the state,' she said. Lois Rodden's comment in *Profiles of Women* is that '… The chart makes as little sense as did her short life.' Janis's own statement, 'Man, I'd rather have ten years of superhypermost than live to be 70 sitting in the same goddam chair watching TV,' reflects neither her Capricorn Sun nor her Cancer Moon … Why did she burn herself out rocketing through five scorching years of 'superhypermost?'

The answer to this question lies in the Draconic, vocational level of the chart. Here, although the Sun is in Virgo, the all-important Moon falls in Aquarius, tightly conjunct the 12th House Tropical Venus and close to Tropical Mercury; opposite the Tropical Sun lies Draconic Mars, carrying all the emotional drive of Cancer, and (as we see so often with public lives) the Draconic MC conjoins the Tropical Moon … bringing with it the angular conjunction of Draconic Saturn and Uranus. Finally, the Draconic Ascendant conjoins Tropical Neptune. The importance of Janis's Draconic patterns is highlighted by the remark made by her friend Nick Gravenites that she gave her public '100% of her physical *and spiritual* body.' (My italics.)

The Tropical pattern certainly shows us the intelligence that put her a year ahead of her peers in school, through the strong Air trines, also the ever-present need to go off on her own at regular intervals for some peace and quiet and privacy, typical of the Capricorn. This side of her meant also that she was drawn to 'father figures'; 'She respected successful people – she listened to them,' David Dalton, her biographer, says of her: '… she did recognise in herself afflictions of that sign – intense introspection and the tendency to go from the heights of ecstasy to the depths of depression, the goat on the peak, the fish in the deep. If she had been named for the two-faced god of this month, Janus, god of gates and transitions, one face toward the past, the other toward the future, the choice could hardly have been more appropriate. She lived in pain, exposed as she was to the embryonic paradoxes of her inner conflicts.' Vis-à-vis the Tropical Moon/Jupiter in Cancer in the 5th, we have Janis's words, 'I was a sensitive child, I had a lot of hurts and confusions,' and Dalton comments that 'if Janis contributed anything at all to our culture, our freedoms even, it was this image of the gigantic child, absorbed in play, willing to let go the monster of self if only it would let *her* go.'

David Dalton's biography is rich and poetic reading, most sensitive to the many facets of the girl whose unique, often coarse, and yet oddly wistful voice comes abundantly through its pages. A vivid picture is painted of the poignant contrasts between the Needing Janis of the Tropical chart, and the Driven Janis of the Draconic. The imagery for the latter is repeatedly electric – fitting the Aquarian Moon she has brought with her out of her past experience to identify with, and to use to express not only her own insistent differentness through her unconventional music (Tropical Venus) and her unorthodox loves, but those of a whole generation. She came to be that. She had something out of the ordinary which magnetised an audience ; she 'sang like a woman possessed, touched by the finger of a naughty god.' Nick Gravenites said that she 'was the only woman I ever met who could sing a *chord*!'

Through the Neptune/Ascendant, she identified totally with the anarchic elements around her, totally involved with all that her rootless, unsettled life had to offer of drinking, drugs, free expression, soul and the formless escapist ideals of her fermenting generation. She was both an escapist, an escape for others, and a legend but something else was there too, for on her own, when she turned back to her other love, painting, it was the imagery of the Bible that she drew on again and again, in complete contradiction to her public iconoclasm. Angular Chiron made her a maverick in everything she thought, felt and did.

And that Draconic Mars/Tropical Sun? – 'I wanna *burn*!' Her philosophy, given freely to anyone who was willing to listen, and to every audience through her songs, was 'Get it while you can, 'cause it ain't gonna be there when you wake up, man!' She was full of the immediacy of life and desire and need, violent with the urgency of living to that 'superhypermost' before burnout. She sought excitement; 'swung between moods of intense creativity and intense self-hatred.' The *Daily Telegraph* critic, on her London appearance, wrote with apparently uncharacteristic fervour: 'Here in fact was the comfortingly embodied voice of love, pain, freedom and ecstatic experience, *a fire that speaks from the heart*, warm rounded flesh …' (my italics.).

And yet, you see, there was also the structure. Capricorn, and that good Mercury/Saturn/Uranus trine, would have their satisfaction – and also the Draconic Virgo Sun with its need not only to be needed (I think she acknowledged this in the importance to her of saying 'Yes' to her friends and her audiences and her publicists) but also for a perfection, and an integrity in her work. 'Sure it's structured,' she says, 'Playing music isn't just letting it all hang out … Playing is like taking a feeling and like turning it into a finished, tight thing that is readable and understandable to the people who are looking at it. It's not just for you, you can't just sing how *you* feel, you've got to take how you feel, sift it through whatever vocal cords you have, whatever instrumentation you have, whatever arrangements you have, and try and create a swelling feeling in the audience.' She knew what she was up to; she believed in it.

Chiron will have played a number of differing roles in Janis's life: most obviously it represents the 'maverick' element, but it will have been much more than that, in its exceptionally strong position conjunct Tropical Dragon's Head and Descendant, and even within reach of her Draconic Sun. Perhaps in her way she was a guru for those who loved her. Perhaps it is the picture of her having to embrace a deeper interpersonal pain than we shall ever realise. Maybe Chiron also speaks of those 'father figures' who would have guided her, were she more docile, into a realisation of her self-destructiveness. For this was the key issue: Tropical South Node exactly rising in Aquarius, and its rulers at the IC in Gemini, implanted in her a dreadful fatalism, a sense of being on a losing ticket even when she was having 'a rocking good time'. It made her restless, voluble, eccentric, and the perpetual rebel that she was. She tried moving into Leo; she did fall in love, there was this odd, private orthodoxy in the subject matter (but not manner) of her painting – but she never quite could let go of the monster; it was 'What's in it for Janis?' and execrating rage when her face was ousted from the cover of *Newsweek* by the death of General Eisenhower. 'Fourteen heart attacks and he had to die in my week. In MY week.'

'Maybe all those cats wouldn't be so scared of me, if I'd shut up, stop telling all I know, what I'm feeling,' she said. And, 'I can't quit to become someone's old lady, 'cause I've had it so big … most women's lives are beautiful because they are dedicated to a man. I need him too, a lolling, loving, touching, beautiful man, but it can't touch, it can't even touch hitting the stage at full-tilt boogie. So I guess I'll stop at this. I'll take it. Can't do without it.' Even the ideal Leo partner could not compete with that wild charge she got from her own Mars loose in the 10th. Even the greatest love and guide she could have had in Christ (of whom I also believe Chiron to be a symbol) was not allowed fully enough into her life to arrest her fall further and further into her own chaotic flight from orthodoxy, away even from the establishments of stardom.

And so she undid herself. Emphasising Aquarius and the rulers in Gemini at the expense of Leo and the ruler in Capricorn, she never stood still nor kept quiet for long enough to really listen to the still small voice of transformative love – the love that demands obeisance from the intellect, the love that asks total personal commitment to that Other whoever it may be, in return for a joy, a peace, an inner understanding undreamt of. Or perhaps it could only be this way? That the only way she knew of throwing herself into the arms of love was into the arms and hearts of her audience, while destroying herself through the abuse of her body.

The big break came for her and her band (Big Brother and the Holding Company) at the Monterey Pop Festival in the August of 1967. She came from almost nowhere and 'did it' three times for her enraptured audience. The Solar Return for January 19th 1967 shows Sun/Mercury in opposition to Jupiter (and sextile Saturn) across 3rd/9th, Moon conjunct North Node, in Taurus, and a rising Scorpio Neptune. But the real drama dazzles from the True Draconic Solar Return of October 13th 1966: not only does the chart echo over and over again her natal patterns in the 12th House Sun, South Node in 1st, and Mars well elevated in the 10th, but also in the Draconic/Tropical cross-contacts this resonance continues with Draconic Descendant conjunct Tropical Chiron and her Aquarian Ascendant echoed by Draconic Ascendant conjunct Tropical Uranus; Draconic Saturn conjoins Tropical IC. The Moon/Venus conjunction repeats the natal tight Draconic Moon conjunct Tropical Venus; Draconic Sun conjoins Tropical Mars to restate Draconic Mars opposition Tropical Sun in the nativity. Was there ever a cue for action! The New Moon signals the beginning of the fame she enjoyed from that point on until her sad death, and at the Draconic level that Sun, Moon and Venus funnel themselves and their midpoint through the 10th House Tropical Mars, co-ruler of the impassioned Scorpio Ascendant and Mercury … and, significantly, the South Node/Neptune conjunction.

The promise is clearly there – and the warning. It may or may not be coincidental that Tropical Saturn falls 4½° square Draconic MC; just over four years from that Draconic Solar she was dead. A cue to include non-axial contacts? One wonders. This is a whole new

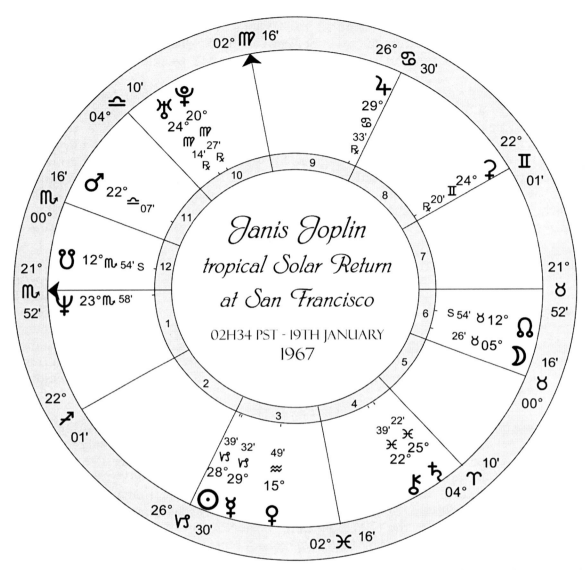

world of astrological understanding. She certainly was to 'have it big', with the Tropical opposition of Uranus/Pluto and Saturn /Chiron lined up with Draconic Ascendant/ Descendant; also the Tropical MC/IC aligns tightly with natal Draconic Moon/Tropical Venus. Draconic MC opposes her natal Sagittarius Mars; Draconic Moon is conjunct her natal Dragon's Head/Chiron/Descendant, offering all that public love.

On October 4th 1970 she was dead from an overdose of heroin. She was happy, the band was cutting a new disc, she had a good relationship going that might have led to stability but clearly something in her could not handle it. Perhaps if everything went right she would be like all the others whose ordinary, contented, comfortable lives she refused to accept or emulate – and her whole reason for living, for being who she was, for doing as she did, the whole point would be lost. She saw that thing that she wasn't as something

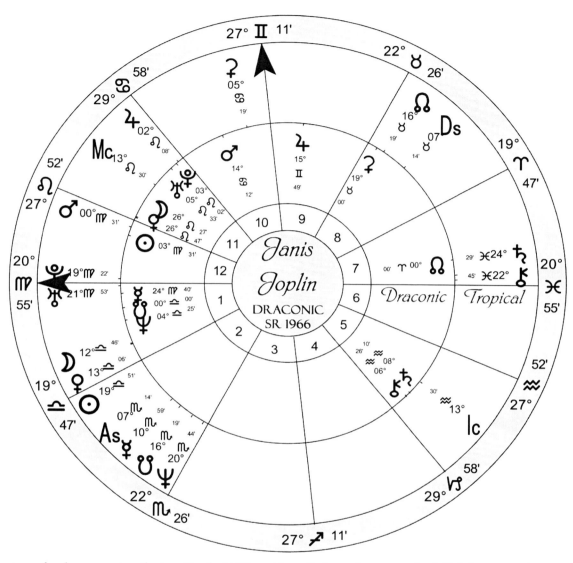

set up for her constantly to attack. Without her fight, what was she? If 'it' won, what was left? Unable to see beyond this profound crisis of purpose, like many another Chironian she took, consciously or unconsciously, her only route of escape.

The familiar Tropical Solar Return of January 1970 is tense with the Sun/Venus-Saturn-Jupiter T-square afflicting her natal Tropical Moon/Draconic Venus conjunction from the Draconic level. The Ascendant conjoins natal North Node, Chiron and Draconic Sun focussing the issue. But again, the Draconic Solar Return on the True Node, for July 29th 1970 – probably at her home in Larkspur, California – foreshadows events with poignant accuracy. The transformation due is heralded by the tight conjunction of Tropical Sun/ Mars/Descendant on natal Pluto; Tropical Neptune/Los Angeles MC configures her natal Tropical Sun by a close sextile. The 7th House is powerful; Tropical Mercury again focusses

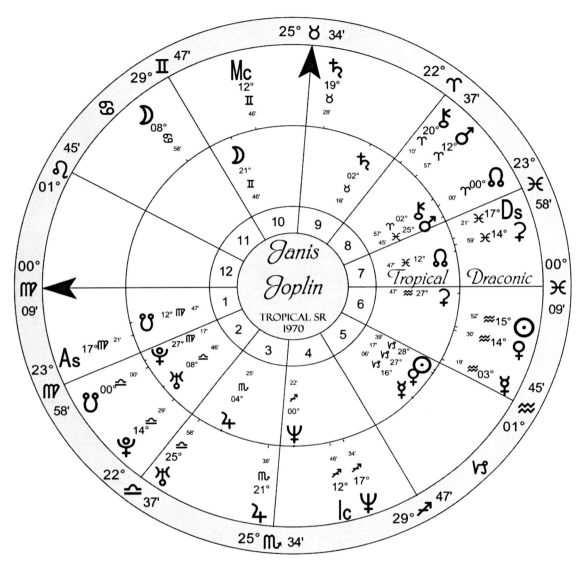

the Descendant/North Node/Chiron of the natus. But the key to the events to follow, perhaps truly inevitable by this stage of her career, whatever free will we each have at our disposal, lies in the eloquent pattern of the Tropical South Node conjunct both natal and current (returning) Draconic Sun conjoined by Mars, plus culminating Neptune (the drug) and Saturn at the IC conspiring to end her earthly progress. At Port Arthur, where her parents still lived, Draconic Saturn is found conjunct the Tropical IC. Janis's natal Sun/ Mars cross-contact is triggered by the Draconic Moon (trine the Tropical Neptune/MC at Larkspur). Does the Draconic Jupiter so close to the Tropical MC speak not just of the good things reaching out to her, but also of the relief in her soul to be freed from the pain of battle?

It was finally time to reckon up, to pay, and/or to let go. She was found in a Los Angeles motel room by her friend John Cooke at 7h30 pm on the day she died. Janis was last

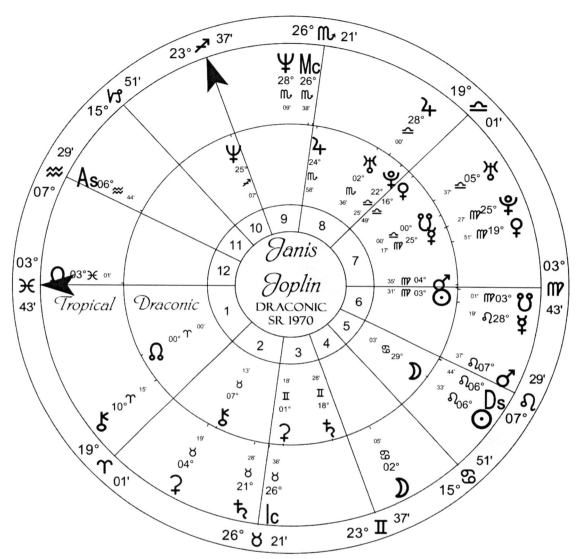

seen by the porter in the lobby at about 1 am when she came out for some change for a five-dollar bill to buy cigarettes. The time of her death was estimated as 1h40 am PDT; the full packet of cigarettes lay near her body. The death chart is poignant; the Tropical Dragon's Tail, still lashing her early Virgo Draconic Sun, had curled seductively round the Draconic Ascendant … 'Let go, Janis!' whispered the dragon, 'Throw it all away!' The Tropical Sun, ruling the Tropical Leo Ascendant as she died, had conjoined Uranus and opposed Chiron, aligning from the Draconic level with Tropical Jupiter; such impulsive energies could easily encourage an act too risky, a leap too far. It was a fateful moment: Draconic Pluto spread his darkness at the Tropical IC as Janis's own Pluto degree rose in Leo; meanwhile that night's gloomy Tropical alignment of Venus, Moon, Neptune and Saturn took over the Draconic meridian, perfecting the pattern for a lethal drug overdose. Suddenly it was all over.

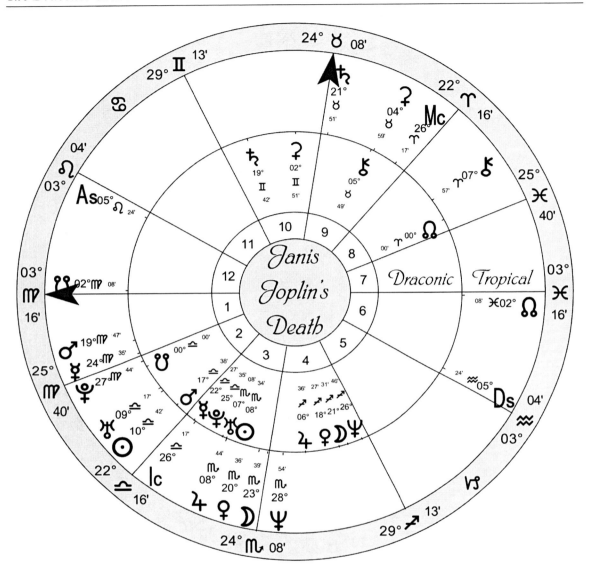

Janis Joplin's Death

Draconic / Tropical

Chapter Fourteen

Draconic Progressions

In looking at the Draconic element in the progressed chart, we shall also include the **daily progressed angles**. For those who are unfamiliar with these, it is enough to remember that over the course of the day in the ephemeris which corresponds in progressions with the year under review, the Midheaven progressing from Midnight to Midnight (or Noon to Noon) moves not just the one degree generally looked on as the annual measure of the progressed MC, but 361°, just as the progressed Moon moves through its natural arc of 12°-15° over the course of that same day/year. You will quickly appreciate that every day of a given year is therefore marked by a fresh pair of angles. The MC moves by just under 1° each 24 hours over the 365 or 366 days of the year, and the corresponding Ascendant moves with it according to the current latitude. To the best of my knowledge, this fact has not been fully appreciated by astrologers until relatively recently; when I started writing about it in the 1970s, I was one of only a handful to realise its importance.

The value of the daily progressed angles is underlined powerfully in an examination of the progressed patterns found for April 25th 1979 in the case of the young man Aaron whose crippling accident we looked at in detail when studying Draconic transits in Chapter Twelve. The relationship that we found at his birth between Draconic Jupiter/Saturn and the Node/Uranus/Venus/Chiron axis of course remains, as these bodies move so slowly over 17½ days. And the Aries/Libra Points in the Draconic pattern – aligned so tellingly with his natal Draconic Sun and MC/IC – have moved by only a degree. But just look at the interactions with these important points in the fully Daily Progressed chart for the day of the accident! The annually progressed Tropical Ascendant and MC/Sun, taken on their own, would tell us little about the life-changing drama that took place; there is only the approach of progressed Ascendant to square natal Moon. But bring in the Draco, and the images begin to form. First, there is a 3° and separating conjunction of this progressed MC/IC axis with progressed Draco Pluto, so we can expect this epoch to have a transformative quality. Next we find the progressed Descendant on progressed Draconic Neptune, with the Mercury/Mars not far back, as they were at his birth in their relationship to the angle, but much closer to Neptune, testimony to a weakening and/or spiritualising of the physical body and all its principal relationships.

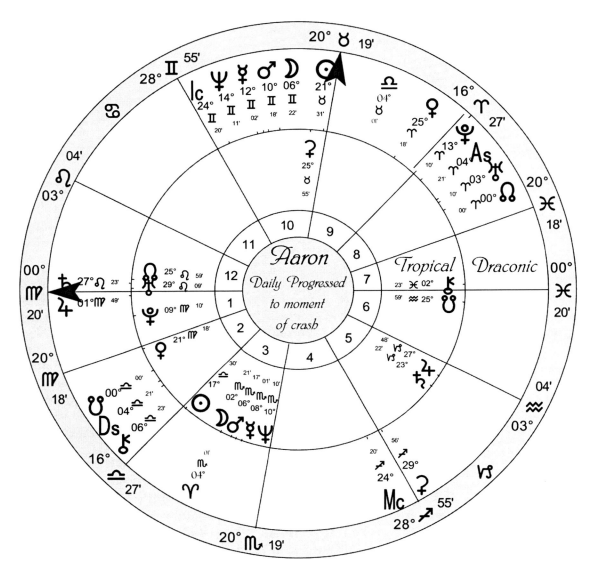

But it is, as I have indicated, in the daily progressed patterns that the meaning and drama really appear: for the Tropical daily progressed MC falls in the 20th degree of Taurus, conjoining the Draconic progressed Sun/MC/IC and the transiting Draconic Sun/Chiron axis on their midpoint; this fixes the date without question as one on which an event of great personal significance may take place. Then we find the Tropical daily progressed Ascendant which corresponds with this MC at the Canterbury latitude exactly conjunct Aaron's progressed Tropical Uranus, plus natal Tropical Uranus/Venus, and in orbs of the Nodal and Chiron axes from their midpoint in 29° Leo. Completing this picture, the Draconic progressed Saturn also lies very close to this angle, marking this day for a potentially sudden, disruptive, damaging and destined event. Because the progressed Sun moves steadily, degree by degree, over the years, this coincidence of progressed Draconic Sun and Saturn/Tropical Uranus-Node could only take place at one given latitude over

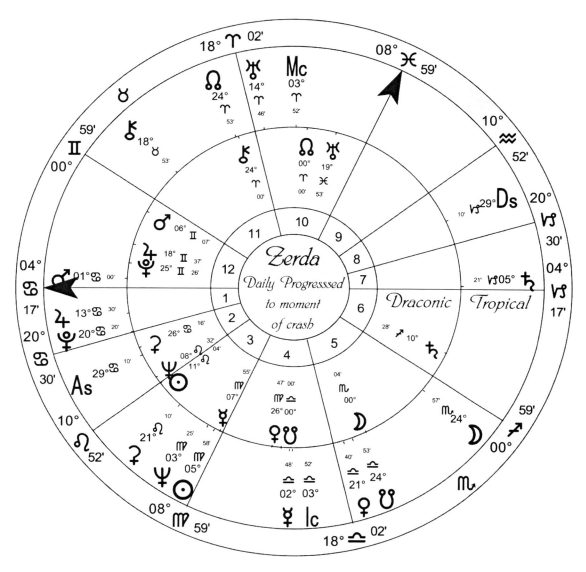

a very few successive years while the Draconic progressed Sun remained in orbs of 20°
Taurus. And of course we know that almost precisely a year earlier a similar event occurred,
but without the dire results of 1979.

What made the difference? In 1978, the progressed Moon had just made its conjunction
with the progressed Sun; a New Moon that heralded a fresh cycle of experience for Aaron.
This progressed Moon was in Libra – as was the transiting Draconic Sun of the first accident.
But in April 1979 the progressed Moon had reached the other hypersensitive point in
Aaron's life-pattern: in 2° Scorpio – so often a sign of intensified experience amounting to
deep suffering and the challenges that transform – it fell on the Aries Point and Draconic
IC of the young man's nativity and opposite his Draconic Sun. It was also close to the
progressed Aries Point and Tropical Mars/Mercury/Neptune, all lying ahead of it. That

fateful day, the transiting Draconic Moon conjoined it and, you will recall, his mother's IC; earlier that morning it had passed over her own epochal progressed Draconic Moon in the last degree of Libra with her natal South Node (also poised for the challenges of Scorpio). Now that Astronomy encourages us to take Ceres seriously as a planet, the position of the suffering celestial mother in any chart may be important. In Zerda's daily progressed pattern for Aaron's crash, the Tropical Ascendant had met Draconic Ceres, with Tropical Mars-Saturn troubling the Draconic horizon – and, significantly, in 5° Virgo the progressed Draconic Libra Point, with its possibly karmic implications, was being joined by the progressed Tropical Sun. She all but lost her son. For Aaron, emotionally ripe for speed, danger, trauma and testing, this was the year of destiny, when Draconic Taurus fixed his own Earth – his body – to a chair, and dared him to find himself a future. He did.

Draconic Progressions: The Death of Janis

If you study your own daily progressed angles, you will find that each time one of them contacts the natal, progressed or transiting Saturn, the passing day demands to be taken seriously; a slower, more deliberate pace is required, more seclusion is necessary (or is imposed by circumstances), practical issues and responsibilities come to the fore, or one must learn that it is time to say 'No', and rest, and take extra care of the health. For on these days above all others one is vulnerable to all kinds of accidents or bugs that can lay one low and put paid to one's plans. For the natally Saturnine person, these days are especially important, as there is usually a message coming through from the Cosmos to which it is wise to attend; and Janis Joplin was no exception.

On the day just prior to her death, she had had a very enjoyable and successful session in a Los Angeles recording studio – but natal and progressed Saturn lay exactly on her daily progressed Descendant, and this ruling planet of hers is conjunct her IC at birth. So this day was likely to throw into painful focus any negativity unpurged from her soul and bring on the distressing loneliness of the Capricorn woman with Cancer Moon who both longs for and fears intimacy. She had gone back alone to her motel room; and we already know how dangerous the transits were for her that night. The annually progressed MC in 2° Capricorn, recently passed by the Draconic daily progressed Descendant, was currently 3° from Draconic progressed and natal Uranus, signalling some kind of change or awakening or shock due to occur near her 30th birthday. But she was not to reach it. The annual progressed angles already threw the progressed Draconic Sun/Chiron/Tropical Neptune alignment into critical focus at Port Arthur, while in California her birth angles were being cruelly echoed. What happened four or five days before death, I wonder, when the Draconic daily progressed Descendant fell on that Uranus? Her personal life was supposed at the time to be very happy – even to the extent of considering marriage and settling down. Had she become frightened and broken her commitment? Or had she been let down in some way? Someone, somewhere may know the answers to these questions. The significant closing conjunction at the latitude of Los Angeles of the Draconic daily progressed Ascendant in Cancer with her progressed Tropical Moon, only 2° past its natal place and 1° before her natal Draconic MC, suggests a time of emphasised emotional need and responsiveness that should (approaching Jupiter) lead to happiness and fulfilment,

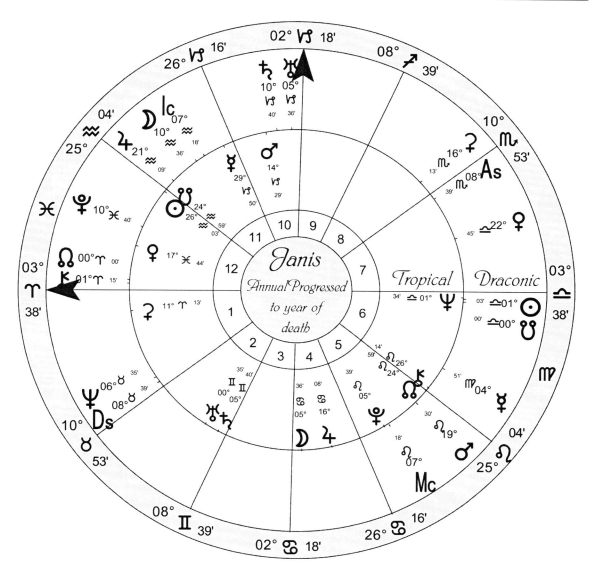

but always the need to devote that softer, creative side of herself to the public, to the recognition that might satisfy her desperate need to feel valued, accepted in all her oddness and uncomfortable forthrightness, and to experience unconditional love.

So there she was, alone in her loneliness, with all these yearnings, accented still further by progressed Pisces/Libra Venus at the daily progressed IC. Was she expecting someone who never turned up? Or was it a deliberate pursuit of solitary self-indulgence when she gave herself that excessive dose of heroin? Or was she frantically seeking a final escape route from the power of her own feelings? She picked up the needle with the transiting Ascendant conjunct her natal and progressed Tropical Pluto; the transiting Sun/Uranus lay provocatively square to the sensitive axis in Cancer/Capricorn; her progressed Tropical Sun was still in orb of her South Node (echoes of the Draconic Solar) and exactly opposite

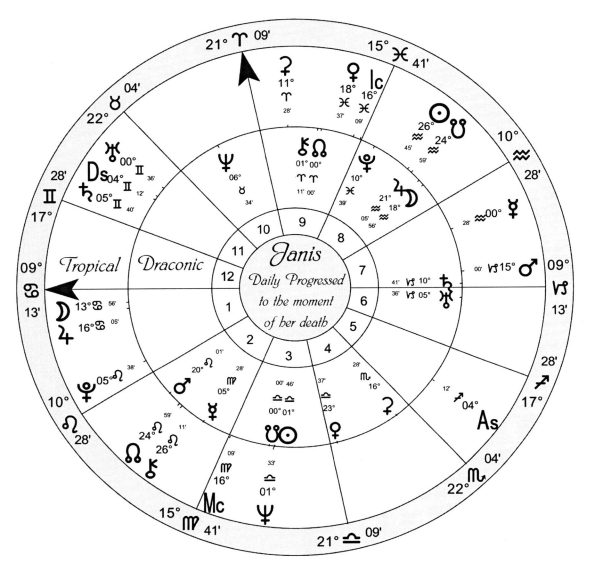

progressing Tropical Chiron. Their Draconic axis fell on natal and progressed Neptune; transiting Chiron in 8° Aries squared her Tropical birth Moon and the daily progressed Ascendant for the latitude of her birth-place, her natal Sun/Chiron quincunx and their progressed opposition was repeated in the sky by the Sun-Uranus/Chiron alignment that day.

Chiron's conjunction with her Dragon's Head at birth so close to the 7th House cusp invites her to leave her privacy behind and suffer the pains and joys of intimacy or suffer indeed. On that emotionally charged day in October 1970 her inner pain must have been unbearable for her to take such a terrible jump into the dark. Even so, it may not have been intended to be so final.

Draconic Progressions and Transits – The Disunited Kingdom!

Look on Britannia (as we often affectionately call the UK) as a 212-year-old lady, and you will see that like all of us she was born with a few problems! Her relationships and her economics are tied up in what is very nearly a Grand Cross of Mars-Neptune-Venus-Saturn in the 8th, 2nd, 5th and 11th Houses. Now, Mars rules her Moon's North Node, so clearly the matter of actively cooperating with her world partners and sharing materially with them (Mars in Taurus in 8th) with no thought of self is going to be quite a challenge, clashing as it does with all kinds of vested interests (Venus, ruler of South Node, in Aquarius in 5th) and negative habits (Saturn in Leo in 11th). That is just the beginning. Her attitude is utterly ambivalent, as with a 10th House Cancer Moon she needs to be seen to care, publicly, and as Draconic Jupiter is conjunct it, with Draconic Moon conjunct MC, she believes strongly in saying 'Yes!' to progress.

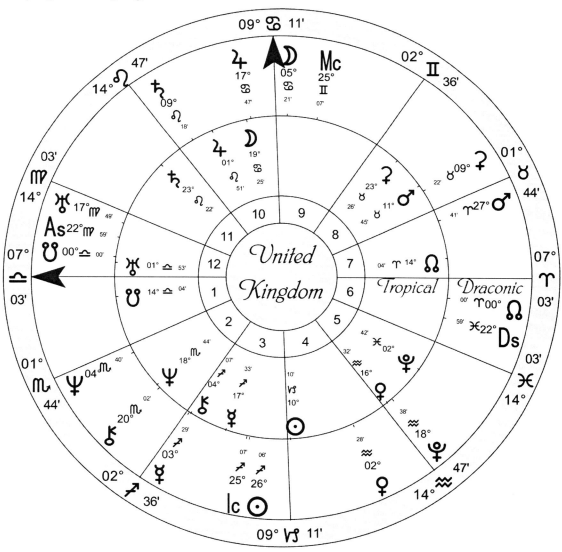

But this is more likely to be in the interest of her own growth, as her Capricorn Sun at the IC places her heart firmly where tradition would expect it – in her own territory, her own history and heritage. The Draconic version of her Sun/IC falls in Sagittarius, which sounds more promising, but it isn't without potential problems: as this is also in the Tropical 3rd House, she will wax eloquent on freedom of opportunity, the value of higher education, the importance of conserving the British heritage and way of life, but her fear of losing control can often be as much a hindrance as a sensible help to her own development and world standing. (Interestingly, this placing resonates with the Galactic Centre, implying a special role in world affairs.) A careful rein is kept at all times on any natural impulse to magnanimity, that a balance be kept between caution and enthusiasm, between expansion and restraint. Actually, these are the qualities of good husbandry! In this part of the pattern, the Tropical/Draconic interactions, there is quite a healthy balance which should in theory keep Mrs. Britannia's household in good order, her aspirations high, her achievements gratifying. But South Node in the 1st always shows us an individual who must learn selflessness, and Britannia clearly has a high opinion of herself and intends to keep it if she can, building on her independence of spirit (Uranus conjunct Ascendant, Tropical Venus in Aquarius, Tropical Saturn in the 11th) and the work ethic which drives both her manhood and her womanhood (Capricorn/Cancer).

It is her deep belief in the spirit of enterprise, in courage, and in the individual's right to a fulfilled life and destiny which is her most hopeful quality. This is the Draconic Mars in Aries, ruler of the Dragon's Head in the Tropical 7th House, which was proved mightily when she threw personal comfort and safety to the four winds in two world wars and showed just what courage, leadership and generosity she was capable of in the battle with the agents of darkness and in the defence of weaker nations. And despite every threat, she with Tropical Mars in Taurus stuck to her guns. Her gift for economy, her natural thrift and ingenuity, became a blessing, and she shared as much as she could. Yes, of course there was a black market – there is in every war – but the British people learned to share. How many of them now look back on those difficult times and remember chiefly the joy people found in their interdependence! Where is that spirit now, though? It flashes out among the wise, and among the youthful. Whenever Britannia is brought face to face with the needy of the world she may be a bit slow off the mark in many instances, and her contribution may be limited for various reasons (as I first wrote this some years ago, there was pressure for even more massive supplies of food and other aid to be air-lifted to the stricken Kosovo refugees in Macedonia and Albania; and while the first edition was being prepared the British public were insisting that generous rations continue to be dropped in Ethiopia, not to slacken) but the instinctive response of her people is heartwarming in its generosity.

However, as well as the creative and inventive brilliance within her (Draconic Pluto conjunct Tropical Venus in the 5th), there is a cussed pleasure-loving streak, which should normally find ample outlet in her social enjoyments, her children, her hobbies, and her love of team and individual sports. But this has gone wrong. It seems to have gone 'South Node' with the advent and mushrooming growth of the electronic society. This too has its intensely creative and beneficial side (witness its many and varied blessings for astrology!) but there is a dangerous move towards depersonalisation through the love and excessive use of machines, which is beginning to bring out many of the least lovely qualities in Britannia's character.

She is in peril of losing her warmth. She is devaluing and discouraging human interrelationship, upon which our spiritual – hence bodily – health depends. Understanding concern has started to give way to manipulative interference; language charged with meaning has become automatic jargon; marriages are being reduced to contracts with escape clauses; the sick, shorn of time with their doctors, may soon be expected to unburden their hearts to a call centre or a visual display unit. Our children, closeted more and more with the screen and keyboard, and forced to share ever fewer – and increasingly undervalued, frustrated and bewildered – human teachers, are cut off from even that source of loving discipline which is already absent from too many homes. Libra-rising Britannia is getting lazy, self-indulgent and self-serving in too many areas of her life; and to prop up her appetite for ease and pleasure, the willing plaything of market forces, she has long been showing her greedy side. 'Hang on to what you get; get more whenever you can; consider no one but yourself' is the message. Contemptuous of authority, uneducated in karmic law, long unthreatened by the wrath of an unloved, timidly represented God, the lower side of Britannia embarks, via social breakdown, on her self-imposed suffering. 2012 brings the slow, inexorable transit of Pluto over her Capricorn Sun: will she come to her senses, and find her heart again? (As I proof-read this at the end of this remarkable Olympic and Jubilee year, there are many encouraging signs that this has begun to happen; there is a growing revolt against unkindness, exploitation, greed and generally poor standards in many areas of British life.)

In 1984-5 there took place one of the most damaging strikes in British history. Almost the entire coal-mining community stopped work. The issue was job security. These long-established and close-knit communities were increasingly (and justifiably) afraid that the Government's economic stringencies presented a real threat to their jobs and whole way of life. For almost exactly a year, bitterness and violence reigned in the villages, on the picket-lines, in associated industries, and in the hearts of those encountering stalemate after stalemate at the negotiating table. It cost the country dearly; not only in financial terms, but also in world confidence and industrial goodwill. In the end it was the miners themselves, worn out and disillusioned by stress, privation, and the most bitter winter for decades, who ended the strike, by drifting back in increasing numbers until the leadership was obliged to make the return official. Each side naturally blamed the other – rarely can we expect much else of human nature, it seems. The miners attacked the Government's unbending policy of restraint, and the Government accused the miners of utter intransigence. Where did the fault lie? To the extent that most of us have blinkered and limited vision, no-one can apportion blame to just one of the parties in such a sad dispute; but one can blame fear.

Let us look for a moment at the man carrying the banner of the miners' cause: Arthur Scargill, President of the National Union of Mineworkers, and, according to *The Sunday Times* of July 15th 1984 '… one of the most important, most admired, most hated, most feared men in the country.' A Capricorn with Sun in the 8th and its ruler Saturn in Pisces square both Mercury in Sagittarius and the axis of Ascendant/Descendant, material distribution of wealth and personal involvement in massive financial matters will not only be close to his heart but a source of painful interpersonal problems, especially in questions of discipline. He does not know where to draw the line, he has a great deal to say, and blends received philosophy and wishful fictions into a rhetoric that to the undiscriminating listener is all too welcome and plausible. With the Tropical Moon in Taurus in the 12th, drawing in the Draconic Sun, and semi-square Tropical Saturn, he has a strong underlying need for material security, a powerful belief in its importance, and a deep fear of its loss. (This was reflected in his devastation at the loss of his mother at the age of seventeen.) Draconic Neptune working through the Tropical Sun turns this into a crusade for an ideal, fed by his Mars/Neptune need to run high on enthusiasm and the injection of emotional power from Mars/Pluto. An additional source of power is the close resonance of these mid-Taurus degrees with the great star Aldebaran; very many people that I meet with this degree-area strong (as you will see later on) are actually or potentially Christ-centred people, but those who are not tend to claim and exercise considerable power, and this often develops into

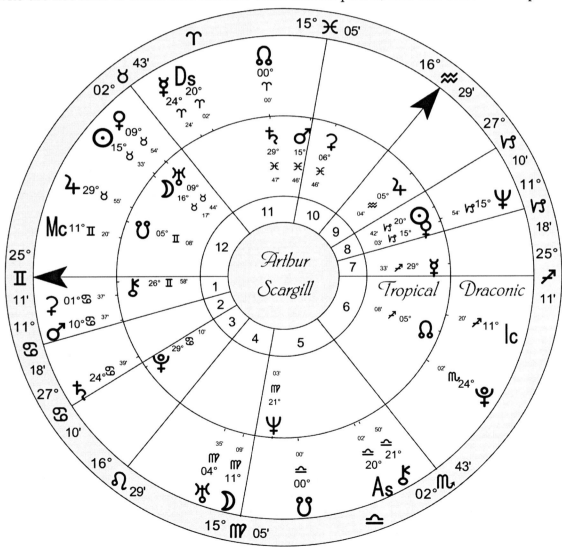

the age-old struggle for the soul between God and Mammon. And even decent Christian instincts can be mis-applied. We are imperfect creatures.

Everything came to a head on March 6th 1984 when the UK's daily progressed MC came within range of Scargill's Tropical Mars, at the same time that its annually progressed Sun/IC plus the Draconic daily progressed Ascendant fell on his Draconic Mars, and approached his progressed Draconic Venus. His time had come – for both the fight and the victory; surely they lay within his grasp? – particularly now that his progressed Draconic Venus had conjoined his natal Draconic Mars. This whole emotive issue was confronting the UK's natal Sun! What laid a grave emphasis on Scargill's role, though, was the mighty involvement of Saturn, 'Lord of Karma', and as we have seen a very prominent and testing element in his pattern. For by annual progression not only had his progressed MC entered a conjunction with progressed Saturn, but the progressed Ascendant with Pluto on the Cancer-Leo cusp was opposed by progressed Tropical Moon and Libra Point in Saturn's sign. On the appointed day his daily progressed MC fell in his South Node. Here began possibly the greatest test of his authority and integrity that he was ever likely to face in this lifetime.

The UK's progressed Draconic Chiron was in Arthur Scargill's natal Dragon's Head by now, its progressed Venus opposite in his progressed Dragon's Tail and aligned with the UK's Draconic Mercury. On March 6th 1984 all these queued up on Scargill's daily progressed MC/IC, thrusting his sense of individual mission before the public and focussing it onto his country's current need to confront, resolve and learn from the continuing wave of financial crises. What he was slow to appreciate – as it appears to me from the pattern – was the part he should have been playing in opening up behind-the-scenes negotiations and providing secret ballots for his union membership when required. Such was his obligation with the now culminating Draconic Jupiter natally linked to his South Node in the 12th. And he could have been more willing to follow his North Node into Sagittarius in the 6th, learning from Britannia's progressed Chiron's guidance to proselytise less and understand and serve more. But with his progressing Tropical Sun in Pisces sitting on the daily progressed Descendant that fateful day, opposite progressed Draconic Uranus so close to the daily progressed Ascendant, he was in no mood to forgo this opportunity to play the social reformer! It was his chance to impose his own ideals on friend and foe alike, with the declared aim of overturning a monetarist Government and blocking any changes that might oblige him and his followers to rethink and restructure their lives as so many of their less protected countrymen repeatedly have to do (thereby growing in experience and understanding).

At this point we come to perhaps the most vital axis of these charts: the Aquarius/Leo opposition. Now, don't be fooled by all this talk of the Aquarian age! Mix with enough Aquarians at all strata of society and you will realise that by no means all are the original, innovative, intelligent, forward-looking, humane, cosmopolitan New Age souls that so many astrologers conceive them to be! It can be a rude awakening to find only the Aquarian Saturn rulership and fixity alive and well and living in its rigid opinions. So Britannia's potentially brilliant Tropical 5th House Venus is in many places and people stultified into a round of habitual pleasures, narrow attitudes, racial intolerance, social gossip, mechanical

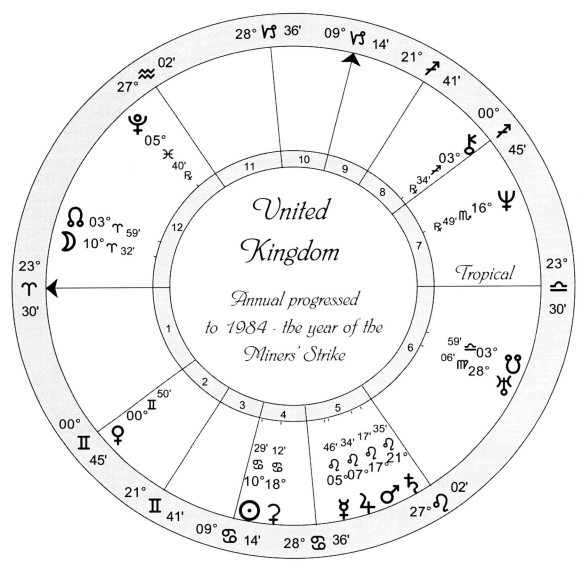

behaviour and a general refusal to look any further than familiar set boundaries. And in March 1984 transiting Saturn came visiting, squaring that Venus, threatening to put a stop to Britannia's pleasures, an end to their tenuous, illusory security (see the Grand Cross). In the same axis of the UK Tropical zodiac, a Mars/Saturn conjunction was inexorably forming in Leo – the Draconic progressed Saturn aligning exactly with the Tropical Mars – and on March 6th transiting Venus joined in from 19° Aquarius, with transiting Draconic Pluto also aligned with the progressed Tropical Saturn in 21° Leo. All this chimed with Arthur Scargill's Tropical MC in 16° Aquarius, and got the go-ahead from his progressed opposition of Tropical Jupiter/Draconic Mars on 16° and 19° of the axis. The battle lines were thus drawn for an inescapable conflict 'that stretched the nation's political system, its method of maintaining law and order, and its economy' (said the aforementioned issue of *The Sunday Times*).

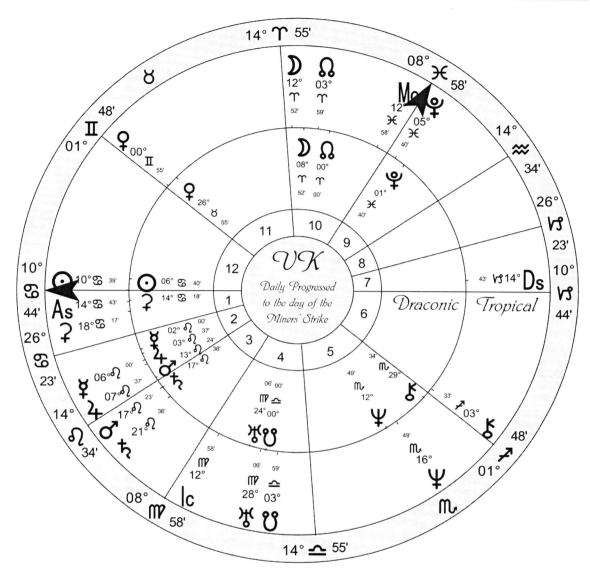

The National Coal Board (NCB), unsurprisingly, was having an annually progressed MC/Pluto conjunction at the same time as its progressed Draconic Sun was entering the South Node. Not a good year, at all. Trauma, upheaval and loss. Time for radical change, time to let go of the past – always costly to those who thenceforth have no future. The NCB was born, like so many British institutions, on January 1ˢᵗ at 0h00, its year 1947. It had a nice pick-and-shovel pattern in the close conjunction of Capricorn Mars with Sun at the IC, and it clearly tried to be fair to its employees, with these planets Draconically in Libra. But Tropical Neptune rose, and Draconic Uranus was 'setting', neither of which boded well for an untroubled history. Ostensibly, Capricornian Scargill had a lot in common with the NCB, which you can see from the links between the two Tropical nativities and their composite. However, move into Draconic, and you find Scargill's Aries Mercury opposite injured Chiron and square obdurate Saturn spoiling for a fight across all the

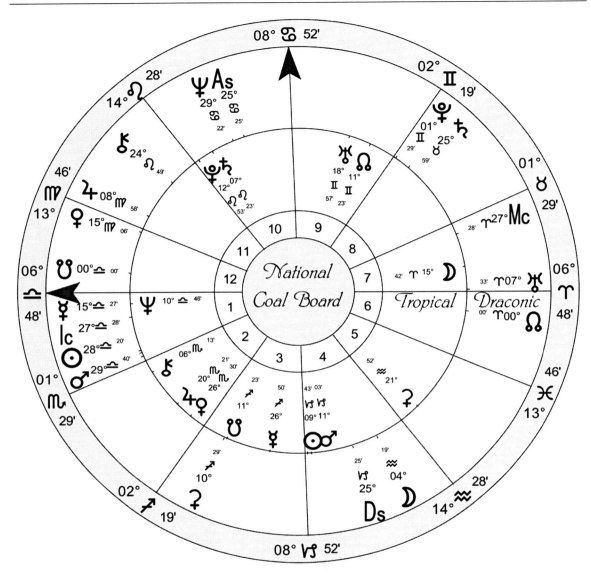

NCB's angles. Comparing the Draconic composite to the natal charts, it is Scargill who is most energised by the clash; for him it brings MC to Sun, Moon to Pluto, Neptune to Ascendant and Chiron, Mars/Ascendant to Uranus and Moon, Venus to Mars. With such an inflated sense of his own power, he would feel invincible. What should have been even-handed negotiation between two Libran parties, developed into an unending confrontational crusade. Now, only while preparing this edition of The Draconic Chart did I consider presenting Tropical and Draconic composites together in a bi-wheel; initially this was simply to reduce the number of tri-wheels and save space, but just look what we have gained! A whole new insight into composite synastry! The combined composites of the NCB and Scargill illustrate so clearly what we previously missed – the mighty power-struggle of Draconic Sun and Tropical Pluto wrestling together in Leo, the Tropical Nodes along the Draconic horizon, pointing firmly to Virgo and service to the public, the

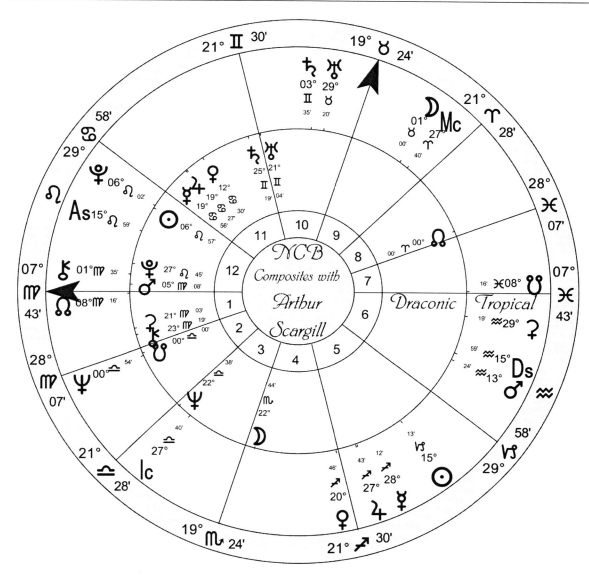

domestic and pay issues around Draconic Cancer Venus/Jupiter/Mercury opposed to the controlling Tropical Capricorn Sun, Draconic Libra Neptune at the Tropical IC dissolving contracts and betraying colleagues. All this with angular Mars and Moon – the entire country embroiled in this Aquarian/Virgoan fight between political groups for the right to continue working and the proper recognition and supply of everyday needs.

On March 6th 1984 the NCB's natal and progressed problem-patterns constellated dramatically as the karmic, Draconic daily progressed angles collected the natal and progressed Tropical Pluto and Neptune, with Uranus setting *in coelo*. The progressed Tropical Moon had almost perfected its square to the progressed Draconic Sun (15′ to go), the daily Tropical Ascendant was on Sagittarian Draconic Mercury, and its corresponding MC with progressed Draconic Venus in Libra, desperate to negotiate. It was all happening.

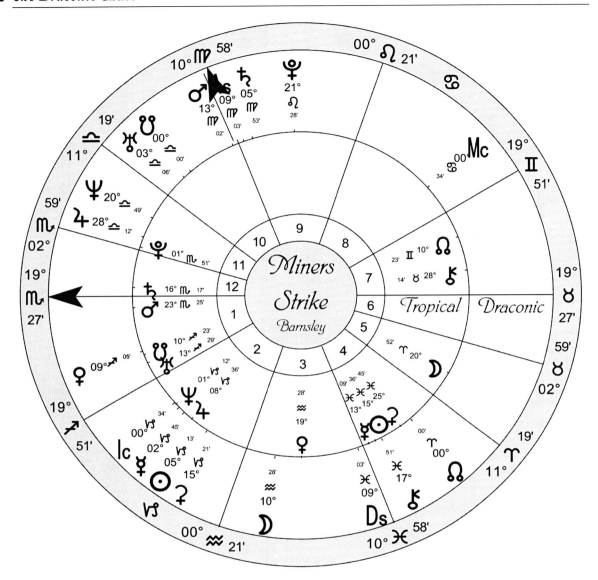

Britannia's progressed Moon meanwhile was working its way through Aries, which it had entered in the spring of the previous year and would leave in the summer of 1985. During the year of the miners' strike it squared natal and progressed Sun/MC from 10° Aries, starting the strike in 12°. Draconic Moon was still near progressed Node, and conjunct the natal Tropical Descendant. Its progressed house position was in the 12th, the UK having been through ten years or so of progressed Aries rising, progressed Ascendant and progressed Dragon's Head conjoining around 1976, with the progressed Ascendant/natal Node conjunction occurring in about 1979. Epochal times for this country, and marked by a disturbing increase in noisy, violent behaviour, aggressive attitudes, and general lack of consideration for others' welfare despite the best efforts of the sensitive minority. And with Mars/Saturn lined up with Tropical Venus in the 5th, a lot of this manifested in the sporting arena where it became commonplace for the slightest advantage to be signalled by the inflammatory raising of clenched fists or crass sexual gestures, and for even the more civilised sports to be marred by mindless shouting. North Node in Aries or not, this could hardly be called progress for poor Britannia. Her Venus/Saturn sportsmanship was once legendary. She used to set an example (an obligation of the Libran South Node) to the rest of the world – but far less so as this chapter was first written. However, the transit of Pluto to Britannia's Tropical Sun is beginning – as I had hoped – to restore her good manners.

So, to return to the miners, it is not surprising that the picket lines demanded such heavy policing over the course of that year in an often abortive attempt to keep the Queen's Peace (and everyone else's!). That the violent Leo/Aquarius axis had moved by daily progression into the 2nd and 8th Houses indicates why the scene of battle was now to be found on the economic/security front. And that Scargill's own Tropical Mars is tightly conjunct the UK's Aries Point, that his Tropical Moon and Draconic Sun are near the UK's Tropical Mars, and his Draconic Mars is close to the UK's Tropical MC, is all highly significant, as is the mutually progressed conjunction of his Saturn/MC to the UK's progressed Node. In other words, if Britannia has a crusade going on, he'll be in front of it to stir things up, spoiling for the people's fight that is his fight; and in 1984 he could have shown his country the way. To what extent he may have done so, and in what measure he just blocked any possible progress, remained to be seen. When I rewrote this chapter in 1999 there were hardly any coalfields left, and the mining communities had to change their way of life probably for ever. Even since 2008 and the looming energy crisis, only a few closed pits have been brought back into production. All that grief in 1984 achieved nothing but even more hardship, and a great deal of public resentment. Arthur Scargill lowered his profile; only a few times in recent years has he put his unmistakeable head briefly and unsuccessfully above the parapet – once in a bid for fresh leadership as General Secretary of a new, militant 'super-union' (a merger of the two principal rail unions and the National Union of Mineworkers) that would directly challenge Tony Blair's New Labour government. But as one miner said, 'It must never happen again.'

The chart for the beginning of the day on which the punishing 1984 strike commenced is eloquent in its own right, quite apart from the transits in force. These included the Tropical Moon, which was in Aries, just past the square to the UK Moon and about to cross the progressed Ascendant and the natal Draconic Mars; and Venus in Aquarius again, almost on the UK's Tropical Venus/Saturn midpoint, right on the UK's progressed Mars/Saturn midpoint, and squaring the transiting Ascendant and Mars/Saturn midpoint. Remember *Venus Victrix*? Here is a pattern declaring that it will try for victory by force; struggle will be the order of the day, and consideration of other people's happiness or convenience can go hang. Draconic Venus is in Sagittarius aligned with the Dragon's Tail; no-one is going to get much joy out of this affair unless they learn magnanimity and to distinguish real need from indulgence, and unless they remember the Gemini end of the axis in the 7th, and keep on talking. It is fascinating to see the key factors in this chart highlighted across the country: most of that fraught and detailed talking will be going on in Westminster at the NCB headquarters and in Parliament: Mercury is doubly angular, and from the Tropical confronts the rising Draconic Mars. Tropical Neptune right on the Draco IC (that pattern again!) sows seeds of confusion, constantly undermining the negotiations. The most

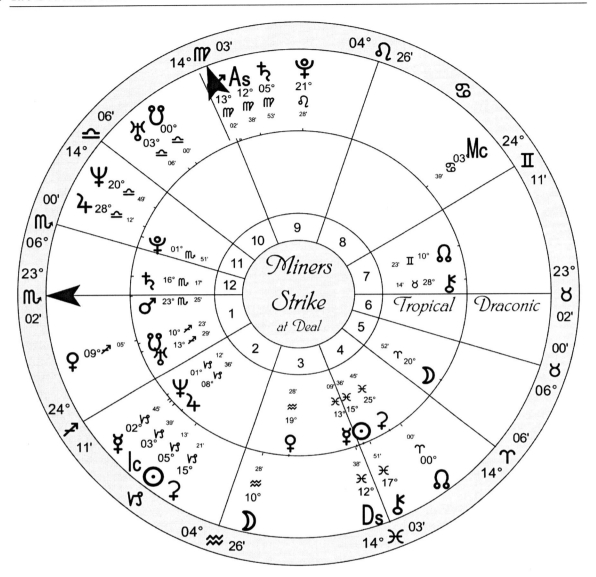

violently troublesome areas were the Scottish, South Welsh and East Kent coalfields, and at these extreme eastern and western edges of the British Isles the Tropical or Draconic angles keyed in powerfully to the hard aspects, as you can see. The most dramatic are those for Deal, Kent, in the South East: this has always been a militant area of the British coalfields, and this could not have been more vividly demonstrated than in the Tropical MC/IC alignment with Draconic Mars and Tropical Mercury, all squaring Tropical Uranus, and the Draconic Ascendant on the same axis, while the Tropical Ascendant exactly conjoins Tropical Mars! The Tropical IC also lies just 1° from the Sun. No wonder the East Kent members of the National Union of Mineworkers took the fight so much to their hearts, and were last to go back to the pits when the strike was officially ended. Interestingly, the Nottinghamshire miners remained against the strike all the way along, and as I was writing, announced their intention to form a breakaway union (which they did.) The angles are almost identical to these shown for Barnsley; they are dealing chiefly, then, with the Venus/Ascendant square, and the Draconic MC is opposite Tropical Neptune – undermining the full efficacy of the strike action! It is also worth noting the 5th harmonic activity in this map between Sun and Chiron, Moon and Neptune, Mercury and Mars, and Venus and Pluto. To me, this highlights the critical importance of making the right moral choices in the handling of power. In 1984 – crunch time for the National Coal Board and a power-hungry antagonist – this proved to be as difficult as ever.

A Note on Dwad Progressions

In Chapter Nineteen, progressions will be extended into the Dwad. At this point it is worth pointing out the following:

It is currently impossible in Solar Fire to create a Dwad directly from a progressed or converse chart. There is a work-around, however, using Solar Fire's Locality function in the Chart menu.

1. Select the progressed chart.

2. Go to Chart/Locality.

3. On the Locality screen ensure the locality and zone of the progressed chart are correct (in Mary's case – in Chapter Nineteen – Nazareth, LMT) Click OK. (You will find that the date and time are now *the ephemeris date and time in the birth year* which correspond to the chosen event date. This can be useful in its own right.)

4. Select the new chart; click Chart/Edit, then Edit Chart.

5. In the blank Name field give it a descriptive name (e.g. 'Mary, daily progressed to Nativity'). Click OK.

6. Select your new chart, and then go to Chart/Vedic/Dwadashamsha. Click OK.

7. When the message box asks 'Create Vedic natal chart first?' choose NO.

8. Your progressed Dwad chart is now in the calculated charts list ready for work!

Chapter Fifteen

The Current Draconic
'This is My Moment – My Destiny Calls Me!'

An Idea

At midnight on February 12th/13th 1989 an idea came to mind of such startling and challenging simplicity that it kept me awake well into the small hours, producing a haphazard sheaf of notes confirming the following concept: that a birth chart may symbolically 'move' in a way perhaps unrealised before, and certainly unacknowledged, which is *in relation to the transiting Node of the Moon.*

The new thought-process ran as follows: The birth chart progresses both Tropically in relation to the Spring Equinox, or Vernal Point, of 0° Aries, and Draconically in relation to the Dragon's Head. But the Dragon's Head *also* progresses, so we find planets moving against a moving Draconic framework, albeit a shift of only a few degrees maximum in a lifetime. I was wondering if one might progress the planets against the North Node as if it stayed fixed in the birth position, when a related question arose as to whether the planets at birth made continuously fresh zodiacal relationships with the *transiting* Node.

This seemed a preposterous idea – until curiosity led me to translate my own pattern into Draconic *as if the currently transiting Node at 0h00 on February 13th 1989 had been the Node at birth.* The pattern that emerged was so striking and potentially apt that it had to be followed up: for the actual natal Node was now directed only 0°4' from the birth Ascendant! The MC was just 0°9' from natal Moon and opposite transiting Neptune, Jupiter was opposite natal Venus, and Uranus opposite natal Mars. Asteroid *Urania* had swung opposite the transit of Uranus, the Moon was entering a conjunction with Pluto, and the Sun, now in the natal South Node with progressed Mercury and natal Draconic Jupiter, fell also in the same degree as the transiting Sun/IC/Draconic Mercury. Pluto was nearly on my natal Draconic Sun. Four hours of compulsive digging into diaries and ephemerides (remember this all started at midnight … this is how astrology gets you!) pulled out pattern after pattern of similarly directed contacts every bit as powerful in significance and timing as their corresponding Secondary Progressions and Solar Arcs. For example, transiting Node positions that draw the author's own radical Nodes together in this way with the Sun, at 26°10′ Aries, 3°50′ Pisces, 26°10′ Libra and 3°50′ Virgo, were associated with the following major life-changes:

Spring 1961

I was entered for the pan-European schools French essay competition; immediately afterwards I was very ill, then learned I had won the Paris holiday during which I bought that first, seminal, astrology book. (5th House Sun to *12th House North Node*)

Autumn 1967

This time I was recovering from the near-fatal delivery of my first (autistic) son. (*6th House South Node* to 5th House Sun)

Autumn 1970

Again, a traumatic birth, of my second son – and the death of my astrological twin. (Sun to *South Node*) To add even more weight to this pattern, the Sun had also moved to the Dragon's Tail by direct secondary progression. This pattern of loss has continued: my son chose to live, work and raise his family on the other side of the globe, and my second grand-daughter was born under the identical Current Draconic in 2007 (my son's Nodal Return).

Spring 1977

This was a crucial time when first I met a friend who was to be very important in building my confidence and stimulating my thinking; then – unrealised at the time – came the first encounter with my future husband, Gerard, who changed my life. (*North Node* to 5th-House Sun)

Winter 1979

Gerard and I bought our first home. We started meeting the people who would set us on our shared spiritual path. (Sun to *North Node*)

Summer 1986

At this juncture I was developing health problems (now largely resolved), and we moved my ageing mother-in-law to Kent. She had her Sun in my South Node. I was also proof-reading the first book *Draconic Astrology*. (6th House *South Node* to 5th House Sun)

Early 1989

The health problems were exacerbated; my father was by now also very ill, and it saw the germination of this idea, the **Current Draconic** – which led to the writing of the first *InterDimensional Astrology*, self-published for several years. (5th House Sun to *6th House South Node*)

Late 1995

A full 18-year nodal cycle since 1977 brought its potent seeds to fruition: this was time spent marooned hermit-like in my study, working harder than I have ever done in my life in a determined attempt to demonstrate (prove?) the phenomena of astrology to the satisfaction of an academic association with stringently high standards in research. I can't say it was successful – but again it led to other significant developments, and enabled me to grow in experience and understanding. (*12th House North Node* to Sun)

Summer 1998

The re-publication of a revised, extended *Draconic Astrology* – this very book *The Draconic Chart* – became possible at last, thanks to meeting Frank Clifford. (5th House Sun to *12th House North Node*)

Winter 2004/5

Very ill with shingles; took all my strength, so unable to continue my beloved choral singing. A close friend got into serious trouble and needed spiritual support. (*South Node* to 5th House Sun)

Late 2007

Very ill again; only just realising that a year unwillingly on statins had been wrecking my entire muscular and nervous system. Preparing to come off them. Intending to broadcast on the new local radio station, but rapidly disillusioned. On the plus side, the birth of my second grand-daughter, and our home resplendent with a new and beautiful front door! (5th House Sun to *6th House South Node*)

The fore-going sample serves to show how powerful this new directional system is; to the above could be added combinations of Moon/Node, Node/MC, Sun/Moon, Pluto/Mercury, whatever you will, but this is not necessary here – it would merely labour the point. Suffice it to add that on the night the idea of the **Current Draconic** came to me, the **CD** Pluto was approaching a multiple conjunction of my radix Draconic Sun, progressed Draconic Mars, and transiting South Node opposite transit Draconic Urania and North Node, which, together with the Urania/Uranus contact, suggested strongly some fresh astrological work to do!

Working with the Current Draconic

The Calculations

The question first to be asked is this: 'If the degree of my Sun is (e.g.) 29° Capricorn, where does that degree lie in a zodiac starting at the currently transiting North Node?' that is, 'What is the *current* Draconic position of my *natal* Tropical Sun-degree?' Next: 'And how do I work this out?' Basically, all you are doing is performing a subtraction, which is:

Natal Sun ° ′ – Transiting North Node ° ′ = Current Draconic (CD) Sun ° ′
or, if the position of the North Node is later in the zodiac than the Sun:
Natal Sun ° ′ + 360° – Transiting North Node ° ′ = CD Sun ° ′

Another way (clarification later, concerning Explements!) is to **subtract the transiting North Node ° ′ position from 360° and simply add the result (*the Explementary angle*) to the Natal Sun ° ′.**

If you are working from an astrological computer program such as Solar Fire which allows you to choose your own arc for Symbolic Directions, all you have to do here is:

1. Choose 'User Arc Directed'.

2. Set the progressed/directed date either to **the subject's birth date or the date of the current event (it will have no effect on the arc.)**

3. Enter the *Explementary degree and minutes of the transiting North Node for the chosen event.*

4. Display the resulting set of CD positions with the natal Tropical or Draconic, in a double wheel, or with both natal charts in a triple wheel.

Once the calculations are done, and the results displayed, you then find that certain of these Current Draconic positions fall on key placements in your birth chart, and tie in with life-events of major developmental importance.

Joining Forces

So, the next question is: 'Where does the transiting Node have to be, in order to move (for example) my natal Sun into *Draconic* Cancer 12°, the degree of my natal *Tropical* Moon?' It turns out to be Libra 17°.

What about the reverse, Moon moving to Sun in the same way? This gives a Node position of Virgo 13°.

Libra 17° + Virgo 13° = 360°. Mathematically these two positions are termed **Explementary Degrees,** *as they add up to the whole 360° circle of which each is a part.* Now, there is another, venerable technique in astrology, in which degree positions are reflected over a Cardinal axis as if it were a mirror: the *antiscia* are reflected over 0° Cancer/Capricorn, and their opposites, the *contrantiscia,* are reflections over 0° Aries/Libra. If you add the starting degree to its *contrantiscion,* the sum is also 360°. *Contrantiscia* are natural Explementary degrees.

Tabulating all the necessary positions of the transiting Node to bring together in CD-to-Tropical contact all possible pairings in the chart, it becomes rapidly apparent that the two different Node-axis placings for each pair (e.g. the Sun and Moon above) are naturally Explements of each other – add them together, and the sum is the complete wheel of 12 signs or 360°.

And of course it goes without saying that whenever you have a full Nodal Return, every 18+ years, the CD positions will again be identical to your natal Draconic – reminding the soul through current events and contacts of the reasons for its incarnation, reinforcing the deeper principles and the vocational drive. A half-return will do the same, as will a quarter; but the message may be less direct, even less comfortable, as on these occasions the CD positions will seem to contradict the nativity through their oppositions and squares.

Making a Visual Aid

At this point comes the realisation that all this calculation and tabulation can be smoothly accomplished by graphing onto rotating wheels; for if you map your chosen chart onto two zodiac wheels, and rotate one against the other to line up the Sun on one against the Moon on the other, the Aries Point will also have rotated against the second circle. Its new position on that circle marks the place where *any* non-Tropical zodiac, including the Current Draconic, has to start in order to join that particular planetary pair from one level to the other. This is, therefore, the position in the familiar Tropical zodiac which the transiting Node must reach to cross-connect Sun with Moon (etc.) in this very special set of Directions.

The corollary to this is that the Dragon's Head transiting the *opposite* points to those already found will bring those same two bodies into opposition – just as crucial as the conjunction.

A most significant and important observation follows on all the foregoing: that the emphasis placed by astrological tradition on the above-mentioned *antiscia and contrantiscia* (and by extension the Parallels and Contraparallels) – those points on the wheel which through reflection lie equidistant from the Solstice and Equinox axes of 0° Aries/Libra and 0° Cancer/Capricorn – is fully justified. They are the essential key to this profound set of bi-dimensional Directions. In my own work, the simpler term I have chosen to use for these is the 'Reflex Points', or more simply, 'Reflexes'.

Life's Rich Tapestry

A tabulation of your own transiting Node degrees as suggested above, and a systematic check on the dates when they have been active through your life, will show you quickly how they pinpoint those periods and moments when you find yourself doing the things which you have come into life to do, to further your spiritual growth and honour your soul's commitments. Entering the Current Draconic dimension we are given a truthful insight into what we may term our 'Fate' or 'Destiny'. How flexible its outworking may be is a matter for much on-going study and debate.

Some Recordable CDs!

The Death of Janis

It is worth looking at patterns of the Current Draconic in other lives now – and where better to begin than with Janis Joplin, and the CDs operative at her death. (Bear in mind that these directions move as fast as the True Node moves – or as slowly – covering any period from a week or two to a couple of months.) Janis, my astro-twin by eight hours and a lot of ocean, also had her progressed Sun in her South Node in 1970, as we have seen. She died; I had a thankfully brief breakdown. Both of us had major relationship issues to deal with at the time … no surprise! But with 25° Aquarius also rising, that CD Sun was not only in her Dragon's Tail but on her Ascendant, pressing on the setting Chiron by less

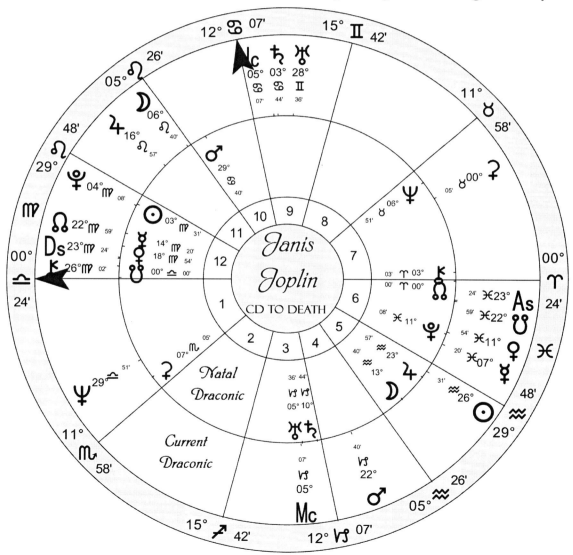

than 2°, and the CD Nodes/horizon/Chiron were squaring radix 10th House Mars. The 5th House Moon had come to Tropical Pluto in the 6th. Already you can see that the Aquarian cussedness that was a hefty personality flaw had come up for a make-or-break moment; she was going to do her own thing come what may, and she would do what she wanted with her poor, self-abused body, if she felt it gave her a kick or a high. But she did it once too often, and threw away with her life the best chance she had had for years of finding out how to love, and at last settling down.

What we must remember now is that the Current Draconic not only impacts on the Tropical, but on the natal Draconic! In Janis's pattern, these contacts are extremely dramatic and revealing. We find no less than Pluto on the Sun, Venus on Pluto, Moon square Neptune, Neptune square Mars, Saturn square the setting Chiron, and MC on Uranus: suddenly it was time for the Great Escape (again), because it was all just too, too much for a soul to bear. '*A lump of pain, like a black mucus, glued onto her since childhood,*' wrote David Dalton. I wonder what happened when she was coming up for nine years old, when this very same pattern would have set a train of inner events in motion? Certainly by or at the time the reverse pattern kicked in, in the spring of 1961, this intelligent, sensitive, paradoxical girl had made her first big escape from home and roots at Port Arthur where she had been shunned and derided for her maverick behaviour, and slipped quickly into the sex, drugs and rock'n'roll lifestyle that eventually killed her.

It is sad to see yet again, and all the more clearly from the wheel, that only 3° of nodal transit before her death (thus in the June of 1970) everything had looked so rosy. We know from her biography and witnesses that she had found a man who made her happy and was winning commitment from the wild child. Life was going to change; she was making uncharacteristically (despite the Cancer Moon) domestic plans. CD Sun had then been on Draconic Jupiter, the CD North Node already passing Draconic Venus, and CD Jupiter aligned with the Tropical Venus and Draconic Moon in the 12th. CD Mars was opposite Tropical Jupiter and CD Uranus just over the opposition with Tropical Mars. Surely this was when Janis really met Love; surely this was when real joy seemed possible. And then, all too soon, the Dragon slid into 2° Pisces where it curled and coiled for the rest of that summer and into the early fall, driving her into what may well have been a massive identity crisis, between public applause and private desires pulling her apart at the seams, crushing her soul with emotional and spiritual demands that she would, in the end, in *this* life, be utterly powerless to meet.

The 1984 Strike

When checking the assorted charts of the 1984 miners' strike for their CD patterns I had such a sense of déja vu that I thought I must have done them before. But of course I hadn't, as CDs were only discovered in 1989 – two whole years after the first edition of *Draconic Astrology* was published! What I was seeing was the extraordinary echo of all those vital DPAs in the added set of Current Draconic directions.

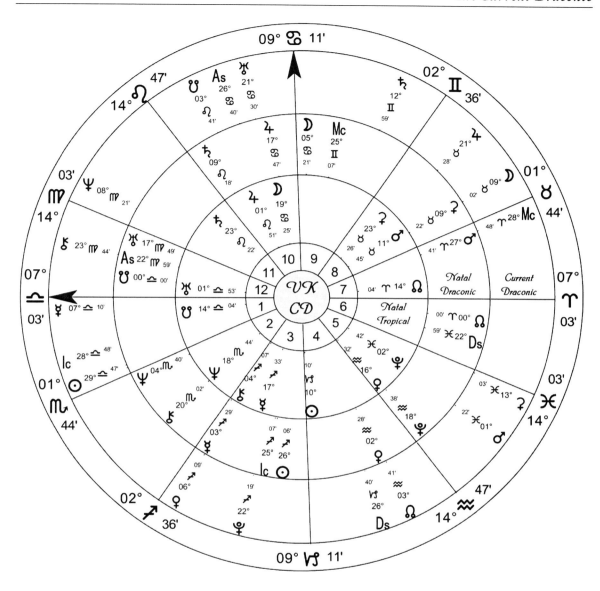

The UK chart is plotted as a tri-wheel to show the impact of the CDs on both Tropical and Draconic radices. The United Kingdom was being treated to CD MC/IC/Sun on Draconic Mars, the Moon, exactly with Draconic Ceres, was running onto Tropical Mars, Uranus was on its Cancer Moon, Chiron conjunct Draconic Ascendant, Venus on the Mercury/Chiron alignment, Jupiter opposite Draconic Scorpio Chiron in the 2nd, Dragon's Head on Draconic Venus with the tail on Tropical Jupiter, and Mars heading for Tropical Pluto. CD Mercury edging onto the Tropical Libran Ascendant keeps negotiations on the table while this protracted, painful (Chiron) battle (Mars) inexorably heats up over job security, resources and status (10th House, Venus, Jupiter, Ceres, Cancer, Taurus/Scorpio, and 2nd-8th Houses.)

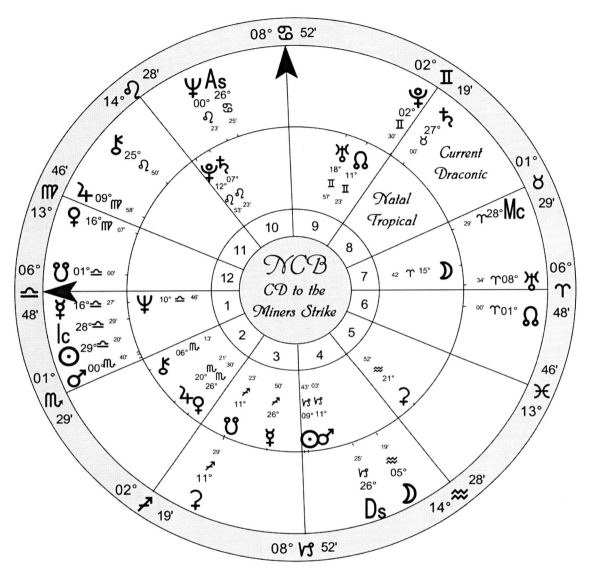

The National Coal Board was having its Nodal Return! So the Current Draconic was a snug fit to the inceptional Draconic – and, sure enough, up came all the difficult issues over changes in working practice and the inevitability of redundancy: CD and natal Draconic Uranus on the Tropical 7th House cusp. With a rising Neptune squared to Sun/Mars at the IC, all being hit by this Uranus, you can see how this could lead to some very dodgy dealing on the part of the Board and management when confronted by any pressure for change. It is interesting to observe that Mars-Neptune afflictions lead from crusading zeal to exhaustion, and here it also illustrates the deep mining (Mars Capricorn IC) that eventually results in exhausted seams (Neptune). And if the seams go, the jobs go. As both Sun and Moon are in Draconic Air, there is also a seam of fair-mindedness and social principle in the NCB – but it is compromised by the squares which risk a less admirable habit of smooth-talking its way out of any financially threatening situation.

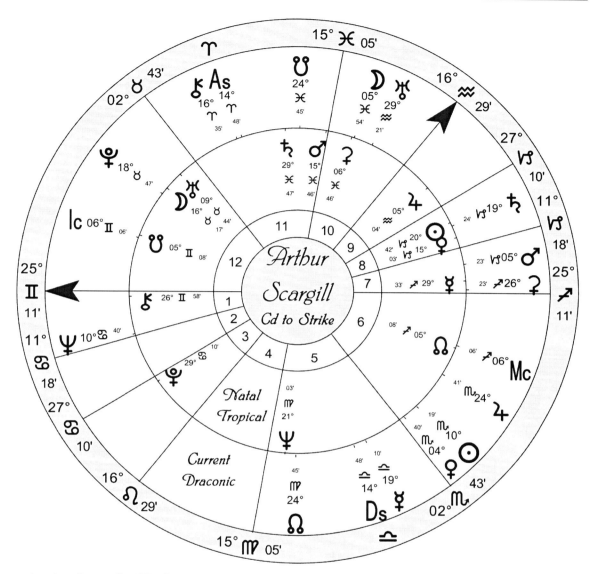

As for Scargill, CD Saturn, natally in that awkward square to the Ascendant, was deep into the 8th between Tropical Venus/Draconic Neptune and Sun. CD Pluto had just delivered its ultimatum to his Draconic Sun/Tropical Moon in security-loving Taurus, and the CD Sun itself was challenging the adjacent Venus/Uranus axis from Scorpio. Jupiter was on Draconic Pluto, Neptune on Draconic Mars (aha! a crusade!), and best of all his CD MC was right up to the Tropical North Node and squared by the CD Moon, as CD Ceres – mistress of resources and of the UK itself – confronted him from his Descendant. At moments like this, a man feels he knows why he has been born! He must rise like a phoenix, proclaim what he stands for, take shared burdens on his own shoulders, and become a Righter of Wrongs. The trouble is that you also have to live in the real world, and this is difficult to achieve when you have Neptune square the Ascendant.

What Happens When People Die?

The short answer is that there is no set pattern. No two lives are identical and no two deaths are identical. Some are sweet, some are painful. Some souls spring gladly into the Light, others struggle bitterly to remain. Eric Morecambe went with CD Pluto at the Tropical MC, Uranus close to the Draconic MC, and CD Chiron on his Descendant, opposite the rising Neptune. This was a mighty, transformative leap from one state of being to another. He was born with both Tropical and Draconic Neptune tightly angular; to find himself suddenly in the subtle body, in the spiritual world, may have been as much a delight as a shocking surprise.

His friend died with CD Sun to Draconic Mars and Tropical Pluto, CD Mars still close to Draconic Ascendant, CD Jupiter on Draconic Mercury and CD Moon conjunct Sun. Yes,

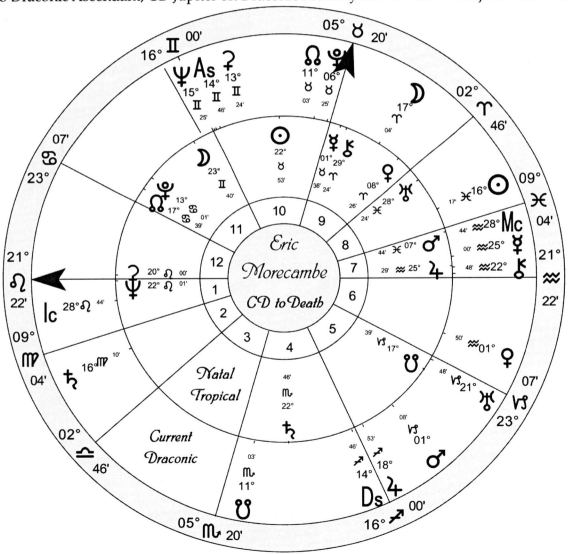

here is the imagery of pain, which had dogged Ernie Wise for months – but again there is the Plutonic dying into new life, and for him clearly the utter joy of reunion. He went from a racked body to greet his best mate and start sharing the jokes again.

Looking back to their very first comedy series on TV, Jupiter is reassuringly in evidence. Ernie's Draconic Jupiter/Venus conjunction in late Virgo has just had the magic wand of CD Pluto/MC waved over it, and the Tropical conjunction is given the go-ahead by CD Mars. As befits a life-changing (and money-spinning!) new venture, we find CD Uranus opposite his 2nd House Sagittarian Sun; and the famous working partnership starts with CD North Node, that started out in Ernie's 10th House, closing on his Ascendant. Obviously busy writing the jokes, too, as the CD Ascendant is tickling the funny-bone of his Tropical Sagittarian Mercury.

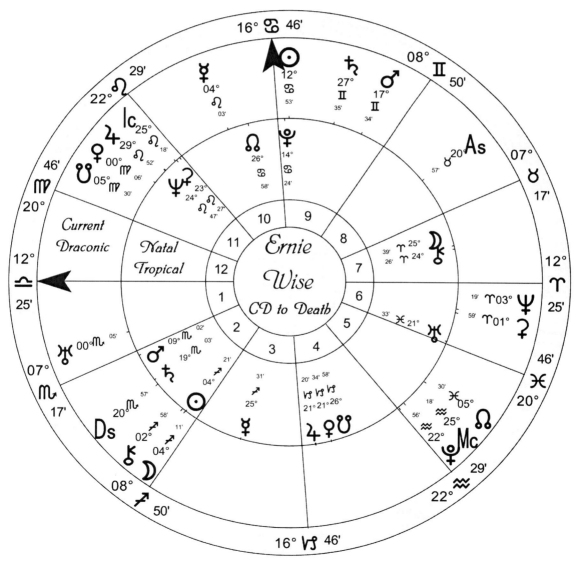

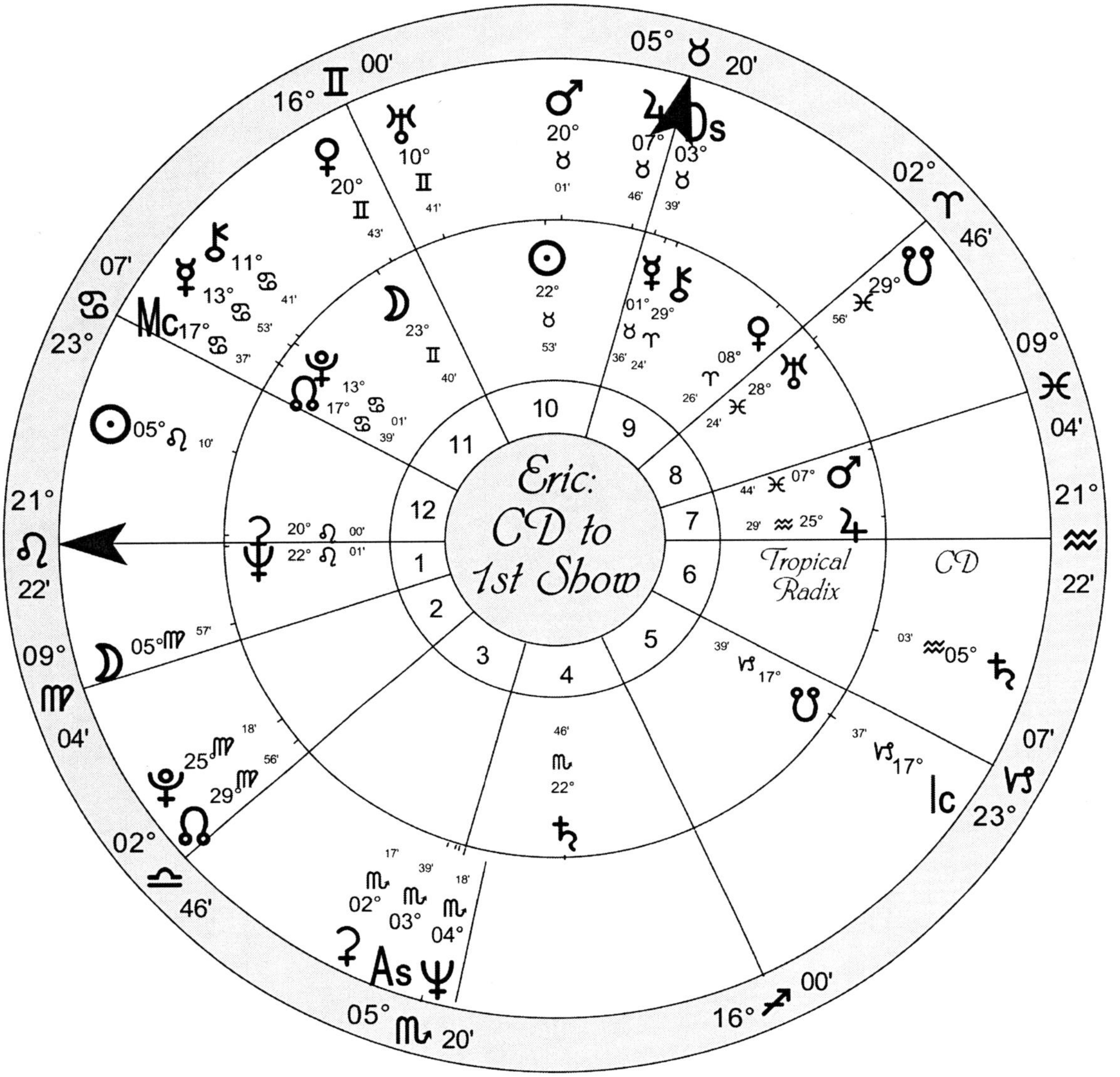

Eric:
CD to
1st Show

Tropical
Radix

CD

As for Eric, CD Jupiter itself, natally angular to his 7th, is crowning the MC right opposite its Draconic position at birth, because he is busy having a Nodal half-return, the other periodic reminder of What We Are Here To Do. So everything significant in his natal Draconic-to-Tropical pattern is CD-constellated: MC to Nodes; Mercury/Chiron to Pluto; his Grand Cross of Sun-Saturn-Jupiter-Neptune-Ascendant impacting the Midheaven; Venus heading for Moon; Moon reaching across to Draconic Mars; Mars driving onto the Sun and the Tropical Grand Cross. Everything Eric was, he became in that seminal April of 1954. It is well-known that this first series of shows, 'Running Wild', received discouraging reviews, and this is reflected in other patterns. But the Current Draconic tells a different story. This could be the start of Something Big!...

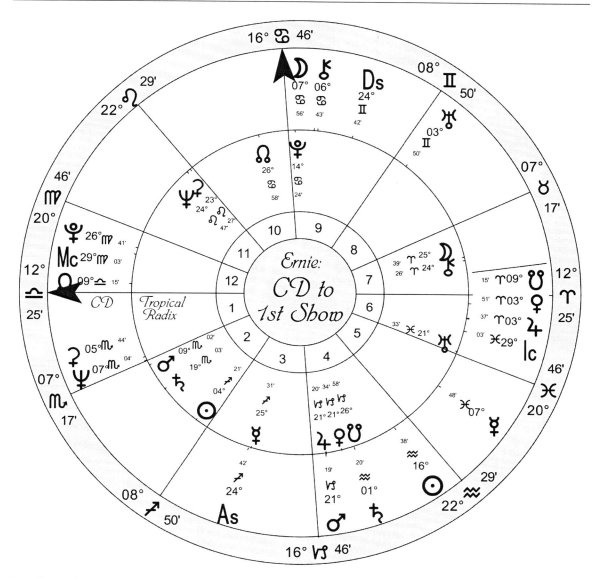

Zerda and Aaron

This is a fascinating picture. If the Current Draconic casts light on the long-term meaning of particular periods in our lives, then Aaron's broken back appears to have everything to do with the consequent relationship between him and his mother. Because both of them have an angular CD Moon! Zerda's has come to her Ascendant, and Aaron's to his Midheaven, and culminating Sun. As you might anticipate, his CD MC/Sun has just met the fateful Draconic Aries Pluto, after his Mercury/Mars met the Draconic Sun/MC around the preceding Christmas (was the motor-bike a Christmas present, I wonder?) and now opposed slippery, inattentive Neptune. So you can see a buildup here of the thrill of having his own wheels, and the dangers to him from now on. That natal Libra-Capricorn square of his between Mercury/Mars and Jupiter/Saturn never augured well

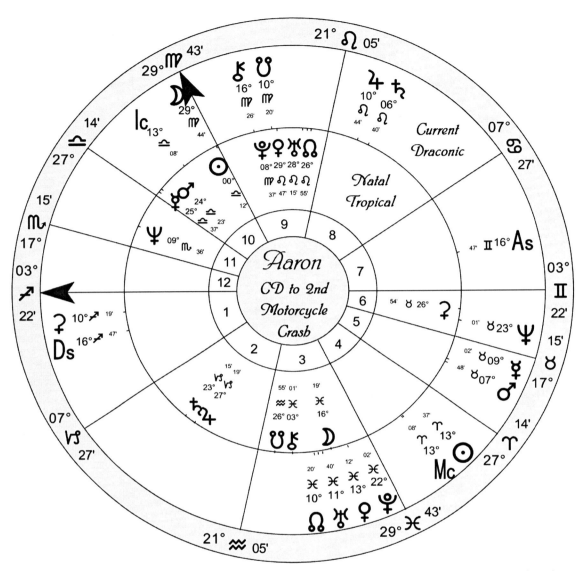

for good coordination and reaction time or efficient braking at speed. It is even the shape of a corner! The CD patterns climax, however, at the moment when the inevitable accident makes him totally dependent on his Moon, his mother, who will from then on set a new and successful course for his life.

Not only has the mothering Moon come to Zerda's Ascendant as her son, so close to independence, becomes totally reliant on her again, but CD Saturn has come to weigh down her Cancer Ascendant-Sun/Pluto alignment. Difficulties and responsibilities loom over her life, and with CD 7th on Neptune, compassion and imagination are called for in her closest relationship. CD IC hits Chiron. Here is the pain; here is her renewed role, as coach and healer to her child back at home. CD Uranus to Draconic Aries Mars and the Nodes wakes her up to the need for decisive action, enterprise, dominance, and the energy

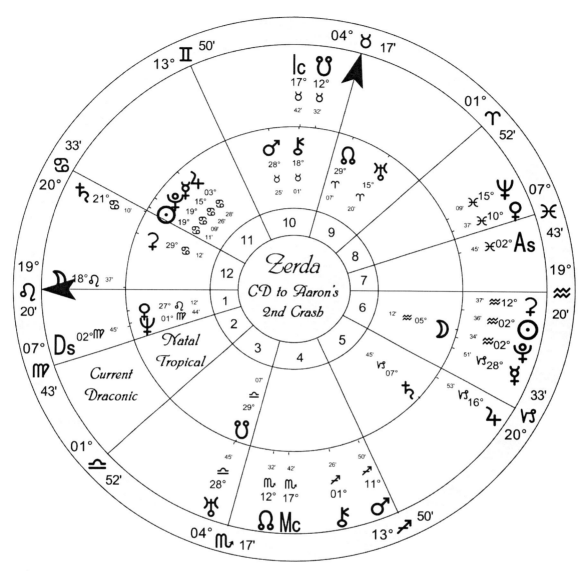

and courage to carry on. Her Sun/Pluto is also opposed to Draconic Neptune, and closing on her 6th House Aquarian Moon. She was always meant to work out radical, imaginative solutions to her family's needs, and now the moment had arrived when this vocation would be put to its greatest test.

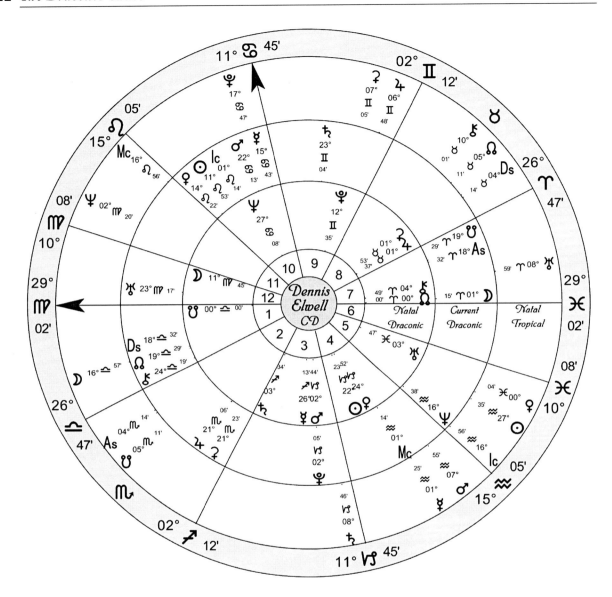

Draco Day!

Dennis Elwell's CD MC was right on his Aquarian Mercury when he gave that lecture back in 1977, and Mercury was running up to Pluto in the 9th – that was about all. No great drama. But what else need we expect? Already then and still today one of our most admired astrologers, Dennis was simply passing on something of interest and value that he had learned earlier. However, the *subject matter* of his Draconic lecture is brilliantly highlighted in that September's CD pattern – of CD Mars opposite his Draconic 3rd House Sun, and CD Pluto on the Draconic Mars; every example he gave was a Draconic-to-Tropical alignment of Mars with Sun!

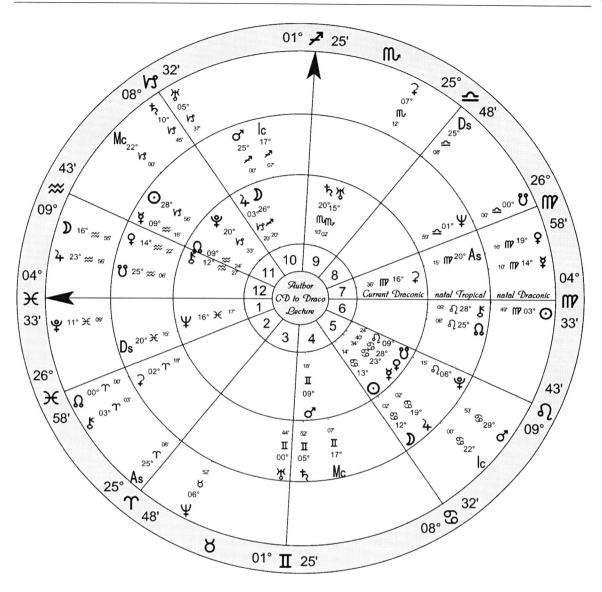

But for yours truly it was possibly the most significant identifiable moment of my astrological life. There have been others of equal importance, and sometimes of greater impact, since – but without that first encounter with the Draconic dimension none of the others could have happened. It was another of those genuinely seminal moments, symbolically graced by the CD Sun's wedding with the 10th House Moon, and CD Venus bonding with Draconic Mars opposite the Tropical Sun. CD Pluto officiated on the Draconic MC opposite Tropical Jupiter in the 10th. The Dragon's Head had, gloriously, come to the conjunction of Tropical 5th House Mercury precisely to the minute of arc – and this is when I am first taught that it generates a zodiac! On the CD Descendant was Draconic Sun in

Virgo introducing me not only to my other self but to years of enthusiastic fine-tuning. CD MC was charged up from 9th House Gemini Uranus; CD Moon had met the Galactic Centre and natal Tropical Mars; Mars was on 9th House Urania: I was firing on all cylinders.

This initial storm of energy lasted for well over two months, as the Dragon hugged 15° Libra to its bosom, only letting it go in November of that year. Back in 1959 when it had last visited the degree it was relatively brief, but ushered in a year that again transformed my life, as nine years in the north of England ended and a new world opened up in the south where everything that had been frustrated suddenly had the freedom to blossom; I was finding out who I was, what I was made of.

The latest visit to Libra 15° was not too long ago, in June 1996 – again quite brief – but it coincided with a number of significant events. During the spring, with the Node approaching its goal through 17° and 16° Libra, and already beginning the sequence of CD alignments, I was working extremely hard to fine-tune and finalise the asteroids for the charts of Jesus, Our Lady, the Crucifixion and the Resurrection in time for the date of the real Christian Millennium on May 7th 1996 (or May 4th, if you take not Jesus' birth date but that of his 1996 Solar Return). A lot of flyers were sent out, and this was when Richard Denton of BBC's *Everyman* documentary series first phoned to talk about the chart of the Nativity. On June 1st, the *Christian Parapsychologist* (edited by Canon Michael Perry) published an article I had submitted at his invitation, and subsequently he invited me to speak at their Millennium conference in Christ Church College, Canterbury. It was in the chapel of this same college where in April 1996 another dimension of life began with acceptance into Canterbury Choral Society; in the June we packed the Cathedral for a performance of Verdi's stunning *Requiem*. I was on such a high by that time, I could have sung it twice!

Bernadette at Lourdes

You would expect some pretty impressive CD configurations to appear in that chart of Bernadette Soubirous, a girl who was granted visions and conversations with Our Lady, Mary, mother of Jesus. The vision first appeared to her on February 11th 1858 down by the river that flows on the outskirts of Lourdes in south-west France. The time is uncertain, but I can offer you this impressive Q-chart: i.e. the day and place of the apparition set for the time of Bernadette's birth, 2h00 pm, highlighting her specific experiences of that day. Fittingly it shows Neptune culminating with the spiritually important North Node, as a Tropical conjunction of Moon and Mercury 'sets' on the Draconic 7th cusp. Aligned with the Moon in coelo are *Riverside*, *Christa* and *Donna*; on the horizon are *Cava*, *Mira*, and *Almamater*; on the meridian are *Aura*, *Carmelmaria* and *Yasue*. In a cave by her local river, Bernadette will be set on her Path, in a state of high attunement, and begin her miraculous relationship with the Divine Mother.

Bernadette was born, according to her birth record, at 2h00 pm on January 7th 1844 in Lourdes at the foot of the Pyrenees, still a most beautiful place despite all the clutter of mass pilgrimage. In her birth chart we find not only an alignment of Draconic Jupiter/

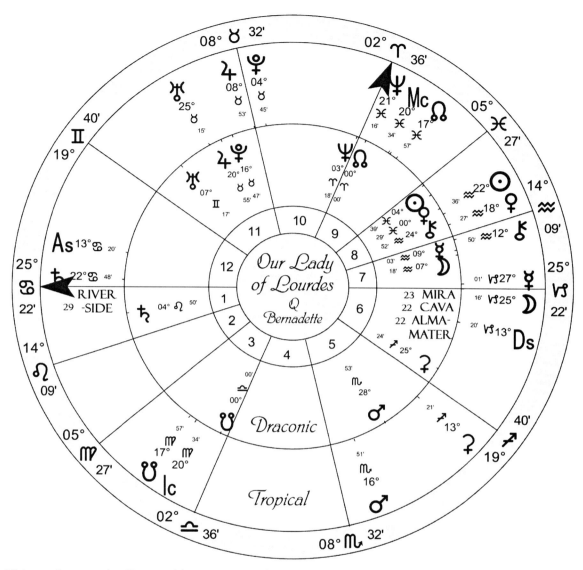

Chiron close to the Tropical horizon (marking her religious life, and constant confrontation with pain) but many strongly-placed and highly significant asteroids. On her Ascendant is asteroid *Maria*; Tropical Maria is conjunct Draconic *Aparicio*. Draconic Christa is close to her Tropical 7th cusp and her Sun, near Mary, is conjunct *Yeshuhua and Draconic Almamater (the nourishing Mother)*, opposite *Yezo*: her heart beats for the Heart of Jesus. Right on her IC with a Leo Moon conjunct Our Lady's own natal Sun, is *Vaticana* opposite a Draconic conjunction in Aquarius of *Donna* and *Basilea*. On her Tropical Midheaven is the healing asteroid *Asclepius* with Draconic *Yasue*. The Draconic MC/Venus-IC/Moon aligns with not only Tropical Ceres – the World Mother – but, close to Mary's own natal Ascendant in mid-Scorpio, the asteroids *Carmelmaria, Paradise, Amor, Devota, Hale* (the old word for 'healthy') and *Bishop*. Opposite in Draconic Taurus, close to Jesus' Sun with ruling Mercury are *Modestia* and *Pia*.

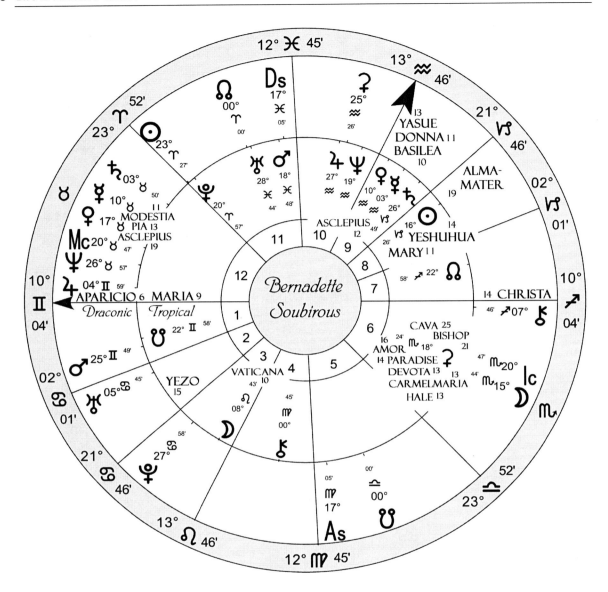

This humble girl was indeed destined to see apparitions of the Blessed Marie, the Madonna, mother of Jesus Christ; and she was to work from her strong Marian root in the Roman Catholic Church to realise Our Lady's requested gift of a great Basilica over the grotto where she had appeared and caused the healing spring to flow.

At the time of the apparition the Current Draconic pattern is almost identical to fourteen-year-old Bernadette's Solar Arcs. The significant natal planets are all in focus. With the setbacks and heavy responsibilities of CD Saturn heading for her Venus and MC in the months ahead, at her moment of destiny she had CD Moon opposite sensitive Neptune and warmed by the transiting Sun. The CD MC was with Jupiter and Draconic Ceres. Chiron was on its way to instruct her obedient Draconic Virgo Ascendant, and her

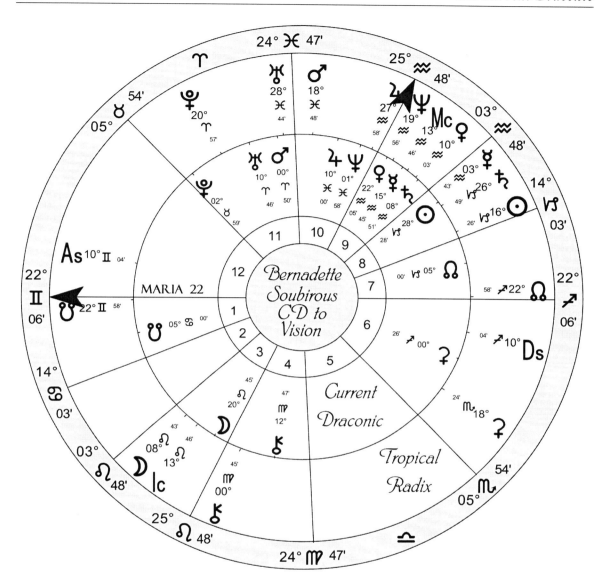

CD Ascendant was conjunct the sacrificial Dragon's Tail. But inseparable from it was CD *Maria*! … who was to receive everything she asked of the devoted girl, at great expense to Bernadette's physical health, but to the eternal enrichment of her patient Christian soul.

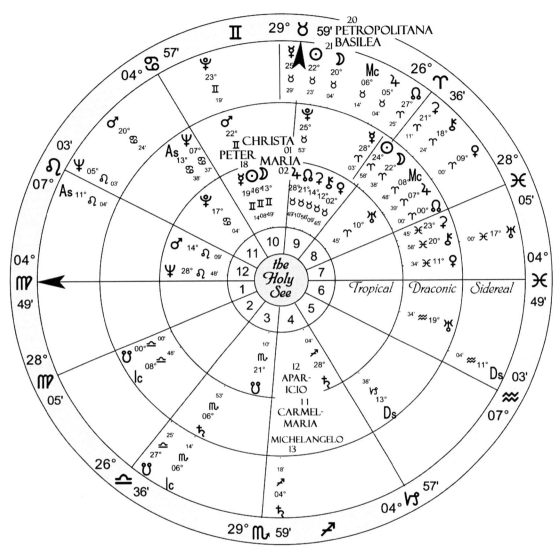

You may like to see what was happening for the Vatican itself at the time. We have a date and time for its political foundation in Rome: June 7th 1929 at 11h00 am CET. It can hardly surprise us by now to find yet another angular *Maria*, in the place of greatest honour where she should be – close to religious Jupiter, and on her Son's Moon, at the Midheaven with Draconic *Christa*. For good measure, *Aparicio* is opposite the Vatican's New Moon with Draconic *Carmelmaria* (so is Draconic *Michelangelo*!) and *Basilea/Petropolitana* (St Peter's Basilica in the City of Peter) is embraced by it. (For reasons of space I have had to display this configuration in the outer Sidereal wheel.) The Draconic asteroid *Peter* (the first Pope) naturally conjoins the Sun. When Bernadette saw Mary, the Vatican's CD MC/ *Maria* conjunction, 12° on from the natal Tropical position, was pointing directly at that Moon, with the CD IC on *Aparicio*; weighty matters were afoot with the CD Sun now opposite Saturn, Venus had come to Ceres, and the shock to the Church's system from

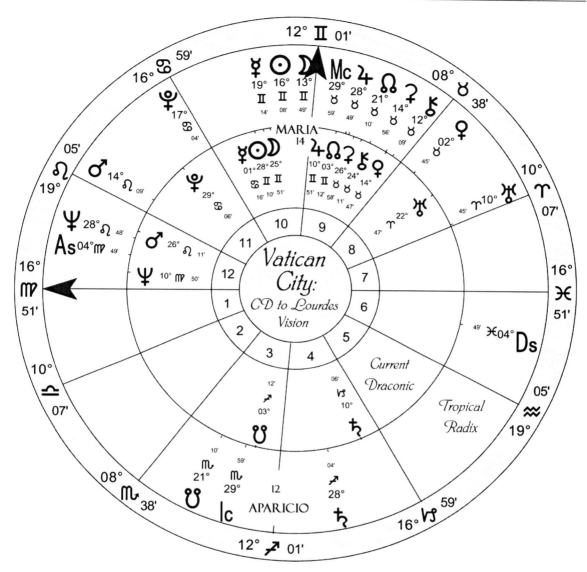

Our Lady's unexpected visitation very apparent from the CD Uranus conjunction to the Draconic Moon/*Aparicio* axis. And the Moon's Ascending Node had come to *Maria*. For the Roman Catholic establishment its purposes had thereby been made very clear: they were to take serious heed of Bernadette's story, and honour Mary with a new Basilica as she had asked.

It will be interesting to study all the other visions that have resulted in a permanent shrine; do the patterns echo this one? It is built into the Vatican's psyche.

You will have realised something else of extraordinary significance about the Vatican's eloquent Current Draconic: it is retrospective! The Vatican itself as home of the Holy See of Rome has existed since the fifteenth century, but the tiny, powerful city state officially came into being *seventy-one years after* the remarkable events at Lourdes. Along with converse progressions and directions, this is further evidence that time and experience take far stranger shapes than any of us can yet conceive.

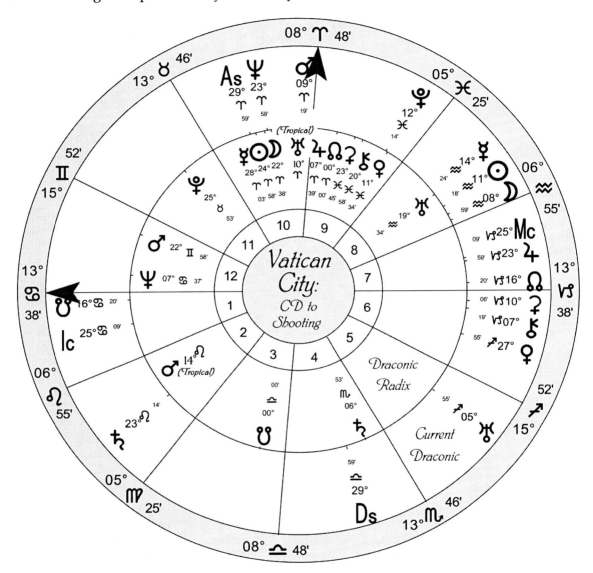

The Pope is Shot

Let's stay with the Vatican for the moment, because another critical event for the Holy See was the day when Pope John Paul was shot by his would-be assassin in St Peter's Square on May 13th 1981.

This time, we would expect Mars to make its aggressive presence felt – and so it does: the Current Draconic Mars has burned its way into Aries and onto the inceptional Draconic

MC/Tropical Uranus; a shot rings out, attacking the very Head of the Church. This is part of the karmic pattern, Draconic Jupiter/MC to Tropical Uranus in the 8th, alerting us to the periodic need for the Vatican to deal with shocks and changes in its hierarchy, dark deeds, irregular fiscal affairs. CD Neptune is doing its best to undermine and weaken the Draconic Sun/Moon, the 20th-century Peter, and can only be overcome by faith and the heart's deep prayer. The Vatican's power over the masses is endangered; the CD South Node is on Pluto, and CD Pluto has netted Draconic Venus among the Fishes. With CD Ascendant on Draconic Mercury in Aries and CD Aquarian Mercury looking down the barrel of 12th House Mars, the unobtrusive assassin is identified, the young man with a gun in the crowd. (His name was Mehmet Ali Agca, born in Hekimhan, Turkey on January 9th 1958.) The Draconic Aries stellium in the Vatican chart co-ruling its Scorpio South Node tells us that the Papacy must always set an example of leadership, zeal and courage through the sacrifices it is called upon to make, while faithfully, unswervingly treading the path of peace. At this cruel test for the Church, the Sun was conjunct the Vatican's Sidereal New Moon/Tropical North Node in Taurus, and the rising Pluto opposed that Draconic New Moon in Aries. Please God, it will not always be so painful a drama.

King is Killed

Another, earlier shooting of a major religious leader was that of the Revd Martin Luther King. King died. His CD Ascendant had met, again in Aries, and in his treacherous 12th House, the karmic Draconic opposition of Mars and Saturn. CD Uranus shattered the Draconic Ascendant in Pisces. He was another born for sacrifice with the South Node in Mars-ruled Scorpio, and Draconic Sun/MC in the same difficult sign, conjoining it. We can only ask, is it their own karma being worked out here? Or are these, like Jesus, willingly sacrificial souls standing bail for humanity, paying with their lives for our mistakes? Martyrdom means even more than this of course; but that is material for a Sidereal book.

War

The last thing that any of us wanted eventually happened. We had another war in Europe. The chief protagonist was Slobodan Milosevic, leader of Serbia, who with his government seemed unbendingly determined to purge adjacent Kosovo of every man, woman and child with Albanian blood. We were back to the Balkans again, one of the festering sores of the world, a Chiron place that never seems able to heal. And taking Nick Campion's 8 pm close-of-poll chart for the Kosovo referendum of September 30th 1991, what do we find? Chiron at the IC. And with 8° Sagittarius setting, 12° Aquarius MC, so newly transited by Pluto and Uranus, we can estimate just how long this purge had been going on.

The chart I am using for the start of NATO's attack on Serbia is not the time that bombs began to fall; in the UK we were shown live pictures from one of the aircraft carriers in the Adriatic just off the Albanian coast as events were coming to a head on March 24th 1999. It was a flawless evening. The BBC's overseas correspondent Kate Adie, usually one of the first to be sent into any war zone, watched with her cameraman the sun sinking scarlet

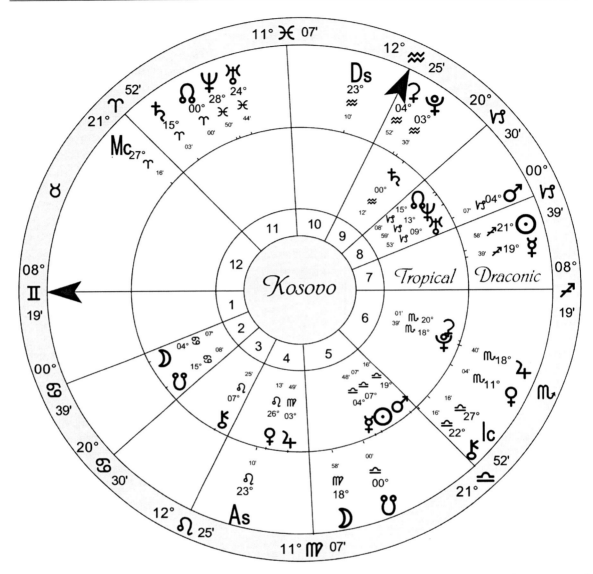

into a kingfisher-blue sea … and then everything was commotion. The NATO command had made the decision to begin preparations for the first missile launch on Serbia at sunset exactly. This is what we all saw, and heard, thousands of miles from the scene. It was pitch dark when the first Cruise missiles blazed and arced into the night sky. I have taken the chart for sunset as my war chart, set for Tirana, Albania, which is just inland from that coast. You will appreciate this chart all the more when I point out that among the asteroids chosen to illustrate the conflict, *Srbija* (Serbia) is on the Draconic MC with *Aeria* (the Air war), and a conjunction of *Beograd* (Belgrade) and *Britten* (Britain) conjoins the Draconic Ascendant … opposite Mars and *Adolfine*. Thought-provoking. Especially when you see, from the Solar Fire tabulated positions, the Draconic collection that 'rises' in the Tropical: *Jewitt, Judith, Flammario* and *Fanatica*. Tropically these four fall in the Dragon's Tail, and opposite at the Head is the Draconic conjunction of the asteroids *Yugoslavia* and *United*

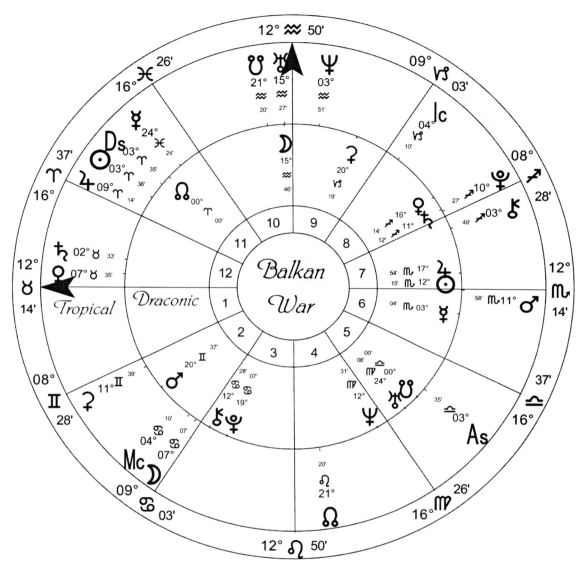

Nations. Europa is a mere 8′ from Draconic Mars. For whatever reason, however protracted or brief the engagement, we were revisiting the issues of two earlier World Wars. With the Nodal axis and Draco so heavily involved, my guess is that unavoidably we had to face the out-working of massive human karma.

The Draconic MC of this war chart, 12° Aquarius, is almost precisely the Tropical MC of **Kosovo**, to which Kosovo's CD Moon has come, echoing the culminating quarter-Moon of the war – image of a shockingly public battle, in the glare of the world's media, conjunct Tropical Uranus by only 19′. Kosovo itself was stricken on the earlier transit of that Uranus. Its CD MC has been over the Draconic Moon, CD Chiron is moving closer to its opposition, the promise of pain to come. The country's trauma started in earnest 6° of Nodal transit before, when CD Pluto struck the Draconic Sun; this would have been November 1998. By

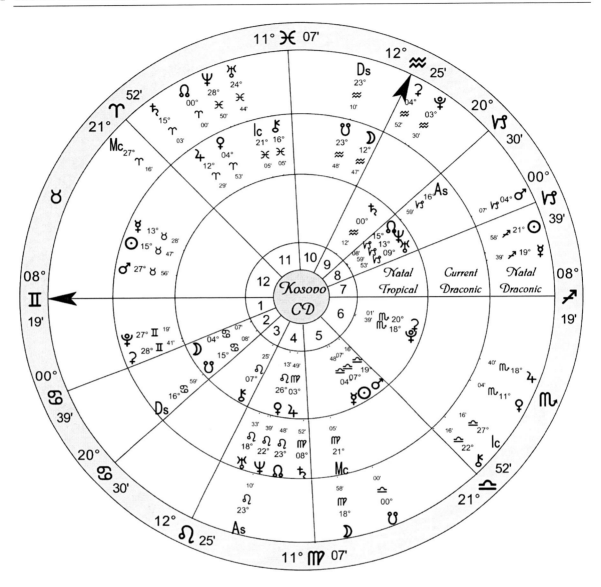

the end of the month transiting Pluto had moved onto Kosovo's Ascendant … and returned there again and again before the end of 1999. As the bombs began to fall on Serbia the CD North Node and Neptune on the Draconic Ascendant caught Kosovo up in its destiny. At the country's inception this conjunction was in the 8th House in Capricorn; these people were to grow through material suffering, yes, but in order to value the spiritual above the material, to cultivate simplicity, patience, faith, compassion and willingness to share. As the thousands began fleeing, leaving behind and losing all the possessions and habitual domestic comforts of South Node in Cancer in the 2nd House, asteroids *Yugoslavia* and *United Nations* were pulling them to the North Node in the 8th. But two more degrees of Nodal travel saw CD Jupiter join Draconic Saturn in the 11th, and the Sun align with Jupiter in the 6th – and it was precisely at this juncture that the massive international aid effort eventually got underway, bringing bedding, clothing, food, medical and other essential supplies to a scattered, exiled, traumatised, starving people.

Serbia was 'born' with Mars in Leo in its 9th House South Node, right opposite Kosovo's Moon and MC, smack on its IC. Of course Serbia wants to rule Kosovo. Of course it will destroy what others would withhold. But this is typical Dragon's Tail behaviour and in the end will only bring Serbia grief. Uranus hits the shared axis, and the payback begins. (It is also working on Milosevic's Moon/Pluto/Chiron.) Here is Serbia, then, with the CD Mars/South Node launching itself confidently into the fray conjunct Draconic Jupiter. CD Ascendant has just passed Draconic Neptune in Gemini; no evidence of sensitivity here, but a lot of deception, and self-deception too. The CD Sun was recently on the Draconic Moon, seeding the new campaign, a new era … but the CD IC was heading for Draconic Uranus, CD Pluto bearing down on the Draconic Ascendant, and as both reached their target the country and its capital were suffering devastating destruction in the escalating air-raids. The Eclipse of August 11th hit Serbia's horizon fair and square. That should have brought a few chickens home to roost – but it did not immediately bring the Kosovans home.

What about **Slobodan Milosevic**? His identification with Serbia is extraordinarily strong, probably going back quite a way. For him it is a spiritual tie, it gives his whole life its meaning; it is the type of Draconic connection we see regularly in married couples, and have seen also in a close working partnership. Here (in a chart calculated for August 20th 1941, speculative time: 10h00 pm Pozarevac, 44N37, 21E11) it is a double bond, with Milosevic's Draconic Sun opposite Serbia's, and his Tropical Sun opposite Serbia's Draconic Moon. Back at the end of October, beginning of November 1998 he too had a 'New Moon' of opportunity, as CD Moon came to his Draconic Sun. The discovery of this in Pisces came as no surprise to me, as every time he appeared on the screen in my living-room all I could see was that negative fishiness, the depraving weakness of a ruined child who had never emotionally matured. In the chaos of his psyche he can never trust, never be trusted; he can never really love, nor ever truly experience love, because in his desperation for that most precious thing he will cheat and charm, and if thwarted will force his way to people's attention. If he cannot have love, then he will take everything else instead. If he cannot have love, then at least this damaged multiple Leo will have pride, and power, and glory, and riches, and stop his ears to the soft voice of his Dragon whispering that the way to love and tenderness is through mercy, humility and service. To be emotionally damaged is no excuse for brutality. We are all given free-will to choose a better way. The Sidereal, of course, reveals even more.

Neptune and Jupiter were both much in evidence as the drama began to unfold: CD Jupiter at his Draconic IC, CD Ascendant in Sagittarius on its way to align with the Tropical gas giant in Gemini. The CD Sun was just waking from a Draconic Neptunian dream, while CD Neptune sowed chaos and fantasy on his Ascendant. And all the while CD MC drew his Leo Sun/Mercury into so much limelight that he would believe he was fully in command, could sweet-talk his way through any interrogation, and would achieve his dream. To look at this pattern, you would notice the weight of transiting Saturn pressing ever more on his agonising Moon/Pluto/Chiron/horizon T-square, but would think this man had little to fear from Pluto, whose CD passage over the Draconic Sun had only brought him power. Once again, if you look, you will find that it is the Sidereal which tells the full story.

NATO (August 24th 1949, 11h42 am EDT, Washington) had also run into drama, with CD Uranus beginning an extended run opposite the 10th House sequence of Draconic Sun, Tropical Pluto, Draconic Moon and Saturn, CD Mars/Jupiter aligning with the Virgo Sun, CD Moon/Saturn in its Aries North Node and on the Draconic Descendant, CD Mercury on the Tropical 7th House cusp, and CD IC on Draconic Venus (Victrix?). Time to flex the muscles of its power, to augment dialogue with planned and uncompromising action. Many people disliked this turn of events, but for NATO action (Aries) is a North Node matter; it really does have to show that it has teeth, that despite an inevitable Virgo-Libra

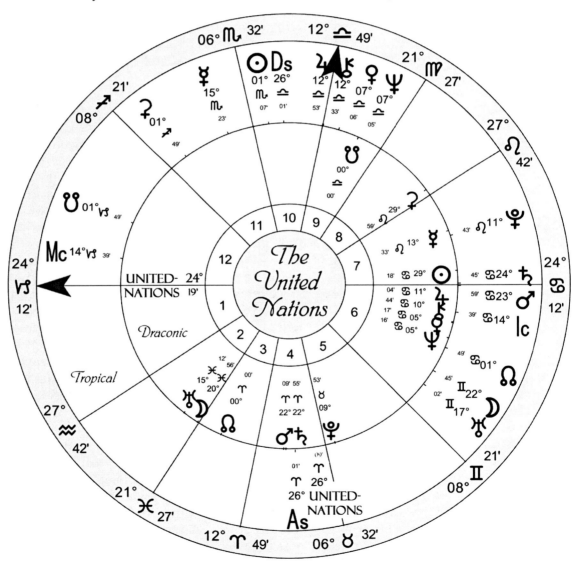

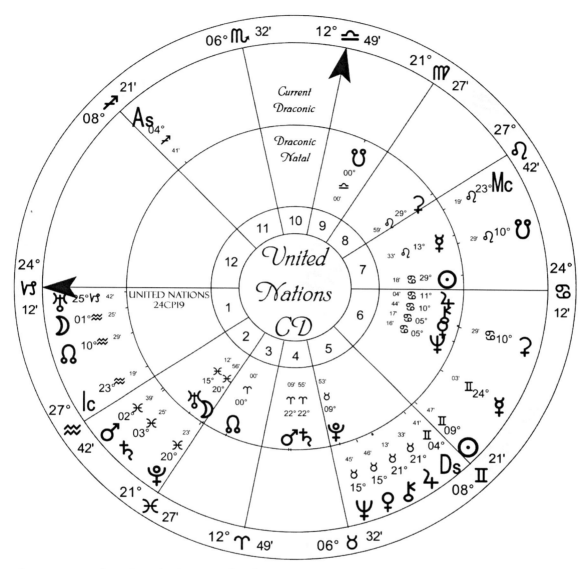

reluctance to abandon diplomacy for force, it has the Draconic Leo Sun's authority to do so, through the power vested in it by Tropical Pluto in the 10th, and military Scorpio rising to confront the oppression of transiting Saturn.

Initially, the **United Nations** were not formally consulted on the proposed aerial strikes. And an examination of the UN chart for October 24th 1945 at 16h45 EST in Washington DC has little to reveal. To me this seemed odd, and wrong. By now, the asteroid named for the international body was in my active file, so I had a look at the position of *United Nations* in the inceptional chart. It wasn't angular, it wasn't aligned to the Lights, even Interdimensionally. This also was odd and wrong. But it was just 6° below the Ascendant – too far to be a really acceptable orb, but close enough to suggest that the time for the UN chart might be in error. All it took was a quarter-hour correction, to 17h00 prompt, for

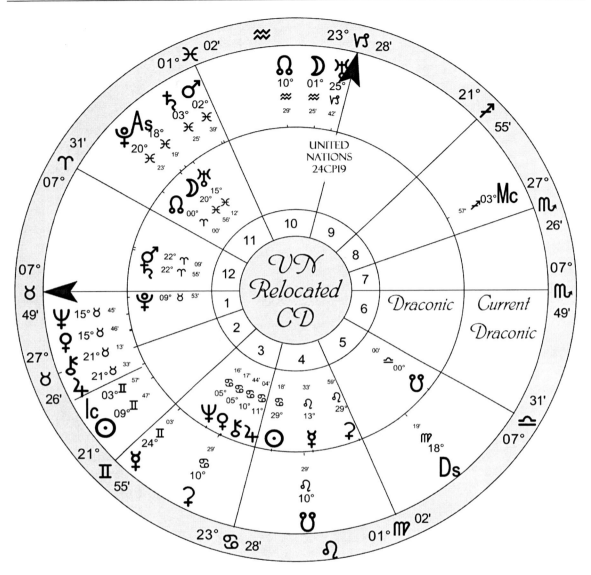

UNITED
NATIONS
24CP19

*UN
Relocated
CD*

Draconic   Current

Draconic

the UN's own named asteroid to rise into the Tropical Ascendant at 26° Aries, confirming its existence and identity. In the process this august body rightly gained an angular Sun, and its guiding, educational, mediating role became crystal clear in the tight conjunction of Jupiter and Chiron with the new Draconic MC. *Its destiny of constant close involvement in conflict and international policing is pointedly obvious from the double angularity of the Mars/ Saturn conjunction from Tropical to Draconic and vice versa; these planets are also the two Ascendant Rulers.*

Now when the chart moved in the Current Draconic to the start of the air war, the cold shock of CD Uranus was felt on the Draconic Capricorn Ascendant as CD Pluto also hit the Draconic Pisces 12th House Moon. Power was being exercised over vulnerable people behind the UN's back. Relocated (why not?) to Belgrade, the corrected chart triumphs again with CD Uranus this time on the Draconic MC, CD Ascendant conjunct Pluto heading for the Draconic Moon here in the traumatic 8th House and, best of all, the CD Nodes stretched across the Leo/Aquarius Ascendant/Descendant, and CD Venus/ Neptune (on Jesus' Taurus Sun) aligns with a 4th House Scorpio Mercury. Here, at this time, the United Nations had to pull together for the common good, take on new roles and responsibilities, help to restructure the disintegrated lives of deeply shocked people through compassion and sharing – through accepting the challenge to love our neighbour … and our enemy.

Now, I don't know which chart you personally prefer for the birth of the **United States**, and I admit to a long-term bias in favour of the July 4th Sagittarius-rising pattern. The Balkan war brought its CD Pluto opposite the Draconic Pisces Sun and CD Jupiter to Draconic Mars, which is appropriate enough for dreams of great victory over great evil! However, a switch to the Yorktown Confederation chart as set for 12h46 pm on November 15th 1777 (time not given by Nick Campion but by David Solté in *The Mountain Astrologer* February and March 1992 and supported by many subsequent articles on 'Scorpionic USA') presents the worryingly vivid picture of a strongly Scorpio nation with Mars in the South Node again, spoiling for a fight. With doubly angular, Airy Tropical and Draconic Moons, the Dragon's Head in Cancer in the 5th, and Leo Jupiter setting, this USA will blossom if it sticks to great entertainment, great food, great sport, great kids, great ideas and inventions, and great humanitarian ideals as proclaimed in its Constitution and enshrined in its Statue of Liberty. But as soon as it picks up the gun, loads the bomb, unless the cause is utterly justified, rigorously controlled and utterly selfless, it risks losing everything that over two centuries it has gained. It has more than it would like to contemplate in common with belligerent Serbia. But Serbia with its Draconic Saturn setting can be cold, hateful and mean; the USA with the Moon/Jupiter alignment to the horizon has a spirit of generosity that, please God, will always come to its rescue – and the rescue of others.

At the time of conflict CD Mars came to that axis, the CD Ascendant/Jupiter to Draconic Mars, and CD Moon to the 11th House Mars/South Node conjunction. This *was* a rescue attempt, on behalf of embattled Kosovo. Only time could tell if it had been justified, or wise, or in any way effective. At the same time, only a month later, with CD Mars still close to the 7th and CD South Node right on it, two adolescent boys ran riot with guns in their Colorado school, murdering thirteen fellow-pupils and staff before turning their guns on themselves. When will this nation come to its senses and melt down its weapons? Enshrining in its Constitution the right to bear arms is the worst error of judgement the United States could ever have made, and until this is reversed America will continue to lose its integrity along with its children.

Chapter Sixteen

Life's Rich Tapestry

Chasing the Dragon

Now, to follow all those examples of the Current Draconic in action in private life and on the world stage, there is more to the story!

In order to track as clearly as possible the sequence of Current Draconic activity over the course of your own life, the next useful job is to mark every one of your significant transiting Node points on a suitably enlarged chart wheel, each point labelled with the planetary pair it will always bring together (just as you would label midpoint degrees.) Such a wheel is eventually, as you can imagine, smothered in data, and very like the 'black chart' once drawn for our entertainment by Geoffrey Dean at an Astrological Association Conference many years ago, with so few noticeable gaps remaining! But life itself has precious few gaps – a point which the author of *Recent Advances In Natal Astrology* omitted to make. A full life is not an amorphous blur of generalised activity, any more than it is experienced in occasional loosely connected bursts of action and reaction. No, indeed, it is made up of a more or less rapid succession of discrete, inter-related inner and outer events that stand out against each other like the bright or subtle colours of a complex tapestry, yet tightly woven.

Weaving Our Way

Looking at such a wheel, then, what does one see? First, that some groupings of planetary pairs, including angles, are tighter than others, so that they are called into action at approximately the same time under the same Nodal transit. At the same time, this shows graphically that each of these pairs is related by the same arc-length of the circle – each two planets are either exactly or nearly the same number of degrees apart. (This demonstrates that in their own Planetary Zodiacs – see Ronald C. Davison's work – they fall on the same pair of degree-axes, and these are the very ones they mark here on this wheel.)

Secondly, the phenomenon of the antiscia/contrantiscia (the Reflex Points) creates a four-fold symmetry in the wheel layout, the same pattern of pairings repeated, but mirrored across the Cardinal axes, on each quadrant of the circle. *This means that the pattern of life-events does not roll on in a repeating one-directional sequence like an ever-turning wheel, but shuttles to and fro in a series of mirrored parabolas about the foci of the Cardinal Points.* I have been intrigued to observe this from my own diaries for very many years, and until this discovery always wondered why it should be so.

An Instant Aspect-finder

Further examination of this special wheel shows how useful it is overall; for added to the above is the rapid reading of aspects:

* Planet pairs found on or near the Cardinal Points are actually conjunct, opposition or square each other in the sky, and therefore in an octaval, dynamic, **4th** harmonic relationship.

* Pairs at 0° of the Fire or Air signs on this wheel are bodily in trine or sextile, so in the harmonious, undemanding relationship of the **3rd** harmonic.

* Pairs at 15° of the Fixed signs relate through the higher octave of the semi-squares and tri-octiles (sesquisquares or sesquiquadrates) – the **8th** harmonic.

* At 24° Leo/Aquarius, 6° Taurus/Scorpio, 12° Gemini/Sagittarius and 18° Cancer/Capricorn, all the **5th and 10th** harmonic pairings are picked out – our giftedness and moral responsibility.

* The **7th/14th** harmonic pairs are revealed at 21°26′ Taurus/Scorpio, 12°51′ Cancer/Capricorn, 4°17′ Virgo/Pisces, 25°42′ Libra/Aries, 17°09′ Sagittarius/Gemini, 8°34′ Aquarius/Leo – the inspirational area of our lives.

All you have to do is work out the natural aspect degrees from 0° Aries and see what is there.

The same applies to all other harmonics: if you read the plotted positions naturally along the wheel from the Vernal Point, pairs conjoining in a given harmonic will be instantly visible. Transparent overlays would serve this purpose very well. Normal orbs apply; the tighter these are, the more powerful and/or immediate their effect.

A number of the pairs will fall in degrees occupied by individual natal planets or angles, either Tropically or Draconically. It follows that all bodies found at or close to the same degree on this wheel will respond more or less simultaneously to the transit of the Moon's Nodes, creating recurring themes in one's life-history. *(It is possible that this effect extends to other types of transit, that is, implying that a planetary body as well as a spatial Node can be the origin of a zodiac – and we are back to Ronald Davison's contention that this is so. To date there is evidence that suggests at least the slow planets from Saturn outwards generate 'zodiacs' in just the same way, and contribute to the destiny patterns at their own level of meaning. I am also persuaded that natal planets and angles can be recalculated from a transiting outer-planetary origin, to give a further set of Directions similar to the Current Draconic. This again is very easy to do with Solar Fire's 'User Arc' option.)*

Nailing Your Colours to the Mast!

One trouble with the plotted wheel as it now stands is its sheer size and visual complexity, useful though this is. Returning to the original idea of rotation, it is a good idea to plot the planetary and angular data in such a way that it is both clear and uncluttered. One way to achieve this is to emphasise the four-fold symmetry by drawing rectangles that join the degrees of planets and angles with their own Reflexes – *antiscia* and *contrantiscia* – and *next, to abolish the clutter of glyphs by* **colour-coding** these planetary rectangles according to tradition (or experience, where tradition is lacking.)

So, if you make two copies of this wheel, either in two sizes, or one on paper and the second as a transparency, you can rotate one against the other to cross-connect Reflex rectangles at their corners. This makes it possible to track planets or angles meeting and joining forces from Current Draconic to Tropical, while from the corresponding shift of the Aries Point you are shown which Tropical zodiac degree will be occupied by a transiting Node to effect this blending of energies.

This still leaves us with a difficulty: it would be useful to be able to plot the signs as well somehow, along with the planetary pattern, dispensing with symbols altogether.

To keep things reasonably simple, the best option has turned out to be a straight change from colour-coding planets to *colour-coding the rectangles according to the sign the generating planet bodily occupies.* When I first tried this approach (after many changes of mind on the most apt colours – should a sign be coloured for its ruling planet? If so, which one? Or should its element be the determining factor?) the outcome was a huge surprise. Once the decision had been made to use the elements as a colour-basis, and three distinct sign-colours had been found for each of Fire, Earth, Air and Water, something was happening as the patterns built up that had not happened with planetary colours alone: they were generating a vivid, ethereal sense of the person's presence. To verify this curious phenomenon more charts had to be tried; and each time the person could still be felt as if they were standing by, invisible but recognisable by the aura they brought with them.

Living Colour

Apparently the chosen colours reproduced vital personal energies that the planets alone, despite their geometry, failed to convey. The *elemental* energy of each occupied sign was communicating a living quality of that person.

To get fully to grips with this, a lot more work was needed. I rapidly abandoned transparencies for paper chart-forms. Another crucial stage was reached when thin lines of colour were rejected in favour of broad bands; these, the width of entire signs, were very coarse and clumsy, but the remedy was quickly found in a further 'fine-tuning' of the colours to a total of three dozen, each identifying one of the thirty-six decanates, giving expression to the nine moods of each element. In this way, 'Life's rich tapestry' has become a living, vivid reality. The decanate holding the planet determines the colour of the now more specific Reflex rectangle, and still offers enough room to combine all four decan-colours involved, should the need arise (there are often two or three.) The presentation of the angles is still something of a problem, as their nature is totally different to planets and so cannot join their geometry. To date, this has been partially resolved by filling any white areas of the map with the decan-colour of the Ascendant, as it is this that is most usually expressed. You may like to experiment. Friend after friend, celebrity after celebrity, has come 'walking through the door' as my initial file of small charts has built up over the years into an extraordinary kaleidoscope of colours. You too can have your personal celestial tartan!

The Kaleidoscope Shifts

But after all that we have explored, this is still barely the beginning.

Look again at the plotted wheel of rectangles, or at the birth map as interwoven colour. If you take just one quadrant of its geometry and actually hold a mirror perpendicular to each of the two radii, visually you will recreate the original symmetries; it will remain the same cosmic mandala. This is exactly what a kaleidoscope does, introducing pattern through double reflection. Here instead we don't have mirrors in a material sense, but **a resonant field of standing waves, with a preferred resonant response equidistant to the two major intersecting axes – the equinoxes and solstices – of the Ecliptic Great Circle.**

The concept of *'Empathetic Resonance'* – a very useful term employed by David Lorimer in his fine book on human spiritual reality, *Whole In One*, and central to his philosophical argument – demands our attention here, as it would seem to underpin so many of the less understood properties of lived experience. From all that we as astrologers know, and all the more from Draconic and other non-Tropical work, just such a cross-dimensional 'empathetic resonance' appears to be a law in the astrological cosmos. **Any transit, progression, direction or synastry contact to a given degree from any zodiac level is bound to stimulate *through resonance* all planets, nodes, cusps, Reflexes and direct midpoints found at that degree or in exact dynamic aspect to it, at any other dimensional level.** And according to this same law, **bodies and active spatial points in certain degrees will cooperate from differing levels in the same nativity, since they are always subject to simultaneous stimulus,** intermittently from planets, and frequently from transiting angles.

My feeling is that there is somewhere a real though subtle boundary in space, defining that Great Circle of the Ecliptic, and that the presence of a planetary influence at any one point (note I am not saying a *planet*) sends two lines of energy out, parallel and perpendicular to the Equator, which 'bounce' at the invisible boundary like snooker balls off the side cushion and run off again at right-angles to meet at the zodiacal point opposite the impelling planet. This would form the Reflex rectangle of *antiscia and contrantiscia.*

Returning to the child's kaleidoscope, if we shake it a little the colourful fragments move, and create instantly before our eyes a totally new pattern of relationships. Its components have not changed, only their arrangement. If we shake our astrological kaleidoscope, even the colours change … and we do this in a sense every time we shift from one level of astrological perception to another, as we do from Tropical to Draconic (or indeed to Sidereal, to Heliocentric, from radix to progressed or directed.) Houses could be included, but these do not function in quite the same way, being the means of locating our activity, which then emanates from one or another level of our being according to the zodiacal framework.

Showing Our True Colours

The realisation that additionally there might be Reflexes working in the Draconic zodiac analogous to those in the Tropical (assuming that any Node generating a zodiac also generates its own cross-axis and dependent resonance field) has meant that the Draconic colours also must be tried; and even more piles of little glowing charts have since accumulated.

Now, as the Draconic chart relates more to one's past self and what it has brought to enrich and inform the present incarnation, one might not expect to re-experience the person concerned 'walking through the door' in the same way as before. And so far, for me, it hasn't happened. Not quite in that way. However, reasoning that just as the Draconic catalyses the Tropical and gives its life meaning, so should the Draconic colours add something recognisable of the inner person to the Tropical, *I have tried holding two patterns up together under a strong light* – and yet again the true individuality shone through, but more profoundly; the sense of a deeper knowledge was indeed there!

Study of the Current Draconic and all its ramifications from start to finish (not that it will ever finish!) has been a transformative process in itself, as it has taken me so fluently from a purely objective, analytical astrology to a wonderfully intuitive, profoundly subjective understanding which had never been open to me before. You may already have made this enchanting journey, in which case you know what delights are to be found! But if you have not yet ventured this way, allow yourself to play for a while, and discover that this astrology is really a living rainbow, and a music, to which – because we are made of the same tones – our souls directly and forever respond.

Chapter Seventeen

Draco and Rectification

The Polish Pope

Pope John Paul II, the late head of the Roman Catholic Church, is known to have been born Karol Wojtyla in Wadowice, Poland on 18th May 1920, but the time of birth has been a matter of some contention amongst astrologers. One astrologer even went so far as to assert that he must have been born six days previously, and produced a great deal of material to 'prove' this! This provoked a positive response from other astrologers, including a letter to *CAO Times* by Dr Hans-Jorg Walter, in which he states that a number of sources in the Pope's family have said that he was born 'about noon' on 18th May, and that this was taken to be reasonably reliable data by European astrologers. However, since that letter appeared many years have passed, and more recently a time was given – apparently from the Pontiff himself – of 5h00 pm.

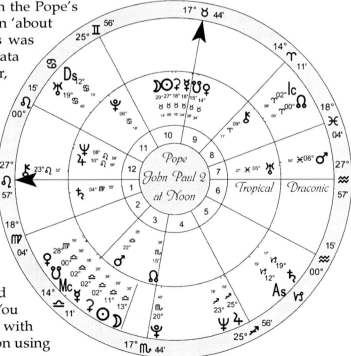

It is always worth considering the use of Draconic material in an attempt to rectify a chart where the life purposes and deeper convictions are sufficiently clear, and so I have applied this method to the chart of Pope John Paul II. You will, I hope, be familiar enough with the techniques of chart rectification using

Secondary Progressed planets and angles, and Solar Arcs. To these I add the natal pattern of Draconic/Tropical contacts, the Daily Progressed Angles (very useful for this degree of fine-tuning) and the natal and progressed Draconic positions, as well as both levels of transits, Quotidian (Q) charts and the Current Draconic. As a reminder, the Quotidian chart in this case is a chart drawn up for the date of a significant event in a person's life, but using the native's own time, and maybe also place, of birth. The resulting wheel shows what that day has in store for the person in question. It is extraordinarily helpful in synastry when the time of birth of one partner is unknown.

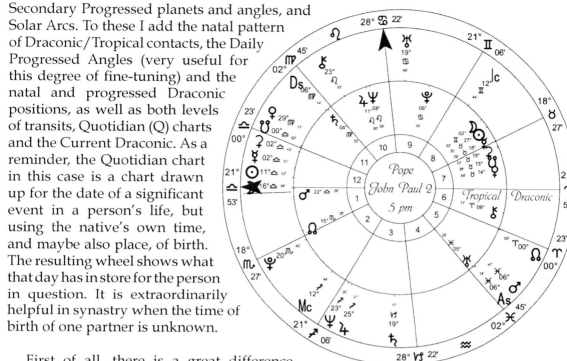

First of all, there is a great difference between the bi-wheels of a noon birth for the Pope, and one at 5h00 pm. Remembering that the Tropical House position of the Draconic Sun is crucial in understanding the area of life from which we each, as a committed soul, make our main appointed contribution, it is hard to conceive of the 2ⁿᵈ house as a key area for this Pope, devoted as he clearly was to the spiritual imperatives of human life. He already has a Taurus stellium, albeit – at noon – in Houses 9 and 10, and while he vigorously engaged with the errant values of the real world, he was a deeply holy man. However, take 5h00 pm, and we have the Draconic Libra New Moon and Mercury in the transcendent 12ᵗʰ House, far more suited to a life that drew its strength and its vocation from spirituality, holy communion and prayer. You can observe this difference mapped in the Current Draconic (CD) tri-wheels that we shall be looking at in a minute.

A Mid-day Chart

First, a quick run through the Daily Progressed patterns for the middle of the day. Four main life events have been taken: his mother's death on April 13ᵗʰ 1929 (progressed date May 27ᵗʰ 1920); his ordination to the priesthood on All Saints' Day, November 1ˢᵗ 1946 (progressed date June 13ᵗʰ 1920); his election to the Papacy on October 16ᵗʰ 1978 at 6h18 pm, Rome (progressed date July 15ᵗʰ 1920); and the attempt on his life on May 13ᵗʰ 1981 in Rome at 5h21 pm (progressed date July 18ᵗʰ 1920).

The radix and progressed charts are set for 12h00 pm EET (2 hours ahead of GMT at that time; Poland's zone standard was unsettled for a while.)

The pattern for **the death of Karol Wojtyla's mother:**

> * This is not totally conclusive; it does show a progression of Moon square Pluto, not quite within the effective 1° orb, insecure Neptune rising, and both Daily Progressed Draconic angles near a radix or transiting Saturn, yet there is also a close conjunction of Jupiter with the Daily Progressed Ascendant, and as he was only nine years old it is hard to see this day as a cause for rejoicing at a new-found freedom.

For his ordination (at his natal latitude):

> * The Draconic Daily Progressed MC opposite his progressed Libra New Moon (on the Crucifixion axis – see Chapter Nineteen), and the wide conjunction of Jupiter and Sun with MC and progressed Draconic Sun in 6°-8° Scorpio of the day's Q-chart, are both consistent with the specifically priestly rôle and the new life he was beginning; so also is the transit of Draconic Sun/Jupiter over Wojtyla's natal Tropical Ascendant.

For his election to the Papacy (at the latitude of Rome):

> * Only by a quarter past the hour do we find Tropical Daily Progressed MC advancing on natal Draconic Jupiter/Neptune and Draconic Daily Progressed ASC in 22° Cancer, collecting a conjunction of his progressed Tropical New Moon and progressed Draconic Uranus. But even then there is no angular pontifical Jupiter.

For the attempt on his life (at the latitude of Rome):

> * The Tropical Daily Progressed MC is still quite near Pluto; the Draconic Daily Progressed MC aligns with his natal Taurus New Moon, and progressed Draconic Chiron has reached the Pope's Tropical Ascendant. The transit of Tropical Mars in his South Node is threatening the MC; transiting Draconic Mars is right on the Draconic Jupiter/Tropical Daily Progressed MC axis.

This does suggest a man whose life is in danger. At noon, we have a birth MC of 17°45' Taurus. Only by about 12h15 pm does the chart generate some convincing patterns: Sun/Mercury/MC (the Pope as orator); Moon/Venus = MC (the worship of Mary in the Roman Church of which he is the head, also the reverence for the life of the Child); Chiron/Pluto = MC (the power of the priest in guiding and healing and educating); Uranus/Neptune and Uranus/Jupiter = MC (the capacity for higher inspiration, wisdom, enlightenment brought into the concept of 'Papal Infallibility', which, let it be said to avoid misunderstanding, is only effective when the pontiff is intentionally attuned to the Divine Source for the guidance of the Church). And Draconic Sun/MC/Mercury all opposing Tropical Chiron from Libra, in support of his teaching, healing, reconciling pastoral rôle.

An Evening Chart

What do we find when we adjust a birth time of 5h00 pm? The chart for 5h11 pm repeatedly throws up persuasive contacts, amongst them a far better daily chart for **the death of young Wojtyla's mother**:

* Draconic Daily Progressed MC conjunct Pluto, and transiting Scorpio South Node; these squared by Draconic Daily Progressed Moon and Ascendant, 3° apart.

* Tropical Daily Progressed Moon opposed by transiting Uranus (invalid in the earlier chart).

* Also the *in coelo* progressed T-square of Sun/Saturn/Uranus hit by progressed Draconic Mars.

* And the transiting Draconic Moon/Tropical Sun hitting the natal Tropical Descendant for this time.

This pattern more graphically reflects the loss of a parent, and the strong daily place of the Moon identifies his mother.

When Wojtyla was Priested:

* Progressed Draconic Sun is still, of course, conjoined by the transiting Jupiter/ Sun conjunction, which is angular, setting like that of the Nativity of the Lord he seeks to emulate, in the Q-chart for that same rectified time on ordination day.

* The Tropical Daily Progressed MC is perfectly opposite natal Jupiter.

* Transiting Moon is past the natal Tropical IC by 1°.

* Daily Progressed Tropical Ascendant is just past the transiting North Node.

* Daily Progressed Draconic Ascendant conjoins transiting Chiron.

BUT! … Another look at these two events suggests something else: that both patterns would be even more descriptive if the time were inched on a little further still, another 3° or 4° of Midheaven, another 12 to 16 minutes on the clock. Let's try. Will it work?

The 17h25 Nativity

After some necessary trial and error fiddling with minutes of time and arc in Solar Fire's Rectification dialogue box, a time of 5h25pm EET (see page 257 for the chart) yielded the following:

The Death of his Mother:

* In Wojtyla's Q-chart, for 17h25 on the day of her death, Saturn is at the IC, square the Ascendant.

* Daily Progressed Ascendant conjoins progressed Moon, squares Pluto, opposes Chiron; Tropically opposed by transiting Uranus.

* Daily Converse Descendant is conjunct his South Node … and transiting Jupiter. We cannot avoid this Jupiter! It could be that the loss of his mother when he was so young in some way sparked the first stirrings of his religious vocation.

* On this day the Sun was conjunct Ceres, who separates parent and child; at 17h25 the Draconic Moon was within 1° of this conjunction.

* And yes! In the Current Draconic based on this new time, CD Ascendant/Descendant aligns perfectly with the natal Tropical Saturn-Uranus opposition in Virgo-Pisces, and CD MC with the all-important transiting Moon.

Ordination to the Priesthood:

* The Q chart still has the Sun/Jupiter conjunction angular to the western horizon in the 6th House.

* But the same Tropical conjunction crowns the Midheaven of the Draconic Q-chart! This is exactly the graphic display of the priestly vocation we are looking for.

* The degree on the Tropical Ascendant is the Jupiter of Christ's Nativity, 1° from His Sun and Wojtyla's natal Tropical Venus.

* In the same sky, Saturn squares the conjunction … and Pluto squares the horizon. Here is the weight of authority and power.

* This *'sweet but heavy burden of the Priesthood'* appears also in a Daily Progressed conjunction of Ascendant/Venus.

* Daily Progressed MC is right opposite progressed Jupiter and the transiting Pluto.

* Progressed Draconic Sun conjoins the transiting Jupiter/Sun.

* Progressed Draconic Saturn/Uranus is collected by the transiting Q Meridian.

* Transiting Uranus is approaching progressed Sun.

* Transiting Q Moon is closing on the natal IC.

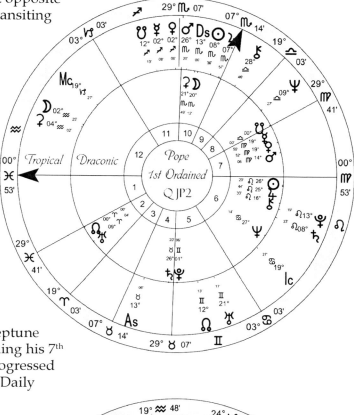

* Current Draconic Jupiter/Neptune is on his Sun, Pluto approaching his 7th House, Ascendant on that progressed Jupiter, transiting Pluto, and Daily Progressed IC.

Powerful stuff! This is what we were looking for.

Election to the Papacy:

The transits for the exact moment when white smoke from the Vatican chimney announced the new Pontiff's election by the assembled Cardinals place Jesus' own Sun (see Chapter Nineteen) exactly on the Ascendant opposite the setting conjunction of Mars/Uranus and Draconic Chiron/Ascendant. The Sun in this chart is Jesus' dwad Sun (and therefore the higher vibration of the Taurus Ascendant). The Draconic Aries Sun is with the Tropical Moon in the 12th –

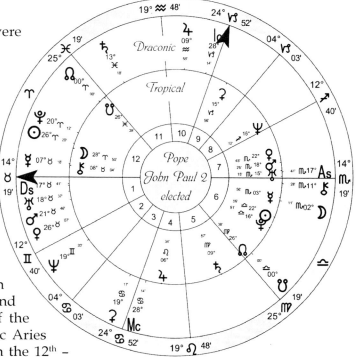

further support for the Pope's own Draconic Sun placement – and these are shining gloriously on his rectified natal western horizon.

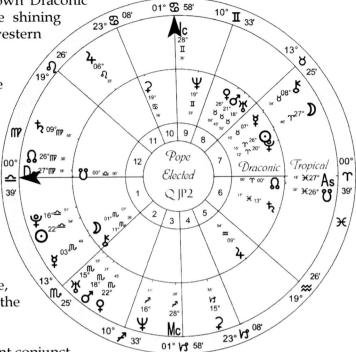

In the Pope's Q-chart for the day, we find, quite properly, an alignment of the Nodes with the horizon, South Node rising. This is a date with sacrifice. It will not only be the sacrifice of the Mass as head of the Roman Catholic Church world-wide, but also the sacrifice of his entire life – very nearly to the point of martyrdom. And in the other patterns, principally Draconic, which for this huge, truly vocational event are far the strongest:

* Annual progressed Ascendant conjunct annual progressed Draconic New Moon in Sagittarius.

* Annual progressed Draconic MC opposite annual progressed Tropical Jupiter.

* Progressed Draconic Uranus conjunct progressed Tropical Sun.

* Transiting Draconic Saturn-square-Neptune just past natal Draconic Ascendant and IC respectively.

* Daily Progressed Draconic Ascendant in 13° Scorpio right opposite the Jupiter of Jesus' Nativity.

* Daily Progressed Draconic MC coming onto the corresponding natal Saturn/Uranus axis.

* Daily Converse Draconic MC opposite Daily Progressed Draconic Pluto.

And virtually all the Current Draconic energies are dynamically active:

* CD Sun opposite Tropical Moon.

* CD Moon square Tropical Saturn/Uranus.

* CD Saturn/Uranus closing on natal Draconic Ascendant/Descendant.

* CD North Node conjunct and CD Venus opposite Tropical Mercury.

* CD Mercury conjunct Draconic Pluto.

* CD Pluto square Tropical Chiron.

* CD Chiron conjunct Tropical Sun.

* CD Mars conjunct Tropical Descendant.

* CD MC opposite Tropical Neptune.

* CD Neptune opposite Tropical Jupiter.

* CD MC opposite transiting Tropical Jupiter.

* CD Ascendant conjunct the transiting Moon.

Overall, we have a repeat of the same planetary energies in focus as for ordination. The main emphasis has shifted, however, from Jupiter to Saturn; this is not another ordination, nor is it a consecration, but an appointment to a position of radically altered responsibility and, as shown by the progressed New Moon and the 'Full Moon' in the Current Draconic, the end of his old life and the start of a completely new cycle.

The Pope is Shot

This happened only five days before his 61st birthday, thus very close to the Solar Return for the ensuing year. The time of the attack is only four minutes short of the proposed birth time. Shooting, attack, is Mars. The shock of it is Uranus. The trauma is Pluto. Its deliberate lovelessness, and ensuing incapacity, is Saturn. The wound is Chiron. Neptune may cloud the scene with subterfuge and duplicity. These should all be in strong positions if our rectified (*nevertheless always speculative*) chart is correct.

Pope John Paul 2 is shot — Tropical / Draconic

This is what we find in the interacting transiting and radix wheels:

* First of all, transiting Tropical Mars is in the magic degree of 13° Taurus: this is an attack not just on Pope John Paul II but on the Papacy, priesthood, Christ Himself. It may also be seen as an attack on power by the powerless; it is close to the sidereal degree of Aldebaran.

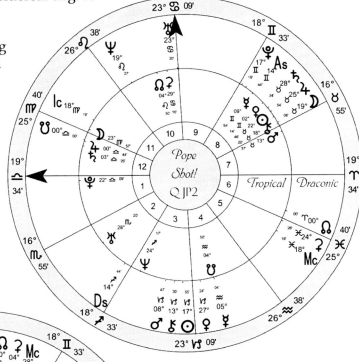

* This Tropical Mars is closing on the Pope's natal Tropical Venus and South Node; we know from experience that the energy of Mars kicks in early: 2° before exact conjunction is typical.

* Transiting Tropical Pluto has reached the Pope's natal, angular, Tropical Mars, and rises, quincunx Sun and exactly squaring the MC as the gun fires.

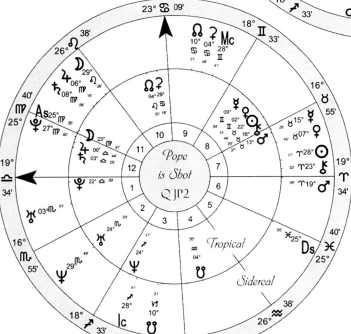

* Transiting Draconic Pluto is on the Pope's natal Draconic IC.

* Tropical Uranus and the closely opposed Draconic Saturn align to the natal Tropical Taurus Sun.

The Current Draconic of the 17h25 birth chart impacts strongly on the Pope's Sidereal pattern: the Current Draconic IC meets Sidereal Mars, involving the pontiff in a very public and historic act of violence which put his life at serious risk. The Current Draconic Dragon's Head had come exactly to his radix Sidereal Midheaven, testimony to the spiritual importance of the event on John Paul's path through this incarnation. It must carry the meaning of the radix North Node in Scorpio so close to Jesus' Ascendant and opposite His Sun; here was the test of a Pope's trust in Christ and his willingness to suffer with Him while forgiving the man who perpetrated this vicious attack. Also present that day on the Pope's Current Draconic IC is radix Draconic Venus. Tropically this is conjunct Jesus' Sun and in the Pope's South Node. The benefic planet protected him; and it also ensured that his love of Christ Jesus sustained him through the trauma and informed his every act and word thereafter.

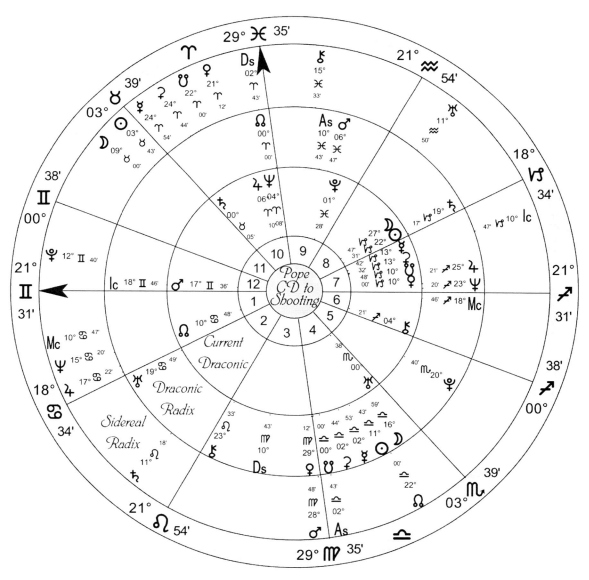

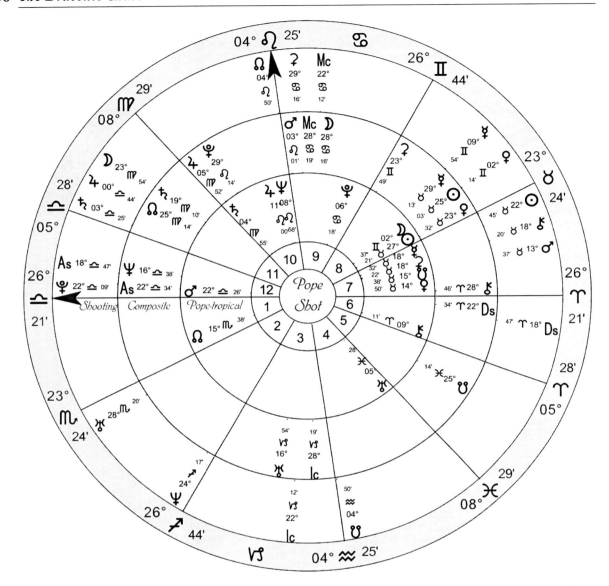

The cream topping comes with an extra tri-wheel for which you may be unprepared, so let me quickly explain: this is the use of a **composite chart** to link a person with an event. But when you use composites, remember that their positions have to be mapped back to the two radix patterns to see what the one means to the other. So, with an event, we are looking at what this moment means, or brings, to the individual involved; conversely, what that person brings to the moment! Here is the composite Tropical tri-wheel for Pope John Paul II and his attempted assassination (a Sidereal composite would make scarcely any difference.)

* Composite Mars conjunct the Pope's MC and transiting North Node.

* Composite Ascendant conjunct his radix Mars and the transiting Pluto.

* A Composite Moon/MC conjunction square Chiron (he is surrounded by crowds of people, as part of his public ministry).

Just to remind you, this means in geometrical terms that the natal arc between Mars and MC at the birth of Karol Wojtyla was 78°01′, and this arc was being repeated by the transit of Mars on the flip-side of his MC, like Mars in a mirror. It was (unsurprisingly) just 2° from exact reflection. Arcs are also, as fractions of the circle, frequencies. Mars/MC was singing a familiar tune that day – twice, as the natal Mars/Ascendant note had also been struck. And when we combine the Draconic and Tropical composites in a bi-wheel the shock and pain of the attack is even more graphic: on the Draconic composite Ascendant lies the Tropical composite Chiron, while exactly on the angle of its IC is the Tropical composite Mars. For the reasons known only to the Godhead and our higher selves, on such days, at such moments, we get what is coming to us, and with such a buildup of supporting directions, Pope John Paul II had a date with destiny.

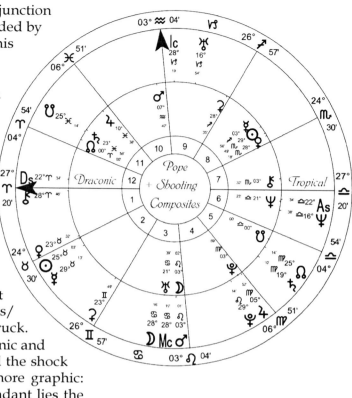

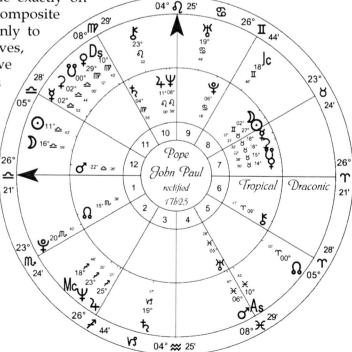

As a postscript, I thought you might like to look at the relationship between the Pontiff and the Vatican; Nick Campion supplies a chart for Vatican City in his *Book of World Horoscopes*. It's beautiful – see the classic culminating Jupiter, in Taurus, conjunct John Paul's Sun and its own Draconic Pluto? This is such a strong signature of his role as one of the Roman Church's most high-profile and influential primates. And then we have the striking alignment of the Vatican's own Ascendant/Descendant to the Pope's Draconic Mars/Tropical Saturn-Uranus: pulled between the old ways and the new, he brought contention and drama to the Vatican.

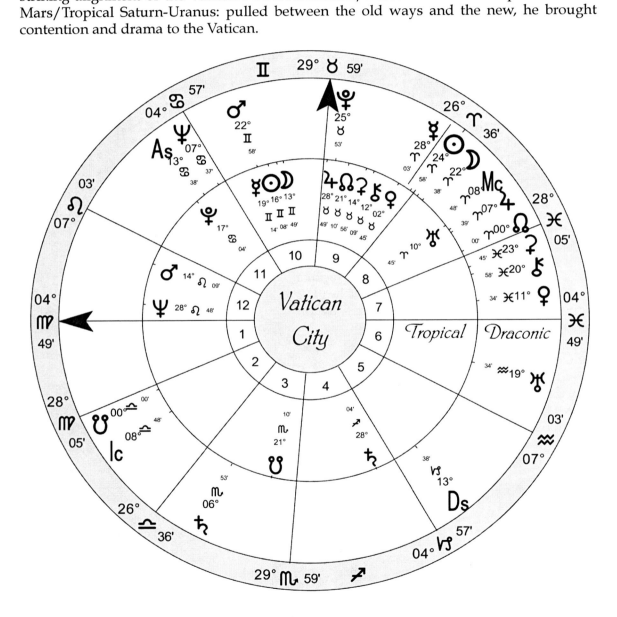

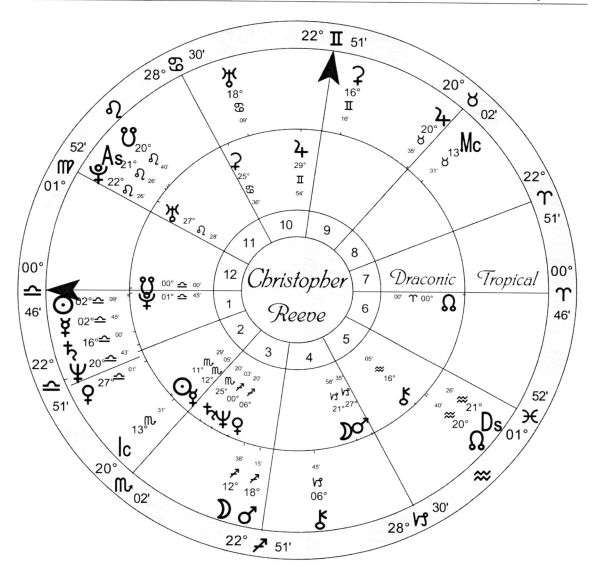

The Fall Guy

My next, briefer illustration is of a handsome, talented, athletic man who at the peak of his career took a dive so catastrophic that it all but killed him (and nine years later, it did.) It is, of course, the late actor Christopher Reeve, who broke his neck in a fall from his horse while out hunting. What this man proceeded to do will pass into legend: not only was his determination to carry on living a full life as a quadriplegic without bitterness a superb example to others, but his faith that he would one day walk again, with help, remains even after his death a strong motivation to continuing medical research. And he did star again in a film – the re-make of the Hitchcock movie, *Rear Window*, which originally featured the late, great James Stewart as the percipient hero confined to one room and his wheel-chair.

We looked at Christopher Reeve in an earlier chapter, so there is no need to elaborate on the remarkable qualities that emerge from his Draconic patterns. Our task is to see again how Draconic rectification adjusts his time of birth. In this book I have in fact been using a rectified time of birth for Reeve of 3h24 am. This falls between two different published times, both quoted as 'A' rated and 'from him': one of '3h30 am' in Lois Rodden's *AstroData II*, the other of '03h12' in Frank Clifford's collection. All I want to do is to present the charts that suggest that neither of these times is correct, and which argue instead for 3h24 am EDT. There are two key dates we can work with: the first radio broadcast of *Superman*, in effect the birth of the fantasy hero, on February 12th 1940 at 17h15 EST in New York (data from Frank Clifford), and the recorded moment of the accident, 15h05 EDT on May 27th 1995 in Culpeper, Virginia. The latter will give us an important Current Draconic, the former some interesting synastry!

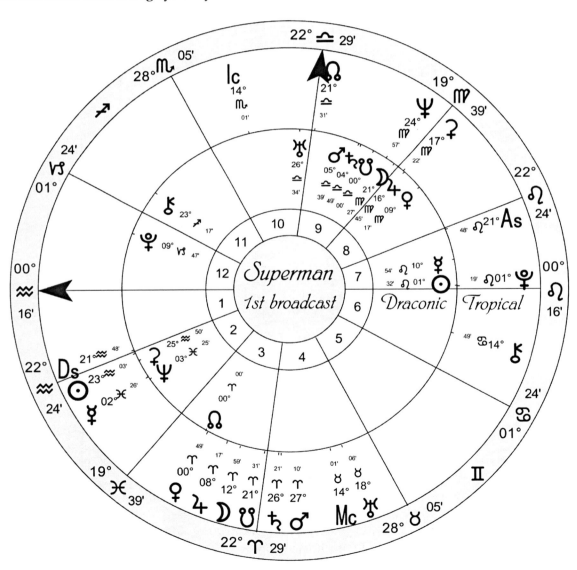

Superman

Superman was born with a setting Leo conjunction of Draconic Sun and Tropical Pluto, also Draconic MC on the Tropical Dragon's Head (conjunct Reeve's Tropical Neptune, the film persona); he will triumph forever in the battle of Good against the forces of Evil! The Draconic Ascendant is very close to Reeve's Draconic Mars. The Tropical angles are 14°01′ Taurus (the Nativity Sun/Jupiter again!) on the MC and 21°48′ Leo rising. The latter is 1° from Reeve's rising South Node, and so I have no reason to see why they should not share an Ascendant of Leo 21°, as he is now so identified with Superman in the public imagination. This is of course repeated in the composite chart – but significantly adds composite Mars to Reeve's Descendant at 22° Aquarius (also appropriately conjunct Superman's Sun!) In the Draconic composite, this becomes a Mars/Ascendant conjunction; also Superman places his Draconic Chiron on Reeve's Draconic IC – together identified, they set the heroic example to generations.

The Accident

Straightforward daily secondary progressions using the new time bring the daily progressed MC onto that 7th House cusp and the North Node, with the daily progressed IC at the Dragon's Tail, Ascendant and Pluto. The transiting Draconic Mars-Pluto square hits his fated Converse Draconic angles, just as the transiting Draconic angles collect the Tropical transit

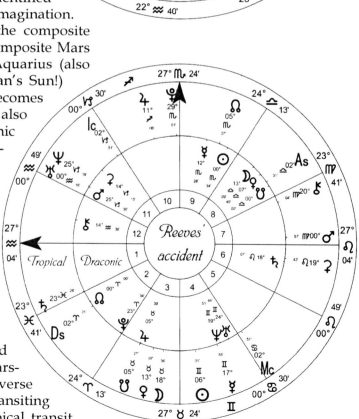

of that same Mars-Pluto square. Meanwhile, transiting Draconic Saturn has come to his South Node, demanding sacrifice for the sake of others. This is the pattern of a day which crystallised in one terrible moment a heroic soul's real destiny. Reeve was born for this day. No other pattern will do. Then, when we add the Current Draconic, we find CD Mars in its familiar 1° approach to the natal Midheaven opposite natal Draconic Sun and Mercury, transiting Draconic Mercury, and asteroid *Stoss (an impact)* at 12°10' Scorpio. For good measure, CD Uranus is only 3' from Reeve's Moon/*Christophe* (12°23' Sagittarius) conjunction; and the conjunction in Aquarius of Current Draconic *Stoss*/Sun/Mercury in their Fixed T-square with his natal Draco Saturn-square-

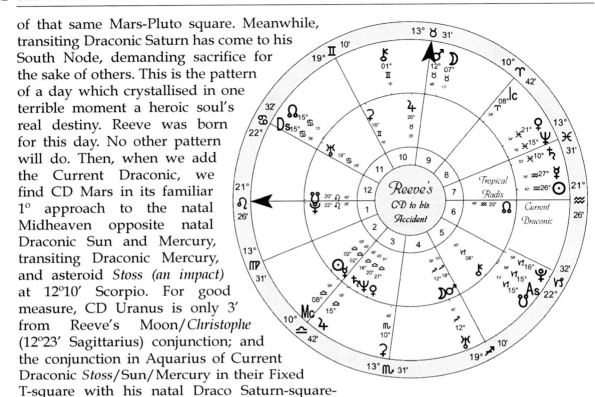

Uranus has just engaged with those harsh transiting Draconic angles. Remarkably, in this same configuration we find natal Draconic asteroid *Huntress* at 26°31' Aquarius and both natal and transiting Draconic *Swift* in 26°48' Aquarius and 27°46' Leo respectively – the most graphic description you could wish for of a sudden traumatic impact while hunting at speed. This is my evidence, which you could almost say is written in stone, given the part played by the asteroids! … And it tells the hero's story.

Superstar

Two particularly nice things happened for the author in 1987; first of all, earlier than expected, the first edition of *Draconic Astrology* came onto the shelves, and six months later the phone rang at a typically inconvenient moment. My husband eventually got the receiver into my hand, and on the other end was a polite voice asking if I was free on the first weekend in July (yes, I thought so) and so would I – and my husband – be able to come to Hampshire, as a speaker was needed for a dinner debate. The proposer was an old astrological friend of mine, and had been invited to bring a seconder of his choice. Transport would present no problem. Mr Lloyd Webber's Bentley would collect us at our front door.

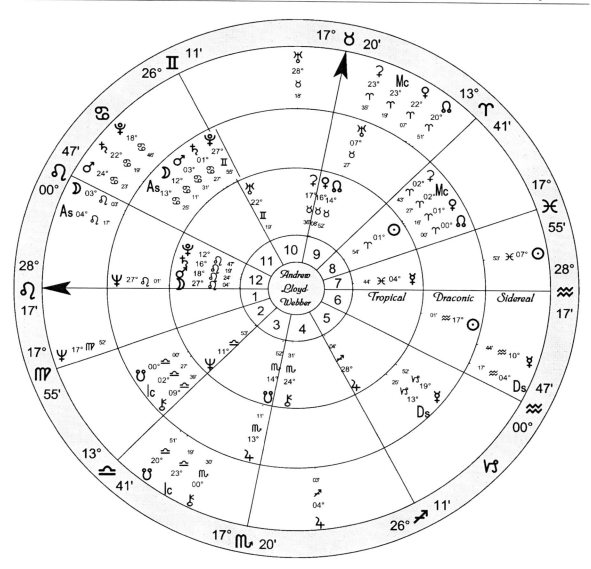

And so, late on the Friday afternoon, with Pluto on the Midheaven, Neptune rising, and Bill at the wheel, we rolled into Sydmonton Court.

We were made most welcome; our room was delightful, our fellow guests animated, interesting and friendly. Breakfast was an informal affair of scrambling eggs and making toast with the family and their friends as we straggled, dressing-gowned, down to the enormous old kitchen and chatted around its big central table. The whole weekend was hugely enjoyable; plenty of music (some of the finest coming from brother Julian's cello), great humour thanks to the presence of Stephen Fry, and several surprises about which I shall remain discreet. Saturday evening saw two banqueting rooms filled with people and at least one astrologer very nervous indeed at the prospect of defending her beloved subject completely off the cuff in such august company, the motion being 'This House believes that astrology is a load of old rubbish!' It meant I had to be funny or die, so caution was thrown to the winds and it developed into a right ding-dong with the opposition, a battle of wits with one respected Anglican politician and the dauntingly brilliant Mr Fry. You will be happy to learn that Urania won the day!

Over the course of the weekend the sun shone gorgeously; there was much strolling and chatting on the lawns and in quiet corners of the lovely old house. I met Sarah Brightman's sisters and her mother, Paula, whom I shall never forget: a vibrant, happy woman, immensely proud of all her daughters. And I met Andrew's mother, Jean. I asked the question every astrologer wants to ask: 'Can you remember what time Andrew was born?' 'It was about 4h00 pm,' she replied, 'in the Westminster Hospital.'

Although the data was given readily, and there was no duty of confidence, for twelve years I kept it privately. As a guest in his house, I felt that to make free with Andrew's data would be in poor taste. However, so many years have gone by, his mother has passed on, and there is so much interest in this chart whose date has been in the public domain for all that time, that I now consider it only fair to make this contribution to the records.

Checking Approximate Data

So we have a date of March 22nd 1948, coordinates of 51°N30', 0°W09', and an approximate time of birth, 4h00 pm BST. Let's have a look.

The first thing that strikes one is the rising Leo Moon conjunct Draconic Neptune. This seems appropriate for a man who is possessed of so much spontaneity, and who expresses emotion so freely and dramatically through composition that his musicals have caught the public imagination all over the world. But it is cuspal – so do we have Leo rising or Virgo? The 8th House Sun is fine: he is a most astute and successful business man. Draconic Venus and MC join the Tropical Sun: he has made millions through a career in music. Draconic Jupiter conjunct the South Node is also close to the IC at 4h00 pm, the Draconic Sun very close to its square from 17°01' Aquarius: again, the promise of success, and a high profile. The 6th House placement of that Draconic Sun is a bit of a puzzle (the 5th

would have seemed more apt for a life in show business) but he is well known for his need to escape the razzmatazz, back to his home, his privacy, his piano, to get to work on the next show. Also, you have to accept a birth well over an hour later if you want Draconic Sun in the 5th, and then you lose all the descriptive contacts that are there at 4 o'clock. There *is* a Virgoan cast to his personality, which could either come from this 6th House or a Virgo Ascendant. The only other source is a Heliocentric Mars. Virgo rising would draw Mercury itself even closer into its conjunction with the western horizon. However, this need for retreat is also a 12th House phenomenon, and he has Moon and three planets there at the stated time. Then there is all that Draconic Cancer: a man handling this sensitive, romantic energy will as often as not prefer to withdraw into his shell to engage with his Muse – bearing in mind that here is an individual with a very strong vocation, and therefore the Draconic (as well as the public Sidereal) will have a lot to say. The other inhibiting factor is the very tight Venus-Saturn square, which at 4h00 pm also configures the Midheaven: much of Andrew's business acumen stems from early anxieties about money and his consequent care of resources, and all this has had a bearing on his career and home life (the MC and IC). Two further factors encourage confidence in this Virgo-rising pattern: with Ceres now classified as a planet, and as Queen of the tiny asteroids surely the co-ruler of Virgo, her presence as Ascendant-ruler exactly on the MC with Venus is a badge of consummate musical success; also Andrew's *Sidereal* Ascendant is where we would expect it to be, in glamorous Leo – in public life he is a Lord!

If the time appears to be about right, is it then possible or desirable to correct it at all? If you read *Fanfare*, Jonathan Mantle's account of Andrew's life, one most intriguing thing stands out – no less than four turning-points have all occurred on the 9th of November: in 1968 the production of *Joseph And The Amazing Technicoloured Dreamcoat* at St Paul's Cathedral, which led to the first meeting with managing agent David Land; in 1969 the release of the single of *Jesus Christ, Superstar*; in 1970 the review in *Time* magazine that catalysed a glittering career on Broadway; and in 1976 a starry gathering was treated to a private performance of *Evita* before the show opened to the public. On all these dates the Sun was between 16° and 17° Scorpio, maybe shining on the composer's IC, and definitely opposite the culminating Venus.

After a long time spent examining Current Draconic patterns, Solar Arcs and conventional Secondary Progressed and Converse charts for the shows, his separation and first two marriages, we are left with two main options, I think. First, 16h00 BST is a very good time; orbs of 1° contact by progression and direction are legitimate and may not mean that it is incorrect. Otherwise, it could well be 16h07, which moves the MC and Ascendant just far enough on to collect some major transits, CDs and Solar Arcs while retaining the original Draconic/Tropical connections. A time of 4h07 pm puts a conjunction of asteroids *Dancey* and *Christine* (referencing both Jesus and the heroine of *Phantom*) right on the Tropical Midheaven from the Draconic, and *Juliana* (brother Julian) bodily at the IC with *Octavia* (musical octaves) instead of *Christa* in that magic degree again of Jesus' own Jupiter, 13° Taurus. But *Christa* is still not far from the angle and is, after all, doubly represented. *Argentina* in 7° Aquarius is only 2° from the Sidereal 7th House cusp, where *in coelo America* (where Andrew has enjoyed spectacular success) and *Terpsichore* (dancing again) align with the horizon more intimately at 16h00 than 16h07. At 16h00, however, *Andersen* (one of two asteroids I have on file for Andrew) is closer to the Draconic Cancer Ascendant, and there is a more closely angular *Sara* – the Helio Sara in 13° Taurus conjunct Venus, and just close enough to the Midheaven. As Andrew has been married to two Sarahs, this is an important consideration! A conjunction of Helio *Andree* and *Doggett* (his devoted Director of Music for many years) in 1° Pisces would still be in orbs of the Descendant of either chart. It is in fact extremely difficult to choose between these two close times; so I am going to leave it to you to make up your own mind, while I continue to work at it in any further way that occurs to me. To help you, here are the relevant asteroid positions courtesy of Solar Fire, followed by some more useful dates (no times are available to me, so I have used either 0h00 or 12h00, or for stage shows a speculative time of 20h00.)

Tropical:

* Albertine 1290	18°57′ Pisces	* America 916	25°47′ Aquarius
* Amor 1221	17°44′ Libra	* Andersen 2476	12°57′ Cancer
* Andree 1296	25°37′ Pisces	* Angelina 64	09°01′ Gemini
* Argentina 469	07°58′ Aquarius	* Byblis 199	28°14′ Pisces
* Chant 3315	23°46′ Aries	* Christa 1015	13°20′ R Scorpio
* Christiansen 8313	19°02′ Sagittarius	* Christine 628	02°53′ Cancer
* Dancey 4021	03°56′ Cancer	* Doggett 6363	25°P33′ Pisces
* Dominique 4020	12°27′ R Leo	* Eva 164	03°49′ R Scorpio
* Evita 1569	09°40′ Aquarius	* Fama 408	10°38′ R Virgo
* Fantasia 1224	14°31′ Aquarius	* Felix 1664	08°20′ Aquarius
* Franke 2824	07°18′ Cancer	* Graham 3541	26°18′ Taurus
* Hall 3299	12°38′ Sagittarius	* Ireland 5029	07°38′ R Leo
* Jack London 2625	18°57′ Aries	* Jeanne 1281	15°54′ R Leo
* Jeans 2763	04°34′ Sagittarius	* Josefa 649	10°12′ Pisces
* Josephina 303	08°39′ Capricorn	* Josephus Flavius	26°46′ Cancer
* Julia 89	06°14′ Pisces	* Juliana 816	22°25′ R Scorpio
* Julioangel 5996	11°12′ Gemini	* Kenrussell 3714	18°31′ R Virgo
* Libera 771	27°27′ Aries	* Liberatrix 125	02°49′ R Scorpio
* Magdalena 318	24°47′ Capricorn	* Octavia 598	21°05′ R Scorpio
* Ops 2736	17°36′ Aquarius	* Orpheus 3361	16°27′ Pisces
* Palatia 415	05°21′ R Scorpio	* Palazzolo 6793	28°05′ Gemini
* Pamjones 4852	20°57′ Gemini	* Paula 1314	26°52′ Taurus
* Philomela 196	22°28′ Aries	* Pia 614	00°01′ R Libra
* Queen's 5457	29°56′ Pisces	* Raphaela 708	08°12′ Pisces
* Requiem 2254	15°48′ Capricorn	* Riceia 1230	08°01′ Aries
* Roberta 335	06°54′ Gemini	* Rockefellia 904	01°57′ Aquarius
* Sara 533	03°25′ Taurus	* Starr 4150	09°51′ Aries
* Stevenson 5211	00°58′ Aries	* Stuart 3874	19°03′ Gemini
* Terpsichore 81	24°34 R′ Leo	* Ubasti 4257	04°28′ R Sagittarius
* Urania 30	06°00′ Sagittarius	* Viola 1076	09°32′ Sagittarius
* Webb 3041	05°03′ Aquarius	* Weber 4152	06°36′ Aries
* Williams 1763	09°42′ Cancer	* Witt 2732	15°40′ Gemini
* Yeshuhua 3241	14°14′ R Virgo		

Draconic:

* Albertine 1290	04°04' Aquarius	* America 916	10°54' Capricorn
* Amor 1221	02°51' Virgo	* Andersen 2476	28°04' Taurus
* Andree 1296	10°44' Aquarius	* Angelina 64	24°08' Aries
* Argentina 469	23°05' Sagittarius	* Byblis 199	13°21' Aquarius
* Chant 3315	08°Pi53' Pisces	* Christa 1015	28°27' R Virgo
* Christiansen 8313	04°09' Scorpio	* Christine 628	18°00' Taurus
* Dancey 4021	19°03' Taurus	* Doggett 6363	10°40' Aquarius
* Dominique 4020	27°34' R Gemini	* Eva 164	18°56' R Virgo
* Evita 1569	24°46' Sagittarius	* Fama 408	25°45' R Cancer
* Fantasia 1224	29°38' Sagittarius	* Felix 1664	23°27' Sagittarius
* Franke 2824	22°25' Taurus	* Graham 3541	11°25' Aries
* Hall 3299	27°45' Libra	* Ireland 5029	22°45' R Gemini
* Jack London 2625	04°03' Pisces	* Jeanne 1281	01°00' R Cancer
* Jeans 2763	19°41' Libra	* Josefa 649	25°19' Capricorn
* Josephina 303	23°46' Scorpio	* Josephus Flavius	11°53' Gemini
* Julia 89	21°21' Capricorn	* Juliana 816	07°32' R Libra
* Julioangel 5996	26°19' Aries	* Kenrussell 3714	03°38' R Leo
* Libera 771	12°34' Pisces	* Liberatrix 125	17°55' R Virgo
* Magdalena 318	09°54' Sagittarius	* Octavia 598	06°12' R Libra
* Ops 2736	02°43' Capricorn	* Orpheus 3361	01°34' Aquarius
* Palatia 415	20°28' R Virgo	* Palazzolo 6793	13°12' Taurus
* Pamjones 4852	06°04' Taurus	* Paula 1314	11°59' Aries
* Philomela 196	07°35' Pisces	* Pia 614	15°08' R Leo
* Queen's 5457	15°03' Aquarius	* Raphaela 708	23°19' Capricorn
* Requiem 2254	00°55' Sagittarius	* Riceia 1230	23°08' Aquarius
* Roberta 335	22°00' Aries	* Rockefellia 904	17°04' Sagittarius
* Sara 533	18°32' Pisces	* Starr 4150	24°58' Aquarius
* Stevenson 5211	16°05' Aquarius	* Stuart 3874	04°10' Taurus
* Terpsichore 81	09°41' R Cancer	* Ubasti 4257	19°35' R Libra
* Urania 30	21°07' Libra	* Viola 1076	24°39' Libra
* Webb 3041	20°10' Sagittarius	* Weber 4152	21°43' Aquarius
* Williams 1763	24°49' Taurus	* Witt 2732	00°47' Taurus
* Yeshuhua 3241	29°21' R Cancer		

Time review: November 9th 1970, 00h00 EST (+5:00) New York 40N42 074W00

Jesus Christ Superstar – USA: October 12th 1971, 20h00 pm, EDT (+4:00) New York 40N42 074W00 (*Andree*/Moon/South Node conjunction, *Webb*/Sun/Uranus conjunction for the First Night! – meaning that the Draconic transiting Andree/Moon would be near 0° Libra opposite Andrew Lloyd Webber's Sun.)

Marries Sarah Hugill: July 24th 1971, 12h00 BST (-1:00) Ashton Keynes UK 51N39 001W51

Jesus Christ Superstar – UK: August 9th 1972, 20h00 BST (-1:00) London UK 51N30 000W10 (*Andree* conjunct Pluto, opposite his Sun and Draconic MC, *Weber* on his Sidereal Ascendant)

1st Sydmonton Festival: June 21st 1975, 12h00 BST (-1:00) Sydmonton UK 51N19 001W19

Evita UK: June 21st 1978, 20h00 BST (-1:00) London 51N30 000W10

Cats UK: May 11th 1981, 20h00 BST (-1:00) London 51N30 000W10

Cats USA: October 7th 1982, 20h00 EDT (+4:00) New York 40N42 074W00

Marries Sarah Brightman: March 22nd 1984, 12h00 GMT Kingsclere UK 51N20 001W14 (*Andree*/Moon/South Node conjunction – again! – square Venus)

Phantom of the Opera UK: October 9th 1986, 20h00 BST (-1:00) London UK 51N30 000W10 (*Andree* on his Sidereal Ascendant)

Phantom of the Opera USA: January 26th 1988, 20h00 EST (+5:00) New York 40N42 074W00

This list is far from exhaustive; a lot has happened since *Phantom of the Opera*, and there is now a third Mrs Lloyd Webber (although since Andrew became a Lord she is now known as Lady Lloyd Webber). But it should give you enough to work with, so that you can try the Draconic rectification system and see the results for yourself.

Chapter Eighteen

Astrology, The Muse and The Dragon
Urania in the Draconic Charts of Astrologers

'*Urania*,' wrote John Addey in his monograph to J. Lee Lehman's Ephemeris in 1981,

> '… is that one of the nine Muses who is said to preside over the 'heavenly sciences', Astronomy and Astrology … Her name means "The Heavenly One" … She was said to be the mother of the great musician Linus, the inventor of melody and rhythm and may also be considered as the female aspect of Uranus … Among the Muses she is the deep thinker about the nature of things and the measurer of all things in heaven and earth … Supposing – just supposing – then, that the asteroid Urania is found to have an astrological value, what should we expect it to be? First and foremost, although it is obvious that not everyone in whose chart Urania is strong will be an astronomer or an astrologer, yet one would expect that students of the "heavenly sciences" ought usually to have it significantly placed, especially those who have a real, deep and lasting interest therein and who are capable of bringing inspired insights into the subject … **It goes without saying that Urania should be strong at the time of important developments in the world of astrology**.'

After just two weeks with the ephemeris, John had seen sufficient evidence to make the validity of Urania in the astrologer's map a tantalising possibility, but declined to publish details of his observations, based as they must have been on an inadequate sample to meet his stringent standards. 'To do so at this stage,' he said, 'would be invidious. In any case one cannot always assess the value of the contribution to astrology of any particular person, or their real involvement in astrology, during their lifetime, and we have no means at present of looking at Urania in the nativities of the great astrologers and astronomers born before 1900.' Until sufficient results were forthcoming that might further encourage the ephemeris-makers, during the 1980s those of us who were inspired to follow John's lead had to do the best we could with the Ephemeris of Urania for this century, and therefore concentrate our researches on the living, whether their best work was known, or yet to come; otherwise we may as well throw away this precious ephemeris and with it any chance of companion volumes for earlier epochs.

Now, however, we are well into a new millennium, and not only have we astronomy software for the PC with which to track the early journeys of Urania for ourselves, but the ability to import into Astrolabe's Solar Fire program the excellent asteroid ephemerides compiled and constantly updated by Swiss Ephemeris, as well as the comprehensive Mark Pottenger collection. Because all these ephemerides go back reasonably reliably to AD 1500, it also means we can at last look for Urania (and also other astrological asteroids!) in the charts of the great early astrologers such as John Dee and William Lilly. Grab yourself a handful of stardust! This is transforming astrology!

The Urania Files

Here are details of some ninety-eight astrologers, many living and some sadly departed, with twenty related charts, to demonstrate simultaneously two important facts:

1. That a consideration of the Draconic level is central to understanding the elements and motivations that give purpose to a life.

2. That the asteroid Urania is outstandingly strong in the charts of fine astrologers: by aspect, in harmonic patterns and through axial contact between Draconic and Tropical. (Of course there will be Sidereal and Heliocentric Uranians too, but they must wait for another book.) Additionally, Urania is prominent, though less powerful, in the maps of those who are active, but not leaders, in our field.

The expression of Urania in the signs begins to show itself a little in this exercise, and the balance of power between Tropical and Draconic. One finds, for example, a most telling alignment in the first decan of **Virgo/Pisces** of three astrologers' Draconic Urania: John Addey, Charles Harvey and David Hamblin. And conjunct the same axis, in Virgo, is Michel Gauquelin's Tropical Urania. All four were in the same line of work, tackling the fine-tuning of astrology through harmonic techniques and painstaking sample analysis. Further on in Virgo is Charles Harvey's own Tropical Urania and that of Deborah Houlding, also the Draconic Urania of Geoffrey Cornelius and Colin Miles; every one of these fine astrologers has been concerned with a precise understanding of the astrological phenomenon. In Pisces, the mystic is showing; here is the inner Charles Harvey, and Joyce Collin-Smith. Another with that all-encompassing vision more overtly expressed is Al H. Morrison, for example, and musically there is Michael Heleus, with perhaps an inductive rather than a deductive vision at work, opening to broad vistas, great ideals.

The **Leo** Urania finds itself at the heart of the astrological 'establishment', and here amongst others we have Julia Parker, Tad Mann, Sir George Trevelyan – teachers, speakers, creators, organisers. Gratifyingly, we discover Draconic Leo Urania in the chart of Dr John Dee – and he was no less than the royally appointed court astrologer to the first Queen Elizabeth! Opposite, in **Aquarius**, we find astrologers who, although very much part of the Uranian community, nevertheless have a highly individual role to play. This can be either because they literally stand out from the crowd, like Noel Jan Tyl, who is physically head and shoulders above any other astrologer I know, or because (and this includes Tyl) they are rather unusual and independent practitioners, often with a marked analytical bent, socially and politically aware, and therefore great with people: such as Roger Elliott, Roy Gillett, Donald 'Moby Dick' Jacobs, and at least two of my favourite maverick friends.

I suppose that if we wish to get the clearest idea of what the Urania sign is saying, it makes sense to look particularly at those astrologers who have both Uranias (Tropical and Draconic) in the same sign. Now the **Libran** example is quite striking: Russell Grant, one of the United Kingdom's most familiar faces and voices throughout the media, who – until *Strictly Come Dancing* switched his priorities – cultivated an extremely affable and intimate approach to his listener, and in the process gave a lot of pleasure to a great many people, mainly the ladies. The double **Leo** is Julia Parker, for several years President of the Faculty of Astrological Studies; double **Gemini** belongs to two astrologers (who wish to remain anonymous), both writers, one familiar to readers of *Prediction* magazine, who share not only a refreshingly unpretentious approach but an often wicked sense of humour and a delight in words for their own sake, which enables them to get astrological ideas across to the uninitiated in a light, bright and enjoyably conversational style.

There are two double **Cancerians** as well: Ronald Davison, the long-standing President of the Astrological Lodge, and Zach Matthews, former Editor of the *Astrological Journal* (in a sense the 'offspring' of Ronald Davison's *Astrology*, inasmuch as the Astrological Association was born out of the Astrological Lodge). Each of these men in his capacity nourished both astrology and astrologers, to become senior members of the astrological family, loved and respected. In Cancer, roots go deep, and perhaps this is why we also find at least one (anonymous) respected astrological psychotherapist (Tropical Urania) here, taking us always further into the origins of our consciousness and the hidden promptings of personal and collective myth; also Michel Gauquelin (Draconic Cancer), that great data-collector and indefatigable investigator who had to see whether the flower of astrology is made of paper or living tissue, and whether it has roots at all, or indeed whether it would do better on a different rootstock like a rose that can be either grown on its own or grafted! And of course he had to see whether astrological patterns run in families. Even one of astrology's oldest 'homes' has Draconic Urania in the 4th sign – the AFA, the American Federation of Astrologers.

The Urania-in-**Aries** people are represented by 'doubler' Suzi Harvey (her Urania in remarkably close conjunction with John Addey's Tropical) who, in common with most of this group, has a flair for getting things going and bringing astrology alive. In partnership with her late husband, Charles Harvey, past President and then Patron of the Astrological Association, she brought great drive and energy into its activities. We surely all know what John Addey's leadership and pioneering astrology have given to the community; but we also find here Sir George Trevelyan, Carl Payne Tobey, Marcia Moore and Tad Mann. Keeping to Fire for the moment, there are no doubles in our **Sagittarian** group; but to underline the religious feeling (in the broadest sense) that is common to most of this small sample, Michael Heleus' Draconic Urania aligns directly with the Galactic Centre. To give a 'home' to his extraordinary, dedicated and brilliant work on *Astrosonics*, he founded the Church of Cosmic Harmony, and on a visit to the zodiac in St John's College Chapel, Cambridge, he was the first person to point out to me (in 1972) the deep significance of the centre of our galaxy. And there is Dr Douglas Baker, of Claregate College, teaching and writing on *Esoteric Astrology*. Elias Ashmole, Jean Overton Fuller, Frank McGillion and Dennis Elwell, among others, share the sign.

I confess that despite two astrologers doubling up in **Taurus** I don't find it easy to pinpoint a clear Taurean mode for Urania except as a source of income! There are hints, maybe, in Al H. Morrison's fascination with the astrology of ancient Irish stone carvings, and three Urania-Taurus colleagues are each in their own way building reliable systems of astrological application on the basis of well-tried psychological technique. (As these are also globally significant pioneers, I suspect that it is their Sidereal Urania in Aries that is showing.) Others have an active interest in economics and the movements of world markets. Surprisingly, we find Edgar Cayce with a double Taurus Urania – maybe it is a matter of offering proof of astrology's reality? The **Libra** group, a much larger one, includes two British astrological poets who thus have Urania ruled by Venus! Earlier, we looked at Russell Grant as the Urania/Libra representative; it is worth examining the idea of Libra and partnership further, to see if any Libra-Uranians need to make a pair for astrological work. The author's own private work on this is very promising. The **Capricorn** group is inclined to 'go it alone' to quite a large extent, efficiently and quietly, seeking high standards of clarity and integrity in the study and practical application of astrology, working for its future, keeping a fairly low profile. There is also an interest in pattern and structure for its own sake, and also antiquity – notably in the case of Robert Hand, with his Draconic Capricorn Urania. Interestingly, five of the sample of ten were all born within less than four months of each other, and so combine this Capricorn motive with Gemini expression, as this was where the Tropical Urania fell at that time – and this they share with the two mentioned earlier, plus Marcia Moore and David Hamblin. The Draconic **Geminis** include, with five other active astrologers, Dr Baker and Alan Oken. Between them, the Uranias of all three of the Air signs have done a great deal to popularise astrology, being especially willing and able to spend long periods on the road, lecturing to students and the general public, and setting down their ideas in print with great regularity and clarity.

One sign we haven't looked at yet is **Scorpio**, and we find that taken together with the other two Water signs the interest in the structures and condition of the psyche and in the esoteric dimension of astrology is very marked, working towards a transformative astrology. Here then are Joyce Collin-Smith (connecting with the esoteric and occult), Jean Overton Fuller whose probing book *Horoscope for a Double Agent* has become a classic, Noel Tyl and Roger Elliott (all Tropical Urania), plus, with Draconic Urania, Dennis Elwell. Our double Scorpio Urania deserves to remain anonymous! … but shows us another face of this sign, in a consuming interest and consummate skill in the area of business and finance.

I feel that the Earth signs are trying to relate astrology to life as we live it – going into depth, yes, but keeping both feet firmly on the ground, maybe treating astrology more as a tool than an experience? … and finding ways to prove its truth to the unconvinced. The Fire people are the front men/women in many cases. They are confident, they are not backward in coming forward; their energy fuels much of the surrounding activity; they are a creative and innovative bunch. Water plunges with its astrology into life's depths, often murky, or takes on challenges many others would avoid. It also cares for and nourishes its own community. And the Air folk? Where else do we go for great PR? They are all out there in the big wide world, talking, travelling, teaching, making friends and making new astrologers.

Urania Synastry

Now, having given ourselves an overview of the elemental flavours of Urania, let me show you something *very* striking. Recall that John Addey's and Charles Harvey's Draconic Uranias oppose each other from 1½° Pisces to 5° Virgo; Roger Elliott's Draconic Urania is close by in 28° Aquarius; and lined up with two Presidents and one Chairman of the Astrological Association (AA) is that very Association's Tropical Urania in 3° Virgo. Trine and sextile to this axis, and again opposite each other, we find two past Presidents of the Astrological Lodge: Ronald C. Davison (Tropical Urania in 1° Cancer) and Geoffrey Cornelius (Tropical Urania in 0° Capricorn), plus another Chairman of the AA, David Hamblin (Tropical Urania 29½° Gemini), and the two journal editors, Ronald Davison again and Zach Matthews (two days the younger). In 28½° Libra again on the Air/Water cusp is Tropical Urania for the Proposal to form the Lodge. Does this Urania synastry work for the Faculty of Astrological Studies? For Julia Parker, one of its past Presidents, emphatically yes; and twice over, in that her Tropical Urania in 12° Leo nicely sextiles the Faculty's Draconic Urania at 10° Libra, and we find a precise square, this time, between her Draconic and the Faculty's Tropical Urania at 24° Leo and Scorpio respectively. Martin Freeman's Tropical 29° Pisces position falls comfortably trine 24° Scorpio, while from its cuspal degree forming a Grand Cross with the Lodge Presidents and Russell Grant (1° Libra) – the latter, of course, was the founding President of the British Astrological and Psychic Society, the Tropical Ascendant of which falls conjunct Russell's Draconic Urania. Last, but by no means least, Michael C. Heleus founded his Church of the Cosmic Harmony when transiting Urania was just 1° past his own! Now that we have our ephemerides, perhaps we astrologers should take a serious look at our Urania Returns.

Let us begin a closer examination of Urania's synastry between three of the charts most closely linked with **John Addey**. As he gave such impetus to the very plotting and study of our own asteroid, it is no surprise to find Tropical Urania in Aries, in the 10th, at the midpoint of his Moon/Uranus square, opposite Mars and the Draconic Moon/*Popastro* (!), sextile his Sun and trine Jupiter! This is the way he responded to his muse – with tremendous energy and enthusiasm. It fired his mind, and he fired the minds of others. He had great fun with it, such as few astrologers have – at least in the UK – so that his humour as well as his knowledge lit up the pages of the *Astrological Journal* for us. But what he would have been unaware of (unless he did have a quiet hour or two with Draco!) is the Draconic Virgo position, which also combines with Mars of course but also with the 8th House Uranus by direct alignment, indicating the nature of his astrological inspiration: to take up the unique challenge of astrology's finest tuning in the harmonics, and the painstaking analysis of shifts of meaning throughout the diurnal circle by the detailed plotting of character traits. This minutely precise, exacting work was truly pioneering; with help from Michel Gauquelin and Charles Harvey he broke new ground for astrology. Mars, Uranus, Urania.

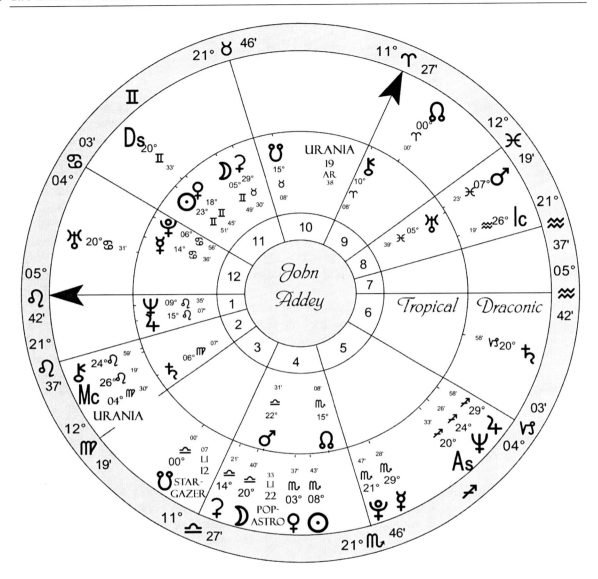

When we look at **Michel Gauquelin**, his contribution becomes clear: it is not just that he also has a Tropical Mars/Draconic Urania contact, in Cancer, moving him to probe astrology's roots, but that his whole Mercury/Jupiter/Chiron/MC alignment, transferred to Draco, falls across that same axis in Virgo-Pisces to feed his Tropical Urania and Neptune. Here, instead of the Virgo *inspiration*, is the Virgo *expression*. John needed a man who loved to handle detail, was supremely qualified for it, and could sift facts out of uncertainty. Astrology more than anything, with all its counting and measuring and sorting, must have been a perpetual fascination for Gauquelin, and, while exercising his imagination, presented an endless challenge to his statistical mind.

I find it intriguing that both men have a strongly placed *Popastro*: Gauquelin's Tropical asteroid is close to his Draconic MC. Neither of them overtly played to the popular gallery,

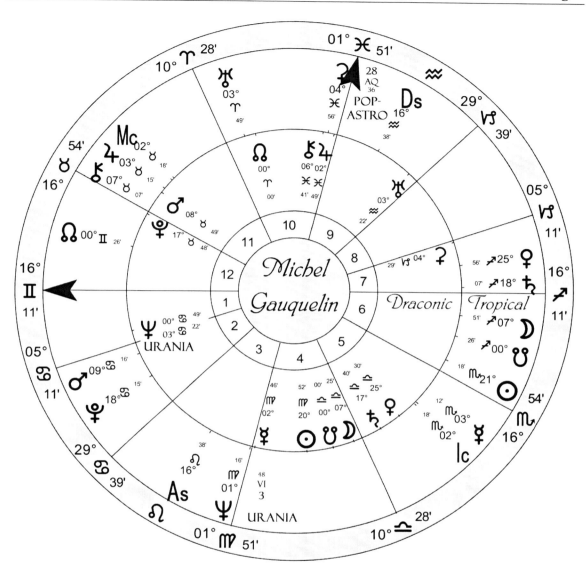

but Gauquelin's work did achieve a measure of the public recognition that he sought, and John Addey's writing remains hugely popular among his fellow astrologers.

A number of years separate the births of Michel Gauquelin and **Charles Harvey**, but each was born with Urania conjunct Neptune – and *at the Draconic level* Charles Harvey's conjunction *also* falls on this critical Virgo/Pisces axis, in 0° and 5° of Pisces, aligning tightly with the Tropical conjunction of Gauquelin and with John Addey's Urania/Uranus contact. (The latter's Tropical Saturn is involved as well, in 6° Virgo; this rules his 6th House and falls in the 2nd, indicating the limitation that John's physical handicaps placed on his resources, but that every crumb of time, energy, attention and spare cash would be fed to this growing body of work, however slender the means at his disposal, however long it should take.) With John's brilliance of mind and application, and Charles' inspiration, and

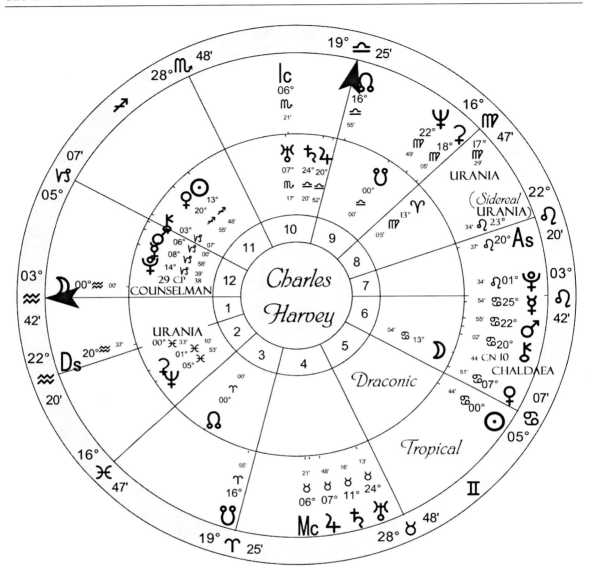

Michel's blend of both, what a team! There is another important link with John Addey's astrology in Charles' chart: the conjunction of his North Node plus Draconic Jupiter/MC with John's Tropical Urania/Mars, and Draconic Moon axis across 19°-22° of Aries-Libra. If ever the professional and ideological destinies of men were more clearly linked, I have yet to see it. Charles' Tropical Urania falls in his 2nd house in a most interesting – if slightly wide – alignment with the Aries Point in the Draconic – which may be the indicator of one's *individual* progress through the incarnation rather than one's dharmic and karmic obligations within the soul-group (Moon's Nodes in the Tropical pattern). Trine the midpoint of the 10th house Saturn/Uranus (signs Ancient and Modern again!) and sextile Chiron, we can see the teacher and guide. But just look at the 7th harmonic patterns of Urania with Sun, Mercury and Ascendant! Inspiration and creativity here must be of a very high order and dominate the greater part of the public and inner life.

Urania on the Angles

Among the astrologers studied, one group in particular stands out: these have a direct Urania/Ascendant or MC contact. There are thirty-four of them in the author's sample: W. Kenneth Brown, who was L. Edward Johndro's colleague by correspondence (Tropical Urania conjunct Tropical Ascendant); Edgar Cayce (Draconic Urania conjunct Tropical MC); Joyce Collin-Smith (Tropical Urania widely conjunct IC); Nicholas Culpeper (Draconic Urania on the Tropical MC); Geoffrey Cornelius (Tropical Urania widely conjunct Descendant); Pamela Crane (Tropical Urania widely conjunct MC); Roger Elliott (Draconic MC opposite Tropical Urania); Dennis Elwell (Draconic Urania conjunct Tropical Ascendant); Jean Overton Fuller (Tropical Urania conjunct Tropical Ascendant); Michel Gauquelin (Draconic MC opposite Tropical Urania); Russell Grant (Tropical Urania conjunct Tropical Ascendant); David Hamblin (Tropical Urania conjunct Tropical IC); **'Moby Dick' Jacobs** (Urania culminating); Marcia Moore (Draconic Urania conjunct Tropical MC); Al H. Morrison (Draconic MC conjunct Tropical Urania); John Partridge (Tropical Urania conjunct Draconic IC); Carl Payne Tobey (Urania conjunct the IC); and **Sir George Trevelyan** (Draconic Urania conjunct the Tropical MC) are found among them.

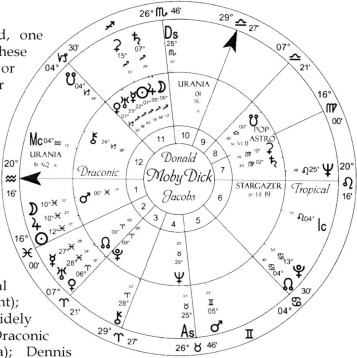

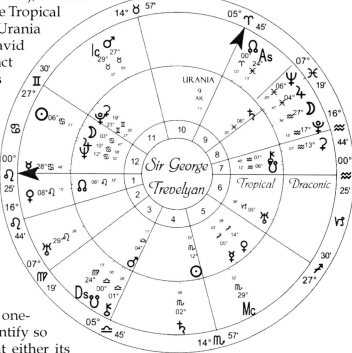

What are we seeing here? Over one-third of our total who clearly identify so strongly with their astrology that either its manner of expression (Tropical) or its inspiring principle (Draconic) becomes blended with part of the outer personality structure. It may even betray an attitude toward the Muse herself, who may at one extreme be given all the credit for the efforts of the astrologer, and at the other be given no credit at all! Those who emphasise Tropical rather than Draconic Urania might risk showing off the wrapping at the expense of the contents (though I doubt whether this is generally true); one might also infer that the IC/Ascendant people have more inner astrological resources than the others who must constantly outreach; also (and I suspect this to be true) these people will apply their astrology far more in psychosomatic study than the MC/Descendant group, who would have a drive to get away from what is already there and use astrology to push back the frontiers not so much of technique or knowledge, but of astrology's application, maybe.

Urania in Lights!

Then there is the *inner* identification to explore, the strongest of which (in terms of 'I am astrology' as well as talent or useful activity) is the alignment of Urania with Sun or Moon. Of our current sample, forty-nine have such contacts, including, for example: John Addey (Draconic Moon opposite Tropical Urania); the AFA. (with both Tropical Urania opposite Draconic Sun and Draconic Urania conjunct the Tropical Moon); Elias Ashmole (Urania/Sun conjunction on the 7ᵗʰ cusp); Dr Douglas Baker (Tropical Moon opposite Tropical Urania); W. Kenneth Brown (Tropical Sun opposite Draconic Urania); Joyce Collin-Smith (Tropical Moon opposite Tropical Urania); Pamela Crane (Tropical Moon opposite Draconic Urania); Ronald Davison (Tropical Sun opposite Draconic Urania and Tropical Moon conjunct Tropical Urania, which was repeated at his appointment as Editor of *Astrology* on February 16ᵗʰ 1959); Dr John Dee (Tropical Urania opposite Draconic Sun); Jean Overton-Fuller (Tropical Moon conjunct Draconic Urania); Robert Hand (Tropical Urania/Sun conjunction with Draconic Moon); Karl Ernst Krafft (Draconic Sun conjunct Tropical Urania); Tad Mann (Tropical Sun conjunct Tropical Urania and Tropical Moon conjunct Draconic Urania); Zach Matthews (Tropical Sun widely opposite, Tropical Moon widely conjunct, Draconic Urania); Colin Miles (Sun/Urania conjunction); Al H. Morrison (Draconic Sun opposite Tropical Urania); and Julia Parker (Draconic Sun conjunct, Tropical Sun widely conjunct Tropical Urania).

To the above list one must next add those who have the Lights linked to Urania by aspect within the chart pattern. As in the foregoing, some will be noted as 'wide' when the orb is 6°-8°. A host of others join those above with Sun/Moon-Urania contacts (and some have appeared before, as they show both interaspects and alignments), including: John Addey (Sun sextile, Moon semi-square Urania); Roger Elliott (Moon sextile, Sun 5/14 Urania); Dennis Elwell (Sun quintile, Moon sextile Urania); Jean Overton-Fuller (Sun trine, Moon semi-sextile Urania); Michel Gauquelin (Moon square Urania); Russell Grant (Sun trioctile Urania); David Hamblin (Sun semi-square, Moon quincunx Urania); Charles Harvey (Sun 3/14 Urania); Suzi Harvey (Sun tredecile, Moon sextile Urania); 'Moby Dick' Jacobs (Sun decile Urania); Marcia Moore (Moon semi-sextile Urania); Al H. Morrison (Sun trine, Moon quincunx Urania); Alan Oken (Moon trioctile Urania); John Partridge (Sun semi-square Urania); Noel Jan Tyl (Sun sextile, Moon quintile Urania).

The septile and semi-septile (7th/14th harmonic) contacts appear notably in the charts of astrologers generally acknowledged to bring considerable inspiration to their work. Add this to strong Draconic activity around the pattern, and you have a formidable ability.

A Uranian Vocation

It would be impossible, and impermissible, to study each of the charts in detail in the present context, but a close look at a few of the most interesting – those who have willingly published their data – will serve to show how active the Draconic level is in pointing to the Uranian vocation. (There are some instances in which not a great deal is going on between the zodiacs, and here one would surmise that astrology may be a new activity for the person in question, not related in any way to qualities and abilities already possessed by the reincarnating soul. Also, there may not be the intensity of commitment that one sees elsewhere, and the astrological life, despite interest and talent, may be less productive. Otherwise, as suggested earlier, strong contacts may exist not with the Draconic but with the Sidereal zodiac, or even the Heliocentric pattern.)

Medium with a Message

First, let us look at two men, each with a very different approach and commitment to astrology. (Again, we have a few interesting extra asteroids to enlighten and entertain us!) One is Russell Grant, very well-known now in the British Isles as an astrological entertainer on television and radio and who has also made successful forays into the USA; the other is Dr Douglas Baker, founder and Principal of Claregate College in the UK, and author of many books on esoteric subjects, including astrology. Two things they have in common, not shared by everyone: 5°/6° of Tropical Libra rising, and a truly uncommon psychic gift, in Russell's case manifesting as clairvoyance (by means of which he was reading birth charts correctly some time before he determined to learn how to go about it in a deliberate and structured way!) and in Dr Baker as the claimed ability to suspend normal sleep in favour of a consciously receptive state in which he has, he says, received the material for all the esoteric volumes he has written and published. Russell's determination to combine his intuitive grasp of astrology with ordered analysis shows in the conjunction of Tropical Urania with Saturn in Libra just above the Ascendant in the 12th. Here it becomes a powerful drive with which he identifies – and is publicly identified. He is fluent and confident, as befits the trine with Mercury. To win his audience, he employs a Venusian astrology; Draconic Urania is also in Libra. It stems from his belief in sharing knowledge and giving (and receiving) pleasure, so his astrology has to be appealing and enjoyable, geared very strongly to a feminine audience, the pill sugared. You could also say it is a matter of making astrology easy for people. His longing was always to bring to the public, through humour and showmanship, an awareness of the serious astrology that was professedly his first love – until BBC TV's *Strictly Come Dancing* 2011 rearranged his show-business priorities.

The T-square of Urania with Chiron and angular Uranus always threatened this kind of upset, even while challenging him constantly to further effort; and the transit of Pluto through early Capricorn has turned this pattern into a Grand Cross that has seen Russell's

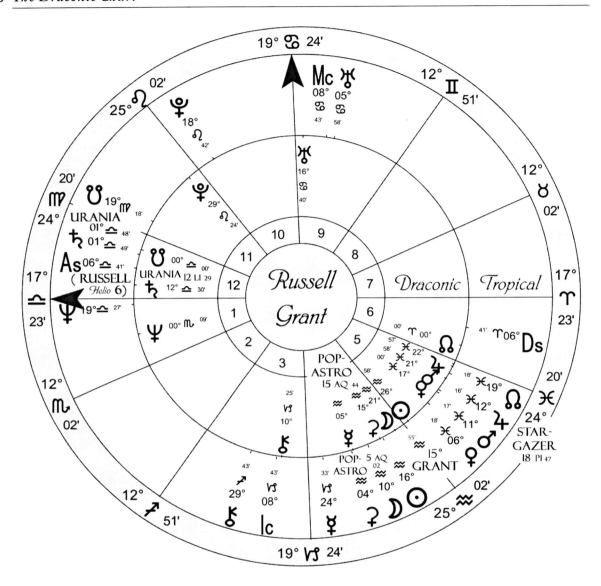

career in the entertainment industry go through the most dramatic and public death-and-rebirth. Can he really relegate astrology to second place? In his Tropical wheel *Stargazer* is with the Dragon's Head, and, spectacularly, Draconic *Popastro* meets his Tropical Sun/ Grant conjunction and the nearby Moon (on *Strictly* he was simply referred to as 'The Grant'!) while Tropical *Popastro* (conjunct Ceres *in coelo*) is with Draconic Mercury. The icing on this star-spangled cake is the conjunction by 5' of arc of Helio *Russell* at 6°36' Libra with his Tropical Ascendant. 'Russell Grant' has become a household name.

The Road Warrior

Dr Baker also believes in communication; his Draconic Urania stands at 21°00' Gemini and so there has to be a great deal of writing and speaking. But he is not so much a media man

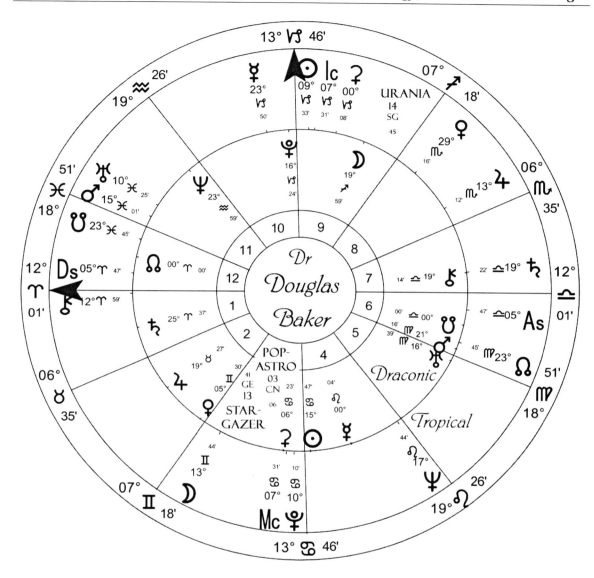

as a lecturer; he travels the country from public platform to public platform. Gemini acts in another way; in his writings the material is arranged in a very accessible manner and is very readable. Though styles may differ, this seems to be typical of Draconic Gemini Urania. The 3rd House placement speaks for itself. Tropical Urania in Sagittarius ensures an exploratory, philosophical interest in the discipline, relating it to the esoteric wisdom. He has produced several volumes of *Esoteric Astrology* to date. His teaching and his intuition come easily to him, with Urania involved in two kite formations – one with Chiron in Aries in the 7th, Neptune in Leo in the 11th, and the Gemini 9th House Moon; the other in the same Grand Fire Tine but with Saturn in Libra in the 1st at its apex. Less easy is the T-square with Mars/Uranus in the 6th in Pisces; like many a powerful and gifted man, he can roar at his students! Like many another human being, he has a bit of a short fuse. But he will use this, too, basing his philosophical tutorials sometimes on his own wartime experiences from which to draw more universal inferences, illustrating themes of personal challenge and victory, physical and spiritual. A most unusual man.

Charles Harvey

Charles Harvey is distinguished by showing no direct planetary alignments of either kind with Draconic Urania, and yet where would one find a more deeply involved astrologer than he? One immediate, obvious answer is that his *Sidereal* Urania lies in 'establishment' Leo, close to his Ascendant. This is highly appropriate to a man who has played so great a part in twentieth-century astrology, identified and is identified with it, and will go down in astrological history. A second, novel suggestion with which the reader is perfectly free to disagree as it is somewhat provocative, is as follows: it is in every way possible that Charles Harvey required no interplay between these higher and lower selves because he was only living his astrological life at the older, higher level, hence the entire Draconic pattern comes into its own, and he expressed his astrology as it moved him. In support of this proposal, let me observe that he never seemed fully to come into his own with the material and detailed presentation of his work (Tropical Urania/Virgo), until, just as water will not be compressed, and always finds its own level, he rose naturally to Draconic Urania in Pisces, excelling in bringing home to us all his vision of the universal astrology, inspiring and uniting his audience, inviting us to consider the mysteries and the unformed possibilities awaiting all astrologers of sensitivity and imagination. It is an other-worldly, rarified, spiritual astrology; and the man who embodied it presented himself to his public far less convincingly as the Tropical Cancerian than as the Draconic Sagittarius/Capricorn, the eternal pilgrim, the aspirant compelled by the grandeur of the universal order. Looking for midpoint stimuli from Draconic to the Tropical, we find only two, but important and active, pairs! Draconic Urania = Sun/Pluto (semi-sextile at birth) and Mercury/Venus (in the subtle aspect of semi-decile), so there is little of the obvious or everyday about the Tropical activity taking place. Just before we leave him, I must mention the remarkable double contact there is between his chart and that of his wife Suzi, of his Draconic Sun to her Tropical Chiron, and his Draconic Chiron to her Tropical Sun. What a lovely and apt teaching partnership they had together.

Editorial Twins

Reference has already been made to the near time-twins Ronald Davison and Zach Matthews, each editor for many years of a major astrological journal; but it is worth adding one or two other items relevant to our theme, namely that in each case the Draconic Urania conjunct Tropical Mars aligns opposite Tropical Mercury (close to *Popastro!*), Venus and Sun in Capricorn, and Tropical Urania receives some effect from Draconic Saturn's 5° conjunction. This ensures that so long as the soul has its way, the man eats, sleeps, dreams, lives astrology, helping by dint of much hard work over a long period to give it a secure framework, to provide it with a family. Ronald Davison's map shows Ascendant/MC directly = Urania in the 5th, descriptive of the considerable creative output of this respected astrologer; while with Urania in the 7th, Zach Matthews spent a great deal of time and energy getting other astrologers cracking with material for publication! This is in addition, of course, to his own editorials, which so often served to remind *Journal* readers of that dimension of everyone's life – not just the astrologer's – which tends in a technological age to be neglected or explained away, namely the spiritual values and realities to which both these men so strongly subscribed. It manifests particularly through their astrology, as Urania configures with Jupiter and Neptune in the 7th harmonic, and Ronald Davison's Cancer/Capricorn alignment fulfils itself in his 12th House, which is most appropriate for the former President of the Astrological Lodge of the Theosophical Society. The importance of Urania is highlighted beautifully at the moment when Ronald Davison was appointed as editor of *Astrology*: not only was there the aforementioned repeat of Moon conjunct Urania, but this fell with a Mars/Jupiter opposition close to his natal MC/IC axis, and the MC at that moment conjoined his natal Tropical Urania. The Urania at appointment was configured in the 7th harmonic with this natal Urania, and MC, Venus and Moon's Nodes in the map.

Cutting-edge Creativity

Roger Elliott's chart is amazing if only for the amount of 5th harmonic activity going on – most of it involving Urania. The dominant pattern is Tropical Urania at the Draconic IC opposite Uranus, quintile Jupiter, biquintile Saturn and biquintile Mercury (plus sextiles to Moon and Neptune); for good measure there are Sun/Neptune and Venus/Pluto quintiles as well. Mars, although a little wide of the quintile patterns, nevertheless lies just in orb of the opposition, and quincunx Mercury. This makes for a startling contrast to Charles Harvey's chart with its powerful 7th harmonic structures and suggests that where Charles was the mystic, Roger was the magician in astrology (the mystic and the magical summarise well the differences between 7th and 5th harmonic activity). And yes, when it was Roger Elliott the personality speaking, the Scorpio Urania did have its way, in an often cutting wit, and a polished repertoire of innuendo; in addition to which his Tropical MC is dominated by our people-pleasing little friend Sidereal *Popastro*, so we can see that Roger Elliott the personality was strongly identified with his role in TV and journalism. Sidereal Urania adds to this cult of popularity, closely conjoined in Libra with the Draconic Sun. Now, the Draconic Urania is in Aquarius: he had come to bring new ideas, modern technology to astrology, and with no direct axis to the Tropical, but two strong midpoints active – Sun/Jupiter and Nodes/Uranus (semi-sextile/quincunx natally) – he did this very successfully, the present author among others being indebted to his original mind for ideas that have subsequently born good fruit. As the one strong Draconic axis in the pattern is between Draconic Jupiter MC/Pluto and Tropical Urania, the personality is likely to appear dominant, as we have seen, and may serve to obscure the real work that goes on constantly when he becomes entirely his higher self. When the Draconic level takes over entirely, governing that creative intellect, Virgo, not Gemini, rises, and Roger Elliott becomes the quieter, deeply thoughtful man that we were also privileged to know, while still feeding and fed by the personality through that powerful conjunction of the Draconic meridian with Tropical Venus/Uranus and Urania/ Mars. At this level his 12th House Venus, which rules the Draconic MC, falls in 3° Virgo – an axis clearly potent in research astrology.

High, Wide and Deep

On that same axis, in Pisces, lies Dennis Elwell's Draconic Uranus; his Tropical Sun conjoins Elliott's Draconic Urania, his Tropical Urania is right on Elliott's North Node. One finds so much potential for mutual enrichment in this study! But to turn now to Dennis Elwell, here again is a magician in our ranks, as Sun, Urania and Chiron join forces in the 5th harmonic. But the mystic is not absent: Neptune bi-septiles Urania from the 10th House. The emphasis is again on a Scorpio Urania, but this time at the Draconic level; and it subtends no less than seven important midpoints, while the Tropical Urania has nothing at all like that to do. Again we find Draconic Virgo rising, and the ruler of the Draconic MC in Virgo in the 12th House of the chart. The Sagittarian expression of Urania is well known to all astrologers who have both enjoyed and been inspired by Dennis' lectures, writings and conversation – always adventurous, often wise, inevitably laced with warm humour. The Scorpio level is constantly busy doing what Scorpio in any context does so supremely well, asking questions, and never letting up until everything is discovered and known that can be known. A fascination with layers, strata, becomes a sensitivity to multiple dimensions. For him, secrets are there to be revealed to the initiate, and to be used in the guidance and healing of others, to bring them to peace. With Charles Harvey he shares Sun/Pluto = Draconic Urania; also active are Sun/Moon, Mercury/MC, Mars/Chiron, Jupiter/ Saturn, Jupiter/Uranus, and the important combination of Chiron with North Node and Draconic Drakonia close to the 7th cusp, which aligns with Draconic Urania to channel its formidable energies.

Incidentally, the first chart which brought to my notice the importance of looking at the Tropical midpoints triggered by Draconic Urania was that of a friend who has been involved in book-selling for many years. There was the pattern, standing out so clearly for anyone to see, at the top of the chart, in the 10th House of career and achievement, in Gemini: Draco Urania = Tropical Mercury/Uranus! If ever there was a plainer signature of a life whose business it is to bring new astrological literature and information to the book-buying public, I have yet to see it! Urania's placement in the 2nd House completed the picture of astrology as a significant source of income.

Celestial Bodies

In the original overview of our sample, by far the largest grouping of Urania positions, at both levels, comprises those found in the signs Leo, Virgo and Capricorn. To me this is highly significant, as it is one indication of the number of astrologers working today who bring to their inner and outer approach an appreciation of the need for the highest standards, for astrology and the astrologer to be scrutinised and not found wanting; to be useful, respectable, accepted, its own house in good order, its practitioners well qualified and ready to teach others (many of the astrologers of this group run their own courses and schools.) It is an education in itself to study the charts of two such establishments side by side; and with this I shall end our survey of the Muse and the Dragon.

These are two of the principal bodies concerned with the teaching of astrology – the Faculty of Astrological Studies, founded in 1948, and the much younger and now needed Advisory Panel on Astrological Education (APAE), 'born' in 1980. I am now no longer sure that one should consider it at all remarkable that things should turn out as might reasonably be expected – so perhaps it

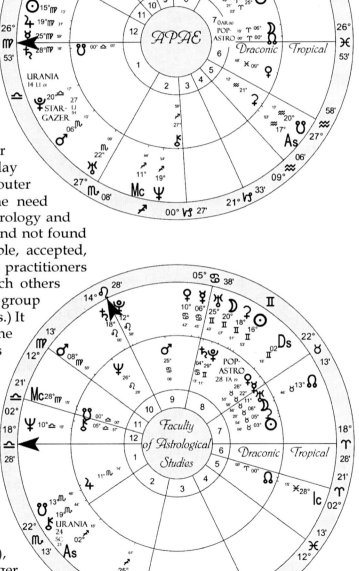

is really no great cause for amazement that, for example, the Faculty should be born with an astrology teachers' Chiron/Urania conjunction that nobody knew was there (is that why it is in the 12th?) After all, the Faculty is there purely and simply to teach astrology, and the conjunction, in a 'Gauquelin Sector', whose meaning we can now read, makes that extremely plain. Nor, therefore, for a similar reason, should we be astonished to find the APAE with Draconic Urania conjunct Tropical Chiron, no longer lurking in the 12th House but decently arranged around the 3rd cusp, and aligned with Uranus exactly. This Draconic Urania is right opposite the Faculty's Tropical Urania; the Faculty's Draconic Urania in Libra is just 3° from the APAE's Tropical. And the Suns are square in the Mercury signs, and the Tropical Chirons are opposite each other; and where the Faculty has Draconic Saturn conjunct Tropical Mercury, APAE has a Mercury/Saturn conjunction *in coelo*. Both have contacts between Saturn and an angle and Neptune and an angle: the Faculty shows Draconic MC conjunct Tropical Saturn (and Pluto), Draconic Neptune conjunct Tropical MC; the APAE has the Draconic Ascendant conjunct Tropical Saturn (and Mercury), Neptune 8° from the MC in the 10th House. The APAE's Chiron squares the Nodal axis; that of the Faculty lies close to the South Node. Both bodies are there to teach, both are governed by an ideal, each advocates serious and disciplined study and has the authority to encourage this in the astrological community. Draconic factors bring their impulse from a higher source, to give a driving motivation to capacities inherent in the Tropical.

That Urania is the tiny star of the astrologer, there can now be no shadow of a doubt; and the 'archetypal or mythic figure … the symbol of the meaning of the "rightness" of … vocation stands no longer behind us, eclipsed by the striving personality, but clearly before us, knowable through the interweavings of two zodiacs'.

Note 1: In the foregoing chapter, every effort has been made to mention by name only those colleagues who have, for either the 1987 edition of *Draconic Astrology* or for *The Draconic Chart* and/or subsequent revisions, given their consent to the author to discuss their data, or those whose birth data is otherwise publicly available for study through books or other literature.

Note 2: The use of asteroids is often criticised; the argument being that even though a chosen asteroid is in a strong and descriptive position, crowded around the same zodiac degree will be many others which have no relevance to the chart. Indeed: but this is no different to the movement of people. If you make a date with your best friend to chat over coffee at Waterstones at 11h00 am on Tuesday, both of you can be expected to turn up there at the appointed time; but the coffee shop will be busy with other people who have nothing to do with you, except for those providing the coffee. You don't complain that all the other folk weren't invited by you and so shouldn't be there! They each have their own agenda at that moment, just as the other asteroids will be relevant to the separate lives of people time-twinning with your chart.

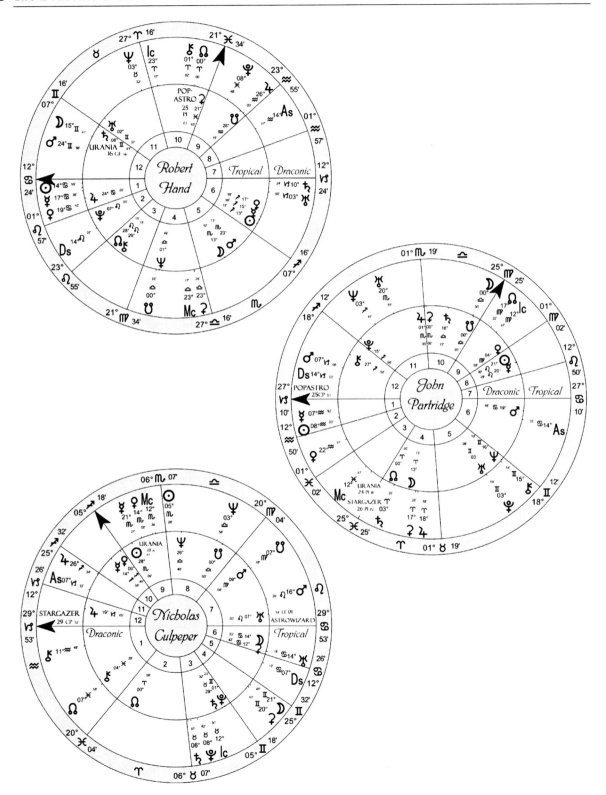

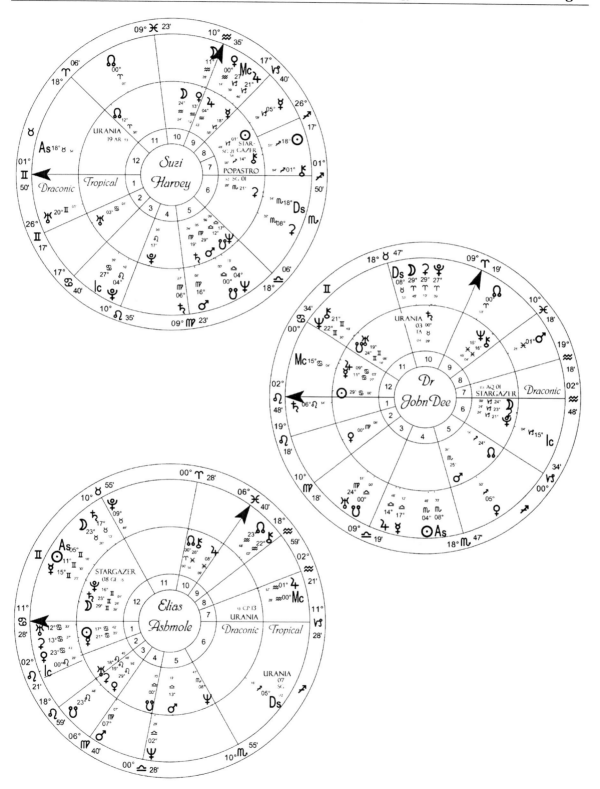

Chapter Nineteen

Stars of Royal Beauty Bright

Draconic's Miraculous Gift of the Birth, Death and Resurrection of Jesus

The birth of Jesus Christ has been a subject of fascinated speculation among astrologers and interested astronomers for a large part of the past millennium. Much of this has centred on the Jupiter/Saturn conjunctions, reports of super-novae, historical records and the few clues offered by the Gospels themselves. That Jesus of Nazareth really lived and died by crucifixion is supported by early historians like Josephus; that something extraordinary happened to his followers is witnessed by their readiness to suffer torture and death for the truth of what they had seen, and by the astonishing spread of his revolutionary teaching throughout the world. Human nature being what it is, the teaching – exoteric and esoteric – has been much corrupted and misunderstood, but still it continues to raise humankind from the brute to the angel.

As all avenues of establishment and fringe enquiry have so far borne little fruit, the idea that occurred to the author on that Sunday afternoon in October 1992, to take a radically different – Draconic – approach to the question of the birth-moment for such an awesome figure, seemed worth pursuing. Accepting that the man Jesus was the earthly vehicle for that emanation of the Godhead which we call the Christ, and assuming that this exalted being must come into the world free of human karma and with no conflicts between his persona and his spiritual nature, it follows that such perfection requires a perfect moment for its earthly incarnation – a moment that is historically unrepeatable. When might such a moment be? The answer indeed turned out to lie not in the search for planetary patterns, nor in the possibility of exploding stars. We only had to look to the zodiacs for our answer.

What I spent hours hunting down by trial and error with the only resource available at that time (my first 386, 25Mhz PC loaded with a first-class astrological DOS program, and an OKI printer) was the only moment in recorded history that could hope to deliver perfection, the exact coincidence of Tropical and Draconic. I knew, from many years of happy marriage to a much more recent example, how unified were the driving principles with outward practice even in an ordinary pick-and-mix, curate's egg of a human being as most of us are. Once every eighteen to nineteen years along comes this particular bunch of people where you pretty well know what you are getting. So, if there *was* a year in the right time-frame for Jesus' historical birth, when 0° Aries Draconic closed in on 0° Tropical, the pattern for the moment of exactitude could be the moment for which all of us had been searching. By 5h25 pm I had at last precisely fine-tuned the North Node's position, entered it into Blue*Star, and only had to wait a few seconds till the chart itself materialised from the printer and displayed its patterns for the first time

This is What I Saw

At 16h23m07s GMT (18h43m55s LMT or 18h50m37s LAT) on May 7th 5 BC (Astronomical Year for computing, -0004) in Bethlehem, Israel, just as the Moon's True North Node reached 0°00'00'Aries, the Sun was setting conjunct Jupiter in the middle of Taurus, between 0° Taurus and 0° Gemini, i.e. 'between the Ox and the Ass.' The Tropical and Draconic zodiacs were precisely aligned for the first time since two other crucial events occurred: the symbolically important conjunctions of Saturn and Jupiter in Pisces, and a highly significant eclipse in the same sign on March 8th 5 BC. Before too long a third event would occur, when the Tropical zodiac aligned with the Sidereal; even on this date the zero points of all three major zodiacs were very close together. (*NB: Solar Fire 4 put the True Node at 0°02' Aries; Solar Fire 7 shifts it to 29°58' Pisces! Halfway between these points is the exact 0°00' Aries position which in Matrix Blue*Star led me to the Nativity in the first place, so I feel no need to dispute it.*)

The lovely setting conjunction formed a Mystic Rectangle in the heavens with the three outer planets, the powerful transcendent energies of Uranus, Neptune and Pluto. Knowing how active these are in the charts of spiritually-minded people, I would have looked for nothing less in our highest Example.

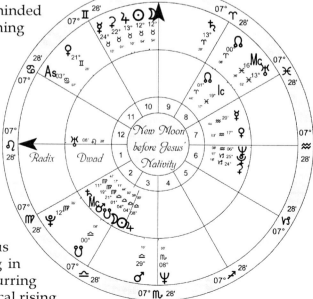

This is How Events May Have Unfolded

The Persian Magi, watching the heavens for signs of the Christ-child's coming, would first observe the triple conjunction and know that the prophesied time was coming near. 'Following his star' they would then have waited for two more signs before they set off on their momentous journey: the Spring Equinox Sun rising in the Dragon's Head (i.e. eclipses occurring close to the Equinox) and then the heliacal rising

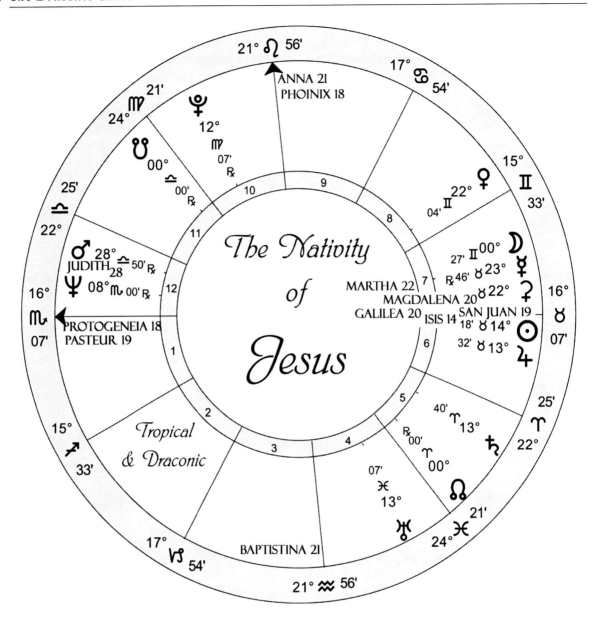

The Nativity of Jesus

Tropical & Draconic

of Jupiter after a New Moon conjunct the mighty Royal Star Aldebaran, 'the Watcher of the East'. Perhaps this is what was meant by 'they have seen his star in the East'? In any case, with Aldebaran in Taurus 11°54', the astrologers would have been able to see its heliacal rising in the East, after the crucial New Moon, on their arrival in Jerusalem. They would have known from this that their calculations had brought them to Bethlehem in good time to pay their homage to the child born 'under' that royal star before his family left to return home.

There could well have been the gift of a lamb by the local shepherds; certainly the flocks would have been back in the hills, and that season's lambs would still have been quite small. But what about the gifts of the 'three kings'? This story may not in fact refer to the Magi, but to those three great symbols of kingship gathered *in coelo* on the horizon – the Sun, Jupiter, and the Royal Star itself – expressed again *in mundo* as material symbols, as gold, frankincense and myrrh.

At this moment the alignment of the three zodiacs was exact (as specified) between the first two, and extremely close between these and the Sidereal – whichever of the main contenders for this zodiac you choose. The De Luce is almost exactly aligned, with the Synetic Vernal Point at only 0°03'01' Aries; the general favourite (and mine, after long and rigorous testing), the Fagan-Bradley, is only off by 3°07'09'. The significance of this triple alignment, intimated above, is that the characteristics of the (Tropical) bodily personality, dependent as it is on that body's metabolic needs and drives, are in total unison with those of the (Draconic) incarnating soul, and very nearly identical with the (Sidereal) 'historic' self that identifies not with its bodily desires, nor with any accompanying karmic drives, but with its duty to the rest of humanity, as far as opportunity affords. (Of which more, hopefully, in a further volume.) The differences that do arise between the Sidereal and the other two zodiacs, allowing planetary cross-contacts from one to the other, bring those other drives and energies into this wider Sidereal scheme.

The Nature of Jesus

What kind of nature, then, does such a uniquely unified being bring into incarnation at this point in history? Common sense and statistics tell us that someone, somewhere, was very likely to be coming into the world at the time. The planetary pattern is amazing, and gives the lie to all protestations that 'undiscovered' planets are invalid in nativities that take place before they were found.

The Sun, the focus of identity at every level, is conjunct Jupiter, royal *Aldebaran* (the 'eye of the bull') and the Descendant in Taurus, opposite the other royal star Antares on the Ascendant and 12th House Neptune, sextile Uranus in the 4th, and in a beautiful close trine to Pluto in the 10th House of the chart. He possesses great power, but resists its temptations and dedicates it to the healing and spiritual enlightenment of others. The conjunction also semi-sextiles Saturn in the 5th. Also in the 5th House are the conjoined Equinox, Dragon's Head and SVP (Synetic Vernal Point).

So immediately we have a figure of tremendous power, sensitivity, originality and spiritual charisma, graced with self-discipline and authority, full of common sense, generosity, wisdom and humour. Now that we have an accurate position for Ceres, the harvest imagery of so many parables is understood – she is closely conjunct his Taurus Mercury! His heart goes out to everyone he meets; his path is one of loving and giving on a global scale. The Fagan-Bradley Sidereal brings that wonderful Sun/Jupiter right onto the Tropical/Draconic 7th cusp to emphasise the importance of one-to-one sharing in this man's principal work. His star, *Aldebaran* in Taurus, grants him the titles of 'King of Kings' and 'Prince of Peace'.

Yet the same Taurus Sun also describes the man Joseph who was earthly father to him, for Jesus was a carpenter – and in those times if a man worked in wood to build homes and furnishings, he also worked in stone as a mason, a builder. (I learned this on our visit to the Holy Land at Easter, 1994.) This was the trade Jesus himself was to follow until the start of his ministry; this Taurean was to be known as the Carpenter – the Builder – of Nazareth.

The Moon in 0° Gemini, still in orbs of conjunction with Taurus Mercury, describes a young and intelligent mother. But she is semi-square the 5th House Saturn, though sextile the triple Node, and quincunx a 12th House Mars … this man can only bring pain to his mother and to any woman in his life, for Venus in Gemini in the 8th also configures the 12th in her tri-octile to Neptune, and its hidden enemies ultimately mean torture (Sidereal Mars Scorpio) and death. Scorpio rising is strong and silent under stress, whatever nature it hides. This is a being who came to love universally, and to suffer in silence. Here is a perfect spirit in an imperfect world.

This is borne out by the impressive Heliocentric chart, where the nativity's Mystic Rectangle is even more perfectly formed than in the Geocentric. It shows Mars no longer in conflict but united with Earth in Scorpio in the configuration of Neptune sextile Pluto and trine Uranus – the spiritual body and blood of the Lord's Supper. Mercury, semi-square Pluto at the time of the previous day's lovely New Moon, has moved to conjoin Neptune and Mars, showing us the profound, spiritual, forceful and compassionate mind behind the friendly voice and plain words.

This is indeed a perfected man, a son of man who is Son of God; who is entitled to say from Scorpio 'I am the Resurrection and the Life', and from the triple zodiacal convergence, 'I am the Way, the Truth and the Life – no man cometh unto the Father but by me', and from the beauty of his pattern, and from the life he lived through it, 'Be thou perfect, even as Thy Father in Heaven is perfect'.

Fine-tuning the chart only adds to the accuracy of its description. I have, over the past ten years, with every chart, made a habit of adding the Dwad. Again, this is a technique which needs – and will hopefully get – a book of its own, but for now you can think of it as a phase-shifted 12th harmonic, for the degrees and minutes calculated are just the same as

Helio Mystic Rectangle of the Solar Christ

those of the 12th harmonic chart, but the signs are different. The sequence of twelve mini-signs within each sign begins with that sign itself, not with Aries. The mini-signs map, in fact, precisely onto the framework of the decanates. (See Appendix.)

These Geocentric Dwad positions for Jesus put the Ascendant into Taurus conjunct Sun/Jupiter/Descendant, completing the identification of self with neighbour. Venus goes onto the Aquarius IC – he is 'rooted and grounded in Love'. Mercury, Neptune and Ceres occupy the radix 3rd House in Dwad Aquarius together with Dwad Capricorn Pluto, opposite Dwad Leo Uranus in the radix 9th., bringing to the picture a visionary teacher; Mars and Saturn align with the radix Pluto-Uranus opposition, introducing the experience of violence; the Dwad Descendant in Scorpio moves near to radix Neptune, drawing followers to Jesus among the fishermen and the 'publicans and sinners'. And the Dwad Sun is conjunct Dwad IC in Libra on the 12th House cusp near radix Mars, graphically depicting the end of his selfless life abandoned and in agony. (Sidereal Dwad Saturn joins this group; here is 'the man of sorrows, acquainted with grief'.)

I have subjected this nativity to almost every test possible; it has been measured interdimensionally against the Crucifixion and Resurrection of 3rd and 5th April AD 33 for progressions, directions and transits; compared directly and in composite with clergy, papacy, saints, martyrs, apostates, faithful, turning-points in Christian history, photographs of the Turin Shroud, and even actors who have played the role of Christ. No matter what I do or how finely these tests are tuned, the resulting patterns behave as though the power, the mind and the love of God are present through the person of Jesus Christ. It will not fall down; I can find no fault in this Nativity, and the supporting research fills more space than I can give it in this book.

However, I shall show you as much as I can! …

Women and Jesus

That womanhood has such a low profile in Jesus' chart, and is subject to such limitations, may disturb some of you. But this is still in accord with the received wisdom, now very much out of fashion and 'politically incorrect', that woman is somehow less than man.

But think about it for a minute – the distress that is present in the feminine part of this pattern comes precisely from the capacity to feel, to respond at a purely human, emotional level, which is after all a woman's special gift. He, being complete, would have this gift; inevitably therefore he would experience – and cause – emotional pain while living a life in the body.

Woman is only 'less' than man because the Earth and Moon are only satellites of the Sun, because body and even soul are necessarily 'satellites' of the true spiritual self in every being, male or female. In the Gospel of Thomas, Jesus says, '*Except a woman become like a man, she cannot enter the Kingdom.*' What are we astrologers teaching, after all, but this very truth – that individuation, true fulfilment in the search for identity, lies in the reunion of male and female in the psyche. Especially it means that a woman, who will tend naturally to find her identity through Moon and Venus, has to become her own Sun, her own man, in order to experience her fullest spiritual life. That relatively few women of Jesus' day would have had our opportunities to desire, to approach and to achieve that fullness of life may be one reason why he chose twelve men as his closest companions – quite apart from the symbolic significance of the twelve Sun-signs encompassing their Sun/the Son, which is unlikely to be accidental.

Asteroids and Identity in the Chart

The latest research into this Nativity, made possible by my friend and colleague the late Jacob Schwartz with his dedicated work on the many thousands of asteroids and their very specific meanings, sheds even more light on its authenticity. *Christa, Yeshuhua, Emanuela, Josefa, Mary, Virginia, Child, Noel, Eucharis, Martir, Anastasia* (Greek *Anastasis* – Resurrection) and many other names and concepts associated with Jesus' life, have been painstakingly run back with all their perturbations to the chart of his birth, the pre-Nativity eclipse, the Crucifixion and the Resurrection. In each chart they are found in tight clusters extraordinarily configured with the crucial axes of horizon, meridian and eclipses, to form in the heavens the key phrases that carry the message of the Gospels … the Words of God.

Rising at the birth of Jesus (as we can see in the Nativity chart on page 292) are *Protogeneia*, the first-born, and *Pasteur*, the shepherd. On the Midheaven is *Phoinix*, symbol of the Resurrection to come, and also *Anna*, his maternal grandmother. At the IC is *Baptistina*; his sacred mission begins with his baptism by cousin John in the Jordan, and John's declaration that Jesus, far greater than he, is to baptise with the Holy Spirit. And – triumphantly – setting exactly where you would hope and expect his closest friends to be (on the Descendant), are *San Juan* (St. John), *Magdalena* and the unassuming, faithful *Martha*. So is *Galilea*, Galilee, the place of his upbringing and focus of his ministry. *Isis*, the Mother of God, is also on the Descendant with her Son the Sun; her Helio position aligns with the mothering Moon. *Judith* is with the 12th House Mars … we have nothing closer than this to the name of Judas.

Heliocentric asteroids are extremely important. This is not the place to launch a Helio tutorial, but once again the Interdimensional Summary in the Appendix will give you a basic grounding in the significance of the Sun-centred patterns. Helio *Phoinix* is still in the Midheaven of Jesus' chart – but now it is joined by *Anastasia*, which is the Greek Anastasis, meaning 'resurrection'. 'Setting' is Helio *Pascal*, which is the Passover, the Christian Easter. Most telling of all is the midpoint inscription of the identity of Jesus as the Christ, thus: *Yeshuhua/Christa = Ascendant.* This is a signature which recurs through all the principal charts relating to his life.

The Prenatal Eclipse

Earlier it was suggested that the Babylonian astrologers, the Magi, would have watched for a spring eclipse. The epochal eclipse in question fell on March 8th 5 BC at 07h04m28s local time at Bethlehem. Here is all the symbolism of Pisces! Its last degree rises with the 0° Aries North Node, and gloriously configured in the spiritual 12th House are the New Moon, Uranus and Mercury, all in the sign of the Fish that is still the emblem of Christians.

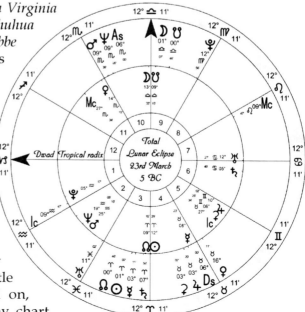

The asteroid signature is vividly prophetic of the birth to come: *Mary* rises, *Modestia Virginia Maria* is the phrase about to set. *Noel Yeshuhua* (the Nativity of Jesus) is at the IC with *Abbe Josefa* (father Joseph). The eclipse itself is conjoined by *Amor*, (love), *Amun* (God), and *Beate Regina* (the blessed Queen). It is in its way the very first tribute to Mary as Queen of Heaven and Mother of God. There is much more, but these are the names central to the drama.

You may well ask if this is not after all the pattern of the Nativity itself – a proper question, and one I asked myself. However, when this chart is tested like the May Nativity in the many ways I am about to describe, there is little or no significant activity. As you read on, and observe how incomparably the May chart behaves, you will appreciate this. A fortnight later on March 23rd at 20h52 LMT the Moon was totally eclipsed in her South Node at 1° Libra. At Bethlehem, in the dwad, the exact conjunction of Mars and Neptune – exactly square MC – was 'rising' opposite a setting Jupiter/Ceres in 3° Taurus. The Sun at 1° Aries was in the North Node close to Mercury and Saturn. On its own, this chart heralds a leader set on a hard path toward high spiritual ideals, and a holy mother bereaved. Add the dwad to this eclipse and the end of that path, the climax of that life, is painfully foreshadowed – the cross of its angles is the very cardinal cross of the Crucifixion to come in 33AD, and the dwad eclipse falls in almost precisely the same positions of Aries–Libra as the Sun and Moon that first Easter. Even Saturn and Jupiter are approaching their Crucifixion positions in Cancer and Gemini.

What Was the Star?

Late in the research, my attention was drawn to the fact that during the fortnight before the Pisces eclipse a most extraordinary pattern had been forming around the Sun. If you track the Heliocentric planets over those weeks, you will see for yourself the unfolding and perfecting of a true six-pointed Star of David carrying within it an inner-planet Cardinal Cross. This must be incredibly rare. At 5h45 pm on March 2nd 5 BC it was at its most perfect, forming lovely midpoint symmetries with the Geocentric angles at Bethlehem. Whatever else was going on in the heavens – comets, supernovae, bright planets, Royal Stars – we have here yet another candidate for the Star of the Nativity, glorifying the Sun, the Solar Logos, itself.

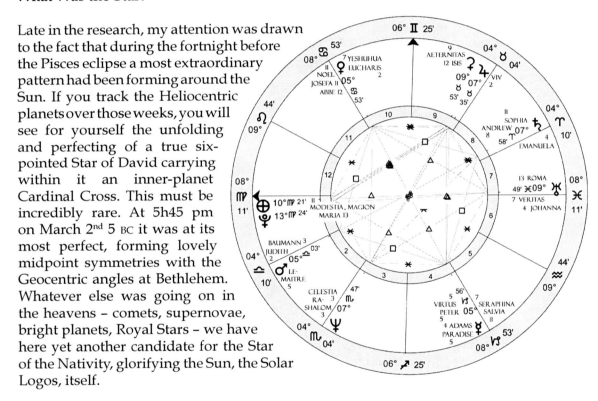

Testing time again – which asteroids would be carried on the points of this peerless Star? Further words at this juncture are unnecessary. Just look at the pattern, and marvel.

Testing the Chart – Jesus' Life, Death and Resurrection

However satisfying any birth chart may be in its symbolism, and however descriptive of its subject, if it is a speculative chart it *must* be tested exhaustively against events and the people with whom the subject is most closely connected. In the case of Jesus, the best material we have with which to test this chart for May 7th 5 BC, is the history of the Christian Church itself, founded by him through his disciples. The life led by Jesus himself is known only through the canonical gospels, a number of other non-canonical writings, and an account by the early historian Josephus of the trial and crucifixion in 'about AD 29'. The only timed event given to us is the family's visit to Jerusalem at Passover when Jesus was twelve years old; this is in Luke's Gospel, and it is also Luke who tells us that Jesus was 'about thirty years old' when John baptised him and he began his ministry.

John the Baptist was preaching in the Judaean desert in approximately AD 26-27, and if the ministry of Jesus Christ began in AD 26, according to this nativity he would have reached the age of thirty-one. The crucifixion of Jesus after a probable three years with the disciples could then have taken place in AD 29 when he was nearly thirty-four years old, or even a year later in AD 30.

However, Church tradition has it that Jesus was born in the year '0' and put to death at age thirty-three; this would date the crucifixion at AD 33 or thereabouts, rather than 29 or 30. If this nativity of 5 BC is correct, then Jesus would have died and resurrected just over one month before his thirty-seventh birthday. So much of the chronology is open to question that at first sight it would appear fruitless to test the Nativity against events in Jesus' life.

Progressed Patterns and the Cross

I believe, though, that we have just enough to work with. Firstly, we can look at the progressions for his twelfth year; either when he was nearly twelve or nearly thirteen his parents and friends took him to Jerusalem in the spring, at Passover – only to lose him after they left for home. He was found eventually, deep in discussion of matters spiritual and philosophical with the Rabbis, the learned men of the temple (a tradition still vigorously carried on beside the temple's remaining Western Wall) and he

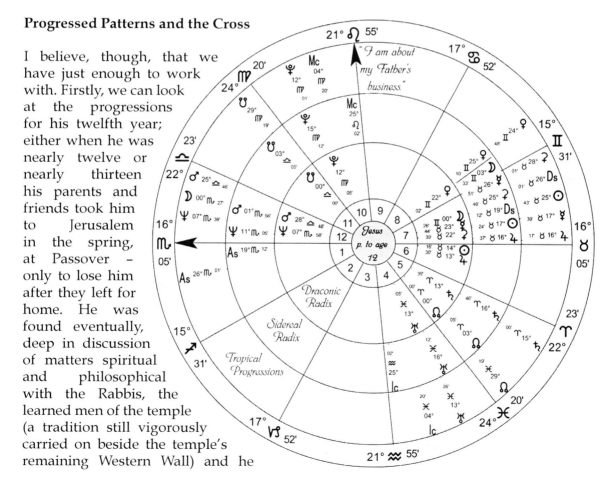

rebuked his parents for failing to realise that he was *'about his Father's business'*, beginning to prepare himself for the unique work decreed by God for his adult life and final years.

What we find is that Jupiter, angular with the Sun at birth, has come exactly to conjoin the western horizon, opening him fully to the religious and intellectual life. At the same time, Mercury retrograde has begun to close with the Sidereal Sun at birth, in 17°24' Taurus, and is also consequently approaching both Sidereal and progressed Tropical Jupiter and the birth Descendant. His Sun, now in 25°/26° Taurus, is at its square to the natal Sidereal MC, and rapidly closing on Sidereal Mercury radix. All this stimulus to key Sidereal positions describes a vital period of development in his world rôle. (As the natal and progressed Draconic positions are actually or nearly identical to the Tropical, it is in the interaction of these with the Sidereal that Gospel history can be seen. To help you, you will find a summary of the Sidereal in the Appendix.)

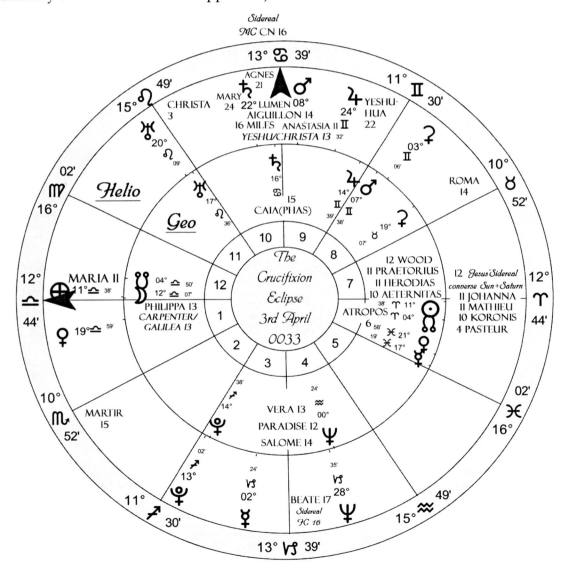

Moving forward to AD 33, first let me present its credentials as the year in which the crucifixion and resurrection of Jesus actually took place. In the science journal *Nature* dated 22/29 December 1983 (Christmas issue) Colin J. Humphreys and W. Graeme Waddington published a paper entitled *Dating The Crucifixion*. Their careful research into the dates of spring new moons in the years AD 26-36 showed that in only two of those years during which Pontius Pilate ruled in Israel as Roman Procurator, did 14th Nisan (Passover) fall on a Friday. Those years were AD 30 and 33; the Moon's Nodes were once again close to the Equinoxes, and on Friday April 3rd (Julian) AD 33 a lunar eclipse was visible at sunset, when 'the Moon appeared like blood' on the eastern horizon, opposite the setting Sun.

When the chart is set up for that eclipse (chart on opposite page), occurring at about the time that Jesus cried out on the cross and his human body died, we find that this eclipse on the Jerusalem horizon fell square to a culminating Saturn in the Tropical and Sidereal degrees conjoining, opposing and squaring Tropical/Draconic (and Sidereal) Saturn in the chart of Jesus, and the Dwad (see Appendix) Saturn was right on the IC, forming a perfect Cardinal Grand Cross. This dwad with its own dramatic fixed Grand Cross adds even more power and pain: its MC, and at the IC *Atropos* the asteroid of death, lines up with the radix Pluto/Jupiter opposition, while Uranus 'rises' and Mars 'sets'. Square to these lies the opposition of *Yeshuhua* (Jesus) and *Galilea/Martir* with *SanJuan* his dearest disciple. The dwad Sun-Chiron axis joins transiting Uranus in Leo – right on Mary's Moon/Meridian in the lovely chart you will see later. The dwad Uranus/Asc/Desc hits her Saturn at the beginning of Virgo. Here is a mother in total shock. In the dwad's 12th house we see not only Jesus' followers' distress but also, in that conjunction of Moon and Chiron in Aquarius, the gift of suffering that offers to redeem the world.

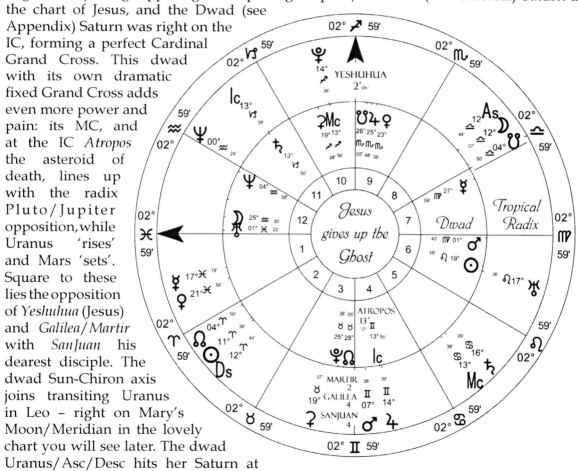

Another powerful Grand Cross appears around the Cardinal points in the Sidereal, focussed by the radix and Dwad Nodal axes which pick up the radix *Draconic* eclipse pattern. Fittingly, AD 33 was the year of Jesus' second, all-important Nodal Return. On the Cancer-Capricorn arm of this Grand Cross lies the cluster of Dwad planets whose energies speak of spiritual power, love and forgiveness; on the Aries-Libra arm is the pattern of the divine man whose triumph is his suffering of the world's pain.

Once again, too, the asteroids set their seal on the drama being played out under that lowering Middle Eastern sky. The actors are all on stage: *Herodias* (Herod, the Judaean ruler) is on the Descendant together with *Praetorius*, the Roman guard attending on the Governor Pilate, *Caia*(phas) the High Priest is on the MC, and *Salome* – exactly as described in the Gospel account – at the foot of the Cross on the IC. Mary and John were there together; and here indeed they are, at the Cross, the Heliocentric *Maria* conjunct the Ascendant and the eclipsed Moon, Helio *Johanna* exactly opposite, on the Descendant (as was San Juan at the Nativity) conjunct the Sun … and *Wood*, and *Atropos*, and *Aeternitas*. Eternity is opened by this death on a cross-beam nailed to a tree.

All through that weekend, the Helio asteroids *Galilea* and *Martir* were conjoined on Jesus' natal Ascendant, opposite *Salvia*, Helio *Roma* and *Tempel*, and his Sun. Through the conspiracy of the Roman authorities and the Jerusalem Temple, he, the Galilean, was martyred for the salvation of mankind. In just such a way are all our great human stories told by the sky. When Jesus said, 'It is Written……' he was not referring simply to the ancient prophetic texts.

Roman soldiers are there; *Miles* is one of the many Helio asteroids resonant with the Midheaven. Others are *Aiguillon* (thorn); *Koronis* (crown) setting; *Agnes* the sacrificial lamb; *Abbe* the Father to whom Jesus cried out as the spirit left his body; *Viv*, the Life; *Lumen*, the Light; and *Ra-Shalom*, the Peace of God to which he went. *Anastasia* (Resurrection) is again bodily conjunct that MC. *Ra-Shalom* is also Jerusalem. Opposite, with *Isis* and Helio *Osiris*, the broken god, is *Paradise*. As death approached, Jesus said to the 'good thief' on his right, 'Today you shall be with me in Paradise.'

Helio *Yeshuhua/Christa* = MC.

Progressions to the Cross

If we map both the annual and daily secondary progressions of Jesus' nativity to AD 33 we find striking support for the events of 3rd-5th April: by annual secondary progression, the MC had come to conjoin that epochal South Node at Tropical 0° Libra, heralding the total surrender of worldly identity to the purpose for which this soul had come into being, the great gift of his life. The corresponding progressed Ascendant in 16° Sagittarius carried the transiting Pluto-Jupiter opposition – and just such a passage of Pluto over Ascendant always brings in one form or another a death and a rebirth. To emphasise the totality of that massive transformation, the Sidereal transit of Pluto nearly opposes the progressed Sun; and on the 5th, the day of the Resurrection, the Dwad position of Jesus' daily progressed IC/MC was 17° Sagittarius-Gemini, right on that Sidereal Jupiter-Pluto axis! (This suggests that with the Dwads we may be dealing with the subtle body rather than with the dense material form.)

Reculer Pour Mieux Sauter

It took a fresh look at my own life to prompt the next, even more important step. Between January 1992 and January 1993 both my parents died. During the course of 1994, a number of fellow astrologers spoke or wrote to me about their use of the converse progressed patterns and I realised how long it was since I really took a good look at these. I was shocked to see what I had been neglecting – my double bereavement had happened over the active period of an unnoticed converse Sun-Saturn opposition.

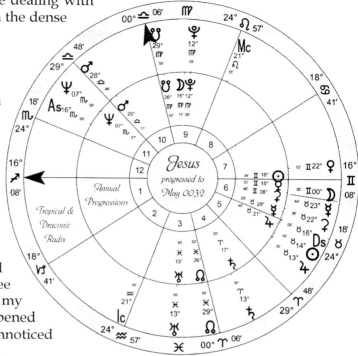

Let us now together go back to the chart of Jesus at the time of his crucifixion – this time looking at its converse progression. It solves the mystery still left after all the work so far: why was only his Saturn hit by the massed forces of that eclipse? In the *converse* lies the answer, for here at last we find what we should have hoped to find at the hardest time of his life, the Sun-Saturn conjunction. *(Again, I shall refer to the Sidereal, and to the higher frequency of the Dwad, which are both summarised in the Appendix. They are important elements in the overall picture. There is a great deal of detail in these converse patterns which may leave your head in a spin! But they are highly significant, so do persevere if you can.)*

Tropically, this mortal conjunction fell in 9° Aries – but even more importantly, the *Sidereal* converse Sun-Saturn was at 11°55'-12°09' Aries on the day of the Crucifixion, so much closer to the axis of the Tropical lunar eclipse that it is almost exact. In the Tropical the conjunction is joined by the converse Dwad Ascendant and North Node in 5° and 8° Aries respectively; the Tropical converse Ascendant at 15°26' Libra is hit directly by the Sidereal eclipse pattern, and squared by the converse MC in Cancer with Dwads of converse Sun, Uranus, Saturn and IC. The 'Judas-pattern' of the 12th House Mars-Neptune has come to fruition in the almost exact conjunction of the converse planets (quincunx the Sun-Saturn) combining in the Dwad with converse Dwad Venus at his natal IC, aligned with the Dwad eclipse and transit Uranus. In the Sidereal converse chart, the Dwad cluster of Sun, Uranus, Saturn, IC moves onto Jesus' *radix* MC in 23°-25° Leo. Here the Dwad Saturn/IC conjunction is exact … and for good measure the dwad Uranus/Ascendant-Mars/Descendant found at the Sidereal Crucifixion falls across his Nodal axis.

Some of the most striking alignments are shown in the triwheel below: in the outer ring is the tropical transiting pattern of the Crucifixion, whose angular eclipse impacts on both Jesus' Sidereal converse Sun/Saturn and the dwad Node/Ascendant of his annual Tropical converse pattern at his birth time on May 7th 0032. In this annual converse dwad we also find the Sun symbolically at the end of life at the IC – and the Draconic version shifts the Sun/Ceres/IC onto the degree of the Crucifixion Saturn in mid-Cancer. The presence of Ceres has a two-fold significance – Jesus' mother at the foot of the Cross, and also the agonising separation of parent and child through physical death.

It all adds up to the picture of a man betrayed, in pain, going through the toughest trial of his life since converse Sun on *radix* Saturn five years earlier in AD 27/28 is likely to have brought him news of the Baptist's murder by Herod. (Remember that not only did John

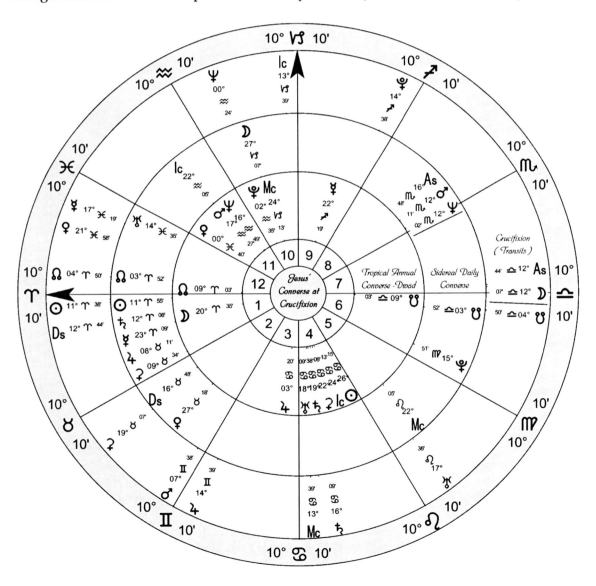

baptise Jesus – probably as the converse Sun began the approach to Saturn – and settle on his shoulders the conscious burden of his ministry, but he was his second cousin and may have been close to him since childhood, as their mothers Mary and Elizabeth were such good friends.) It is a picture of heavy destiny, a mission completed, an agonising physical, mental and spiritual ordeal before the joy of transformation. It would be difficult to imagine a pattern better fitted to the death and resurrection of Jesus – and even harder to find one.

Regarding John the Baptist – as his mother was said to be about six months into her pregnancy when Jesus was conceived, he would consequently be approximately six months older than Jesus. A birth in Scorpio 6 BC seems very appropriate for a man who subjected himself to the privations of desert life; so I offer you this speculative chart for November 11ᵗʰ 6 BC when, sextile a demanding Mars-Pluto conjunction, there was a New Moon at 16° Scorpio – the degree of Jesus' Ascendant. A noon chart has late Capricorn rising; John is said to have wandered the Judaean desert in goatskins. This Ascendant collects the Dwad South Node and Neptune, marking him out for self-sacrifice and holiness; the Dwad Sun/Moon/Descendant

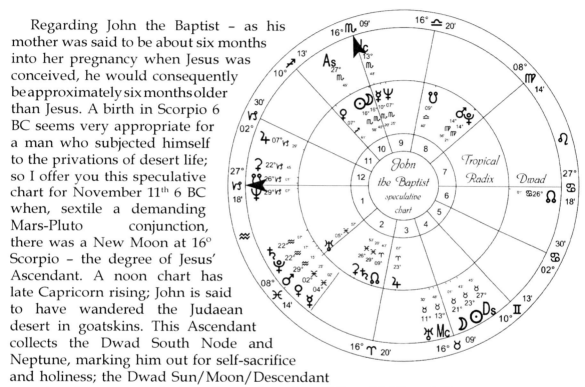

promises fame – or notoriety; the conjunction of Dwad MC and Uranus in mid-Taurus depicts one man's unorthodox, turbulent life serving his cousin and his world-changing message.

But if you want yet further proof of the 5 BC Nativity, I can offer you more.

The Composite Pattern

Most of us have discovered the value of composite charts in clarifying the dynamics and viability of relationship; but have you made composites of people with *events*? There is every good reason to do this, as the most significant function of a composite is to show that the planetary energies of one space-time event (which may or may not be the incarnation of a person) *are mirroring those of another, and therefore they mean something to each other*. So you would expect the composites of the Crucifixion and Resurrection with Jesus to show us the same trauma, the same pain, the same sacrifice, the same transformation as the forgoing patterns have done.

In the Crucifixion composite we have a triple conjunction of Jupiter-Saturn-Uranus in the 8th House; the Moon is very publicly on the MC, square rising Pluto and setting Sun with dwad Saturn and the Nodes all aligned tightly with natal 12th House Mars. The Sidereal pattern is the most dramatic, as a dwad Sun/Mars conjunction – again conjunct natal Tropical Mars – closes in on that rising Pluto from the 12th, opposed by Pluto in the dwad conjoining the radix 'setting' Sun. In the dwad the Moon is with the Ascendant embracing Jesus' natal setting Sun, and the Dragon's head points to the 8th house Gemini stellium on his natal Moon. Yes, this moment *does* mean destiny, sacrifice, agony and a very public death. Here is our Jesus graphically crucified across the sky.

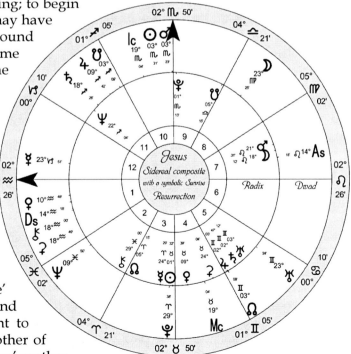

We are given no exact time for his Resurrection on the Sunday morning; to begin with we can only surmise that it may have happened symbolically at or around the rising of the Sun. Such a time gives us a composite where the Sun-Pluto opposition – especially in the Sidereal again – realigns dramatically with the meridian; the man is no longer stretched across the sky, but becomes a surge of mighty energy rising upwards from the tomb of Sun/ IC/dwad Saturn.

The Events of the Resurrection

Now, it was 'very early on the Sunday morning, just after sunrise' that Mary Magdalen, Salome and 'Mary, the mother of James' went to the sepulchre. (If James was a brother of Jesus, then this may have been Jesus' mother herself.) When they discovered it empty, and were told by an angel in white robes that Jesus had risen, 'they hurried away from the tomb in awe and great joy, and ran to tell the disciples.' On their way back, Jesus himself appeared to them to tell them that they would see him again later in Galilee. This moment meant his rising through the power of God, and the imminent transformation of his companions' lives.

There was a moment during that early morning, at 6h39 am local time, when the Moon in 0° Scorpio (conjunct the Sidereal Mars of Jesus) was exactly setting. This is the picture of an encounter with a woman. Now, here is the wonderful thing! When the asteroids were run back (so very, *very* carefully) to that world-shaking moment, *Maria* is with that setting Moon, at 2° Scorpio right opposite the rising *Virginia* at 3° Taurus; *Salome* is in the Midheaven at 15° Capricorn, and an opposition of *Twilley/LeMaitre* has not long left the horizon. Here *is* Mary! ... but 'the Virgin Mary', and with *Isis* (and Helio Osiris, the broken god!) simultaneously on the MC it looks as though Jesus' mother was there before the Magdalene arrived; it was another twenty minutes before the angles turned to place the equally important Helio positions of *Mary* and *Magdalena* simultaneously and exactly on IC and Descendant.

The inclusion of *Twilley* is a reference to the twill shroud in which the body of Jesus had been wrapped; *LeMaitre* is 'the Master' (echoed in Helio *Rabinowitz*, also 'setting'). If you recall, when Mary first saw the risen Jesus she failed to recognise him, thinking he was a gardener. Then the light dawned, and she is said to have exclaimed, 'Master!' Her exclamation at the encounter, her name, his identity, all meet in the phrased alignment of asteroids.

There is much, much more in the asteroid patterns, but most of them must wait for another book. Except for the remarkable account they give on the Resurrection morning at 04h58 LMT, two hours before the possible arrival of Mary Magdalen, which you really must see: on the angles of this pre-dawn chart are all the words that describe the Biblical Jesus. No less than twenty appropriately named asteroids simultaneously occupied these four crucial positions. In pairs or groups they match the very words used in St John's Gospel and in the Revelation of St John to describe Jesus Christ. As we know, another very important descriptive point in an astrological chart lies at the midpoint of the horizon and

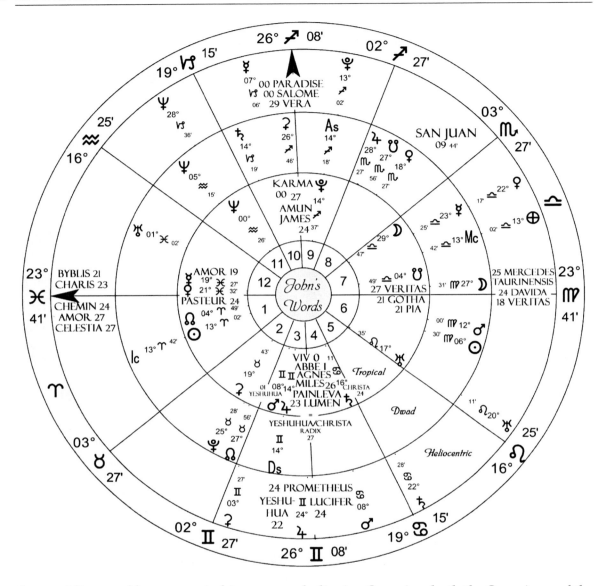

the meridian; and here, even in his own symbolic sign Scorpio – both the Scorpion *and* the Eagle – is the Helio position of St John's asteroid *San Juan*. The phrases found on the angles are as follows:

'Behold the Lamb (*Agnes*) of God (*Amun*) who taketh away the sin of the world (*Karma/Prometheus*).'

'I (Jesus, *Yeshuhua*) am the Way (*Chemin*), the Truth (*Veritas*) and the Life (*Viv*). No man cometh unto the Father (*Abbe*) but by Me.'

'I and the Father (*Abbe*) are one.'

'I am the Light (*Lumen*) of the world.'

'I am the Bread (*Painleva* – uplifted bread) of Life (*Viv*) that came down from Heaven (*Paradise*).'

'I am the Good (*Venus*) Shepherd (*Pasteur*).'

'I am the bright and morning star **(**Venus itself conjunct Ascendant as the Morning Star).'

In addition, through *Vera/Amun* and *Vera/Prometheus*, Jesus (*Yeshuhua*) is described as both truly God and truly Man. As *Protogeneia/Amun* he is the first-born of God. He is Love (*Amor*), Mercy (*Mercedes*), and the fulfilment of the Scriptures (*Byblis*) and by the same token, The Word. And as in Jesus' Nativity, we find his name's sensitive midpoint on an angle; this chart is stamped with the identity '*Yeshuhua/Christa* = MC'.

These are the only named asteroids among the 9000 or so currently on file that embody these specific ideas.

The Resurrection is in effect the real birth of Christianity, and while the sunrise chart carries so much symbolic planetary power, this extraordinary chart is a stronger contender for the real moment, as it sums up everything that has remained central to Christian belief and practice, the example set by Jesus for all human beings to follow. At the same time it demonstrates the reality and spiritual relevance of astrology, the significance of the tiny asteroids, the insignificance of time as we know it, and the vivid presence of God in human history.

Degrees in the Nativity

Bearing all the foregoing in mind, it would be interesting to see if any of the several books devoted to degree-meanings have anything significant to add to the Nativity of Jesus. Two of these seem to me to be more than usually reliable in such a subjective field: one is the excellent synthesis achieved by Esther Leinbach after long study of the available sources, and the other is the series produced in 1917 by Isidore Kozminsky. This is what they have to offer:

For **Taurus 14°** Kozminsky offers the image of '*A student with lamp in hand, standing at the entrance of a cavern from which issue clouds of soft, light, rosy vapour*' to which he adds his own understanding of the degree: 'Denotes a person whose tastes and desires are directed to the understanding of the secrets which rest beneath the veil. He has brought to earth from other sources the knowledge which enables him to find the entrance to the cavern of hidden jewels … the gateway is guarded by sublime and intense colours caused by more excessive vibrations than can be endured by the human body … it is a symbol of initiation.'

Leinbach agrees that 'This degree seems to encompass some mystical tendencies. The native may either seek companionship or retire to some monastic situation where he meditates on seeing mystical truths. It would seem that the influences here are meant to blend the two extremes ... he usually does all he can to benefit society.'

These readings are appropriate; discipleship for Peter, James, John and the rest of the chosen few, was a constant series of initiations into the secret teachings Jesus brought with him from the Divine Life. On our journey through the holy places over Easter 1994, we came to a rocky cavern in the hillside where Jesus would retire with his close companions to initiate them secretly into the deeper mysteries that were denied to the crowd. It is my personal conviction that these would have included many of the teachings restored by the 'New Age' – the truths of reincarnation and the evolutionary journey of the soul, the symbolism of astrology, enhancement of sensitivity, ways of spiritual and physical healing, meditation and prayer ... many things cast out from the so-called Christian Churches. Jesus would only teach these things openly by using the symbolic imagery of the parables, so that *'those that have ears to hear'* would understand, and the developmentally unready would not. To the latter, only the exoteric meaning would be plain. One of the images Jesus used for the spiritual understanding yearned for by the seeker is *'the pearl of great price'*. This is the hidden jewel which, once found, is purchased by the sacrifice of everything less valuable. At his physical death on the cross, *'the veil of the Temple was rent'* as a sign that, in that act and from that moment, Heaven was offering freely to humanity the spiritual treasure hidden in the religious establishment. In Holman Hunt's famous painting 'The Light of the World' (*'Behold, I Stand At the Door and Knock'*) Jesus is shown with lamp in hand waiting for his knock to be answered, and another of us to journey with him, by the light of his love and his knowledge, into the caverns of our own initiation. For many years in my dreams I came upon hidden treasure – here it is. It is also for you.

Of **Taurus 17°**, the degree of the Sidereal Sun, Leinbach says that 'it seems there is a message here concerning violence and non-violence ... This degree has characterised individuals as swimming against the current ... the real power of non-violent action is active goodwill. There are few people who can live such a demonstration. When they succeed with their own lives *we call them Saints.*' (My italics.) And bearing in mind the unique mission of the Christ in the person of Jesus, it is remarkable that Kozminsky's reading adds this: 'Within him is *a continual war between good and evil, and victory depends on himself alone.*' Jesus spent forty days on his own in the Judaean desert in parching heat tussling with the voice of worldly temptation; he quelled it with all the scorn of his spiritual integrity and power. He had to do it alone. Non-violence and active goodwill are cornerstones of his exoteric and esoteric teaching: *'Love thy neighbour as thyself'*; *'Do not set yourself against the man who wrongs you. If someone slaps you on the right cheek, turn and offer him your left ... Love your enemies and pray for your persecutors'*; *'Blessed are the peacemakers'*. He was teaching the laws of the repayment and non-perpetuation of karma. Had he followed the current of his time, there would have been no Crucifixion, no Resurrection, and two thousand years of human history void of the Christian drama. Jesus knew that his historic (Sidereal) impact on the world, challenging every convention, every value-system, every selfish, belligerent bone in our bodies, would polarise love and fear in the world. *'I come not to bring peace, but a sword.'*

It is worth looking at the readings given by Kozminsky for the Tropical and Sidereal degrees of the Ascendant, surrounded as they are by adjacent degrees whose meanings seem to be quite negative, and certainly not appropriate.

For **Scorpio 16°**: 'Denotes peculiar birth conditions, but a gifted person who, though threatened with danger, overcomes and produces worthy works. His powerful and energetic soul is blended with idealism, poetry and beauty. There is firmness in all he does, and a power which gives it penetrative force and excellence.'

For **Scorpio 19°** the image is of '*A handsome boy, climbing up a ladder, looking upwards to the heavens* … Denotes one especially favoured and of magnetic personality who raises himself by his own efforts and indomitable mind. He gains by right, scorning base and unworthy actions, and gains in spite of obstacles which are raised against him …' – even the world's mockery and the cross.

A further reference to degree-significance appeared among my papers, a translation by Mary Vohryzek of work by Elspeth and Reinhold Ebertin, detailing the anatomical correlations of the 360 degrees. To **Taurus 14°** they assign '*the true vocal chords*' and to **Scorpio 16°** the head of the cochlea in the inner ear. This again is remarkable, since Christ is identified as 'the Word', and he said to his followers '*I am the Way, the Truth, and the Life*'. The act of correct listening was emphasised constantly in his teaching: '*He that has ears to hear, let him hear!*'; '*Heaven and earth shall pass away; my Words shall never pass away.*'

Finally there was the defining moment when, at the 1995 AMASS conference in Philadelphia, Lynda Hill took one look at the chart of the Nativity and said, 'You do realise what that Ascendant degree means?' I waited expectantly – Lynda's work on the Sabian Symbols is famous now! 'A woman the father of her own child! The virgin birth!'

How much more do we need?!

Men and Women of God

A long and ever-ongoing study of the charts of practising and closet Christians has thrown up much excellent synastry with the Nativity that founded their faith. There are far too many clergy, clients and friends for me to include here, but having looked through my growing collection it is striking how many who clearly love their Lord Jesus have Sun or Venus on or opposite his Sun (and I continue to find this in every authentic Christian soul I meet), how many who preach the Suffering Christ or the mystery of the Resurrection share his Scorpio Ascendant (Tropical or Sidereal), how many who teach his Way have Mercury on these axes … and where Taurus-Scorpio is empty, the squares from mid-Leo/Aquarius (which are Jesus' Reflex degrees) or the degrees of Jesus' MC/IC axis will be fully alive.

The mid-Aquarians can be a problem, even though they are the Antiscia of the Taurus degrees, for their very spirit of independence can drive them away from full acceptance of Jesus' example and they may come late into the fold! Leo knows how to love … but pride can put up its own resistance. As with the clergy and faithful, the inceptional charts of many churches and parishes share the same Fixed angles as the Jesus they serve in the Tropical, Sidereal and sometimes the Draconic pattern.

For example, Billy Graham's Sun is at 14°40' Scorpio; Mother Teresa (beatified in 2003 and now known as Blessed Teresa of Calcutta), being a woman, has her *Moon* conjunct Jesus' own Moon; also her Sidereal (historic) Sun is at 9° Leo, the place of the Sun on the birthday of Mary, mother of Jesus (about which, more a little later on!).

Edgar Cayce, that extraordinary and committed Christian, has not only his Draconic Moon on that of Jesus, but his Lord's Sun crowning his MC conjunct the Tropical Taurus Moon, and his rising Uranus on Jesus' own Midheaven. For such individuals, the *imitatio Christi* must be that little bit easier.

Archbishop George Carey, former Primate of the Church of England, even though not obviously a devotee of the Mother of Jesus, has a Sagittarian Jupiter on Jesus' Moon axis; and of course it is he who has expedited the ordination of women to the priesthood of the Anglican Church. He is another Scorpio with Sun close to the Nativity Ascendant at 20°.

The Rev Dr Chad Varah who founded the Samaritans is another of the Scorpio Christians, his Sun conjunct Jesus' Ascendant opposite Saturn, driving him to tackle humanity's most intractable problems. His Mercury is opposite Jesus' Moon from

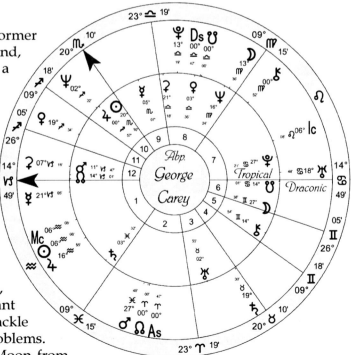

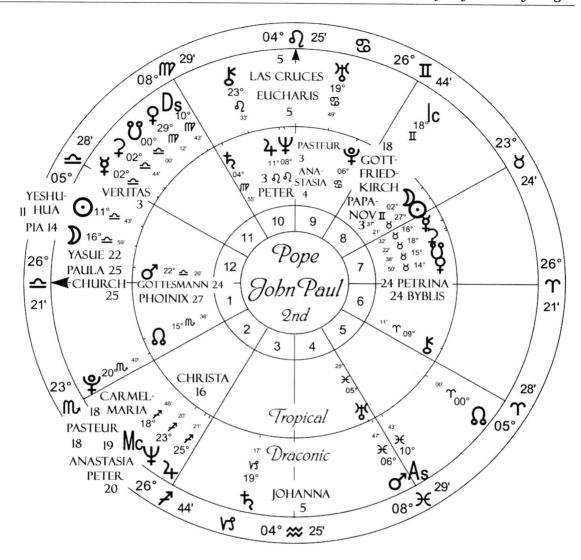

frank, resilient Sagittarius; he can be brusque! At 0h00 on November 2nd 1953, the hour the Samaritans came into being under a purging, transformative rising Pluto, the Draconic Moon was on his Sun – and the Jupiter/Sun of Jesus was on the MC.

The late **Pope John Paul II** is another with the same early Gemini Moon; he has Venus, South Node and Mercury on Jesus' western horizon and the Draconic New Moon in Libra opposite the Saturn of the Nativity and of course on the eclipsed rising Moon of his Lord's crucifixion … also aligned with his own Tropical *Mary* (to whom he was devoted.) All this, plus the North Node in Scorpio, ruled by his risen Mars on the Dwad Sun in Jesus' chart, ensured much suffering bodily and inwardly, which he endured with exemplary patience. He has *Yeshuhua* exactly (to 0°02') conjunct his Sun. When he was shot, Pluto was on his Libran Mars, and a conjunction of Mars and Chiron attacked that Christian South Node. At the moment of his election, Jesus' Sun was exactly rising.

One of the UK's most famously public practising Christians is Sir Cliff Richard. Born Harry Webb in India in 1940, the World War II Draconic Uranus galvanises his committed Scorpio Mercury – aligned beautifully with Jesus' Sun and their shared Jupiters! This man uses his music to convey the Christian message; Saturn is at 12° Taurus, giving manifest form to its evangelical spirit.

A life in stark contrast was that of **Bishop Oscar Romero**. He was murdered for his faith. His birth chart is a moving witness to that Christian devotion: Sun conjunct Jesus' Midheaven; Draconic Sun on Jesus' ruling Venus; Draconic Ascendant conjunct Jesus' Sun, with Tropical Jupiter opposite close to his Lord's Ascendant. His massive Leo stellium stretches across that of Our Lady … and his Tropical, physical angles poignantly carry the Cross of the Crucifixion.

I can't leave out one of the most exemplary Christians of our time, **Sister Wendy Beckett**, born in Johannesburg, South Africa on February 25th 1930 (no time available). But although the Draconic level of her chart shows us much, it is unsurprisingly the Sidereal that paints the most vivid picture of this unusually public hermit. First of all, in a Sidereal Q-chart for the time of Jesus' Nativity her profound identification with the Jesus she loves is manifest not only in her inner Tropical dwad Sun at 16TA12 but her culminating Sidereal Jupiter/Ceres/ Wendy with the Sidereal Dwad Moon/IC, all

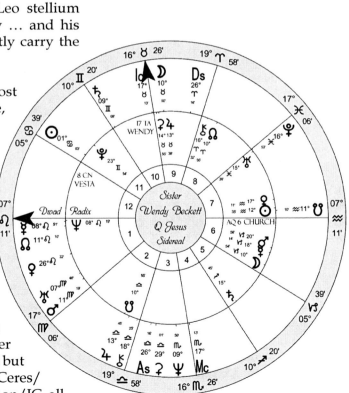

on the same mid-Taurus-Scorpio axis. Rising is Leo Neptune with Dwad Mercury opposite a setting Aquarian Sun/Venus and asteroid Church conjoined by the dwad South Node. Opposite her Capricorn Moon is Vesta. What clearer portrait could we find of a unique, dedicated virgin and anchorite, who sacrifices her cherished solitude to the explanation of Jesus' life through her speaking and writing on Christian art. All is an act of prayer; since she was four, her whole life has been offered totally to God.

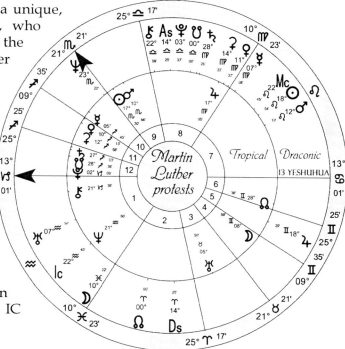

Martin Luther's puritanical Venus/Saturn conjunction is only 2° from Jesus' Taurus Sun, and when he **nailed his protest to the church door** in Wittenburg at noon on October 31st 1517, Mars was approaching their opposition, the Sun stood on Jesus' Ascendant, Neptune on his IC in 21° Aquarius, and the IC conjoined his Gemini Moon.

As a consequence of this act, forty-one years later at the decree of Queen Elizabeth I of England, the Church of England – via **The Act of Supremacy** – came officially into being. Not surprising that it also has Capricorn rising at 0h00 LMT on April 29th 1559 … nor that feminine Venus is now on Jesus' Moon and Protestantism's IC, nor that the Sun is exactly facing the 1517 Sun on Jesus' Descendant with Mercury on his Sun and revolutionary Uranus opposite!

When Secundo Pia saw his **historic photograph of the Turin Shroud** for the very first time at 11h00 pm on May 28th 1898, Uranus was opposite Jesus' Moon – a new and astonishing image! – and the conjunction of

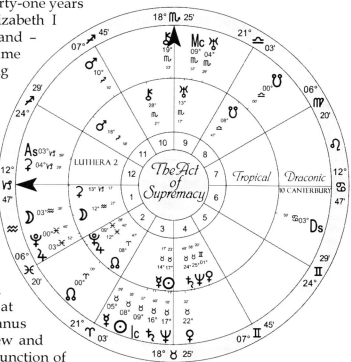

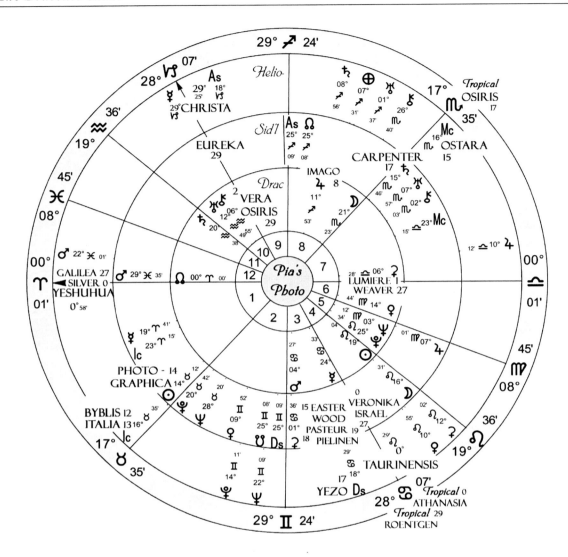

Draconic Sun and Pluto was on his Midheaven. The MC at that moment was the horizon axis of the Nativity, and Mercury at the IC was conjunct Jesus' Jupiter and Sun. Draconic Saturn had come to his IC; so often I have noticed a strong, angular Saturn when the spiritual has manifested in the material world. Like the priesthood, it is a 'sweet but heavy burden'. I have also to tell you – because it is so important – that the Sidereal, historic, Sun was itself in 14° Taurus; also the vital Helio *Yeshuhua* and *Christa* are on the angles. This is why I have never doubted the authenticity of this piece of linen as the shroud of the crucified Christ. Carbon dating is useless where the great energies of a light-body may have transformed not just the appearance but the material structure of the cloth. That very energy is implicated by the presence of Tropical asteroids *Roentgen* and *Athanasia* (immortality) conjunct the Draconic IC with Helio *Taurinensis* (Turin's Latin name) and Sidereal *Veronika* (the true image). The whole interdimensional picture of this moment is extraordinary: aligned with the above asteroids from the Draconic MC are Helio *Christa*,

Draconic *Vera* and *Osiris* (the true broken god) and Sidereal *Eureka* … which speaks for itself!
The nature of the photographic medium, the historic cloth and Jesus himself are identified
across the Draconic Ascendant/Descendant by
Helio asteroids *Silver, Galilea, Yeshuhua* and
Draconic *Lumiere, Weaver*. Across the
Tropical meridian – crowned by *Osiris
in coelo* – we find that vital Sidereal
Sun conjoined with *Photographica*
and opposite *Carpenter*, and Helio
Byblis/Italia opposite *Ostara*.
On the Tropical Descendant are
Sidereal *Easter, Wood, Pasteur*
and *Pielinen* (holy cloth) with
Helio *Yezo* – another asteroid
which identifies Jesus/Jesu/
Iesu in Christian charts.
Beautiful.

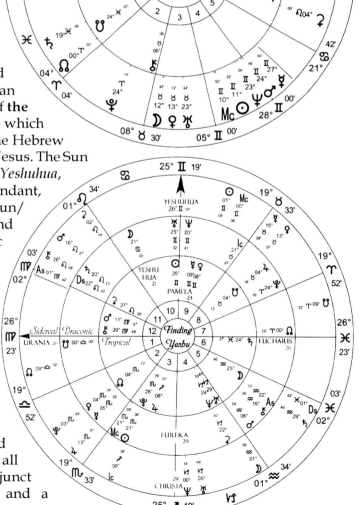

There are significant events,
too. Again, many occurred
through the course of Christian
history. One nice one is the date of **the
discovery of asteroid *Yeshuhua***, which
is the closest match we have to the Hebrew
name, with its many spellings, of Jesus. The Sun
was less than 1° from Draconic *Yeshuhua*,
Uranus was conjunct Jesus' Ascendant,
and opposite, conjoining his Sun/
Jupiter, were Draconic Moon and
Venus in mid-Taurus. Draconic
Uranus was 0°01′ from Jesus'
Mercury!

(I can't let the opportunity
go, either, to show you what
happened in the sky when
'the penny dropped'; when in
the pages of Jacob Schwartz's
Asteroid Name Encyclopaedia I
**saw the word 'Yeshuhua' for
the first time** and realised this
was the name for Jesus that I had
been searching for. You can see it all
clearly in the tri-wheel: MC conjunct
Pamela and Draconic Uranus and a
historic Sidereal *Yeshuhua*, which is opposite

Christa and Draconic *Eureka* at the IC, while Sidereal *Urania* 'rises'! And the Draconic Moon embraces Tropical Yeshuhua from 21° Cancer. My goodness! And of course ever since that moment it has been possible to guarantee the identity in his charts through that *Yeshuhua/Christa* midpoint – whose Sidereal position is also dominant here, within less than 2° of the Tropical Ascendant.)

There is one well publicised episode in recent years that has prompted many folk to suggest that God does indeed hurl his thunderbolt, and that was of course the moment on July 9th 1984 at 2h10 am BST when **lightning hit York Minster**, and the entire south transept burned down. It was barely three days after the installation in the Cathedral of the new Bishop of Durham, the Right Reverend David Jenkins (with Saturn opposite Jesus' Sun!) who seems to have done more than many other men of the cloth to undermine

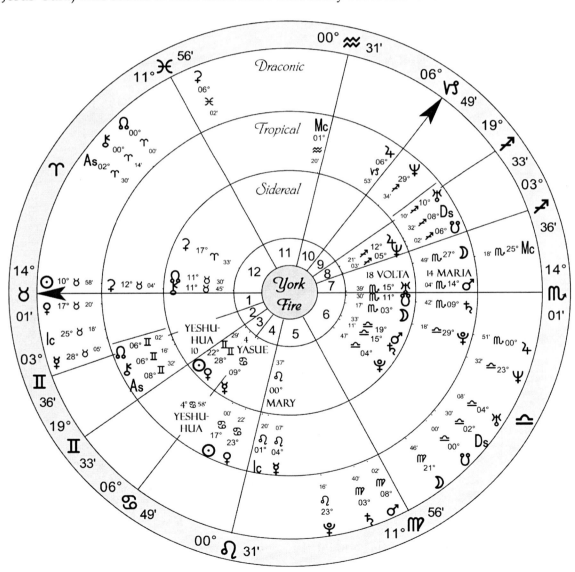

the traditional teachings of Christianity in favour of a presumably well intentioned but confused intellectualism. Also, in common with many Cathedral churches, there was commercial activity within the anciently hallowed walls; the souvenir shop was in that very transept, and we know what happened when Jesus found the same sacrilege within the holy spaces of the Jerusalem Temple.

When the bolt struck, the Sidereal Ascendant was 14°01' Taurus with Aldebaran, a conjunction of Chiron and North Node close by at Taurus 11° (Aldebaran at Jesus' Nativity) with the Draconic Sun, and Draconic Venus at 17°25' Taurus. Setting was Sidereal (historic) Uranus in Taurus 15°, conjunct Tropical Mars at 14°04' Scorpio. Tropical Pluto was transiting Jesus' Libran Mars, and the Sidereal Sun was on his ruling Venus. In the Tropical chart, the Dwad Descendant conjoined *Christa*. And there's more – setting in coelo with *Uranus is Volta, the lightning bolt; Maria* is with Mars; Tropical *Yeshuhua* and Sidereal Yasue are on the Sidereal IC; Sidereal *Yeshuhua* graces the Draconic Ascendant; and Sidereal *Mary* is almost precisely on the Tropical IC. *Now* do you believe that God, Our Lady, and Jesus the Christ, intervene in the world?

There was a deeply unpleasant period in English history when in 1647 Puritan Parliamentarians enforced a total and brutal **ban on all Christian festivals**. The dated document was unrolled before the viewing public on Christmas Day December 2008, when UK composer Howard Goodall presented *The Truth About Christmas Carols* on BBC 2 television. In the absence of a recorded time, I have set up the Q-chart for the time of Jesus' birth (as it would have been in our islands); his Sun/Jupiter degrees are setting with Sidereal Mercury, opposed by a disruptive Sidereal Uranus. Close to this axis is that of the Draconic Mars/MC in

Taurus; this, conjunct Tropical *Christa*, is directly involved with Sidereal Pluto/*Laetitia*, while the Scorpio IC and Ceres come together with Sidereal Neptune. The names of the festivals – *Easter, Ostara* and *Yule* – are all on angles as you can see, and *Noel* is with *Yasue* and the North Node *in coelo*. A higher power, in this case the State, is attacking, stamping on and undermining popular celebration; the Sidereal IC on Draconic Saturn in Aquarius is a mutinous killjoy, and the Tropical Moon in her South Node and her Detriment presents a miserable populace, divorced for fourteen cold, dark years from the traditional Christmas celebrations of the Cancer North Node.

Happily, England got her festivals back with the restoration of the monarchy in 1661! And one Christmas, in the city of Truro, a new tradition was begun: **the Service of Nine Lessons and Carols.**

Once again it is the spiritual Draconic chart that carries the life of the pattern on its angles. At the centre of a tri-wheel, onto its Ascendant-Descendant are gathered Tropical *Yeshuhua* with Venus-Moon, Helio *Christa* and *Christycarol* with Sidereal Mercury, and *Massinga/Noel* – Draconic, *in coelo* with rising Uranus and setting Jupiter. At the IC, Draconic *Christa* also conjoins the Sidereal Jupiter/Descendant; on the Tropical MC are Helio *Chant* and *Gaudium*; Tropical *Christycarol* is on the Sidereal Moon. To all this joyous celebration is added the Sidereal Sun in Sagittarius with Tropical Mercury; Draconic Saturn is firmly relegated to the Sidereal South Node. Let joy be unconfined! The Draconic Sun in Pisces invites men to come closer to God; Draconic Moon in Leo with Pluto blesses everyone with the power of love. Of course we in the UK have for decades enjoyed the Festival of Nine Lessons and Carols every Christmas from King's College Chapel, Cambridge; this became the Service's permanent home from Christmas Eve 1918.

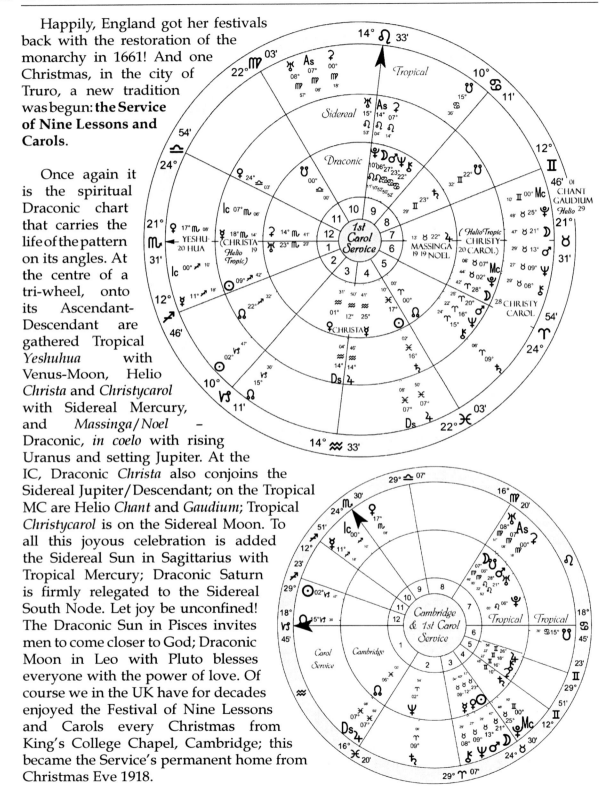

The relationship between that first celebration in Truro and the 1207 chart for **the city of Cambridge** is extraordinary! Each carries the Nodes of the other on its horizon, and their stellia conjoin – that in Taurus a gift of voices to Jesus, on his Sun/Jupiter and Mercury. This was a musical marriage made in heaven.

My last example here will perhaps come as a surprise to one reader – if he reads it! Many years ago I was friendly with a fellow Capricorn astrologer who shares the name of the actor most famous for his portrayal of Jesus in Franco Zeffirelli's *Jesus Of Nazareth*. The actor is Robert Powell – whom I have also encountered, briefly, but alas not conversed with – whose historic Sidereal chart has so many striking resonances with that of Jesus.

This other **Robert Powell**, however, has distinguished himself by studying Christian astrology for many more years than I have, and this has borne fruit in an exceptional book, *Chronicle of The Living Christ*. We differ, of course, on the date of the Nativity of Jesus, but the work he has put into this massive astrological history is admirable. He gave me his birth data all those years ago; so let him see himself now in the mirror of the May Nativity! It is not his Tropical chart that we look to, but the Draconic, those things that are dear to his soul. Here are his 16° Scorpio Sun, 14° Scorpio Mercury, 13° Scorpio Mars, and Pluto conjunct Jesus' Moon in 1° Gemini. Of course he would dedicate his life and his skill to working and writing for Jesus Christ.

You may wonder where your author fits into all this. It isn't obvious. It is *Urania* herself (Sidereal), Tropical Uranus and both Sidereal and Helio Mars, plus the Moon's North Node. These make direct contacts. But it's on the invisible corners of the cosmic rectangles, the Reflexes, where Moon, Sun and Venus show their allegiance to Jesus. Also when the idea first came, secondary progressed Moon was right on the 13° Taurus Daily Progressed MC. That day's New Moon fell conjunct Jesus' own progressed Sun which had reached 0°01' Scorpio (the Draconic Ascendant of my Q-chart for the day was Scorpio 0°07'); and in the discovery chart – the moment when the Nativity chart first appeared from my printer – at Tropical Scorpio 1°50' embraced by the Tropical New Moon at the Draconic IC we find the confirmation of Jesus' identity: the all-important *Yeshuhua/Christa* midpoint. On the Draconic Ascendant was a Tropical conjunction of *Gottesman* (God's man) and *Christa* opposite the setting Mercury/Pluto; Tropical *Papacosmas* (heavenly Father) and

King were both on that eloquent Libra-Scorpio cusp; within ½° of the Tropical Ascendant was Helio asteroid *Betlem*, which is Bethlehem.

Finding Mary

Here and there in the course of this narrative I have referred to the birth chart of Our Lady, Mary/Maria, the mother of Jesus. And earlier in the book her name came up in the context of the author's journey. You may remember that I referred to a dream in which her name was associated with the date of August 4th. (According to the account of one of her dialogues with the visionaries at Medjugorje in Bosnia she told them that her birthday was August 5th; now, the Roman Catholic Church has always celebrated Our Lady's birthday on September 8th, so there was no wishful toeing the party line here!)

Once I had the necessary equipment, I did explore various August 4ths between fourteen and about twenty-four years before the birth of Christ; but remained unsatisfied, uncertain.

And so things remained; work continued on the Nativity and I put everything I had found into an A4 book that was published from home. Until 1995 … when, one glorious May day Gerard and I took a coach trip to Brighton to see Torvill and Dean's ice show, *Let's Face The Music!* Returning after an afternoon of magic, the courier came down the coach from seat to seat handing out pink raffle

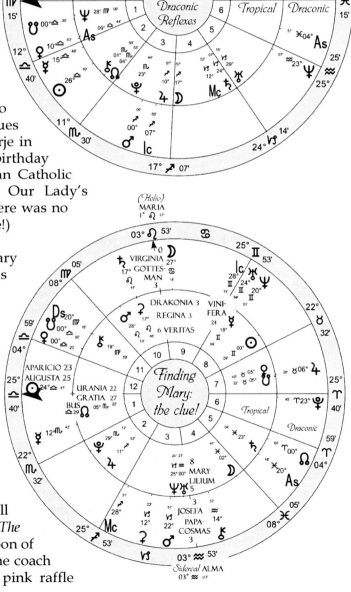

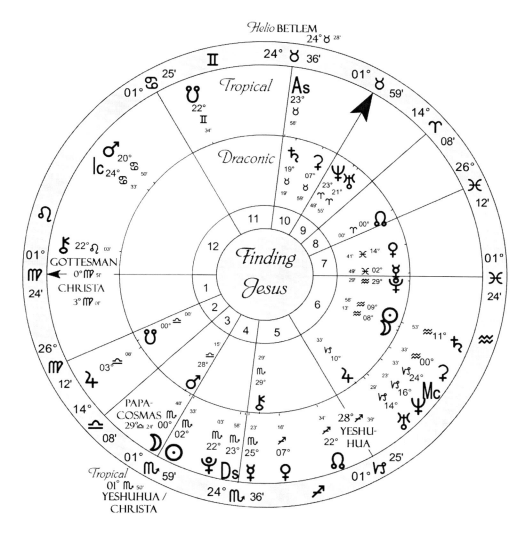

tickets. These she had already torn from their stubs and thoroughly shuffled; the prize was a bottle of red wine '…to thank you for travelling with us,' she smiled. Her name was Alma.

We were sitting near the back, two of her last customers. The ticket she pressed into my hand was Nº 570; I smiled at Gerard and said 'Look, she has given me Jesus!'– 5, 7 being forever now May 7th. Gerard took his own slip and scrutinised it: 840. I was in 'date mode' still, and found this highly amusing. He had August 4th! '… and she has given you Mary!' This was highly appropriate, as he has always had a special love for Our Lady; in fact that very morning we had drunk our coffee from what I call our Jesus and Mary mugs, which actually have birds on them – but one is the Robin Redbreast, symbol of the Crucifixion, and the other the Wren, Our Lady's bird. So we chuckled at this for a while, enjoying 'Upstairs'' little joke on this very pleasant day, until I had a giddying thought. Suppose it *wasn't* a joke?

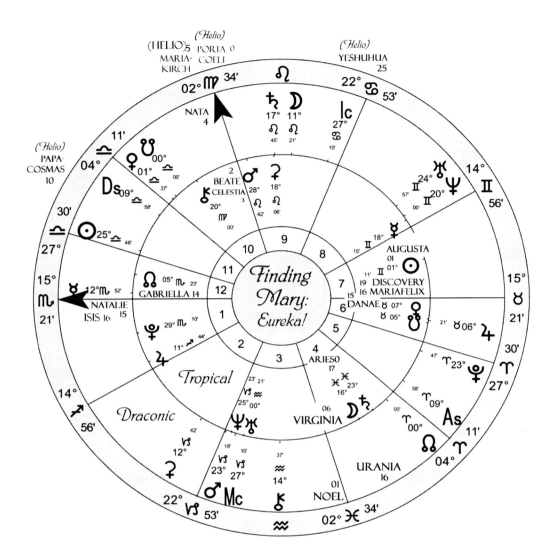

Both these numbers ended in zero. Why? Did it connect them in some way? Did it mean something? What were our ingenious invisible friends trying to say? In the context of May 7th, and Jesus, what was zero? It was pretty obvious when you come to think about it, as I actually pin-pointed the Nativity by searching for two zeros that had to coincide: Zero Aries Tropical with Zero Aries Draconic! Now, here was Mary's possible birthday also linked to a zero. Surely they weren't telling me to look for *her* now, the same way?

We were late home, and tired at last. No time even to consider switching the computer on to check this wild idea. It had to wait till the morning. Straight after breakfast, on went the laptop, up came Solar Fire's on-screen ephemeris (what a change from the laborious process two-and-a-half years before!) and it took only a few minutes to scroll back through the appropriate years BC, watching the Moon's True Node as it moved through the signs.

I could see the end of Pisces approaching. Would there be three passes of the Node over $0°$ Aries as often happens, or just one? And would it be in a suitable year? What kind of pattern would it bring?

The True Node hit $0°$ Aries just once, uniting the Tropical and Draconic, in the year 24 BC. It happened on the 4th of August.

The moment this came up on the screen, $15°$ Scorpio was rising and the IC had reached the place of the Moon when I held ticket 840 in my hand – also the Draconic Ascendant when I first saw the chart of Jesus. By now totally dependent on the help clearly being given, I asked for a time and was shown that she was born with mid-Scorpio ascending like her Son. This put the dramatic conjunction of Sun and Pluto in her religious 9th House, and the day-old Moon (another one!) close to the Midheaven. Truly, this was 'a woman clothed with the sun' as St. John the Divine describes in his book of Revelation. Her love of God, her transparency to His power, and her imperative motherhood dominate her life. It remained to study how her chart behaved against events and in synastry; you have already seen her Sun-degree strong in some of the Christian patterns above. But it was the asteroid work that clinched it. As with Jesus, the tiny bodies carrying the Gospel scripts were patiently and scrupulously run back over the centuries to her birth, over and over again, day and night for weeks on end, adding higher degrees of precision every time, until no matter how exacting the standard, the results from run to run scarcely varied and the positions stabilised. Suddenly there I was looking at the astonishing proof we needed. Asteroid *Mary* was conjunct Our Lady's Sun by only $1°$! What was more, in her important Helio chart, the other asteroid, *Maria*, was precisely opposite, $1°$ from the Earth. Her Nativity was secure.

I would, however, do just one more run. I think it was the seventh; months had passed since the first, much quicker, test. If I was born a Capricorn to learn patience, this exercise was very good for the soul! At last we were there again, at August 4th 24 BC (i.e. – 0023) and here was the asteroid *Mary* – not, as I fully expected, out of orbs after all, with the eight-fold increase in accuracy, but this time right in the Sun's degree! Where was helio *Maria*? Exactly conjunct the Earth!

I first wrote this chapter in early spring 1999; the morning of March 27th was the first time I had looked at the asteroids for the finding of Mary back in May four years previously, and it is worth showing you the pattern for that moment, because once again it is a shining example of how our lives are scripted in the heavens. During the previous days while I was concentrating on the Nativity of Jesus, *Yeshuhua* had been – unknown to me – accompanying Mercury over my 7th cusp; and now I found *Mary* also there, closely following him, prompting this account of her own birth and discovery!

Here then, are all three of the discovery charts. They show, beside the various names for Mary ('full of Grace' – *Gratia*), Jesus, heaven and the heavenly Father, asteroids connected to the astrology and to the other people involved, including *Alma*, the *Bus*, *Gabriel*, *Drakonia*, *Urania*, *Augusta*, plus versions of 'truth' and of nativity (the second chart with its conjunction of Draconic *Urania* with Tropical *Aries0* and Moon, as *Discovery* sets and

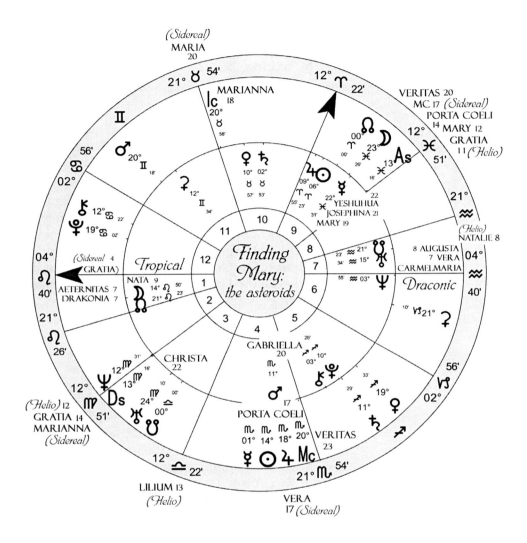

Augusta meets the Sun, is particularly delicious!). The patterns are so graphic that they should by now be self-explanatory.

However, the asteroid positions for the third chart (set for the moment when I checked the asteroids for the first chart) are simply *extraordinary* (you can see in the diagram what was going on in 22° Virgo-Pisces with the Draconic Moon-Uranus/Tropical Mercury! ... and that the Draconic Sun that day was opposite the Sun of Jesus' Nativity). As there is insufficient space on the wheel I am listing here all the names and positions I have found strung like jewels across the dimensions on the Draconic horizon, Sidereal Midheaven and axis of the Draconic Moon(13°, 17° and 23° Pisces-Virgo, the signs abbreviated below to 'pi' and 'vi' for simplicity. *13° Pisces is the degree of Mary's natal Dwad Moon/Ascendant conjunction.*) It is as if this moment was the culmination of everything that started with Dennis Elwell in Cambridge in 1977. Here goes – including Reflexes, remembering that radix and reflex bodies occupy corners of the same celestial rectangle in a given zodiac, and act as if in conjunction or opposition.

Tropical: Pax 8pi30, Pamjones 8pi49, Angel 9pi10, Crane 9pi15, Archilochos (the first Word) 10pi26, Pamela 11pi01, Astronomia 11pi17, Baumann 12pi19, Carpenter 12pi24, Lamb 14pi08, Cambridge 14pi18, May 15pi13, Bennett 15vi14, Rosa 16pi08, Magion 17vi19, Las Cruces 17pi32, Mary 19pi20, Papacosmas 20pi00, Almary 21pi00, Josephina 21pi08, Christa 22vi16, Yeshuhua 22pi20, Trueblood 22pi23, Veronika (true image) 22vi53, Pia 24pi 16, Byblis 25pi14, Conscience 25pi56.

Tropical Reflexes: San Pedro (St Peter) 9vi19, Rabinowitz (Rabbi) 11pi06, Charis (grace)13pi42, Probitas 14pi39, Karma 15pi14, Veritas 15pi18, Josse (another name for Jesus)19pi14, Amun 19pi27, Marianna 20vi24, Porta Coeli 21pi05.

Draconic: Salvia 8pi19, Roentgen 8pi47, Denise (Dennis) 9vi21, Elisabetha 12vi18, Stargazer 12vi28, Noel (Christmas) 12vi38, Bishop 14pi02, Carmelmaria 15vi37, Gotha (Golgotha) 15vi49, Aeternitas 15pi46, Drakonia 16pi10, Hill (Calvary) 17pi24, Elias 19pi08, Union 23pi37, Taurinensis 23pi44, Horus (the son of the goddess Isis) 24vi06, Coelum 24pi08, Angelica 24vi27, Betlem (Bethlehem) 26vi16, De Sanctis 27pi17.

Draconic Reflexes: Carpenter 8vi59, Baumann 9vi04, Astronomia 10vi06, Pamela 10vi22, Archilochos 10vi57, Crane 12vi07, Angel 12vi12, Pamjones 12vi34, Pax 12vi53, Josefa 13pi58, Peter 15vi44, Jessenius 16vi26, Child 17vi08, Baptistina 18vi03, Wisdom 19pi37, Angelina 21vi44, Mira (miracle) 22vi04, Gratia (grace, thanks) 22pi18, Martha 23vi07, Jerusalem 23vi28, Judith 24vi03, Aiguillon (thorn) 24pi33, Isa (Arab Muslim name for Jesus) 25pi27, Mentor 26vi03, Amor 26vi46.

Sidereal: Gerarda (my devout husband, without whom *none* of this would ever have happened! … only15' from Tropical Crane) 9pi00, Skepticus 13pi05, Fides 13vi18, Porta Coeli (the gate of heaven)14pi10, Marianna 14vi51, Astrowizard 15pi41, Amun 15pi49, Josse (another asteroid for Jesus)16pi01, Veritas 19pi57, Karma 20pi01, Probitas 20pi36, Charis (grace) 21pi34.

Sidereal Reflexes: Dennispalm 11vi30, Osiris (the broken god)12pi06, Regina 13pi31, Ostara (Easter)15vi25, Emanuela 20pi04, Jordaens (river) 20pi08, Protgeneia (first-born) 22pi39, Galilea 23vi50, Saint-Marys 26pi38.

Helio: May 8pi23, Las Cruces 11pi55, Gratia 11vi56, Mary 12pi04, Almary 13pi37, Wisdom 15vi04, Trueblood 15pi31, Josefa 15vi58, Josephina 16pi10,Yeshuhua 17pi40, Pia 19pi37, Bennett 22vi19, San Juan 25pi18.

Helio Reflexes: Charis 10pi10, Probitas 10pi13, Karma 11pi32, Veritas 12pi24, Amun 13pi31, San Pedro 14vi21, Josse 16pi47, Josephus Flavius17vi14, Astrowizard 18pi02, Porta Coeli 20pi08, Marianna 21vi15, Fides (faith) 22vi33, Abbe 26vi32.

I could do the same for the Scorpio-Taurus axis carrying the Draconic stellium and MC, if only to point out the activity of the Helio Reflexes in particular. Another of Jesus' names comes thereby to 20° Scorpio, the exact Draconic Midheaven – *Yasue* (the Arab Christian name for him being Yasu). Close to it at 23° is *Santa*, and at 18° *Martir*. *Signe* is at Scorpio 19°. At the opposite end of this axis in Taurus on the same Helio Reflex rectangle, are *Compassion* at 19° and *Spirit* at 22°. If you are feeling adventurous you may like to explore these patterns for yourself; it is fairly easy now to build up a collection of useful asteroids, and Solar Fire's own database gives its user a good start. And it makes no difference if an asteroid – such as Spirit, named in 2004 for the Mars exploration rover – was given its name long after these events took place!

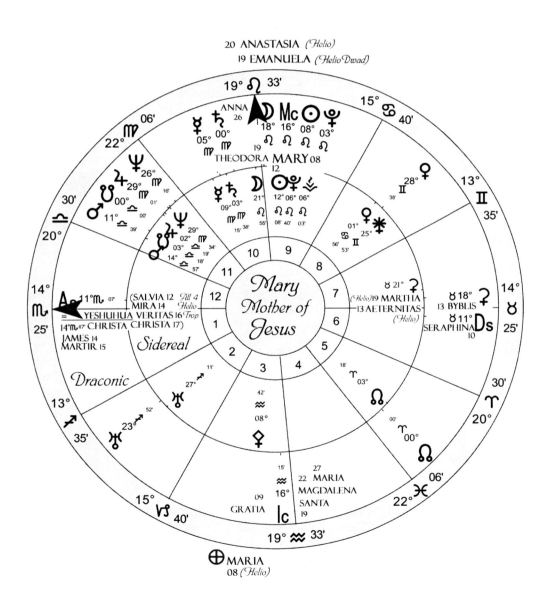

A Fresh Look At Mary

As this new edition of *The Draconic Chart* was first being prepared in the spring of 2009 it occurred to me to take a fresh look at Mary's pattern. While, for all the technical and spiritual reasons given above, I was then perfectly happy with the date and approximate time, the years had taught me to be critical of discarnate guidance; even where this is present and benign, the human mind can be a faulty receptor, and where it is possible checking should be done. I had of course worked on the chart of Jesus' Mother using the dates we have from the Gospels, but had not always been fully satisfied with the results. Some rectification might well be in order.

After many hours of testing, I now have a chart which appears to respond far better to fine-tuning, progression and stimuli. I have moved Mary's time back to 12h33 LMT, which shows that New Moon embracing the Midheaven, while a slightly earlier degree of 11°03' Scorpio now rises. **And we now have Ceres!** (But not, alas, Chiron, who is far too erratic.) The Swiss Ephemeris has, it appears, sorted out Ceres' tricky orbital behaviour (which prevented me from using her back in the 1990s) and the position of the bereaved Mother Goddess in the chart of the Mother of God is perfect. She is in the 7th House in Taurus 18°, (the degree that was just about to set at Jesus' Nativity), and falls in a tight square to the Leo Moon, describing Mary's nature and foretelling the agony of separation from her son. The other **three major asteroids** only add to her status: Juno is with Venus, and an opposition of Pallas to Vesta lies in orbs of the Leo Sun. The **reflex** chart (contrantiscia) dramatically unites Moon with Ascendant. This life is all about motherhood.

The **Sidereal angles** of this modified chart connect powerfully to **Mary's asteroids**. In the accompanying diagram (168) I have placed this Sidereal wheel at the centre, as it concerns her vital place in history, with the Draconic/Tropical on the outside. Scorpio 14° is rising (with Helio asteroid *Mira*, a miracle) – therefore her son's Nativity Sun is almost exactly on her 7th cusp. This Sidereal Ascendant/Descendant axis also carries the Draconic/Tropical *Yeshuhua/Christa* midpoint that is central to all these charts. Jesus' brother *James* is also there, with asteroid *Martir*, both Draconic. With *Mira* on the Sidereal Ascendant are three more Helio asteroids – *Salvia, Veritas, Christa*; opposite are Helio friend *Martha* and *Aeternitas. Seraphina*, the announcing angel, and *Byblis*, the Bible, are setting *in coelo*. Over and over again we find Sun-centred asteroids contributing vividly to the interdimensional picture. The Sidereal Midheaven is crowned with Mary's Draconic/Tropical Moon and *Theodora* (who adores God), Helio *Anastasia* (immortality) and Helio Dwad *Emanuela* (God with us). Opposite the Sun/*Mary* conjunction is *Gratia* – grace; at the Sidereal IC is Draconic *Santa* – holy; and her (Draconic) friend *Maria Magdalena* aligns with *Anna*, her mother, close to the axis of the Sidereal Moon.

If the chart is valid, then its **Reflex** patterns should highlight that life's outstanding characteristics. Indeed this is so in Mary's case: in the modified Draconic/Tropical chart the Moon, whose symbolism is central to her life as woman, as mother, as goddess (and almost exactly square the other symbol of motherhood, Ceres) reflexes with her Ascendant almost precisely, by only 24' of arc.

The new chart should relate significantly to that of Jesus; a **'Q' chart** is always a crucial test. Setting up Jesus' map for Mary's birth time confirms their relationship: although at her previous, slightly later time his Moon was on the MC, we now find his Midheaven conjunct both Mercury and Ceres while Juno rises. The Queen of Heaven brings him into the world, and Mary is the mother from whom he has to separate to fulfil his destiny.

The Dwad of Mary's revised chart is startling. The Moon now 'rises' in Pisces, opposite a harsh trio of Saturn, Pluto and Uranus, all squared by Ceres. Here is the inner reality of this consciously spiritual, tender woman born to unique burdens as a mother, and ultimate sorrow. But she experiences the indwelling strength and stability of Sun/Mercury in Scorpio opposite Taurus Venus and trine Neptune sweetly configured with that embattled Ascendant. They form a classic kite pattern in Mary's inner sky. The Midheaven conjoins Mars, with Jupiter at the IC and conjunct the radix MC; this young woman will always know God, and accept suffering – there will be no joy without pain. And of course the Sun/Venus opposition describes the son she is born to bear; close to her own radix horizon, it is almost exactly his Sun/Ascendant axis, and was conjoined by the New Moon in 12° Taurus that immediately preceded his birth. It forms a Grand Cross with the angular Jupiter and the radix Sun/Moon/MC. The eclipse in March 5 BC fell right on her Dwad Ascendant/Moon.

Key asteroids are powerfully placed in this wheel also. In the Dwad a conjunction of *Veritas/Mary* combines on the Draconic Ascendant with the Dwads of Mercury, *Gratia* and the Sun opposite a Dwad stellium of *Tempel, Patientia, Anna,* Venus, *Galilea* and Helio Dwad *Maria*. With the Dwad Moon/Ascendant are *Santa* and *Paradise* opposite friend *Salome*. A Dwad conjunction of *Virginia/Seraphina* combines with all the groupings in Leo opposite Dwad *Vera/Lumen* (true Light) and *Amor* on the mid-Aquarius angles. In coelo, aligned with the Moon from the IC, is Mary's symbol, *Rosa,* the rose.

The chart below shows you the **Sidereal chart** of Mary, its **Dwad** at the centre with Ascendant/Moon opposite Jupiter, Uranus and Pluto. On the Dwad 7th cusp are radix *Porta Coeli* and *Elisabetha, Mira* and *Salvia*. This axis alone tells of a uniquely destined woman who, with her cousin, through a miracle will open the gate of Heaven for mankind's salvation. At the Dwad IC is *Virginia,* with radix *Vera* and *Patientia;* opposite in the radix are *Child* and *San Juan*. This young girl was truly a virgin, and the child who would be baptised by his cousin St John was to bring her deep suffering. Who was he? Clustered around the historic Sidereal Dwad Sun in holy Sagittarius are *Yeshuhua, Christa, Veritas, Mary* (opposite *Patientia*); all these conjunct the radix Uranus, *Carpenter* and *Martir*. Here is the story of Jesus, son of Mary, Carpenter of Nazareth, the Anointed One who incarnated Truth, suffered, was martyred, and is the living Christ. The aid from Elisabeth and John can be seen in the Dwad at its North Node, with the radix 14° Taurus Descendant; at the Dwad South Node on her radix Sidereal

Ascendant is the holy child Mary gives to the world, *Santa/Child,* and also there in the radix is *Peter,* as close to her as to her son – in fact exactly on her Draconic/Tropical Ascendant. Opposite the shining Leo Midheaven and Mary, in radix Aquarius is Peter's other name, *Simona;* and so is *Horus,* son of the goddess; and *Gratia,* grace. Dwad Aquarius brings to the radix IC *Noel, San Juan* and *Sophia* – the births of Christ and St John, and the wisdom that guided their upbringing.

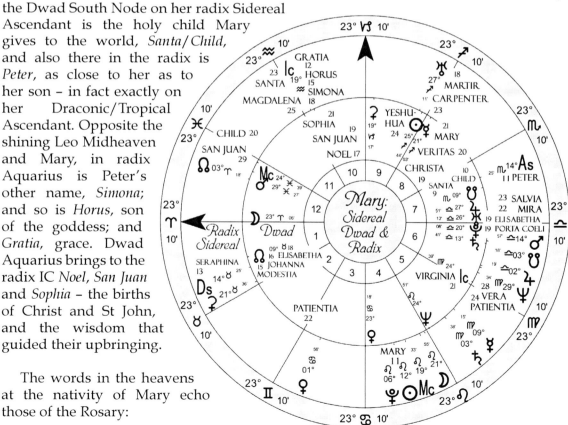

The words in the heavens at the nativity of Mary echo those of the Rosary:

'Hail Mary, full of Grace! The Lord is with Thee. Blessed art Thou among women, and blessed is the fruit of Thy womb, Jesus.'

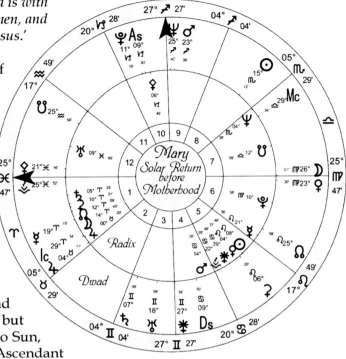

Recently I have extended the use of Dwads to **Return charts**. Just look at Mary's Solar Return for August 4th 6 BC, close to the time of the Annunciation, nine months prior to the birth of Jesus. 'A virgin shall bear a child' – and here is a Dwad Vesta-Moon, opposed by only 9' of arc, exactly on the Ascendant/Descendant axis. The Mother/Goddess is written all over it! Not only is she embracing her destiny, with the Moon/Ceres/North Node *in coelo* trine Sun and Venus in the 5th House of children, but Dwad Ceres joins that glowing Leo Sun, transformative Pluto is with the Ascendant in the Dwad, and a stunning Grand Cross of Dwad Moon/Venus, Mars/Neptune, Pallas/Vesta and Juno clings to the angles of the radix Return chart bringing heaven to earth. The burden she must bear is also there, in the Return's **Reflex** of Saturn to Ascendant.

Not only the Solar Return is active: the **Lunar Return** in April 5 BC puts Dwad Ceres/Ascendant on the Return MC opposite Saturn, and also in the Dwad we find conjunctions of Sun/Pluto and Moon/MC, this last opposite Dwad Venus and radix Pluto. Asteroid Vesta is making a strong showing here – you will find her busy in many of the following maps. She is of course, through her priestesses, connected with virginity!

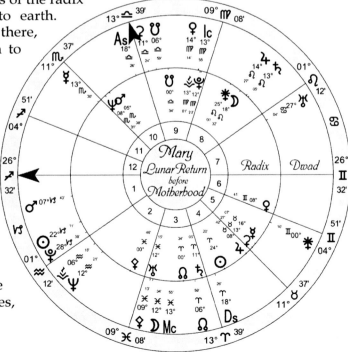

Possibly the most dramatic pattern of all is found in Mary's **Moon/Sun Phase Return** which occurred on the very morning of the birth of Jesus: we have of course the Sun/Jupiter conjunction of that day – and it is rising, with the degree of the recent New Moon on the Ascendant. The Moon is in the 1st House tightly conjunct Ceres and Mercury, angular to the fast-moving Dwad IC. In the Dwad the Moon is joined by Mercury and – intriguingly – Vesta. The Dwad Ascendant/ Descendant carries the 0° Aries Nodes; and on the Midheaven there is a close conjunction of Ceres and Pluto. *Everywhere* you look in these charts the significators of motherhood are signposted by the angles. The repeated strength of Pluto flags up a world-changing event.

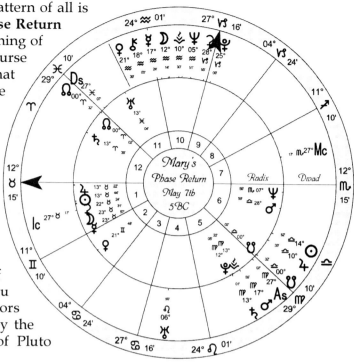

You would hope to see the Grand Cross recur at the crucifixion of Jesus, and it does: it is formed by Moon, Neptune, Mars, Ceres in his mother's **Dwad Solar Return** of August 3rd AD 32 preceding the first Easter. This is a strange pattern – there seems to be far too much joy in it for so sombre a destiny; this is when the Mother has to endure bereavement of her Son. And indeed the mental torment and loss of her child is graphically shown in the radix Return with its **Reflexes** of Mercury/ Saturn to MC and above all Ceres to Ascendant. But the body's torment and death on the material cross was followed by the uttermost spiritual reward, the resurrection into eternal life that was God's promise to struggling humanity, and Mary knew what had been achieved. She knew in her soul what a great

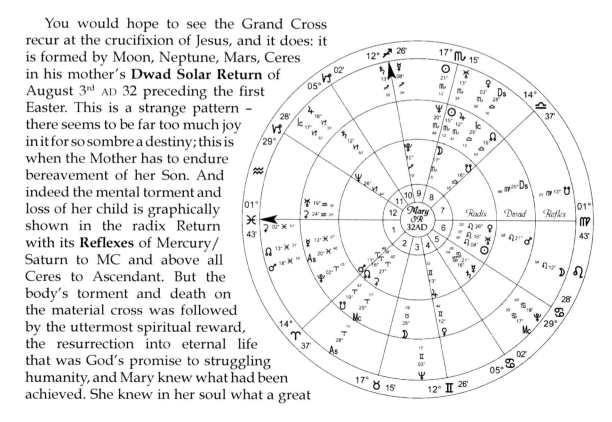

gift of love had been given through her sacrifice. So here, in Pluto/Jupiter on the radix meridian conjoined by dwad Venus, in the dwad Sun/Jupiter/Neptune conjunction with the Return's Moon on her son's Scorpio Ascendant, and in radix Ceres on the dwad MC, we see all the poignancy of the mother's pain, all that love – and that transcendent joy.

On March 30th AD 33 Mary had her **Lunar Return**. The Ascendant axis is the very axis of the lunar eclipse that darkened the Crucifixion, and Uranus has joined her Moon, squaring Ceres. The Sun is with the Dragon's Head, close to the Dwad MC; and near the radix MC, in their cross with that prophetic horizon, are both radix and Dwad Saturn. The Son is completing his work, he and the sorrowing mother are wrenched apart. The 'setting' Moon in the Dwad is right on Mary's own Dwad Ascendant and her Son's prenatal eclipse. Two eclipses bounding a uniquely historic and holy life. 'In my end is my beginning.'

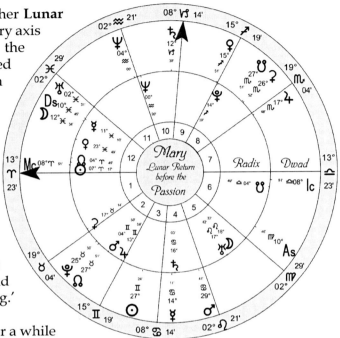

I realise that we have departed for a while from the Draconic theme of this book, but this chapter is an opportunity to offer proof of the historicity of the main Gospel narrative – at least among the astrologically literate. It is necessary to look now at progressions for Mary; and once again it is the addition of the Reflexes and the Dwads in each that brings the chart alive. I had noticed this with my own annuals and dailies – often there seemed nothing strongly descriptive of the day, but when the Dwad and/or Reflex of the progression was added everything fell into place. Perhaps we are looking at the inner significance of outer events? We have eight charts to work with: Mary's annual and converse progressed charts plus her daily progressed and daily converse charts, for both the Nativity of Jesus, and for his Passion.

First the Nativity: the **annual progressed chart** has little Dwad activity, but the **Reflexes** are powerful. A progressed opposition of Moon and Mars, just right for child-bearing, reflexes with the Midheaven (recently conjunct Saturn – marriage to the elderly Joseph?) and more importantly the Ascendant has come to its reflex with fateful Pluto. The annual converse pattern has nothing special to add.

Looking at the **daily progressions** for the date of Jesus' birth, the **direct** pattern brings reflex Moon to oppose the Sun, a time of fulfilment. But it is the Dwad which is remarkable this time, with more intense activity from Pluto and the signature of doomed motherhood – Ceres conjoins the Ascendant in the Dwad opposite radix Pluto and square the radix

Taurus Moon, and a radix conjunction of Ascendant and Mercury meets Dwad Uranus and Pluto. The **daily converse** angles have just separated, by 2°, from reflexes to Saturn and Moon, which may reflect the exhaustion of a woman close to term and, desperate for rest and shelter, having to accept second-rate accommodation. But oh, look at the Dwad again! Here we can see the real appointment Mary is keeping on May 7th 5 BC, in the glorious double Jupiter! Jupiter conjunct Neptune radix joins a Dwad MC flanked by mothering Ceres and Uranus; Dwad Jupiter smiles on the daily converse Descendant. The day has brought joy and holiness to the world.

And then we come at last to the Cross. The **annual progressions** are fascinating, because they show the progress of her son's earthly ministry over the three or four years leading up to its world-shaking climax. Four years/degrees back we can see three things happening at once: the shock of Uranus on the progressed Ascendant; the joy of Jupiter in the Midheaven; and the Sun beginning its journey over Neptune, the South Node and the South Node reflex. Progressed Sun to South Node is always a time of self-sacrifice, and in Mary's life it is a sacred duty. Neptune calls her to transcend normality and fully immerse herself in the spiritual mission of her son – God's Son. Now her Sun has completed this vital parabola and come to Neptune's reflex: she must give her son back to God. You cannot hold what Neptune refines, nor what the South Node requires you to surrender. The spiritual duty of this mother is echoed in the meeting of progressed Dwad Ceres/ Pluto/MC/IC with her progressed Nodes and that reflex progressed Sun. Also in the Dwad, Sun squares Neptune. The same message is repeated in the **annual converse** prior to the Passion: shocking Uranus is at the IC, Jupiter and Neptune rise, and that Ascendant reflexes to the South Node. The **Dwad** horizon of the converse chart carries an opposition of Mercury and Moon, tied to disruptive Uranus in the radix and squaring all that late Virgo-Pisces activity. A Dwad MC/Ceres conjunction insists again on the tragic separation to come.

Mary's **daily progressed chart** (overleaf) for Christ's crucifixion is all love and grief and loneliness. Saturn's cold hand is on both angles of the **Dwad** – flanking the MC with the Sun in the Dwad pattern itself, and conjunct radix daily progressed Mars, while radix Saturn, Venus, Moon and Dwad Moon all meet on the Dwad 7th cusp. **Extraordinarily this point is at 1° Virgo, whose Sabian symbol is a white cross on a hill. And if the Moon is parallax corrected it moves a degree or so to join it.** But by Resurrection day that Dwad horizon will have moved 24° to conjoin Dwad Pluto and the radix Neptune/ South Node! The greatest spiritual revelation awaits her! Momentous days, momentous patterns. The **Dwad converse** brings MC and Pluto together near radix Saturn to the IC, and the Sun into the grasp of Mars and the South Node. The Dwad horizon holds the radix Nodes. Drama, pain and sacrifice. The patterns of the Passion are inescapable: go back to the Crucifixion itself, centre it on the Dwad, and yet *again* you find Ceres on the MC, lined up with radix Pluto-Jupiter, a painful Uranus-Mars across the horizon, and the Dwad lunar eclipse square an alignment of Venus/Jupiter/Nodes and Pluto. *Where is that Dwad horizon again, burdened with the sudden agony of Uranus and Mars? Across the axis of the white cross.* Change the time to 12h33, a Q-chart for Mary, and in the Dwad you *still* find the same energies in sharp focus: Ceres on the Descendant, MC/IC with Venus/Jupiter/Nodes and Pluto.

The revised chapter was completed, fortuitously, on April 3rd 2009, the anniversary of the Crucifixion. When I opened Solar Fire that morning to add the three final extraordinary lunar charts, alive with Ceres and Pluto, to the extended work on Mary, the Nativity and the Passion, Pluto was setting and Ceres was at the IC in 1°-2° Virgo again, the Sabian degree associated with a white cross dominating the landscape. The 'setting' Dwad Mars at the Crucifixion was in the very same degree. What more can I say? The patterns speak for themselves; and without the Draconic chart this extraordinary journey of historic and spiritual discovery could never have started.

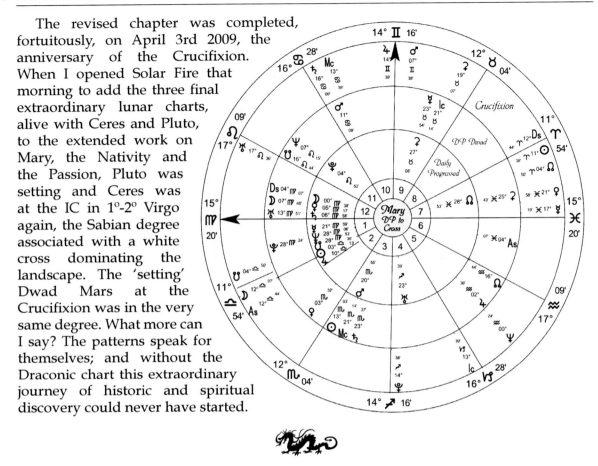

Meanwhile, in the Groves of Academe ...

Finally, there is also academic support (if you still need it!), at least for the May 5 BC Nativity. In the summer of 1995, I discovered (well, more correctly, it turned up under my nose in just as odd a way as the paper on the Crucifixion) a twenty-page article in the October 1993 *Science and Christian Belief,* by the same Professor (now Sir) Colin Humphreys who co-authored that earlier paper, explaining that the documented appearance of a tailed comet, plus many historical and environmental factors, finally decided his own choice of March to early May 5 BC for the birth of Jesus. He and I have kept in touch.

Whether or not you are persuaded to believe, after all this extraordinary evidence, that Jesus was born at that place and time, and exercised his world-changing ministry, two things are incontrovertibly true: one, that something unprecedented happened to catalyse the phenomenal spread of Christianity, and two, that there truly was a moment in celestial history that held the spiritual power to set an ideal pattern for human growth. Even on these terms alone, the skies of both the 7th of May 5 BC and the 4th of August 24 BC repay our study, but to some of us they will from now on and forever speak of the coming of Christ.

Chapter Twenty

In My End is My Beginning

We have reached the end of this first volume of Interdimensional astrology; but it can only be the beginning of a whole new world of astrological experience for many of us. The greatest world-encircling dragon, Ourobouros, wisely keeps his tail in his mouth!

If we wish to take our discipline into the twenty-first century, we need to add to the twentieth century's understanding of the Tropical, 'horizontal' dimension of self, this 'vertical' dimension of understanding which through the Draconic zodiac links each soul's behaviour in the past to its fruits of karma, principle and vocational drive in the present. Upon the blend of these (and other) aspects of self, and our deepest spiritual will, we build our future.

'For each entity in the Earth is what it is because of what it has been,' said Edgar Cayce, 'and each moment is dependent on another moment; so a sojourn in the Earth … is as a lesson in the school of life and experience.' Elsewhere he said: 'Hence again the injunction, look upon all phases; for there is the mental, the material, and the spiritual, and these are the phases of man's reaction and man's activity. Do not apply the law of the spiritual in material things, nor the material in spiritual things. Remember that Mind is the Builder, and the Spirit giveth Life; and as ye use and dwell upon such, be sure thy ideal is in Him.'

'When he gets up on that stage he's a different person!' is the kind of remark that is often heard, and is more significant in the light of the foregoing statements than many people realise. We are at least two different people, depending on the level of ourselves at which we are living, the experiential Tropical level or the vocational Draconic level. (There are also the Sidereal and the Heliocentric, which we have touched upon in several earlier chapters, and hopefully will be covered in later volumes.) Although we can combine their energies, as we have seen earlier in numerous examples of lives richly lived, we clearly have constant work to do to learn to distinguish carefully and thus effectively between our material and our spiritual responsibilities. Cayce's words echo the meaning of Christ's words: *'Render unto Caesar those things that are Caesar's, and to God those that are God's.'*

So it is not always appropriate to strive to reach into our Draconic self; we are here to create and perfect a new personality as well as to share with our spiritual kin those gifts, whether of Grace or of many lives' learning, which will be of value, or to play an appointed rôle, fulfilling a wider and higher purpose than our immediate personal concerns. Similarly, we must not cling to our immediate Tropical needs when life demands that we step into our greater rôle. Sometimes in the course of such undertakings martyrs are made; the Dragon of myth is traditionally propitiated by human sacrifice, and it is indeed in honouring the soul's commitments, the vows binding us each to the inner dragon-quest, that we continually sacrifice ourselves. Sacrifice only ceases when we have exhausted our karma, we spring from the wheel of *samsara*, and as heroes are brought rejoicing home to the heavens. Yes we may, and frequently must, *combine* the material and spiritual energies – but we must not *confuse* them. I am personally convinced that in the Draconic and Tropical dimensions of self we are looking at two out of the three minds that Cayce describes: the 'mind of the soul' and the 'mind of the physical body.' The third is the mind of the spiritual entity, and may be related to higher levels yet of astrological understanding … or bear no relation whatever to this wheel of life upon which we take turn after turn.

If there is one thing of value which insight into the meaning of the Draconic zodiac gives us, it is this timely and vital reminder of our own spiritual nature. And if Cayce is to be believed, with his extraordinary access to truths in which his conventionally Christian waking mind was untutored, this is the royal truth of our human condition: '*As has been indicated by some, ye are part and parcel of a universal consciousness or God and thus all that is within the universal consciousness, or the universal awareness; as the stars, the planets, the sun, the moon.*' (This would seem also to have been the Essene view.) '*Do ye rule them or they rule thee? They were made for thy own use, as an individual – yea, that is the part, the thought which thy Maker, thy Father God thinks of thee. For ye are as a corpuscle in the body of God; thus a cocreator with Him, in what ye think, in what ye do.*'

Mankind is in the gravest danger yet again of falling as a result of his own hubris; he is so in love with his clever brain and all its wonderful machines, so excited by his gatecrashing of Genesis and the gene, so full of his knowledge! We must none of us allow ourselves to become so blind to our true origins and our ultimate destiny that we can no longer guide others safely along their path. We must not forget, either, that the greatest guidance comes not *from* us but *through* us, as many who heal and counsel already know. In an age when spirituality is so often confused with psychism, let the astrologers reassume an ancient and dignified mantle as the guardians of a spiritual wisdom which in its many guises has ever informed and illumined human affairs. Isn't it time, too, that we were sufficiently committed to that which we know to be true, that we gave up wasting energy in trying to convince our profane Shadow on its own terms that astrology is fact? Stuck in the mud of materialism, we can never hope to reach the holiest stars. Give proof, when asked, to the sincere doubter and to the neophyte, but then move on.

For this journey will have no end; some of you reading this will already have reached a new crest, from which tantalising fresh vistas stretch out before you to yet another horizon. Life, consciousness, understanding pour forth from the very centre of Being, filling all manifestation and overflowing to the round brim of the universe, pushing its limits back as lava lifts and moves our continents. Man's soul is a part of the continuous creation, our journey is to the ever higher understanding of our discipline, and each human being is on his or her particular and perplexing star trek.

On the way, *'the dragon will speak to you in riddles, and will seem to know as much about you as you know yourself'* (Peter Dickenson in *The Flight of Dragons*) *'and the traditional answer to the Riddle is 'Man'.' 'Man, know thyself.'* To answer the riddle of the Dragon is to grasp its head and its tail firmly in the present, subduing its threat – our own vice and error – through the fullest comprehension of our long past, and delight in the vision of our future. And it is to understand that the higher, older Draconic self that has grown out of our past experience comes with us as the voice of conscience and conviction. *'... when a soul reaches the highest spiritual stage short of absolute absorption into the One Spirit,'* says Yogi Ramacharaka in his book *Mystic Christianity*, *'it is no longer a person, but exists as a principle.'* (My italics.) But that principle is not an inanimate mechanical force – it is a living, knowing, active principle of life.

This occult fact cannot be explained in the words of men, for no terms have been coined by which men can speak of it. Even the advanced student may grasp the fact only indirectly. He speaks here in the context of the vivid presence of the Christ principle in the world today – as it has always been – but also, in 1918, anticipates what the discovery of the Draconic zodiac has opened up for us. A new level of awareness has been reached; we need no longer be driven by incomprehensible passions, we need not doubt our sense of a vocation, we need no longer deny our spontaneous inner wisdom, unaccountable as all these voices may have seemed for centuries. We may know at least two of our selves now, begin to understand our history, and rejoice in the knowledge that the fragmented flames of the human spirit have begun to blend, burning in ever greater and more glorious fires of united vision on their way back to God.

It is not the end, then, because we pass from one room to another, from one consciousness to another.

'For, so is it is proclaimed in that promise. Though we live in the physical consciousness, we pass – as this entity has oft – into those consciousnesses of Venus, Mercury, Jupiter, Uranus; for these are but stepping stones to the greater consciousness which He would have each soul attain in its relationships with and usage of its fellow men.'
Edgar Cayce (2282-1)

'Like the ocean is your godself; it remains for ever undefiled. And like the ether it lifts but the winged. Even like the sun is your godself; it knows not the ways of the mole nor seeks it the holes of the serpent. But your godself dwells not alone in your being. Much in you is still man, and much in you is not yet man, but a shapeless pigmy that walks asleep in the mist searching for its own awakening.'
Kahlil Gibran, *The Prophet*

THE ASTROLOGER'S PRAYER

♈ Teach me how to be,
   and be aware, ♎
♉ Teach me how to have,
   and how to share, ♏
♊ Teach me to understand
   as well as know; ♐
♋ Teach me how to root,
   and how to grow. ♑
♌ Teach me how to love
   - and to be free - ♒
♍ To be of service;
   and to come to Thee. ♓

Rev Pamela Ann Frances Crane

Appendix

Interdimensional Astrology: A Summary

Most of the following techniques are now available in all the major astrology computer programs; here follows a summary of the main Interdimensional principles.

1. **A ZODIAC IS IDENTICAL OR ANALOGOUS TO A STANDING WAVE IN THE TWELFTH HARMONIC, GENERATED AT ANY ECLIPTIC NODE.** E.g. Tropical Zodiac generated at the Spring Equinox Node; the Draconic Zodiac at the Moon's Ascending Node; the Oriental Zodiac of the Houses at the Horizon/ Ecliptic Node.

2. **A ZODIAC BEGINS WITH ITS OWN SIGN.** This rule includes the DWAD – a micro-zodiac generated at the nodal point of a Sign-cusp in its 'parent' macro-zodiac, the RADIX, and which begins with the Radix Sign in which it is formed.

    As the 'parent' zodiac of twelve standing waves begins with Aries, the same principle applied in the opposite direction identifies the Ecliptic Circle as a whole as ARIES – the Generator, the Creative Origin out of which the Zodiac springs, and thus as a manifestation or symbol of the Father. Within this circle is generated the TRIANGLE – the Three-in-one, the Trinity – of ARIES the FATHER, LEO the SON, and SAGITTARIUS the HOLY SPIRIT.

    This triangle of the first, fifth and ninth signs in each of the Dwads creates the familiar DECANATES.

3. **A SIGN, WHETHER AT HIGH OR LOW FREQUENCY, IS A DISCRETE PACKET OF MEANING.** I.e. There is discontinuity of characteristics at the nodal point where one Sign ends and the next begins. This is demonstrated by the missing Sign between any two Dwads; for example, the Dwad in Radix Taurus finishes with Aries, and the following Dwad in Radix Gemini begins according to the rule with Gemini, the sign in sextile. A Zodiac does **not** behave like a spectrum with a gradual progression of meanings that overlap and blend into each other.

4. IDENTICAL AXES OF LONGITUDE IN TWO OR MORE ZODIACS RESONATE TOGETHER.

If two bodies in their respective zodiacs – macro or micro – are found in or very close to the same degree of the same Sign, they are 'on the same wavelength', 'striking the same chord'. If one is in the opposite degree, half the circle away, its resonance with the first has something in common with musical notes separated by an octave. Tight squares to an axis can also be strongly active. Again we have a division of the circle (the 'string' of the zodiac) by two, raising its 'note' by a further octave. In music, the same note played on several instruments or sung by several voices is powerfully reinforced as they all resonate together. In the same way two or more planets or angles 'playing the same note' on their respective zodiac strings (Tropical, Sidereal, Draconic, Heliocentric, Dwad etc) have their energies (their 'voices') combined and amplified by the unison.

The image of fingers moving on a musical string and producing octaves of its original note is perhaps closer to reality than we have imagined; physics now teaches that every object bends its local space. So every planet and energy-point may interrupt the basic resonance of the ecliptic to make the music of the spheres.

Orbs of aspect to an axis should ideally remain within 5° on either side, and within 2° for squares. Clearly, the tighter the contact, the purer the unison of energies, and the more dramatic their combined action when triggered by progressions, transits or Solar Arcs for example.

Putting all this into practice means working habitually with not just one zodiac at a time, but TROPICAL, DRACONIC and SIDEREAL together, plus HELIOCENTRIC – and sometimes with the GEOSOLAR – the zodiac generated within the calculated Radix chart from the position of the Sun – or the ORIENTAL, discussed further on.

THE TROPICAL CHART (in my own terminology the **GEOTROPIC** or **GT**) is the one with which we are all familiar, and expresses the 'new creation', the 'growing tip' of our self, the embodied and environmentally conditioned personality of the current incarnation and its consequent psychology. At this level of self we have maximum free will to shape ourselves through coping or failure. This is the 'little' self which we must master at all costs, or become increasingly the slaves of our bodily drives and desires. Even when it is full of positive qualities, this Tropical identity is essentially selfish, and has always to be directed or monitored by higher levels of the will.

In synastry, contacts between Tropical charts show compatibilities or potential conflicts of interest, similarities or differences – but these do not in the end determine the strength, importance or longevity of a relationship even though they affect it. The stock phrase 'this thing is bigger than both of us!' in fact holds the key: the strong relationships are the deep ones, based in the soul or in shared vocation, and to see them we must look to the other levels.

THE DRACONIC CHART (the **GEODRACONIC** or **GD**) is calculated by taking the Dragon's Head (Draco), the Moon's North or Ascending Node, as the first point of Aries. The formula is as follows:

PLANET/ANGLE – NORTH NODE = DRACONIC PLANET/ANGLE

This self is a vital core of strength for each of us, as it expresses all that is of current value that the soul has brought with it from the far and/or recent past into this incarnation to be used, or to be resolved (for there is karma here), and to be drawn on in times of need. Many of one's most deeply-held principles are found here, in what amounts to a personal belief-system and may even extend to an enduring self-image. As it is older and more central to the consciousness than the Tropical, this is bound to be true for much of the life, until the new experiences begin to lay down their own deep patterns in the self's core, adding to all that has gone before. Using DRACO in counselling restores meaning and purpose to lives that are almost cracking apart.

There is less freedom of will at this level – it is conditioned by the commitments made by the soul prior to the incarnation, which must not be neglected. This involves the more important relationships – between souls who have come back together to resolve old issues or do particular work together. Contacts between the Draconic charts will show the bonds and the kind of work to be done. SUN–MOON alignments (conjunction or opposition) are commonly found from Draco to Draco or from Draco to Tropical, as well as Tropical to Tropical, where there is or has been a marriage between the two.

THE SIDEREAL CHART (GEOSTELLAR or **GS**) is the basis of Hindu astrology, and is used by a growing number of Western astrologers. However, the nodal starting point of this zodiac is still a mystery, and only by much careful research has the Synetic Vernal Point (SVP) been established (the degree in the Sidereal Zodiac at which the Tropical Spring Equinox is found at a given epoch). This point is listed in the 'Phenomena' section in the Michelsen and Rosicrucian ephemerides. Having worked to fine tolerances with this, the Fagan-Bradley version of the SVP, I am personally persuaded that it yields the correct Sidereal positions. The AYANAMSA is the degree of the Tropical Zodiac where the start of the Sidereal Zodiac is found. AYANAMSA + SVP = 360°, so to find a planet or angle's GS position all you need to do is either subtract the Ayanamsa, or add the SVP.

The Sidereal chart and its alignments appear once again to describe the new self – but this is a greater self, no longer ego-centred in the manner of the Tropical but one that takes its identity from the role it plays in the socio-cultural whole, for which it may be remembered, even in some cases revered. Generally this is an unselfish level of selfhood, and freedom of the will is only exercised as far as it does not interfere with the person's current duty as a member of the human family. If his or her identity is entirely founded on this contribution to the whole, duty is pleasure; but if this is all the person lives for, then private life can suffer, and important personality or karmic issues may not be tackled when they should be. It can be seen from this how vital it is to live consciously – and conscientiously – at all levels of our being, even when one of the several identities is bound to predominate for much of the time.

It is worth remembering that nowadays the GS planets and angles are mostly a sign behind the GT positions, so to assume that all Aries and Scorpio men, for example, are ideally suited to military life or other areas of challenge or leadership is quite, quite wrong. This is why most tests of astrology and vocation fail so miserably (and, alas, so publicly as a rule!) for in the above example only the body-self is cut out for such work, and the greater self is intended for the more sensitive pursuits of Pisces and Libra! The Taureans and Sagittarians are the ones in public life who have hidden strengths, with their Sidereal Suns in signs of Mars. These days, the iron hand almost always comes in a velvet glove ... the wolf in sheep's clothing.

Synastry between people who work together or who are thrown together by events, should always include the Sidereal; and it is essential in work on Mundane astrology, especially events and individuals of historic significance.

THE GEOSOLAR (GSL) is calculated thus:

PLANET / ANGLE – SUN = GSL PLANET / ANGLE.

This is not the same thing as a sunrise chart; the overall feeling from this pattern is that of the unconditioned person, the spontaneous child, the self at its most free ... and selfish! It is fascinating to compare this chart with the actual childhood behaviours of the individual and to see where they arise in adulthood! The phenomenon of 'isolated and congested Suns' is highlighted here by the presence or absence of planetary clusters in Geosolar Pisces/Aries.

It must be pointed out that at all these Radix levels the geometry between the planets and angles remains the same; all aspects and midpoints remain the same, describing the fundamental dynamics in the psyche that run through all shifts of identity, all changes of experiential context.

THE ORIENTAL CHART (OR) is identical with the twelve Equal Houses, starting from the Ascendant, with this important difference – not only are the Houses treated as Signs, but Planets have exact positions within these Oriental Signs as they would in any Zodiac. This is one of the most personal of all the zodiacs, and on investigation seems to show what the person actually wants – not what they feel moved to do (GT) or driven to do (DR) or obliged to do (GS). It adds detail to the picture painted by the Houses, of the main action taking place in chosen corners of life's stage. In practice, these choices vary very little throughout life, though they may express themselves in a variety of ways. Once a fifth-house person, always a fifth-house person! – although drawing may give way to sports, then to love affairs, then parenthood, then to creative renewal or running a children's playgroup, for example. And the Signs through which all this activity is expressed will vary according to the dimensions of self which dominate at various times.

THE HELIOCENTRIC CHART (HELIOTROPIC or HT) seems to be the most 'fated' of all the patterns, with the possible exception of karmic Draco. It is a pattern of blessings and curses on our lives over which the ego has little or no control, having no option but to accept and come to terms with it. It really seems to be our good and bad luck.

But there is more to it than simple fate, because the hard aspects in this dimension also describe with painful accuracy our deepest flaws, and the easy aspects do match the parts of our nature that are problem-free and parts of our lives that always seem to work out well – often enviably so. Some of the flaws appear to be areas of inadequacy which reflect a lack of development and a need for experience and training; some are blocks which prevent us from being as kind and considerate as we could be; some are vicious corners of the psyche where old jealousies, fears and hatreds are still alive and well and sowing our lives and all other lives we touch with the bitter seed of violence. Some flaws are the remains of ancient greed for attention or power or sensual pleasure.

What seems to happen to many people is that they behave so badly that in the end they are brought sharply face to face with their faults, and are so shocked and remorseful that they try very hard from then onwards to become a far better person. Once this will to change is registered in the deep heart of the spiritual conscience, the eternal Self which is most closely approached by the Heliocentric chart, the hard patterns cannot manifest any longer as sins. Instead, they are channelled into our lives as illnesses, disabilities or other personal problems that are as difficult to escape as that old self once was. This would seem to be the price we pay for our refusal to love. With the acceptance of Love, at last, and the hope of spiritual healing, material suffering must also be endured. The only relief from this is the act of Grace, an answer to prayer; and for many this will never come during the lifetime. Only when the body and the material world are cast away in death may the spirit at last spring clean and free from its self-made prison.

It is necessary to add that some relatively unblemished souls may incarnate with difficult Helio patterns to work with as a voluntary challenge, a willed burden that may either be needed to provide others with the opportunity to grow through help and caring, or to lift some of the karmic weight from the world. Also that some of the errant behaviour described above may in fact result from innate hormonal/metabolic imbalances rather than spiritual ignorance or downright wickedness. The issues in the Helio chart are very important, and central to our basic viability and vitality as whole beings; they do tend to marry with our fundamental physiological makeup with which the personality is supported or hampered. Therefore it is crucial not to make hasty moral judgments, but explore the physical and attitudinal issues here with discernment, honesty and care. I do believe however that at the Heliocentric level, we can 'know ourselves as we are known'; deep in the heart of our own spiritual truth, we are under the gaze of God.

ALL THESE LEVELS INTERACT through axial alignments, sympathetic zodiacal resonances. The dimension from which such an axial contact comes, shows the area of self that is making itself felt. A study of violent criminals has turned out to be most interesting in this respect, as time after time clusters of 'malign' planets collected around angles; yet different levels would be emphasised, showing how one man could have chosen to live a better life (GT), another was making a mess of his karma (GD), one needed to be remembered no matter what the cost (GS), another was driven by his fate to face the awful darkness in his soul (HT).

AT EACH LEVEL a precise description of the individual is given by the **DWAD** and (where possible) its refinement the SUPERDWAD.

As in the twelfth harmonic, to calculate the Dwad, each chart factor is multiplied by twelve and converted back to degrees and minutes of longitude – but its Sign is found visually from its original, radix, sign position; every 2½ of the 'parent' sign becomes a micro-sign, and the sequence (as explained earlier) starts with the parent sign itself. Aries starts with Aries and ends with Pisces, but Taurus starts with Taurus and ends with Aries, Capricorn starts with Capricorn and ends with Sagittarius, and so on.

For example, a Sun in 22°21' Sagittarius will now fall in its LEO sector:

12 x 22°21' = 268°12' = 28°12' Sagittarius … however, it is not now in this sign but in 28°12' LEO.

The Dwad is very powerful in its description of the specific interests and character of person or event; transits, progressions and other directions to the Dwad from radix planets and angles, and vice versa, are an important element of fine-tuning, and the use of selected asteroids from the available list of many hundreds will show you quickly and clearly just how accurate these descriptions are. For example, musical asteroids in the charts of singers, composers and other players are always very strongly placed, and in the charts of comedians and humorists the asteroid HILARITAS combines dramatically with the Lights and Angles.

The Dwad seems to show us the *idea* behind the form – it is often less obvious, less immediate, but on closer acquaintance it introduces us to the deeper, subtler but far more specific characteristics of the person or the phenomenon. The ***real self*** emerges to add depth and detail to the broader picture given by the radix, in any and all of the Dimensions. To study any chart without adding the Dwad is to risk generalising at the expense of necessary accuracy. The more refined and particular you can make your analysis, the more relevant it is going to be – and the more testable, in this critical age.

It will be appreciated that reasonable accuracy is needed for Dwad work; to study the Superdwad, time and place must be very close to exact, otherwise error-free work is impossible. Accuracy *in the Radix* to the nearest minute of arc creates a margin of error in the Superdwad of up to 1¼° either side. If you can work to decimal minutes, this will be improved ten-fold.

TO SUMMARISE

The authentic spiritual Self (HELIOCENTRIC) manifests through the incarnate personality (GEOCENTRIC) with a Role to play (SIDEREAL), Karma to resolve (DRACONIC) and a body/new identity (TROPICAL) to work through, master, and learn from – all of which are essential facets of the *whole* Identity, and whose activity is focussed and encouraged by the HOUSES. The RADIX chart at all levels describes the self at its most material, most dense, most general; the DWAD at all levels adds specific detail of the real, subtle self, the mind, the idea animating the form.

There are still further dimensions and details – but those above form the essential structure.

A USEFUL IMAGE TO WORK WITH IS THAT OF A TREE IN A FOREST:

The **Root** of the tree from which all growth initiates and continues, and which anchors it in the life of the world around it, is the Helio chart. Even if the tree is felled, life can begin again from its root if it is healthy. If it is diseased or inadequate, life will always be a struggle, even in optimum conditions.

The **Crown** of the tree with its unique annual growth of leaves, flowers and fruit is the Tropical chart, whose life of individual growth then adds a layer of experience to …

The **Trunk** of the tree – the Draconic – which carries the memories and strengths of all previous growing seasons.

The tree as **part of the Forest** is the Sidereal chart, contributing to the ecosystem, the collective life, and affected by its experiences.

Use of the **Transiting** Dragon's Head produces the **CURRENT DRACONIC,** where the radix chart is zodiacally related to that point, producing a very powerful and important new set of Directions concerning Karmic events or stages in soul-growth.

In **Synastry** between subject A and subject B, a Draconic chart can be set up for A using B's North Node, and vice versa. I call this the **'EXCHANGE DRACONIC'**, or **X Chart**. So far, it seems to be showing us what A expects of B, and B expects of A, in terms of principled behaviour and spiritual response. Such expectations can lead to profound disappointment in relationships, so these charts may well be worth careful study.

When I first tried this it seemed a wild idea – but Oh, how clearly peoples' expectations of each other came into view! The Draconic/Tropical energies within a nativity show whether we are likely to practise (Tropical) what we preach (Draconic). Your chart pinned to my N. Node shows how I expect you to think, feel and behave – and if this bears no relation to your InterDimensional radix and threatens your integrity, then I should be on a hiding to nothing except disappointment. However!... having looked at some good test cases, it is also clear that the qualities thrown up in Exchange charts can actually be brought out in the other person, at least in terms of behaviour; expectations can indeed be met. In fact it even looks as though my presence in my partner's life inevitably steered him in certain directions and significantly characterised our relationship. As he is 'wysiwyg' with the Dragon's Head at the beginning of Aries, he in his turn cannot help but encourage other people to be fully themselves, with no other expectations whatever!

We can legitimately expect transits to Exchange charts to bring all such issues into focus.

REFLEX POINTS

This is the term I have adopted to comprise the under-used techniques of Antiscia/Contrascia. It is a more useful term (and easier to pronounce!) because it describes the phenomenon of planets and other points reflected across a significant axis as if this were a mirror. The axes generally used are the Cardinal Points of 0° Cancer/Capricorn, 0° Aries/Libra respectively, and as the latter axis also generates the Parallels and ContraParallels as well as creating with its paired Reflexes reciprocal degrees that add up to 360, this is the axis I far prefer of the two.

Study of a chart's Reflexes reveals defining characteristics that you know should be present, but are often unaccountably 'missing' from conventional analysis. You miss a huge amount of information if you don't check Reflex connections between charts in Synastry. I cannot stress the importance of these points strongly enough, and find the rectangular symmetries displayed thus across the ecliptic utterly fascinating.

It is possible to portray a nativity purely as a plaid of uniquely-combined colours filling the Ecliptic circle using this property of all zodiacs. When shown to the chart's owner, the colours are always recognised as favourites.

Q-CHARTS

Here is another vital technique that I believe would be of immense help to many astrologers, especially those specialising in Synastry and often struggling with missing or vague birth-times. Learn this simple approach to chart comparison and you will find light cast in many a dark corner of relationships. I call these charts Q-Charts as an abbreviation of Quotidian Charts, since the idea stemmed from the use of one's birth-time to create a chart, known as the Quotidian, for each day that passes and thus understand the personal meaning of that day.

All you need is to set up one chart of a loving, warring or collaborating couple for the corresponding birth-time of the other (i.e. with time zone corrected to match so that both are synchronised to UT, or BWT, or JST, or whatever) – and then see how the planetary energies are distributed. If A at B's time has a Venus/Jupiter conjunction on the 7th cusp, you can be certain that B's presence in her life is a joyous and rewarding one. If Saturn is on B's MC at A's time, A is going to bring some heavy stuff into B's life – maybe serious career responsibilities, or constant belittling and frustration, or just plain misery, among other possibilities. You get the picture. I have found people with couple issues greatly clarified and helped by this.

It means that if one of the pair has no birth-time, the other time can legitimately be used – and even other times that are significant to that person, such as the time they clock on every day, or the time they always rehearse for the next gig. If both times are known, these extra charts show clearly what each will come to see in or associate with the other, and so what the fundamental nature of the relationship will always be. The insights can be stunning. A Composite of the two Q-Charts is also worth doing, to look deeper into the dynamics.

CHART LISTING – THE DRACONIC CHART

1. 1st Christmas Carol Service	Natal, 24 Dec 1879 NS, 22:00, UT +0:00, 50°N16', 005°W03'
2. A Healing Centre	Natal, 21 Feb 1984, 10:00, GMT +0:00, 51°N20', 000°E53'
3. A.F.A.	Natal, 4 May 1938, 11:38, EST +5:00, 38°N54', 077°W02'
4. A.P.A.E.	Natal, 7 Sep 1980, 18:37, BST –1:00, 51°N28', 000°W59'
5. Aaron	Natal, 23 Sep 1961, 12:45, BST –1:00, 51°N20', 001°E25'
6. Aaron's 1st Crash	Natal, 24 Apr 1978, 17:15, BST –1:00, 51°N17', 001°E05'
7. Aaron's 2nd Crash–Broken Back	Natal, 25 Apr 1979, 12:30, BST –1:00, 51°N17', 001°E05'
8. Albert Einstein	Natal, 14 Mar 1879 NS, 11:30, –0:40, 48°N24', 010°E00'
9. An Inner Event	Natal, 7 Oct 1978, 06:10, BST –1:00, 50°N16', 005°W03'
10. Andrew Lloyd Webber	Natal, 22 Mar 1948, 16:00, BST –1:00, 51°N30', 000°W09'
11. Andrew marries Sarah 1	Natal, 24 Jul 1971, 12:00, CET –1:00, 51°N39', 001°W51'
12. Andrew marries Sarah 2	Natal, 22 Mar 1984, 12:00, UT +0:00, 51°N20', 001°W14'
13. Archbp.George Carey–SunMC	Natal, 13 Nov 1935, 11:43:35, UT +0:00, 51°N32', 000°E10'
14. Arthur Scargill	Natal, 11 Jan 1938, 14:00, GMT +0:00, 53°N34', 001°W28'
15. Bernadette Soubirous–tropical	Natal, 7 Jan 1844 NS, 14:00, LMT +0:00:12, 43°N06', 000°W03'
16. Betty Callaway–SunMC	Natal, 22 Mar 1928, 12:07:40, UT +0:00, 51°N30', 000°W10'
17. Billy Graham	Natal, 7 Nov 1918, 15:30, +5:00, 35°N13'37", 080°W50'36"
18. Bishop Oscar Romero	Natal, 15 Aug 1947, 03:00, CST +6:00, 13°N46', 088°W16'
19. Cambridge	Natal, 8 May 1207, 00:00, LMT –0:00:32, 52°N13', 000°E08'
20. Cats–UK	Natal, 11 May 1981, 20:00, BST –1:00, 51°N30', 000°W10'
21. Cats–USA	Natal, 7 Oct 1982, 20:00, EDT +4:00, 40°N42'51", 074°W00'23"
22. Chad Varah	Natal, 12 Nov 1911, 12:00, UT +0:00, 53°N41', 000°W27'
23. Charles Harvey	Natal, 22 Jun 1940, 08:16, GMT +0:00, 51°N18', 000°W20'
24. Christian Festivals banned QJesus	Natal, 8 Jun 1647 OS, 16:23, LMT +0:00:36, 51°N30', 000°W09'
25. Christopher Dean–SunMC	Natal, 27 Jul 1958, 13:11:06, BST –1:00, 52°N58', 001°W10'
26. Christopher Reeve–(rectified)	Natal, 25 Sep 1952, 03:24, EDT +4:00, 40°N46', 073°W59'
27. Church of England	Natal, 29 Apr 1559 OS, 00:00, +0:00:40, 51°N30', 000°W10'
28. CRUCIFIXION	Natal, 3 Apr 0033, 18:20, –2:20:56, 31°N46', 035°E14'
29. Dennis Elwell	Natal, 16 Feb 1930, 23:40, GMT +0:00, 52°N30', 001°W50'
30. Dennis Elwell on Draco	Natal, 3 Sep 1977, 16:30, GMT +0:00, 52°N13', 000°E08'
31. Discovery of Chiron	Natal, 1 Nov 1977, 10:00, PST +8:00, 34°N08'52", 118°W08'37"
32. Donald "Moby Dick" Jacobs	Natal, 3 Mar 1927, 06:00, CST +6:00, 38°N51'31", 093°W53'26"
33. Dr. Edward Bach–SunMC	Natal, 24 Sep 1886 NS, 11:59:43, GMT +0:00, 52°N28', 001°W56'
34. Dr. John Dee	Natal, 13 Jul 1527 OS, 04:35, LMT +0:01:04, 51°N28', 000°W16'
35. Dr.Douglas Baker	Natal, 31 Dec 1922, 23:55, GMT +0:00, 51°N30', 000°W10'
36. Dr.Ludwig Zamenhof	Natal, 15 Dec 1859 NS, 01:50, –1:32:36, 53°N09', 023°E09'
37. ECLIPSE–5BC	Natal, 8 Mar 0005 BC, 07:04:28, –2:20:48, 31°N43', 035°E12'
38. Edgar Cayce	Natal, 18 Mar 1877 NS, 15:03, +5:49:57, 36°N51'56", 087°W29'19"
39. Edgar Mitchell	Natal, 17 Sep 1930, 04:30, CST +6:00, 34°N48'54", 102°W23'50"
40. Election–Healing Clinic	Natal, 21 Feb 1984, 10:00, UT +0:00, 51°N20', 000°E53'
41. Elias Ashmole	Natal, 2 Jun 1617 NS, 03:28, +0:07:12, 52°N42', 001°W48'
42. Elvis Presley	Natal, 8 Jan 1935, 04:35, +6:00, 34°N15'27", 088°W42'12"
43. Equal Pay For Women	Natal, 29 Dec 1975, 00:00, GMT +0:00, 51°N30', 000°W09'
44. Eric Morcambe–death–SunMC	Natal, 20 May 1984, 13:05:25, BST –1:00, 51°N53', 002°W14'
45. Eric Morecambe–tropical	Natal, 14 May 1926, 11:58, BST –1:00, 54°N04', 002°W53'
46. Ernie Wise–death	Natal, 21 Mar 1999, 07:00, UT +0:00, 51°N31', 000°W36'
47. Ernie Wise–tropical	Natal, 27 Nov 1925, 02:57, GMT +0:00, 53°N50', 001°W35'
48. Evita–UK	Natal, 21 Jun 1978, 20:00, BST –1:00, 51°N30', 000°W10'
49. Faculty of Astrol. Studies	Natal, 7 Jun 1948, 19:50, BST –1:00, 51°N30', 000°W10'
50. Finding Jesus–tropical	Natal, 25 Oct 1992, 17:25, GMT +0:00, 51°N20', 000°E53'
51. Finding Mary–1–the Clue!	Natal, 21 May 1995, 17:30, BST –1:00, 50°N50', 000°W08'
52. Finding Mary–2–Eureka!	Natal, 22 May 1995, 18:15, GMT +0:00, 51°N20', 000°E53'
53. Finding Mary–3–asteroids	Natal, 27 Mar 1999, 12:24, GMT +0:00, 51°N20', 000°E53'
54. FindingYeshuhua	Natal, 17 Jun 1995, 12:55, BST –1:00, 51°N20', 000°E53'
55. First Sydmonton Festival	Natal, 21 Jun 1975, 12:00, BST –1:00, 51°N19', 001°W19'
56. Friedrich Nietzsche	Natal, 15 Oct 1844 NS, 10:00, LMT –0:48:32, 51°N15', 012°E08'
57. Harold Evans–SunMC	Natal, 28 Jun 1928, 13:12:01, BST –1:00, 53°N30', 002°W15'
58. Healers–Husband–draco	Natal, 15 Dec 1931, 07:12, UT +0:00, 53°N45', 002°W29'
59. Janis Joplin – death	Natal, 4 Oct 1970, 01:40, PDT +7:00, 34°N03'08", 118°W14'34"
60. Janis Joplin	Natal, 19 Jan 1943, 09:45, +5:00, 29°N53'55", 093°W55'43"
61. Jayne Torvill–SunMC	Natal, 7 Oct 1957, 11:52:35, GMT +0:00, 52°N58', 001°W10'
62. JesusChristSuperStar–UK	Natal, 9 Aug 1972, 20:00, BST –1:00, 51°N30', 000°W10'

63. JesusChristSuperStar—USA   Natal, 12 Oct 1971, 20:00, EDT +4:00, 40°N42'51", 074°W00'23"
64. JESUS—tropical   Natal, 7 May 0005 BC, 18:43:55, −2:20:48, 31°N43', 035°E12'
65. John Addey   Natal, 15 Jun 1920, 08:15, BST −1:00, 53°N33', 001°W29'
66. John McEnroe   Natal, 16 Feb 1959, 22:30, CET −1:00, 50°N05', 008°E14'
67. John Partridge   Natal, 28 Jan 1644 NS, 14:27, LMT +0:01:12, 51°N28', 000°W18'
68. John the Baptist spec   Natal, 11 Nov 0006 BC, 11:44, LMT −2:21:12, 32°N42', 035°E18'
69. Kosovo   Natal, 30 Sep 1991, 20:00, CET −1:00, 42°N53', 020°E52'
70. Leonard Nimoy   Natal, 26 Mar 1931, 20:28, EST +5:00, 42°N21'30", 071°W03'37"
71. Martin Luther   Natal, 10 Nov 1483, 23:00, −0:46:08, 51°N31', 011°E32'
72. Martin Luther King Jr.   Natal, 15 Jan 1929, 12:00, CST +6:00, 33°N44'56", 084°W23'17"
73. Martin Luther King Jr.Shot   Natal, 4 Apr 1968, 18:01, CST +6:00, 35°N08'58", 090°W02'56"
74. MARY, mother of Jesus   Natal, 4 Aug 0024 BC, 12:33, LMT −2:21:12, 32°N42', 035°E18'
75. Maurice Ravel   Natal, 7 Mar 1875 NS, 22:00, LMT +0:06:44, 43°N23', 001°W41'
76. Michel Gauquelin   Natal, 13 Nov 1928, 22:20, +0:00, 48°N52', 002°E20'
77. Morecambe & Wise Show   Natal, 21 Apr 1954, 21:40, BST −1:00, 51°N30', 000°W14'
78. Mother Theresa   Natal, 27 Aug 1910, 14:25, CET −1:00, 41°N59', 021°E26'
79. National Coal Board   Natal, 1 Jan 1947, 00:00, GMT +0:00, 51°N30', 000°W09'
80. New Moon 6 May 0005 BC   Natal, 6 May 0005 BC, 08:23, LMT −2:20:48, 31°N43', 035°E12'
81. Nicholas Culpeper – draconic   Natal, 28 Oct 1616 NS, 12:12, LMT +0:01:28, 51°N09', 000°W22'
82. Nicholas Culpeper   Natal, 28 Oct 1616 NS, 12:12, LMT +0:01:28, 51°N09', 000°W22'
83. No man cometh...but by Me   Natal, 7 Oct 1978, 06:10, BST −1:00, 50°N16', 005°W03'
84. Nottingham   Natal, 28 Jun 1449, 00:00, +0:04:40, 52°N58', 001°W10'
85. Olympic Gold! for T&D   Natal, 14 Feb 1984, 22:00, CET −1:00, 43°N52', 018°E25'
86. Orson Welles   Natal, 6 May 1915, 07:00, CST +6:00, 42°N35'05", 087°W49'16"
87. Our Lady of Lourdes Q Bernadette   Natal, 11 Feb 1858 NS, 14:00, LMT +0:00:12, 43°N06', 000°W03'
88. Patrick McGoohan (thePrisoner)   Natal, 19 Mar 1928, 04:31, EST +5:00, 40°N46'19", 073°W55'50"
89. Phantom—UK   Natal, 9 Oct 1986, 20:00, BST −1:00, 51°N30', 000°W10'
90. Phantom—USA   Natal, 26 Jan 1988, 20:00, EST +5:00, 40°N42'51", 074°W00'23"
91. Pope John Paul elected   Natal, 16 Oct 1978, 18:18, CET −1:00, 41°N54', 012°E27'
92. Pope John Paul shot   Natal, 13 May 1981, 17:21, −2:00, 41°N54', 012°E27'
93. Pope John Paul–5h25pm   Natal, 18 May 1920, 17:25, EET −2:00, 49°N53', 019°E30'
94. Protestantism   Natal, 31 Oct 1517 OS, 12:00, −0:44:16, 53°N31', 011°E04'
95. Reeve's Accident   Natal, 27 May 1995, 15:05, EDT +4:00, 38°N28'23", 077°W59'49"
96. RESURRECTION—John's Words   Natal, 5 Apr 0033, 04:58, −2:20:56, 31°N46', 035°E14'
97. RESURRECTION—Mary-tropical   Natal, 5 Apr 0033, 06:39, −2:20:56, 31°N46', 035°E14'
98. RESURRECTION—Mary-tropical   Natal, 5 Apr 0033, 06:39, −2:20:56, 31°N46', 035°E14'
99. RESURRECTION—Sunrise   Natal, 5 Apr 0033, 05:49:45, −2:20:56, 31°N46', 035°E14'
100. Rev.Dr.Chad Varah–SunMC   Natal, 12 Nov 1911, 11:45:56, UT +0:00, 53°N41', 000°W27'
101. Richard Dimbleby–"midday"SunM Natal, 25 May 1913, 11:57:22, UT +0:00, 51°N30', 000°W10'
102. Robert Hand   Natal, 5 Dec 1942, 19:30:11, EWT +4:00, 40°N38'01", 074°W24'28"
103. Robert Powell (astrologer)   Natal, 18 Jan 1947, 20:31, GMT +0:00, 51°N28', 000°W59'
104. Roger Elliott   Natal, 25 Jun 1937, 03:15, BST −1:00, 50°N28', 003°W30'
105. Ronald Davison   Natal, 10 Jan 1914, 08:44, GMT +0:00, 51°N24', 000°E02'
106. Rt Revd David Jenkins Q Jesus   Natal, 26 Jan 1925, 16:23, UT +0:00, 51°N24', 000°E02'
107. Russell Grant   Natal, 5 Feb 1951, 21:35:35, GMT +0:00, 51°N33', 000°W29'
108. Satya Sai Baba–SunASC   Natal, 23 Nov 1926, 06:26:35, IST −5:30, 14°N15', 077°E45'
109. Sex–the Husband   Natal, 8 Nov 1928, 03:26, GMT +0:00, 51°N08', 001°E19'
110. Sex–the Wife   Natal, 29 Mar 1935, 01:13, GMT +0:00, 51°N08', 001°E19'
111. Shroud–Enrie's Photo   Natal, 3 May 1931, 23:12, CET −1:00, 45°N03', 007°E40'
112. Shroud–Pia'sPhotograph   Natal, 28 May 1898 NS, 23:00, CET −1:00, 45°N03', 007°E40'
113. Sir Alexander Fleming   Natal, 6 Aug 1881 NS, 02:00, LMT +0:17:12, 55°N37', 004°W18'
114. Sir Cliff Richard–SunMC   Natal, 14 Oct 1940, 12:00, IST −5:30, 26°N51', 080°E55'
115. Sir Freddie Laker–SunMC   Natal, 6 Aug 1922, 13:01:27, BST −1:00, 51°N17', 001°E05'
116. Sir George Trevelyan   Natal, 5 Nov 1906, 21:25, UT +0:00, 51°N30', 000°W10'
117. Small World–tropical   Natal, 3 Mar 1998, 17:30, GMT +0:00, 51°N20', 000°E53'
118. Solar Partial Eclipse (NM)   Natal, 6 Apr 0005 BC, 19:16:57, LMT −2:20:48, 31°N43', 035°E12'
119. Star & Cross around the Sun   Natal, 2 Mar 0005 BC, 17:45, LMT −2:20:48, 31°N43', 035°E12'
120. Star Trek on NBC   Natal, 8 Sep 1966, 19:30, PDT +7:00, 34°N03'08", 118°W14'34"
121. Star Trek–UK Rerun   Natal, 19 Sep 1978, 18:50, BST −1:00, 51°N30', 000°W10'
122. Stephen Hawking–SunMC   Natal, 8 Jan 1942, 13:11:38, BST −1:00, 51°N46', 001°W15'
123. Subject A   Natal, 13 Aug 1917, 23:29, CST +6:00, 39°N09'43", 084°W27'25"
124. Subject B (no time/place)   Natal, 16 Jan 1919, 12:00, EST +5:00, 36°N50'48", 076°W17'08"
125. Subject C   Natal, 26 Feb 1915, 17:56, EST +5:00, 36°N50'31", 076°W00'48"
126. Subject D   Natal, 13 Aug 1917, 23:29, CST +6:00, 39°N09'43", 084°W27'25"
127. Subject E (no time/place)   Natal, 16 Jan 1919, 12:00, EST +5:00, 36°N50'48", 076°W17'08"

128. Subject F	Natal, 26 Feb 1915, 17:56, EST +5:00, 36°N50'31", 076°W00'48"
129. Superman–1st Broadcast	Natal, 12 Feb 1940, 17:15, EST +5:00, 40°N42'51", 074°W00'23"
130. Suzi Harvey	Natal, 23 Dec 1949, 14:47, PST +8:00, 37°N29'41", 120°W50'44"
131. Sydmonton Festival	Natal, 21 Jun 1975, 12:00, BST –1:00, 51°N19', 001°W19'
132. Synastry: the Husband	Natal, 8 Nov 1928, 03:26, GMT +0:00, 51°N08', 001°E19'
133. Synastry: the Wife	Natal, 29 Mar 1935, 01:13, GMT +0:00, 51°N08', 001°E19'
134. The Miners Strike	Natal, 6 Mar 1984, 00:00, GMT +0:00, 53°N34', 001°W28'
135. The Miners Strike–Kent	Natal, 6 Mar 1984, 00:00, GMT +0:00, 51°N14', 001°E24'
136. The Miners Strike–Wales	Natal, 6 Mar 1984, 00:00, GMT +0:00, 51°N38', 003°W57'
137. The Prisoner – Rerun	Natal, 1 Oct 1978, 13:00, BST –1:00, 50°N16', 005°W03'
138. TIME Review	Natal, 9 Nov 1970, 00:00, EST +5:00, 40°N42'51", 074°W00'23"
139. Total Lunar Eclipse (FM)	Natal, 23 Mar 0005 BC, 20:42:32, LMT –2:20:48, 31°N43', 035°E12'
140. United Kingdom	Natal, 1 Jan 1801 NS, 00:00, GMT +0:00, 51°N32', 000°W09'
141. United Nations–UN	Natal, 24 Oct 1945, 17:00, EST +5:00, 38°N54', 077°W02'
142. VaticanCity–tropical	Natal, 7 Jun 1929, 11:00, CET –1:00, 41°N54', 012°E29'
143. War	Natal, 24 Mar 1999, 17:52, CET –1:00, 41°N20', 019°E50'
144. Where Is The Motorbike?	Natal, 27 Apr 1974, 09:15, BST –1:00, 51°N13', 001°E24'
145. William Lilly	Natal, 11 May 1602 NS, 02:00, LMT +0:05:04, 52°N50', 001°W16'
146. William Shatner	Natal, 22 Mar 1931, 04:00, EST +5:00, 45°N31', 073°W34'
147. World Gold for T&D	Natal, 24 Mar 1984, 22:55, EST +5:00, 45°N25', 075°W42'
148. YeshuhuaDiscovered	Natal, 28 Nov 1978, 03:49:27, GMT +0:00, 32°N00', 119°E00'
149. York Minster Fire	Natal, 9 Jul 1984, 02:10, BST –1:00, 53°N58', 001°W05'
150. Zach Matthews	Natal, 12 Jan 1914, 05:30, GMT +0:00, 50°N43', 001°W59'
151. Zerda – Aaron's Mother	Natal, 12 Jul 1930, 07:51, BST –1:00, 51°N30', 000°W10'

14 essays on psychological, traditional, mundane and evolutionary astrology from contemporary writers including Gary Caton, Frank Clifford, Rebecca Crane, Nick Dagan Best, Maurice Fernandez, John Green, Tony Howard, Mark Jones, Keiron Le Grice, Eric Meyers, Wendy Stacey and Branka Stamenkovic.

Business astrologer Faye Cossar reveals how the birth chart can be used to create a tangible product – a Vocational Profile – which enables you and your clients to: identify talents, blocks and style; create a CV, website and logo; define goals and awaken life purpose and passion.

In *From Symbol to Substance: Training the Astrological Intuition* learn to: develop creative and spontaneous interpretations for any placement; enhance intuitive faculties when analysing charts; and think creatively when exploring symbolism and correspondences.

A complete guide to horoscope synthesis – designed to help astrologers identify, prioritize and synthesize the components, themes and storylines of any chart. Packed with original ideas and observations, this textbook includes 150 horoscopes and profiles showing astrology in action.

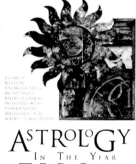
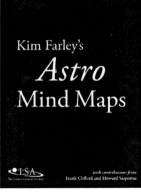

Sue Tompkins (*Aspects in Astrology*) presents an authoritative guide to chart interpretation, with an in-depth exploration of the planets, zodiac signs, houses and aspects. Included are biographies and step-by-step instructions for synthesizing the main horoscope factors.

From an award-winning psychological astrologer comes the definitive book on the astrological houses. This new edition of the best-selling handbook remains a firm favourite among students and professionals. With a new foreword by Dr. Liz Greene and tribute essays from astrologers.

Based on over 30 interviews with researchers and leading astrologers, this landmark, thought-provoking volume examines the lives and work of contemporary astrologers, and considers many of the issues facing this ancient and systematic art.

An exceptionally handy booklet packed with info including: mind maps for the signs, planets and aspects; Mercury Retrograde advice; a history of the outer planets through the signs; an outer planet ephemeris; and easy-to-use Ascendant and MC calculators.

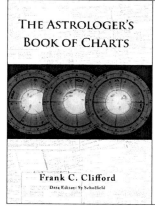  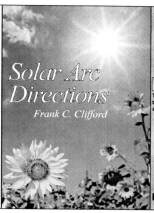 

From Dolly to Dali, Nixon to Manson, George Galloway to Greta Garbo, Christine Keeler to Monica Lewinsky. 150 accurately timed and sourced horoscopes and worksheets. With charts presented in both Placidus and Equal houses. Includes new data.	An ideal companion for students and fans of the famous. Enjoy the charts, meticulously sourced data, personal quotes, dated events and biographies of over 800 prominent personalities from the worlds of film, theatre, TV, comedy and music. This 2003 ed. has many additional features.	All you'll ever need to know about Solar Arc Directions is packed inside this informative and popular manual, presented clearly and concisely. There are numerous examples and an intro to Shadow Transits, an indispensable new method that connects directions to transits.	This acclaimed, fully illustrated textbook offers immediate access to the mysteries of the hand. In 4 easy-to-follow-steps, this innovative, fully revised edition presents: The Palm Detective; Timing Techniques; Love, Health and Career; and Palmistry in Action.

Astrology The New Generation: Essays from 14 Rising Stars of Astrology by various contributors (2012)
Using Astrology to Create a Vocational Profile: Finding the Right Career Direction by Faye Cossar (2012)
From Symbol to Substance: Training the Astrological Intuition by Richard Swatton (2012)
Getting to the Heart of Your Chart by Frank C. Clifford (2012)
The Contemporary Astrologer's Handbook by Sue Tompkins (2007)
The Twelve Houses by Howard Sasportas (2007)
Astrology in the Year Zero by Garry Phillipson (2000)
Kim Farley's Astro Mind Maps by Kim Farley (2010)
The Astrologer's Book of Charts by Frank C. Clifford (Flare, 2009)
British Entertainers: The Astrological Profiles by Frank C. Clifford (1st and 2nd ed., Flare, 1997; 3rd ed., 2003)
Solar Arc Directions by Frank C. Clifford (booklet, Flare, 2011)
Palmistry 4 Today by Frank C. Clifford (fully revised edition, Flare, 2010)

Other titles from Flare:
Jane Struthers' 101 Astrology Questions for the Student Astrologer by Jane Struthers (2010)
Jupiter and Mercury: An A to Z by Paul Wright (2006)
The Sun Sign Reader by Joan Revill (2000)
Shorthand of the Soul: The Quotable Horoscope by David Hayward (1999)

Coming Soon from Frank Clifford and Flare:
Humour in the Horoscope: The Astrology of Comedy
The Astrology of Love, Sex and Attraction with Fiona Graham (revised edition of *Venus* and *Mars* booklets)
The Midheaven: Spotlight on Success

www.flareuk.com

LSA

The London School of Astrology

— the students' choice in contemporary astrological education —

- Accredited Foundation courses for beginners in central London
- Accredited Diploma courses for those with more experience
- Saturday seminars, residential courses and other events
- Short courses in tarot and palmistry (modern hand analysis)
- A distance learning course in palmistry

Learn astrology, palmistry and tarot in a fun, supportive environment
with the UK's most experienced astrologers/tutors

To find out more
Visit our website www.londonschoolofastrology.co.uk
Email: admin@londonschoolofastrology.co.uk

London School of Astrology
BCM Planets, London WC1N 3XX

Telephone: 0700 233 44 55

Fun, self-knowledge, spiritual development, vocational training

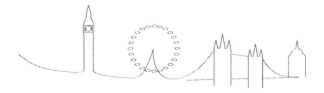

Lightning Source UK Ltd.
Milton Keynes UK
UKOW010228250213

206705UK00005B/100/P